Catching the wave

Catching the wave
Workplace reform in Australia

John Mathews

Cornell International Industrial and Labor Relations
Report Number 26

ILR Press
Ithaca, New York

Published in Australia by Allen & Unwin Pty Ltd

Library of Congress
Cataloging-in-Publication Data

Mathews, John (John A.)
Catching the wave: workplace reform in Australia/John Mathews.
   p. cm.—(Cornell international industrial and labor relations report; no. 26)
   Includes bibliographical references and index.
   ISBN 0-87546-707-5 (cloth).—ISBN 0-87546-706-7 (pbk.)
   1. Industrial relations—Australia—Case studies. 2. Industrial management—Australia—Case studies. 3. Australia—Manufactures—Technological innovations—Case studies. I. Title. II. Series: Cornell international industrial and labor relations reports; no. 26.
HD8846.5.M37 1994   94-25504
331'.0994—dc20

Copies of this book may be ordered through bookstores or directly from the publisher.

ILR Press
School of Industrial and Labor Relations
Cornell University
Ithaca, New York 14853–3901

(Telephone 607–255–3061)

Set in 10/11pt Garamond by DOCUPRO, Sydney
Printed in Malaysia

5 4 3 2 1

Contents

Figures, tables and illustrations

Figures

Tables

Illustrations

Selected abbreviations

ACTU   Australian Council of Trade Unions
ATO   Australian Taxation Office
CAD   computer-aided design
CIM   Computer-Integrated Manufacturing
CNC   computer numerically controlled
CSD   Client Services Division, Colonial Mutual
DISC   Dynamic Integrated Service Cells
ELS   Electronic Lodgement Service, ATO
FMS   flexible manufacturing system
IT   information technology
JIT   Just-In-Time
LPS   lean production system
MPS   mass production system
OCR   optical character recognition
Q1   'quality first' Quality Assurance programme
QA   Quality Assurance
QC   Quality Control
STPS   sociotechnical production system
TQM   Total Quality Management

Acknowledgments

This book results from case studies conducted through a research programme at the University of New South Wales and published in the series *UNSW Studies in Organisational Analysis and Innovation*. Funding for the programme was provided originally by the Business Council of Australia, then in 1991 and 1992, by the NSW Education and Training Foundation, and in 1993 by the Australian Research Council. The assistance of all these sponsoring bodies is gratefully acknowledged.

I wish to thank my colleagues at UNSW who provided intellectual sustenance and assistance in the course of the research programme. These include Professors David Plowman and John Niland who helped me get started, Professor Dexter Dunphy, who shared the results of his own case study research programme with me, and Professor Stephen Frenkel, who debated all the issues with me in spirited fashion.

Andrew Griffiths was my research assistant and collaborator throughout the study programme. He assisted with all the field work, and was co-author of some of the case study monographs which are the source for Part 2 of the book. He has commented extensively on successive drafts of the text, and in every way has been an exemplary collaborator. He will take many of the ideas further in his own doctoral work.

Special thanks are due to the business leaders who were instrumental in providing access to their organisations and their experiences. They are acknowledged in the case study monographs, but special mention should be made of the roles played by Chris Barry,

Trevor Boucher, Michael Carmody, Peter Fancke, Peter Fritz, Graeme John, Pat McCarthy, David Murphy, Tom Pettigrew, and Moira Scollay. Justice Bill Fisher, President of the Industrial Relations Commission of New South Wales, has been a constant source of support. On the union side, special thanks to Michael Costa, Sue McCreadie, Max Ogden, Peter Robson, Paul Watson, and Bruce Wilson, Director of the Union Research Centre on Office Technology, for their encouragement and assistance. Both Neil Watson and Kate Nash at the former 'Workplace Australia' have been fine colleagues and collaborators in opening doors and discussing issues, while the 1991 *Workplace Australia* conference was instrumental in bringing many of Australia's best practice stories to light.

The concepts and arguments of the book have been presented at numerous seminars and colloquia where they have received helpful criticism. Special mention should be made of the conference of the International Industrial Relations Association held in Sydney in September 1992; the Colloquium of the Culture and Production International Research Network (CAPIRN) held in Bremen, Germany, in April 1993; and the Colloquium held by the Asia Pacific Researchers in Organisational Studies (APROS) in Honolulu, in December 1993.

Helpful comments on an earlier draft of the book were provided by anonymous referees. As with my previous books, I owe a special debt of gratitude to my father, Alwyn Mathews, who has carefully scrutinised the entire text and queried anything he found obscure; I hope the final text meets his exacting standards. Special thanks for their reliability and accuracy in their assistance with preparation of the manuscript to Caterina Manea and Marie Kwok. My thanks also to the bibliographically-demanding editor, June Ohlson.

This book provides me with the opportunity to acknowledge the pioneering efforts in workplace reform conducted in Australia by Fred Emery and Bill Ford, both of whom have been inspirational leaders for the generation now leading the change programmes of the 1990s.

Preface to the American Edition

This book tells the story of how a pioneering band of Australian organisations have transformed their operations over the past decade. They have broken with traditional segmented and hierarchical organisational structures, and instead have introduced more flexible, more focused organisational networks of self-managing teams. They are reaping the gains in terms of greatly enhanced levels of quality, productivity and efficiency.

Why should such stories be of interest to an American audience? Surely there have been many such cases of organisational renewal and improvement in the United States. Indeed there have—the interest of these stories lies not so much in what was done, but in how it was done. Just a few years ago, these organisational transformations would have been impossible in Australia and, for the most part, in the United States as well. For they are stories of organisational innovation that have depended for their success on advanced levels of commitment and trust between management and workforce

The commitment and trust was not established easily, and it was not the work of the organisations alone. It arose partly through a mechanism that is also operating in the United States—fear of foreign competition. But more to the point, it arose as a result of fundamental changes to the institutional framework within which business is done in Australia. In particular, the industrial relations system has been transformed, so that it now favours collaborative outcomes reached at enterprise level, instead of the previous contested processes orchestrated at a centralised national level. More and more organisations in Australia are taking advantage of these new conditions to improve their internal organisation and thereby enhance their competitive performance. Organisational participation has been good for business. This is the relevance of the stories of how six such organisations were able to harness participation and make it work for them—the major subject of the studies reported here.

As this book goes to press, the US is being swept up in a major debate over the future of its industrial relations institutions and processes. The New Deal structures set in place in the 1930s under the Wagner Act, which have provided a successful framework for the best part of six decades, are now seen to be in urgent need of reform. A top-flight committee chaired by Professor John Dunlop has been charged by the Clinton administration with outlining the major directions of change. But what kind of model should the US be pursuing? Should it take the best from these systems, and perhaps add something from the Swedish model? What emerges clearly in these debates is a sense that the industrial relations system should not be considered in isolation from its wider economic and productivity effects. The reason that the German and Japanese models are so prominent in discussion is not difficult to fathom: it surely has something to do with the fact that these countries have developed extraordinarily efficient production systems in the post-war era, and that industrial relations have made these systems more, rather than less, efficient. The emulation of this achievement in Anglo-Saxon countries is widely seen as becoming a matter of national economic survival.

In these debates, there is a case to be made for looking closely at the experience of Australia over the past decade. In this short period, Australia has transformed itself from a sleepy haven of sheep farmers, iron ore mines and sun-bronzed life savers, to a dynamic, export-oriented country that is striving to secure a future for itself in the Asia–Pacific region. Not the least of the astonishing changes wrought in Australia during this time has been the transformation of its industrial relations system.

In the early 1980s, industrial relations in Australia was confrontationist, with high-wage settlements followed by a government-imposed wage freeze. Unions and employer organisations pursued their own agendas through a rigid and centralised negotiating framework, consisting of awards handed down by the Australian Conciliation and Arbitration Commission. This Commission had been one of the first agencies established by the Commonwealth after federation of Australia's colonial governments in 1901—and its operation had changed very little in the intervening decades. High wages, union protection and 'infant industry' protection through tariffs—each facet feeding off the others—formed the cornerstone of this essentially closed inward-looking industrial system.

In 1983 a new government was elected with a mandate for change. One of its assets was an Accord reached between the trade unions (represented by the Australian Council of Trade Unions) and the Australian Labor Party government, governing prices and incomes management. This Accord, still in force at the time of writing (albeit much modified), has provided the broad framework within which a cooperative and production-oriented industrial relations system has been established in Australia. Wage settlements have been moderated and brought into line with productivity improvements. In return, the 'social wage' has been extended, through reforms to the social security, health care, childcare and general welfare systems. Unions, employers and government have been formed into tripartite structures to determine future strategies in manufacturing industry, superannuation (pension) arrangements, and overall economic management. At the same time, industry has been exposed to the full force of international competition, through a relentless winding back of tariff protection.

The award system, which was the bedrock of the national industrial relations system, has been transformed. Through successive decisions of the Australian Industrial Relations Commission, wages and employment conditions have come to be settled in a more decentralised manner, reflecting enterprise needs and productivity. First there was a set of 'national wage principles', handed down by the then Conciliation and Arbitration Commission in 1983, setting wage-fixing and employment conditions on an orderly, centralised footing. This was extended through the second tier decision in 1987: wage increases were allocated through a first tier that offered a flat increase to all workers, while a second tier linked a further increase of up to 4% to productivity offsets at an enterprise level. This was followed by the 'award restructuring' decision in 1989, in the form of a new Structural Efficiency Principle (SEP) being added to the existing wage fixing principles. Under the SEP, award provisions have been extended to cover negotiations concerning technological change, skills formation, work organisation and job design, and a host of other issues that are raised as soon as firms seek to introduce 'best practice' in management and human resources strategies. Firms were forced to address these issues by linking wage increases to their successful negotiations. In 1992, a further Enterprise Bargaining Principle was added to the wage-fixing guidelines, ensuring that most aspects of employment conditions would be settled through local negotiation at enterprise level, but within the framework laid down by national standards and the national wage-fixing principles. Finally, in 1994, a new industrial relations legal framework came into effect, further driving the system towards enterprise negotiations by establishing a fast-track enterprise bargaining division within the national industrial relations tribunal. This new framework allows the most flexible outcomes for firms but still within a regulated system.

The unions themselves have been, for the most part, strong supporters of these changes. They have drastically reformed their own internal structures to cope with the new system, for example by enhancing the skills and knowledge of their workplace delegates. They have also transformed their macro structures; the overwhelming majority of union members are now enrolled in no more than 20 industry-based major unions, whereas prior to the Accord there were over 300 bickering craft-based unions. This has made unions much more efficient partners in negotiations with firms that are seeking to bring their operations to world best practice standards.

These changes have, of course, been contested. There have been some employer groups, and indeed some unions, which have bitterly opposed them. The Business Council of Australia has been prominent in these debates. In the latest report from its Industrial Relations Study Commission, it urges firms to enter into individual contracts with employees, bypassing the industrial relations system altogether (Hilmer 1993). Throughout this period of change the political opposition has held out an alternative framework of a totally deregulated labour market. But the strong coalition of government, major firms that favour the new collaborative industrial relations and a majority of unions, has prevailed in these debates, and the process of transformation continues.

Beyond the industrial relations system, further changes to the institutional framework within which firms operate have been introduced. In particular, government has intervened to promote the diffusion of best practices. Firms have received government assistance in opening themselves up to mutual benchmarking activities. A battery of tripartite study groups, either from individual firms or from whole industrial sectors, consisting of management, union and government representatives, have been sent to North America, Europe and East Asia, scouring these regions for techniques and lessons that can be applied in the Australian context. These study missions have had a major impact on the level of awareness in Australia of international trends. Overall, the Australian Best Practice Demonstration Programme, based on the concept that firms learn best from each other, has been most effective in exposing Australian firms to the best of international manufacturing and service quality standards.

At the centre of these transformations lie changes to production systems. In Australia, firms seeking to introduce new production systems are faced with inescapable choices. On the one hand, they can seek to emulate the lean production system first perfected in Japan and now spreading its influence world-wide. On the other hand, they can look to their own traditions in establishing an indigenous version of team work that gives firms flexibility while drawing on the skills and commitment of their employees.

In the United States, similar choices are recognised. For example, in their 1994 book on the 'new American workplace', Eileen Appelbaum and Rosemary Batt discuss the experiences of a small but growing number of US firms that have succeeded in transforming their production systems. They identify two major trends: first an American version of lean production, and second, an American version of team production which combines ideas of team-based collaboration with those of quality engineering, and places greatest emphasis on the decentralised management of work.

In this book, I term these the competing paradigms of lean production and 'sociotechnical' production, named after the sociotechnical school of management and organisational change where many of the current ideas of transformation have originated. Both choices need to be contrasted with the continued dominance of the segmented, hierarchical organisational systems that arose in the period of dominance of the mass production system. In both Australia and the United States the intellectual overhang from this system continues to dog efforts to make work systems more adaptive and quality-oriented. The way in which a small group of firms have overthrown these shackles in Australia, utilising the full panoply of institutional supports to do so, provides the principal interest of the studies reported in *Catching the Wave*.

Of course, the differences between Australia and the US are considerable. Australia is a comparatively small country with a small economy, while the US still has the largest economy in the world. But the upheavals the two countries face as they seek to come to grips with the new competitive challenges posed by, for example,

Japan and the Asian Tiger economies, are strikingly similar. What emerges repeatedly in the US and the Australian debates is the economic effect of the wide range of options enjoyed by firms; they can seek to reach accommodations with their workforce and their unions in the name of cooperative productivity enhancement, or they can simply evade such issues by relocating or outsourcing or through good old-fashioned union-busting. The freedom of choice at enterprise level leads to a debilitating weakness in imposing standards at the national level.

It is in this crucial interaction between enterprise flexibility and national employment standards that Australia's experience is surely relevant. A country with similar Anglo-Saxon traditions to the US, with a similar bias towards pragmatism and the good life, it has nevertheless been able to erect a system of national standards (covering employment conditions, wages, training levels and employment conditions) that shapes the competitive strategies now pursued by firms. When simple-minded cost-minimising strategies are put out of reach through imposition of such national standards, firms are forced to develop more sophisticated strategies, based for example on quality improvement. These are the profound, and immediate, economic implications of the changes that have been wrought in the Australian industrial relations system.

The point is that in a democratic system there are advantages in requiring firms to negotiate in an orderly fashion with their employees, and to seek consensus, or at least some legitimacy, for the changes that must flow from the introduction of new production systems. Participation within a firm can be translated into business advantages, for example in the rapid deployment of new technologies that have already been discussed and agreed upon. The firms presented here were able to work within the framework established by the industrial relations system, making it work for them; they were able to derive business advantages from the commitment engendered in their workforce towards achievement of organisational goals. These striking features are documented in the stories of best practice discussed in this book.

1

Introduction

A wave of technological and organisational change is washing through both manufacturing and service activities in the industrialised world. Some firms are learning to ride this wave, adapting their organisational processes to constant but managed change; they are emerging as winners. Others are being left behind, locked into organisational structures designed for less turbulent times; they are drifting back towards oblivion.

It is the world of production—factories, workshops, offices—that is undergoing the most profound transformation. Job structures and management processes inherited from the past, which previously were seen as a source of strength, are now seen as fetters, restraining the flexibility and market responsiveness that firms need to survive. The talk now in management and production circles is of 'new production systems', of 'world best practice' and of a 'new workplace culture'.

For ten years debate has raged over the prospects for the mass production system, perfected in the USA but now under great stress. The Japanese challenge has been recognised and assimilated in what is called the 'lean production system', and is seen as a world-historic successor to mass production.

In Europe a skills-based, human-centred alternative is also being discussed and promoted: the anthropocentric production system, or what I am calling the sociotechnical production system. It is a view espoused by firms which see their success based on quick responses by skilled staff to changing circumstances, using technologies that extend their skills rather than replace them. The sociotechnical view

1

utilises the possibilities of information technology to integrate tasks that were previously fragmented, building them into a coherent whole through a process that has come to be called business process re-engineering (in services) or cellular manufacturing. This view sees efficiency not so much in quantitative terms of productivity, but more in qualitative terms of timeliness, responsiveness, quality assurance and innovation, achieved by skilled people working collaboratively in self-managing teams that adapt continuously to changing circumstances.

These sharply diverging paradigms are intellectual constructs, but they reflect real divergences in production strategies, in work structures, in management styles, and most fundamentally, in the business strategies pursued by firms. There is no longer a 'one best way' to the perfection of production efficiency. A more complex world now demands a more complex approach to the design, negotiation and implementation of production systems.

In the current period of turbulence, as markets become global and more sophisticated, there is seemingly no end to the round of exhortations driving firms to improve their performance—by introducing 'new technology', or by adopting 'best practice'. The familiar battery of acronyms is summoned up as saviours: CAD, CAM, FMS, CNC, TQM, JIT, and most comprehensive of all, CIM. Government programs offer strong incentives to firms which are prepared to install such systems. But there is by now abundant evidence that it is not these systems themselves that are responsible for improved performance. It is the way in which they are used, or more exactly, the way in which they mesh with the organisational and business strategies being pursued by the firm that counts.

For example, it is not 'new technology' itself which rejuvenates a firm, but the way in which computer-based, programmable systems are used and implemented. They can either enhance flexibility or they can intensify existing rigidities. Simple approaches to rationalisation and labour-shedding automation, or frank deskilling, might seem attractive to firms which see their competitive advantage lying in extending their production runs in order to reduce their costs. But firms which see their future more in terms of enhanced quality, product differentiation and rapid response, are more likely to be interested in using programmable systems to extend the flexibility of their existing skills-based work systems, utilising a very different organisational architecture and strategy.

These choices lie at the heart of the transformations which are currently revolutionising production systems. What confuses the issue is the intellectual baggage that firms bring with them from a time when things were simpler. The competing paradigms of production systems reflect contested views of what it is that constitutes productive efficiency.

The dominant view is still that efficiency is associated with the division of labour, with fragmentation of jobs, with the embodiment of routines in programs and automation that eliminate the 'uncertain' factor of human work from the production cycle—the old dream of the workerless factory. In this book I argue that such views are not simply 'mistaken'—even though they drive firms in sometimes grievously mistaken directions. They have a rationality of their own that connects them with certain business strategies, and with the intellectual overhang from a time when mass production strategies could be expected to lead to business success. The problem is that in a more complex world, such strategies are a recipe for failure.

In the changed circumstances of the 1990s, when products have shorter life cycles, and are developed with shorter lead times; when products are more closely attuned to customer and market demands; when product variety, diversity and quality are the determinants of competitive success—under these circumstances, it is firms which are prepared to adopt new production systems which gain a competitive edge. Such firms are prepared to experiment with non-authoritarian teamwork structures that dispense with traditional supervisory and surveillance systems; they are prepared to experiment with new programmable routines for switching products and services as market preferences change; they are prepared to enter into closer collaborative relations with both their customers and suppliers. They are prepared to utilise computer-based systems to enhance the decision-making powers of skilled, responsible workers, rather than seeking to eliminate them. They seek to achieve these heightened states of awareness through managed, negotiated processes of change, rather than through top-down, 'big bang' transformations. Thus the organisational imperatives of the future will be for workplaces that maximise creativity, innovation and cooperation.

NEW PRODUCTION SYSTEMS: ORGANISING AROUND WORK CELLS

The new production systems are emerging everywhere. Let us look at some examples, before going on to discuss their common features and the forces that are driving their development.

Take the case of cellular manufacturing based on semi-autonomous teams as it has developed in the metals industry.

Case 1: Cellular manufacturing

New production systems have emerged in the metals industry in the form of flexible manufacturing systems (FMS) utilising computer numerically controlled (CNC) machine tools under various forms of programmable loading and operating controls. The CNC tools can perform different operations as the programs are changed or modified, thus removing the set-up times and costs associated with changing tools. The FMS provide the opportunity to regroup work away from its traditional functional division of tasks (such as grouping all the milling machines in one section) and provide instead a functional integration of operations within a self-contained manufacturing cell. The cell consists of a small group of machines and team of workers collaborating in the production of a well-defined set of products or components, carrying responsibility for planning their operations, ensuring the quality of their output, and responding to unusual circumstances. Cellular manufacturing is illustrated in Figure 1.1.

Cellular manufacturing enables operators as a group to regulate their activities, since they are in charge of producing a given range of finished products or components. This compares with previous batch systems, where operators on specific machines simply performed the same tasks over and over again on different pieces, without ever knowing where they came from or where they were to be despatched, unless the shop was very small. Flow production through the cell makes it ideal for the adoption of Just-In-Time (JIT) manufacturing, responding rapidly to customer orders. The approach calls for multi-skilled operators who are given responsibility for thinking about their work rather than simply executing orders.[1]

The metals industry is of course far from being the only aspect of manufacturing. The new production systems are also emerging in many other branches of manufacturing and process industries. One area which has not traditionally been associated with highly skilled 'craft' work is textiles, clothing and footwear, yet here too the new production systems are beginning to appear.

Case 2: Garment cells in the clothing industry

The traditional clothing factory saw long lines of operators (mostly

Figure 1.1 Cellular manufacturing vs functional layout

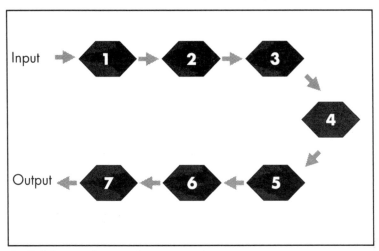

1. Cellular production: the new production concept
   All the operations involved in producing a product are
   self-contained and laid out clearly and sequentially.

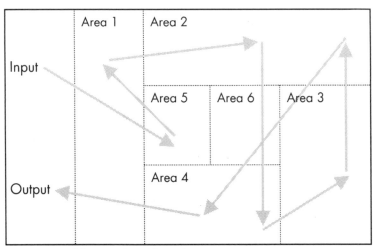

2. Functional layout: the old production concept
   All the operations are grouped by function, so that different
   products follow different zig-zag production paths.

women) working at sewing machines, performing detail work, such as sewing hems, pockets or collars, on bundles of garments that were moved from one operator to the next. The women would perform the same operation hundreds of times a shift, goaded on by piecework payment systems that paid according to individual productivity. The production system as a whole would consist of bundles of semi-finished garments moving from one workstation to another, tying up large quantities of capital in work-in-progress and requiring long production runs to be economic.

One approach to 'modernising' such a system is to install overhead conveyor systems and computer control of individual pieces through microprocessor additions to sewing stations. This enhances surveillance and control but does nothing about the coordination problems presented by such an extreme division of labour.

The new production system has come to the clothing industry in the form of a reorganisation of work in small product-focused cells. Each cell, consisting of perhaps five operators working ten machines, is responsible for a whole garment. A single piece moves through the cell, handed or moved from one operator to the next, in a finely programmed sequence of steps. The 'bundle' is dispensed with in favour of a single-piece, continuous-flow production system involving small groups of multi-skilled operators. The operators handle several different tasks, overlapping with each other as needed to keep production in balance (i.e. avoiding build-ups) which is the bane of traditional mass production. In order to emphasise the compactness of the group, such cells are frequently laid out in a U-shape.[2]

In the processing industries, which operate continuously to produce chemicals, paper, food, and many other processed goods, the same principles are starting to be applied. Take the case of automotive components production.

Case 3: Cellular processing in the automotive components sector

The new production system has come to the automotive components industry again through cellular, team-based production. In the production of friction materials for automotive brakes and clutches, for example, the previous batch processing methods called for functionally differentiated tasks to be carried out in various parts of the factory: moulding, grinding, painting, packing. Operators would perform their processes over and over again on materials as they came through, in the time-honoured division of labour.

In cellular, team-based production, a group of operators takes responsibility for producing a distinct product or range of products, and the products are produced in sequence, again frequently in a U-shape configuration to emphasise the unity of the group. Large batches are replaced by small batches which are moved from processing point to point along conveyor systems. The group as a whole is responsible for its own scheduling, and for ensuring the quality of each finished small batch. Product diversity is obtained through operators being multi-skilled in switching from one processing configuration to another.

We shall study a successful case of transformation of a traditional system of production to cellular production at the friction products firm Bendix Mintex, described in Chapter 5. The new production cell at Bendix Mintex is shown in Figure 5.2.

There are of course many other examples of new production systems in manufacturing and processing, which will be discussed throughout this book. But the concepts that drive the new production systems are not confined to manufacturing; on the contrary, they are also emerging in various services sectors, and can be expected to transform services work through the 1990s. One area in particular that has been affected is financial and insurance services.

Case 4: Client-centred service cells in the insurance industry

The functional division of labour has been taken to extraordinary lengths in the insurance industry where, by the end of the 1980s, most firms resembled white-collar paper-processing factories. Clerical operators would handle fragments of policyholder business, such as data entry, address changes, verifying accounts, transferring payments, and so on. Each function would be dictated by a particular computer system, and the whole service production system would be coordinated through extreme hierarchies of supervisory control.

One way of 'modernising' these systems has been to centralise customer operations in large telephone pools, where operators have access to all the computer systems in order to respond to a range of policyholder queries. All necessary processing is passed on to the existing clerical staff. These computer-driven 'telemarketing' units themselves become factory-like, with operators placed under tight surveillance and computer control.[3]

A complete break with such an approach involves forming customer-focused service cells, or 'one stop shops', so-named because a group of operators cater for all the needs of a particular set of clients, in this case policyholders. This new production system can work if all the clerical operators share tasks and have access to all computer systems, through menu-driven desk-top computer workstations. The cell members take responsibility for dealing with clients directly, and respond on the spot to such matters as claims, policy changes, or renewals. The cell as a whole takes charge of the quality of service, in this case measured through promptness, cycle completion times, and other non-traditional measures of quality and productivity.

We shall examine a successful transition to such cell-based services work in the case of the insurance firm, Colonial Mutual, discussed in Chapter 6.

These organisational innovations are transforming work and the workplace. They represent a powerful restructuring of human relations at work, through a restructuring of the relations between people, organisation and technology. They are taking the place of 'old' production systems where the emphasis is on repetitive processing of materials, goods or information, with people performing narrowly defined tasks, subject to command and control coordination through supervisory hierarchies. Why? Because they offer firms which introduce them greater levels of quality, flexibility, adaptability and efficiency, which can be translated (with adequate management expertise) into better competitive performance and profitability. To the workers themselves, they offer a renewal of the quest at work for meaning, dignity and responsibility—aspirations that were marginalised with the triumph of the mass production system and its canons of productive efficiency.

PART 1: A NEW WORKPLACE CULTURE

The task of Chapters 2, 3 and 4 of this volume is to identify the most important elements of best practice organisations, and to account for the systematic manner of their appearance. It is by now relatively uncontroversial to claim that a new production system is emerging in industrialised countries, based on high quality, quick response and high value-added product strategies. These are the elements of 'best practice', which we shall explore in some depth in subsequent chapters. It stands in contrast to the standardised low value-added production system, based on mass production that has dominated the twentieth century until the most recent decade. The lineaments of the new production systems are by now reasonably familiar.[4]

As an example of this new consensus, we may accept the arguments advanced by the Massachusetts Institute of Technology Commission on Industrial Productivity, in their hard-hitting 1989 book, *Made in America* (Dertouzos et al. 1989). The Commission's analysis was centred on the role of mass production in shaping the prevailing concepts of productivity and efficiency, and in determining the prevailing patterns of industrial relations. As the MIT Commission noted, 'The great success of the American economy in the twentieth century was a system of mass production of standard products for a large domestic market' (Dertouzos et al. 1989, p. 47). Competitive advantage lay with simple, low value-added products that could be produced at low cost in large numbers for undifferentiated mass markets.[5]

This system was replicated, with varying national adjustments, in virtually all OECD countries during the post-war period. It called for narrow jobs and the pursuit of efficiency through the division of labour, for detail work to be regulated by machine and by close, untrusting supervision, for skills to be appropriated by Organisation and Methods engineering departments, and to be confined to narrow 'trades' protected by demarcation and the 'front end' training model of apprenticeship. Deskilling was pursued as a conscious strategy, in order to cheapen labour and hence reduce production costs; technological innovation was pursued to further deskill and eliminate the labour 'factor' in the production process.

The paradigm shift in manufacturing captured in the phrase 'new production concepts' owes its origins to a wide array of forces. On the demand side, these include the trends towards market segmentation and product innovation; on the supply side, there has been the pursuit of flexibility and quality assurance through the development of new work organisation systems such as teamwork and programmable flexible manufacturing and assembly systems. In the realm of complex value-added goods and services, these organisational innovations have given firms adopting them a competitive edge over firms which are still wedded to large-scale mass production as their strategy.

The elements of the new production systems are likewise relatively uncontroversial. Firstly, production (of goods or services) is demand-driven or demand-regulated. This means that production is linked to customer demand, rather than allowed to accumulate in stocks which are periodically cleared. This represents a fundamental shift which appears in a new focus on the customer and on 'quick response' as a generalised strategy. Secondly, competitive strategy is based on product and process innovation rather than cost minimisation and repetitive production. Such a strategy calls for, thirdly, flexibility of process and adaptation of employees to different tasks, achieved through teamwork, multiskilling, and complemented by technological innovations such as programmable flexible manufacturing systems and flexible service cells. Fourthly, it calls for devolution of responsibility, autonomy and authority, which is best expressed through self-managing teams and, in any case, through broadened job descriptions and elimination of middle levels of supervision. This broadening of tasks is achieved through the integration of functions that were previously fragmented, and the building in of functions (such as quality assurance) that were previously functionally distinct. Flexibility demands new management techniques such as JIT and Total Quality Management (TQM). Finally, the system's dependence on worker commitment and adaptability comes to be reflected in more cooperative industrial relations and recognition of workers' contributions, e.g. through skills- and performance-based pay.

New production systems—common features

The new production systems are no passing fad or 'flavour of the month'. They are here to stay. A number of factors are at work here.

Firstly, the new production systems as innovations differ from previous management innovations such as matrix structures or 'management by objectives' in a fundamental way. Important as these initiatives may have been, they did not engage directly with the way that work is productively performed. *Rather than reforming the management of inefficient work procedures, the new production systems represent a reform of the work structures themselves.* And by getting to the fundamentals of reorganising the way that work is performed, they bring in their wake an equally fundamental reform of the process of management itself. In place of command and control structures designed to enforce rigidity and compliance, the new production systems call for management that offers facilitation, guidance and coordination between self-managing groups of employees who are capable of looking after the details of production for themselves.

Secondly, the new production systems also differ sharply from the various job redesign and quality of working life (QWL) initiatives that were popular in workplaces in the 1970s—such as job rotation and job enlargement. Important as these initiatives may have been, they never got to grips with the fundamentals of *why work was structured in such a fragmented way*. The QWL initiatives grappled with the symptoms, but not with the cause of workplace inefficiencies. They never came to grips with the fundamentals of enhancing the responsibility carried by employees for achieving better results, which is the issue that underpins all the new production systems.

Thirdly, the move to new production systems is concerned with the quality of the outputs of the production process, rather than being obsessed with the cost of the inputs. Traditional approaches to productivity improvement have almost always taken cost cutting as their driving feature. But if the outputs are not being improved— which is the goal of the new production systems—there is little scope for competitive advancement through cutting the costs of inputs, other than by sliding down to a cheaper level in the market place. And this is a slippery slope that most firms would want to avoid.

I concur with the Harvard scholar, Wickham Skinner, in his characterisation of the traditional cost-cutting approach as generating a 'productivity paradox'. Following his ground breaking publications on manufacturing, Skinner was concerned to review the efforts made by US organisations in the early 1980s to improve their productivity levels.[6]

Skinner observed the enormous efforts these firms expended in seeking to motivate their workforces, coupled with enormous efforts to cut back costs and in particular direct labour costs—and yet the results were uniformly disappointing. He concluded that the exclusive focus on costs was, in the end, not just unsuccessful but was positively counter-productive. It focused attention on the wrong issues. It saw productivity improvement in terms of behavioural change, whereas the real breakthroughs were to come from structural change and a totally different perspective. *It is the new production systems that have now resolved Skinner's productivity paradox.*

So the new production systems represent a substantial shift in techno-organisational paradigm.[7] They involve a restructuring of work, and through this, a reconceptualisation of management. They go beyond cosmetic changes to engage with the fundamentals of work responsibility and quality assurance. They focus on outputs rather than inputs, and they seek functional flexibility rather than 'external' flexibility (such as unrestrained ability to hire and fire), as summarised in Table 1.1.

11

Table 1.1 New production systems

Common approaches

- Changes to work *vs* changes to management
- Enlargement of responsibilities (maintenance; quality assurance; collaboration) *vs* task specialisation
- Focus on output *vs* costs of inputs
- Integration of tasks *vs* functional division of labour
- Functional flexibility *vs* internal rigidity, external flexibility

Building on the quality revolution that was the necessary prelude to their emergence, the new production systems are therefore concerned with the structures and processes through which work is performed efficiently. They represent a rethinking of the fundamentals of human creative activity, motivation and aspiration. Michael Hammer calls it nothing less than the *re-engineering of work*. Like Skinner before him, Hammer (1990; 1993) argues that firms which seek productivity gains through labour-shedding automation are responding to symptoms rather than causes. They see their problem in terms of inefficient workers, whereas their real problem is inefficient structures and systems. They have to re-engineer these systems and structures, to release the productivity and creativity that is constrained by the traditional structures. Simply automating processes to remove labour, even with the very latest computer technology, will not solve the problem; *if anything, it will make it worse*, by building further rigidities into a system which is already close to seizing up with rigidity. Again, the real challenge emerges as one of changing the underlying structures.[8]

To change these structures means taking some pretty drastic steps. It means dispensing with supervisory hierarchies, and replacing them with the direct, self-managing coordination of teams. It means dispensing with professional demarcations, and bringing such tasks as programming, quality control and maintenance into the ambit of shop floor teams themselves. It means dispensing with a model of productive efficiency that is grounded in division of labour, and opting instead for maximal integration of tasks. It means dispensing with the idea that quality can be achieved through inspection, but instead structuring work so that quality is achieved at source, by entrusting workers with the goals and performance measurement of their work systems. All this and more is entailed by the concept of 'new production systems'.[9]

Our questions are: why have these strategies been so popular in the past, and why do they continue to be the dominant strategies chosen in the present—despite the evidence of the superior efficiency of the new production systems? Such strategies cannot simply be mistaken; they must have some rationale. Why is it that firms have viewed productive efficiency in the past, and continue to see it in most cases, as deriving from the fragmentation of tasks, their coordination through rigid hierarchies, and the elimination of labour altogether wherever possible through automation? The answer is this. They made sense when large firms secured unbeatable business advantages through the scale of their production systems, and when such large firms could secure competitive advantages through reducing their costs, based on being able to mount long production runs and amortise capital expenditure over these long runs. They made sense within a particular form of production system, and within that system only. That system is mass production. It rose to dominance in the twentieth century, so that its canons of productive efficiency came to be seen as universal. But as the mass production system loses its dominance, so too do the business and workplace strategies that made sense within it. Hence the salience of the new production systems.

There is a wide sweep of history summarised in this paragraph, and it calls for justification. We shall attend to this in a moment. But consider for the moment how the dominant notions of efficiency, encapsulated in such strategies as concentration, centralisation, vertical integration and fragmentation of tasks, derive from the canons of mass production. In this system, the concept of returns to scale makes formidable economic sense. Chandler (1990) has described in magisterial terms how firms were formed in the last quarter of the nineteenth century and first quarter of the twentieth century which were able to organise production on a scale never before witnessed nor attempted. Standardisation was the key to their success. Standardisation of product was matched by standardisation of process (achieving a pinnacle in Henry Ford's moving production line) and a standardisation of labour, achieved first by Frederick Winslow Taylor. The strategy of producing huge runs of identical products through repetitive processing, with people performing the same fragmented tasks over and over again, called for massive investments in supervisory hierarchies whose sole task was to reduce variation and impose uniformity. The rigidity of this system was its strength.

Now, in different circumstances, when rapidly changing markets call for quick responses from firms, this very rigidity becomes a source of weakness. Strength and rigidity no longer confer competitive advantage. The canons of mass production, which derive their rationale from their rigidity, thus become of questionable relevance as the system of mass production loses its dominant position. A variety of 'new production concepts' are thus able to emerge.[10]

So, to understand why new production systems are emerging now, we first need to understand the nature of the system they are replacing. This brings us to the question of the rise of the mass production system, and its supersession by alternative production systems. We shall offer first a (very compressed) historical account followed by an analytic discussion of the rival production systems. We shall identify three such systems through which firms compete in the 1990s: the mass production system, its rivals in the lean production system which arose in Japan, and the sociotechnical production system that arose in Europe.

The approach I intend to follow is to contrast the different strategies pursued by firms in terms of their underlying models of productive efficiency; these I will generalise as three competing models of production, or production systems. The argument does not depend on any dating of production eras, nor on any idea of production paradigms succeeding each other in some grand march of history. On the contrary, it is to be expected that paradigms as 'visions of efficient production' will co-exist and indeed offer alternative sources of competitive strategy. It is this co-existence that underpins the otherwise puzzling notion of 'competing production models', used as shorthand to depict the competitive advantages sought by firms in their adoption of different visions of productive efficiency.[11]

But we still have to find an answer to the question of why the shift should be so noticeable now. If the imperative for organisational change is so great, then the attentive manager or union official is entitled to ask: Why now? Why not before? There seems to be no end to the stream of books appearing on management shelves urging firms to restructure in order to meet the 'new international competition'. There seems to be a tremendous urgency to these injunctions to 'change now, and bring employees into the decision-making process, before it is too late'. Yet we know that the same arguments have been developed by the sociotechnical school at least since the 1960s, and earlier than that, in the 1940s and 1950s by the Human Relations school. Why were they ignored then, and yet be promoted so assiduously—without attribution, without sourcing, with scarcely any acknowledgment at all—in the 1990s?

Sociotechnical production systems: then and now

Consider the example of Australia's great proponent of change in work organisation, Fred Emery. He was involved from the beginning in the formulation of sociotechnical ideas at London's Tavistock Institute in the 1950s, and then in the first major national attempt to de-bureaucratise industry, through the Norwegian industrial democracy programme, in the 1960s. Writing in 1974 in the influential US journal *Organizational Dynamics*, he reflected on these experiences, and sought to account for the entrenching of bureaucratic ideas of management in industry. He was one of the first to point the finger decisively at Frederick Winslow Taylor and his associates, such as Gilbreth and Gantt and the engineering school that developed Organisation and Methods engineering departments in factories, as the real founders of the modern approach. This was linked to the rise of big business in the 1880s and 1890s in the USA and its ability to tap unprecedented economies of scale and to utilise unprecedented sources of power in unleashing a new wave of productivity expansion. In this way he equated mass production with scientific management as the twin foundations of the 'modern bureaucratic corporation', which he saw as the principal enemy of further progress and the source of so much 'turbulence' in the social domain. He was absolutely correct in his formulation of the alternative to such bureaucratisation, locating it in the reform of work structures that re-emphasised the role of individuals and at the same time promoted the concept of semi-autonomous work groups. As Emery put it:

We have firmly based scientific knowledge of what a job needs to provide if a person is to develop greater self-reliance and self-respect and achieve a sense of dignity. The job must provide optimal variety, opportunity to learn on the job and go on learning, adequate scope for decision making, mutual support and respect from co-workers, a meaningful task, and the opportunity for a desirable future. It is precisely these things that are negated by a bureaucratic organization of work. Optimal variety is knocked on the head by standardization of effort; continued learning is defeated by job simplification; elbow room on the job is restricted by shifting all possible controls to supervisors and staff planners; mutual support and respect are replaced not by the impersonality with which bureaucracies are usually charged, but by invidious inter-personal comparisons as individ-

15

uals seek to ease or improve their personal lot and by self-serving cliques that form to improve their lot vis-a-vis their co-workers; meaningfulness of the individual's task tends to disappear in the interest of job simplification and the centralization of responsibility for 'whole tasks' in supervisory hands; the desirable future of job security and promotion that the industrial and administrative bureaucracies hold out to middle-level and lower-level employees becomes in fact something of a *Pilgrim's Progress*—a life of endless vicissitudes on the way to Heaven (Emery 1974, p. 9).

In this striking passage Emery puts his finger on virtually every topic that the latest management texts parade as novel and urgent. His message then fell on largely deaf ears. Now it is all the rage—albeit with little acknowledgment. Something has obviously changed. It is of course the world itself that has moved on, leaving behind the giant bureaucratic corporations that Emery in the 1970s feared could take over and reshape the world in their own image.

First of all, in East Asia and Latin America new sources of mass production arose which could compete on equal technological terms but with drastically lower labour costs. This was the first shock for the over-bureaucratised and standardised mass producers of Europe and North America: the undermining of their markets from below.

Then there was the rise of networks of small and medium-sized enterprises which were able to complement these monolithic giants and open up market opportunities that had lain dormant in the era of standardisation. Such networks arose in Italy and in Germany, and at the same time they emerged in Japan, Taiwan and other East Asian economies. This was the origin of the specialisation and fragmentation of markets that has proven to be so troublesome for the giant bureaucratic corporations; it was the invasion of their markets from 'above'. They were now being squeezed from both ends. Increasingly they could be seen as omnipotent only in a world created in their own image.

But the real coup de grace was delivered by Japan, in the form of a comprehensive competitive alternative production system that delivered superior quality, superior market responsiveness, and superior levels of innovation, built on unprecedented levels of commitment of multi-skilled staff to productivity enhancement and efficiency improvement. This was a combination that the bureaucratic giants, so feared by Emery, could not hope to match. And they have paid the price, going down to defeat after defeat in the 1980s and increasingly in the 1990s, staging something of a comeback (such as in the cases of Motorola or Xerox) only when they have thoroughly absorbed the lessons of the Japanese lean production system and systematically applied them to their own operations.[12]

So although sociotechnical theory was elaborated to deal with a world dominated by giant bureaucratic corporations, it is finding its relevance in a world today where flexibility, adaptability and responsiveness are the keys to competitive success. And this is just where sociotechnical innovations such as semi-autonomous work groups find their niche and application.

PART 2: WORKPLACE REFORM IN AUSTRALIA

Chapters 5 to 11 of this book report the findings of studies I conducted into organisational innovation in Australian enterprises. These are real organisations grappling with the all too real problems of a rapidly changing world, and in one form or another, they are generating examples of sociotechnical change in the process that is called in Australia 'workplace reform'.

Workplace reform has been one of the great success stories in Australia during the past decade. While the rest of the Anglo-Saxon world devoured itself in an orgy of free market liberalism, financial excess and de-industrialisation, Australia quietly put in place the elements of a manufacturing consensus culture—something long postponed during the years that the country rode to prosperity, as we say in Australia, on the sheep's back.

The path to reform in Australia has not been easy. The country's economic and industrial institutions provided little incentive. A unique integration of trade policy, industry policy and industrial relations policy was effected at the time of federation, and it stuck with some resilience right through to the 1980s. The former Tariff Board played its role in maintaining protective tariffs, originally imposed to protect 'infant industries' but increasingly becoming a costly barrier behind which Australian industry grew fat and lazy. Tariffs and wages became locked together in a peculiarly Australian model of industry development.[13]

The industrial relations system was held together in tightly regulated fashion by the Australian Conciliation and Arbitration Commission (now the Australian Industrial Relations Commission) which was able to hand down 'awards' covering workers across whole industries. Periodic adjustments to national wages were effected through regular National Wage Cases, where the unions, led by the Australian Council of Trade Unions (ACTU), argued the merits of wage increases with the employers.

Enterprise-level considerations rarely entered the minds of the industrial partners who put together this protective framework. It was a cosy, conservative, inward-looking consensus, disturbed occasionally by outbreaks of ferocious class battles when unions such as the Metal Workers launched periodic wage campaigns in a situation where an artificially high standard of living was maintained by high world commodity prices. But as commodity prices fell in the 1970s and 1980s, Australia's low levels of industrial sophistication became embarrassingly obvious, and its cosy arrangements (which could be described not so much as neo-corporatist but rather as pre-corporatist) came under sustained reformist attack.[14]

The 1980s saw an inexorable shift in the 'centre of gravity' of the industrial system to the enterprise level. Tariffs affecting whole industries were wound back, while new institutions like Austrade dealt not with industrial sectors but with firms. The Australian Manufacturing Council (AMC), established as part of the 1983 ALP–ACTU Accord as the voice of the unions in industry matters, increasingly took a firm-level export-oriented approach to policy, through issuing such major reports as *The Global Challenge* (Australian Manufacturing Council 1990). The industrial relations system was gradually pegged back from national and sector-level adjustments, and brought more and more into line with productivity performance and enterprise-level results, through such wage principles as the Restructuring and Efficiency Principle ('second tier'), the Structural Efficiency Principle ('award restructuring') and finally the Enterprise Bargaining Principle.[15]

In the mid-1990s, Australian enterprises and their performance are clearly the focus of the country's industry policies and industrial relations bargaining, albeit with much controversy.[16]

It is in this context that there has been a proliferation of research at the enterprise level to find out how enterprises actually work in the Australian system.[17] At the same time, these same enterprises and their advisory bodies have opened themselves up as never before to 'benchmarking' experiences comparing themselves to the rest of the advanced manufacturing world. The exchanges between Australian firms and their counterparts in Japan, Scandinavia, Germany, Italy and other European countries, and now increasingly in the East Asian 'tiger' economies, have been intense. Many of these delegations have been bipartite and tripartite, reflecting the new level of cooperative accommodation between unions and employers in Australia, which in turn reflects the maturity of the unions and the constructive role they are playing in the country's industrial renaissance.[18]

Australian enterprises are calling on a little recognised but precious intellectual resource, namely a strong tradition of cooperative workplace reform. Australian social scientists and reformers like Fred Emery worked with the world's best to fashion the concepts of sociotechnical organisational change that now dominate the innovation strategies of firms pursuing a democratic model of adjustment. Through the 1970s and increasingly in the 1980s, Australian firms have joined the ranks of the world's leading organisations in mastering the challenges of change. This legacy, which is now embodied in dozens of restructured firms themselves, in dozens of consultancy firms pursuing sociotechnical reform strategies, in unions and in the academy (but as yet with little penetration of government or its agencies), is one of Australia's great assets as its enterprises gear up to face the further restructuring challenges of the 1990s.[19]

The watchword of change in Australia is *workplace reform*—meaning that it starts with the reorganisation of jobs and technology, and from that basis proceeds to the renegotiation of company structures, strategies and production systems. There have, of course, been all too many examples of the top-down variety of organisational change, pursued with some vigour in the 1980s, but few of these remain to tell of their success, and many have crashed, bringing the good name of their companies down with them. But the number of firms committed to participative change, and achieving sometimes astounding improvements in organisational performance as a result, has been steadily growing.

The stories of a selection of these successful cases of workplace reform are told in the following chapters. They are not all 'good news' stories. The mistakes made were sometimes appalling. Improvements were sometimes fitful, and organisations took as many backward steps as they did forward. Lessons were sometimes learned hard and at great cost. But through all this adversity, the stories are there to tell. The successes are real.

I have been fortunate in being able to take a close look at the companies whose experiences I discuss. Through my research programme of UNSW Studies in Organisational Analysis and Innovation, conducted between 1991 and 1993, I have been granted access to the inside stories of real change processes in selected organisations The object of the studies has been to provide a fair representation

19

of the organisation's own experiences, set within its commercial and industrial context, and to attempt some generalisation of this experience against the predictions and insights of the organisational and industrial relations literature.[20]

Like the Australian experiences themselves, these UNSW studies have spanned manufacturing and services sectors, both public and private. The cases selected for presentation here are exemplary of the Australian workplace reform experience of the last five years. In most cases, there are telling contrasts between the gains of the past five years and the setbacks and mistakes notched up in the past. Sociotechnical organisational reform is thus alive and well in Australia.[21]

PART 3: SOCIOTECHNICAL ORGANISATIONAL INNOVATION

Chapters 12 and 13 form the third part of this volume. This last part attempts to draw out some of the lessons of these stories of change, seeking to generalise the patterns of adaptation and negotiated transformation undertaken within firms that are sometimes struggling to keep abreast of developments. In this, there emerges a curious disjunction between the two great streams of thought flowing from industrial relations and from organisational analysis.

On the one hand there is already a substantial literature on the topic of organisational change in the business and organisational press, where the emphasis is on strategies and processes for accomplishing change. On the other hand, there is a great deal of debate concerning the transformation of industrial relations, which in Australia has focused on the issue of 'enterprise bargaining' but which everywhere is concerned with the issue of 'flexibility'. Yet it is rare to find the two streams of thought engaging, such as in a discussion of the constitutional foundations and legitimacy provided to a programme of change by first seeking a mandate through the negotiation of a development agreement or enterprise agreement. In the real world, these issues are inseparable.

The third part of this volume, then, seeks a synthesis of industrial relations and organisational innovation, in the concrete setting of the case studies of real organisational change. It is the transformation of work that underpins the current wave of organisational innovation. And it is the negotiation of this transformation that constitutes the foundation for the new industrial relations. In place of previous concerns with collective wage bargaining and grievance procedures, there has emerged a new industrial relations of skills formation, of work organisation, and ultimately an industrial relations of technological and organisational change. These issues provide the new substantive matters for negotiation of workplace reform.

Thus the synthesis emerges through seeing the substantive issues of human resources management and of organisational development in a new light, as matters for negotiation within an industrial relations framework. Such an integrated approach achieves a twofold advantage over the traditional intellectual division of labour between these disciplines. On the one hand, it provides the change issues with a constitutional foundation that gives their practices a legitimacy never before accorded them. And on the other hand it generates a new content for the subject matter of industrial relations, taking it beyond its sterile concern with distributive bargaining and engaging instead with productivist bargaining concerns at the enterprise level. It is at this level that the threefold synthesis of strategic human resources management, strategic industrial relations and strategic management of change, find their common ground and common purpose.[22]

The final chapter probes the notion of organisational innovation at a more abstract level. In it I present a model of organisational innovation (conceived as an analogue of scientific and technological innovation) where the common features are those of probing of the environment, experimentation, learning, and the embodiment of results in some institutional form. It is my purpose to demonstrate how the successful, adaptive and responsive 'best practice' firm is starting to look like a conscious experimenter, utilising procedures that bear a striking resemblance to those of the scientific laboratory and engineering design studio.

The discussion proceeds with a very concrete examination of what all this means for organisational design. What indeed can we expect to be the shape of the workplace of tomorrow, and to what extent will it successfully embody such notions as learning organisation, intelligent manufacturing and human-centred systems? What will be the organisational architectures shaping these activities, and the new patterns of organisation that drive them?

CORE PROPOSITIONS

Let me close this introduction by distilling the argument of the book into five core propositions. They are as follows.

1 The structures of control found throughout industry are mod-

elled on nineteenth century organisational innovations developed in mass production sectors of manufacturing, where they were designed to produce outcomes of uniformity and standardisation. The intellectual overhang from these past successes bedevils current efforts by firms to generate market responsiveness and innovation in turbulent environments.

2 The record indicates that firms have everything to gain by dispensing with the organisational structures of control and implementing instead frameworks that encourage creativity, collaboration and continuous improvement. This means embarking on a new round of organisational innovation informed by a new, sociotechnical vision of productive efficiency.

3 There is no 'one best way' to design or implement this new vision of productive efficiency. It is best seen as the outcome of a process of renegotiation of work organisation systems, technology, skills formation, and management coordination. Significant advantages are seen to accrue to firms which successfully manage such a legitimated process of change.

4 Innovative structures such as self-managing teams and inter-organisational networks provide firms with possibilities for strategy adjustment that are in turn conditioned by frameworks of public policy and administration. This is the complex business environment within which the continuous adaptation of a 'learning organisation' provides competitive advantage. Such public frameworks are constructed by the operation of the political systems, and entail major choices over the allocation of public resources.

5 The probing and testing of options that are the hallmarks of adaptive learning give the process of organisational innovation strong links with innovation in the cognate fields of science and technology. It is the mutual enrichment of each of these three great creations of modernity, united in a common recognition of the primacy of values over various determinisms, that offers the possibility of a rational synthesis of innovation processes that protects their strengths and defines their limits.

There can be no 'proof' of the validity of these propositions but my purpose is to provide the most convincing justification for their validity, based on the research literature that is now available, and on the direct evidence of the case studies which have engaged me over the past three years. The book will have served its purpose if these propositions eventually come to be taken as self-evident.

Part 1

A new workplace culture

2

Competing models of productive efficiency

Mass production systems, lean production systems, sociotechnical production systems

In production systems operating around the world, in factories, offices and shops, there can be found today three competing and irreconcilable models of what it is that constitutes productive efficiency. Whereas once there was seen to be 'one best way' of organising for efficiency, today there is confusion among firms over the structures needed for efficiency. This mirrors their confusion about which strategies to follow to remain successful.

The dominant view remains one of efficiency being associated with the division of labour and the imposition of hierarchical control. This leads to production systems characterised by fragmentation of jobs, specialisation of tasks, and command and control structures designed to achieve standardisation and uniformity of output. This is how most workplaces are organised today, whether they are found in heavy industry, in banks, in fast food outlets, or in government agencies.

A second view is that efficiency is associated with leanness, meaning the elimination of all non-value-adding activities, combined with functional flexibility and total quality assurance. This leads to production systems like that pioneered in Japan by Toyota, with its reduction of inventory costs through Just-In-Time delivery systems, its reduction of overhead costs through sub-contracting, and its reduction of product variation costs through the use of multi-skilled teams of operators taking responsibility for the quality of their own output. This second view, known as the lean production model of efficiency, is sweeping the world, based on the extraordinary industrial success of Japan.

There is a third view that contests the dominance of the mass production view, but refuses to go all the way with the principles of lean production. This is the approach that calls for skills-based systems where computer integration, for example, extends the capacities and capabilities of operators, rather than seeking to eliminate them or turn them into machine-minders without any real role to play.

Which view of efficiency is right? The answer is that each model of efficiency has its sphere of applicability. We shall look in some detail at how these models tie in with, or mesh with, certain kinds of business strategies and approaches to organisational change, human resources management and industrial management. But first I wish to develop each view, or 'model' of productive efficiency, in its historical specificity. We shall then be in a position to compare and contrast the different models, and probe their relevance for firms that are restructuring today.

THE MASS PRODUCTION SYSTEM

The term *mass production* describes a system in which product, process and labour are all standardised. The standardisation allows for long production runs, which lowers unit costs, which in turn allows prices to be cut and markets to be extended. Thus, as Adam Smith predicted, the extent of the market becomes the determining influence over the form of production. The original pioneers of mass production, such as Henry Ford, created not only new products, but new markets. Ford's practice of lowering prices for his Model T cars went against the commercial wisdom of his time (which held, naturally enough, that if you want to increase profits you increase prices).[1]

But lowering prices was essential to extending markets and that set the conditions for producers being able to lengthen production runs. The longer the production run of a standardised good, the greater the possibility of recouping costs sunk into design, development and capital investment in assembly facilities. This is the system in which the notion of 'returns to scale' makes formidable economic sense. It was so successful that it drove its competitors, based on craft and batch production, out of the market.

Let us first consider the real mass production system (henceforth MPS), which arose as a historical fact in the early years of the twentieth century, and became a dominant industrial force throughout the world.

There is by now an impressive literature which documents the rise to dominance of the MPS.[2] This literature documents the origins, rise to dominance and loss of dominance of a system based on standardised production. It has been extended to encompass the impact mass production techniques have had on management practices, in particular on accounting (Johnson & Kaplan 1987), as well as on culture more generally (Harvey 1989). In the recent work of Chandler (1990) and Lazonick (1991) this literature has been given a definitive comparative dimension, utilising the general categories of a 'competitive managerial capitalism' which arose in the USA and a 'cooperative managerial capitalism' as found in Germany, both superseding the 'personal' or 'proprietorial' capitalism of nineteenth century Britain; managerial capitalism has in turn been succeeded as the dominant system by the 'collective capitalism' of Japan and the Far East in the later twentieth century.

Briefly, the MPS as a category encompasses some of the common features which emerged in industry at the turn of the century, allowing firms to capture systematically what Chandler (1990) calls economies of scale and of scope. It was put together from three main sources.

Firstly, there was the 'American system' of manufactures, developed in the mid-nineteenth century, which introduced the novelty of interchangeability of parts, replacing the unified nature of craft-produced products. Manufacturers of the new standardised products, such as the Colt revolver, the Singer sewing machine, or the McCormick harvester, enjoyed considerable economic advantages because of this standardisation.

Secondly, there was the standardisation of labour, achieved through the efforts of Frederick Winslow Taylor and his disciples such as Henry Gantt, Harrington Emerson and Frank Gilbreth. Under the banner of scientific management, these pioneers sought to break work tasks down to their basic, elemental components through time study and motion study, and then resynthesising them as work routines embodying the 'one best way'. Taylor, in particular, strove to enhance productivity by taking as many of the production decisions as possible out of the hands of workmen and placing them instead in a production department made up of engineers and professionals.

Finally, there was the standardisation of process, through the development of the moving assembly line, first introduced in manufacturing by Henry Ford at his Highland Park, Michigan, auto plant in 1913. It traced its lineage back to the moving conveyor lines of

27

the Chicago meat works and to the continuous refining methods pioneered in the oil industry by such giants as Standard Oil. Its major accomplishment was to embody the demands of supervision in the technology of the conveyor system, presenting the task to be done repeatedly to the worker by mechanical means, thereby providing a technical foundation for time and motion study. The world has never been the same since.

It was actually Henry Ford who coined the term 'mass production', in a ghostwritten article he published in *The New York Times* magazine in 1927. The term caught on, and has been with us ever since. It is actually a misnomer, because the essential feature of the system is standardisation; its mass character came from the market opportunities created by this innovation.

It was the standardisation of products, labour and process that allowed the MPS firm to break tasks down into smaller and smaller components, for each of which less skilled labour could be employed. This approach to productivity, first realised systematically after 1913, was actually spelt out clearly by the British mathematician and political economist, Charles Babbage, in 1832, in his influential text *On the Economy of Machinery and Manufactures*. Babbage enunciated his principle in these terms:

> That the master manufacturer, by dividing the work to be executed into different processes, each requiring different degrees of skill or of force, can purchase exactly that precise quantity of both which is necessary for each process; whereas, if the whole work were executed by one workman, that person must possess sufficient skill to perform the most difficult, and sufficient strength to execute the most laborious, of the operations into which the part is divided (Babbage, 1832).

Most scholars are agreed that the mass production system became an economic force during the First World War, particularly in the munitions industry, and then spread its militarisation of production to other sectors of the economy, first in the USA, and then in Europe, through firms becoming multinational (such as Ford), through the activities of consulting firms, and through political developments. (Taylorism was taken up with greatest enthusiasm in Fascist Italy, Nazi Germany and the Communist Soviet Union.) In the period after 1945 it spread through various national adaptations to the entire industrialised world, East and West, through the agency of multinationals and the rise of competitive mass producers first in Japan and later in Taiwan, Hong Kong and South Korea. The period up to the mid-1970s constituted what has been termed the 'golden age' of mass production and of the Fordist system it spawned (Marglin et al. 1989).

The methods of mass production were also taken up systematically in sectors unrelated to manufacturing, such as retail food, banking and financial services. The success of McDonalds in the 1970s and 1980s, for example, rests on the same principles of standardisation (in this case, of a hamburger product and the process for producing it) and the creation of a novel mass market, which Henry Ford had pioneered 50 years earlier. Schlesinger and Heskett (1991) call this the application of an 'industrial model' to services in both the public and private sectors, and undoubtedly it was competitively very successful.

But the very successes of mass production sowed the seeds for alternatives and competitors which increasingly made themselves felt in the 1970s and 1980s. In manufacturing, low cost competitors emerged in the Far East who could install factories utilising the latest mass production techniques but employ labour at very much lower wages, leading to lower costs of production and lower prices. Their successes were notched up in one field of consumer products after another. At the same time, the mass markets opened up by mass producers created opportunities for new competitors offering greater variety or quality or innovativeness, in ways which contradicted the standardisation principles of mass producers. Thus firms following mass production strategies found themselves caught in a pincer movement, undercut by lower cost producers on the one hand, and bested by producers offering superior products on the other. These are the origins of the pressures which drove large firms to look for rationalisation solutions in the 1970s and 1980s, which Schlesinger and Heskett (1991) graphically call a 'cycle of failure' afflicting firms in manufacturing as well as in services.

Limits to the mass production system

In retrospect, we can see how the success of mass production was underpinned by wider social and economic structures such as Keynesian policies, designed to maintain the strength of purchasing power and wage levels. One by one, these structures came under pressure from the shifts in markets and competitive strategies in the last two decades. The advent of new information technologies such as programmable computerisation and telecommunications was another factor in the breakdown of the conditions for the supremacy of mass producers. Scholars such as Jaikumar (1986) have documented how Japanese firms employing computer numerically controlled machine tools were able to exploit their flexibility to a much greater extent than their counterparts in the USA because of the adherence by the latter to principles of rigid production which no longer made sense with the possibilities of programmability.

There is, thus, an astonishing range and conjunction of forces that have undermined the supremacy of the mass production system, and created the conditions of turbulence faced by firms today as they seek to restructure their operations. In such conditions, organisations inevitably face choices between competing options, and the choices they make carry strategic implications.[3]

Seen from this perspective, the MPS is revealed as being extraordinarily rigid and dependent on a favourable, stable commercial environment. Of course the policies pursued by the major MPS firms in the inter-war and post-war years were designed to achieve this stable environment, and they were remarkably successful for several decades. But as the environment changed, the vulnerability of the canons of productive efficiency became all too evident: high-wage MPS firms in the USA and Europe found themselves undermined by low-wage MPS firms in Asia; as markets and consumer tastes became more diverse, long runs of identical products became less and less commercially successful. And so we have an analysis of mass production as a system whose canons of *productive efficiency* are as shown in Table 2.1.

Taken together, these canons of efficiency have come to dominate the discourse of productivity in the twentieth century. It is now taken as virtually self-evident, at least in the popular mind, that efficiency is synonymous with division of labour, with centralisation of expertise, with hierarchies of control—all features of the MPS system. Within the MPS system proper, they had a clear rationale—even if in practice they led to extreme social conflict and sometimes inhuman working conditions, particularly where Taylorisation was combined with rationalisation of jobs in large bureaucracies. But outside the MPS system which, after all, never attained a majority proportion of productive activity in any country—not even the USA—these canons of efficiency had no purchase at all. Yet they have achieved almost total dominance as the preferred first approach, being seen to apply to batch-based production work and even to the activities of public sector agencies such as transport and health systems that have nothing in common with the MPS. This is the paradox of the twentieth century, and one which is only being addressed now, as the economic dominance of the MPS sector moves into decline.

Table 2.1 The mass production system

Organisational features:
- Standardisation of product
  (competitive advantage based on price)
- Standardisation of labour
  (Taylorism: divorce of conception from execution)
- Standardisation of process
  (moving assembly lines; long, stable production runs)

Outcomes:
- Low quality, low cost products
- Functional division of labour
- Labour rigidities and demarcations
- High inventories and buffer stocks

Inputs:
- Low trust, arm's length customer and supplier relations
- Centralised authority/hierarchies
- Low trust industrial relations

Alternatives to mass production

Our understanding of current best practice in workplace reform and organisational innovation starts with an appreciation of the limits to the mass production system, and hence of the reach and applicability of its canons of productive efficiency. The next step in the argument is to consider the real alternatives that have arisen to mass production. This means looking beyond the superficial innovations mentioned above, such as matrix management and quality of working life (QWL) initiatives, for these did not engage with the logic of mass production, but merely sought to soften its effects. Nevertheless, genuine alternatives have arisen, which is one of the reasons that the mass production paradigm is now under such strain.

THE LEAN PRODUCTION SYSTEM

Historically, the first comprehensive alternative to the mass production system emerged in Japan. Evolving out of a replication of mass production systems in the USA, the Toyota production system in particular was already, in the 1950s, developing a markedly different model of productive efficiency. The reasons for this are now coming to be understood after a lengthy period of miscomprehension that veiled Japanese developments because of lack of contact.

For a start, the Japanese market was much smaller than the American market, and so extreme dependence on long runs of identical products was never seen as an option. Secondly, early on Toyota conceived of its comparative advantage over American and European mass producers in terms of the skills of its workforce, so it never sought the extremes of deskilling that were pursued in North America. Building on these skills, it strove for continuous, incremental improvement in its production processes, ignoring the Taylorist injunction to seek and stick with the 'one best way'. The reliance on skills also led in a natural progression to an emphasis on building quality into production work. Out of this flowed the notion of reducing inventories which other plants needed as a buffer between poor production and disrupted supply. Thus was born the Just-In-Time (JIT) approach which, in retrospect, can be seen as a powerful joint learning technique involving collaboration between a producer and its components or raw materials suppliers.

While none of these elements on its own could be said to mark a decisive break with the technoeconomic base of mass production, together they amounted to a rupture with the model of productive efficiency associated with Frederick Winslow Taylor and rigorously adhered to in the west at the time that Toyota was developing its alternative.

In a thoughtful review of these developments, Kaplinsky (1988) identifies seven central features of what he calls the *Toyotist* mode of production, and which we now term the lean production system (LPS). They are as follows. Firstly, production is demand driven, rather than being driven by supply considerations and amassed in stockpiles. Secondly, functional flexibility in both product and process is sought, for example via mixed assembly lines. Thirdly, this calls technically for quick change-overs, and organisationally for Just-In-Time production, rather than the 'Just-In-Case' buffer production strategy of the mass production system. The fourth feature is the multi-skilling and multi-tasking approach, which is designed to achieve functional flexibility needed for rapid response. These arrangements demand high levels of quality assurance, with the goal of 'getting things right first time', which is the fifth feature. Sixthly, workers are expected to make their contribution to quality assurance and quick response strategies through exercising higher levels of responsibility, in place of employers vesting all skills and responsibility in engineers. Furthermore, the engineers are expected to work on the shop floor, in contact with daily production problems. This leads to the seventh feature, which is worker involvement in continuous improvement, as opposed to the 'big bang' change philosophy espoused by traditional mass producers. These we can take as representing the canons of productive efficiency of the LPS.

It was with great surprise that American and European car producers discovered the features of the Toyota system (which was rapidly spreading to other Japanese producers) in the 1960s and 1970s, learning that the source of Japanese superiority lay not, as they imagined, in more advanced technology, but in a more efficient organisation of work. Rather than relying on the capacity of an engineering staff to anticipate and predict all aspects of production, leaving operators no scope other than to take orders, the Toyota system integrated the skills of workers into a cohesive system of expanded job content and continuous improvement.[4]

Shimada and MacDuffie (1986), in their analysis of Japanese-owned plants in the USA, coined the word 'humanware' to describe this unique interdependence between technical and human resources in the Japanese system. They characterise the Japanese approach to manufacturing as 'fragile', in the sense that its success is predicated on the continued input of skill and commitment from the workforce. This is opposed to the 'robust' approach typical of comparable US plants, where disruptions from the workforce are guarded against through measures such as holding large buffer stocks, bringing in extra employees to cope with absenteeism, ensuring quality through surveillance of products by Quality Control (QC) staff, and filling narrowly defined jobs with interchangeable workers.

The system developed by Toyota has since been picked up by other Japanese manufacturers in the automotive industry and beyond and this is the system that is now called the lean production system. This term was coined by the Massachusetts Institute of Technology researchers who conducted the five year MIT study of the world automotive industry, published as *The Machine that Changed the World* (Womack et al. 1990). This is certainly a book that has changed the industry. It has been widely studied by automotive firms themselves, as well as by wider sectors interested in penetrating the secrets of Japanese success.

It is now understood how the LPS model of productive efficiency has underpinned the astonishing successes of Japan. Features such as JIT enable firms to reduce their inventory costs while subcontracting networks allow them to reduce their overheads. The dynamic feature of these initiatives lies not so much in the cost savings, important as these are, as in their capacity to harness joint learning between principals and suppliers. This is the interactive, inter-organisational learning that is so sought after in the West (Lundvall et al. 1992).

The lean production system is seen as a total system that encompasses fundamentally new approaches to running the factory (the production system), to designing new products (the new product development system), to coordinating the supply chain (involving relations between suppliers and manufacturers), to linking customers with other aspects of the business (the sales and marketing system), and finally to the management of the total enterprise (the global management system). See Table 2.2.

Table 2.2 The lean production system

Organisational features:
- Diversified mass production
  (competitive advantage based on price, quality and responsiveness)
- Flexibility of process
  (quick change-over; Just-In-Time)
- Functional flexibility of labour
  (multi-tasking)

Outcomes:
- High quality, low cost products
- Functional integration of labour
- Low inventories and buffer stocks
- Labour flexibility, continuous improvement

Inputs:
- High commitment, close customer and supplier relations
- Team-based hierarchies
- Medium-trust industrial relations
- High worker commitment to company

The MIT group argue that the LPS is an integrated system that will become the dominant paradigm in the twenty-first century. They argue that these paradigm shifts take decades to accomplish: for example, it took 50 years for mass production to diffuse from the USA to Europe and Asia. The lean production system has taken the best part of three decades to develop in Japan; it started to spread quickly to the USA and Europe in the 1980s and will become, they say, a global force in the 1990s.

The best indicator so far of the success of the lean production system outside Japan is in the so-called Japanese transplants such as the automotive companies run by Toyota, Honda, Mazda and others in overseas countries. The Japanese 'transplants' have now been studied and their output measured. Krafcik (1988) found that Japanese automobile plants in the USA required 19.6 hours on average to produce a vehicle, compared with 20.3 hours in Japan and 24.4 hours in other US plants. This is the material effect of a lean production system. In other words, the transplants have achieved a level of efficiency comparable to that obtained in their home base. Efforts are now being made by automotive manufacturers to go beyond 'transplants' and embody some of the LPS principles in their own operations. A group of European manufacturers has formed the European Automobile Initiative Group to promote such changes.[5] But in my view, the real significance of lean production will be felt *beyond* the automotive industry, in manufacturing more generally and most broadly in the services sector, as firms find their 'mass production' approaches becoming counter-productive. Now LPS principles are being extended into general manufacturing by such agencies as engineering consultancy firms.[6]

Limits to the lean production system

As a system, the LPS has successfully overturned the Taylorist canons of productive efficiency erected by the MPS in firms seeking diversity and quality of output. But in their place, it has established a new and potentially dangerous orthodoxy, namely that the system is more important than its component parts. In the tightly-integrated lean production system, operating on razor-sharp Just-In-Time principles, the least variation leads to seizure of the production apparatus. Apart from the (very real) contribution that people make to improvements via 'quality circles' and other forms of involvement, the contributions that they make on the job are tightly constrained.[7] These systemic constraints are widely seen, both within Japan and externally, as constituting the limits to expansion of the LPS.

In Japanese LPS companies, workers on assembly lines still perform short-cycle repetitive operations that can be executed in less than one minute. In such cases, the LPS can only be described as a modified form of Taylorism. Critics of the LPS outside Japan such as Berggren (1992) and Dohse (1990), point to these features as being the essence of LPS, and hence as drastically opposed to

Western traditions of job redesign in its most participative mode. European alternatives such as those presented by Volvo, with its team-based assembly systems at Kalmar and Uddevalla, have long been seen as constituting the case against the endless expansion of production facilities based on LPS principles.[8]

Of even greater significance, the LPS is under exacting scrutiny in Japan. It is now recognised by many parties in Japan, including the Ministry of International Trade and Industry (MITI), that the JIT system carries heavy social costs such as small transport vehicles making hourly deliveries clogging the roads. The system of externalising costs through sub-contracting is also coming under scrutiny, and pressure is being applied to final assemblers to take on more of the costs themselves. It is significant that the MITI-favoured automotive producer appears no longer to be Toyota, which still adheres fairly strictly to LPS principles, but Mazda, which is now making efforts to internalise many of the social costs imposed by the LPS.[9]

Critics in Japan point to the alienating features of work organised along strictly LPS lines outside the automotive industry. Nomura (1992), for example, has described the case of automated assembly work in an electronics factory where printed circuit boards were being fabricated for television sets. Masami Nomura, from Okayama University, and colleagues argued that the approach to productivity enhancement in this factory followed traditional rationalisation and automation lines, with automation seeking to eliminate jobs, and the workforce being divided into a core and periphery that followed gender divisions. High productivity was maintained by long working hours. The conclusion was that 'The division of labor in Japan is a kind of Taylorism which will hardly be maintained under pressure from abroad'.[10] If this is the case, what kind of alternative can be construed as a genuine successor and competitor to both the mass production system and lean production system?

SOCIOTECHNICAL PRODUCTION SYSTEMS

A quite different intellectual tradition is involved in the generation of the third alternative production system paradigm. This is the tradition that derives from 'human relations' insights, which all through the twentieth century have been at odds with Taylorism. This paradigm is fundamentally concerned with the role of people at the centre of the production process. It has variously been called human-centred, anthropocentric or sociotechnical. It traces its lineage through the semi-autonomous work groups and industrial democracy experiments associated with the Tavistock Institute (Trist & Emery), back to human relations organisational theorists such as Douglas McGregor and Kurt Lewin. In honour of these intellectual antecedents, I propose that this model—or ideal type—be termed the sociotechnical production system (STPS).

The clearest expression of the STPS is found in team-based cellular production systems, appearing in various manufacturing, processing and services sectors, where the team members carry authority and responsibility for achieving production targets, for ensuring quality standards, and for following through all the scheduling and coordination issues involved in meeting these targets. Computer systems and other forms of information technology are used in such systems as extensions of the skills already acquired and used collaboratively by cell members. Numerous examples of such production systems have been described in the literature.[11] The cases that I have observed myself are described in Part 2 of this volume.

While various aspects of the STPS have been analysed in management, manufacturing and services literature, I wish to emphasise the common model that informs all of these developments, and above all, the constitutional legitimation of such systems through a framework of industrial relations founded on what Kochan and Dyer call 'mutual commitment'.[12]

Like its predecessor, the human relations school, the STPS provides both a positive model of new production systems and a critique of dominant practices, reminding the parties to industrial negotiations that the human element must always be central to production. As its name indicates, it calls for a balance between the social and technical dimensions of the change process.

The point of calling this a system alternative to LPS is that (at its best) it incorporates all the insights of the LPS regarding the elimination of wasteful activities, but it does so with a firm understanding that ultimately people constitute the source of productivity improvement. In the STPS, machines are devised to extend the capacities of productive people, whereas in the MPS, people are seen as mere extensions of a machine, or in the LPS, people are frequently sacrificed to efficiency through systemic coordination.[13]

There are a number of intellectual sources for the STPS. We may identify at least four streams of thought and experience:

- the human relations school;

37

- the sociotechnical school;
- new production concepts in Europe; and
- human-centred production systems.

Let us look briefly at each and then consider how they fit into current episodes of restructuring associated with the advent of information technology using intelligent manufacturing and business process re-engineering.

The Human Relations school: Mayo, Lewin, McGregor, Herzberg

The Human Relations school has existed as a source of critique of Taylorism ever since the 1920s and 1930s, when it was becoming clear that firms organising their production systems by the rigorous application of Taylor's methods could not hope to sustain their competitive advantages. While conventional organisational behaviour theory traces the origins of human relations thinking to Mayo and the Hawthorne experiments conducted at Western General Electric, it is more fruitful to base the arguments on the work of Kurt Lewin and his practical demonstrations of the contribution made by teamwork and the effect of different leadership styles on the work of teams. Through original notions such as 'group dynamics', he was able to strike a blow at the very foundations of mechanistic notions of productive efficiency.[14]

The Human Relations school eventually became subsumed within the Organisational Development school in the USA, which, in its insistence on participation without leadership and its studied ignoring of industrial relations, has largely departed from the realistic assumptions of human relations, and is not counted here as a source for the STPS. This stream terminated in the ideas of job enrichment and job enlargement propagated by authors such as Herzberg, and which came together in the broad notion of quality of working life (QWL) improvements. In retrospect, this can be seen as an evolutionary dead-end that had little practical impact on workplace reform and innovation.[15]

Sociotechnical school: Trist, Emery, Thorsrud, Gustavsen

The term 'sociotechnical' derives from the school of that name developed at the Tavistock Institute, London, in the 1950s and 1960s, and since exported around the world. While there have been many alternatives proposed to Taylorism and work bureaucratisation, the sociotechnical approach was the first to be promoted systematically and successfully as a practical alternative to the prevailing paradigm.

It was in fact promoted explicitly, by exponents such as Trist and Emery, as 'the emergence of a new paradigm of work' (Emery 1978a). Nothing that has happened since has invalidated this view. The more recent arrival of information technology innovations has merely underscored the basic soundness of the original sociotechnical insights.[16]

The Tavistock Institute of Human Relations had been founded in 1946 with the aid of a grant from the Rockefeller Foundation as a novel, interdisciplinary, action-oriented research organisation. It was set up for the specific purpose of actively relating the psychological and social sciences to broad social concerns. Pioneering studies had been conducted of the social system of factory work, published as the celebrated Glacier study (Jaques 1951), but as yet the action-oriented researchers had not formulated a specific link with technology and so were unable to propose a work system as an alternative to the mass production model.

In 1950, as part of a government-funded research programme investigating organisational innovations that could raise productivity in industry, Eric Trist and his group 'discovered' the existence of self-regulating groups in underground coal mines, leading to the formulation of the notion of the 'semi-autonomous work group' which has been central to sociotechnical theory ever since.[17]

The Tavistock researchers went on to generalise this discovery, and the principles of *joint-optimisation of the social and technical systems* of work soon became well established as alternatives to the prevailing Taylorist approach (which sought to optimise the technical system alone) and to the human relations approach (which sought to optimise the social system alone). As Trist put the matter in his 1981 overview of the entire sociotechnical experience, this joint approach could be enunciated in the form of seven principles:

1 The *work system*, which comprised a set of activities that made up a functioning whole, now became the basic unit rather than the single jobs into which it was decomposable.

2 Correspondingly, the *work group* became central, rather than the individual job-holder.

3 *Internal regulation* of the system by the group was thus rendered possible rather than the external regulation of individuals by supervisors.

4 A design principle based on the *redundancy of functions* rather than the redundancy of parts, introduced by Emery, characterised the underlying organisational philosophy which

39

tended to develop multiple skills in the individual and immensely increase the response repertoire of the group.[18]

5 The *discretionary*, rather than the prescribed, part of work roles is valued.

6 The individual is treated as *complementary* to the machine rather than as an extension of it.

7 *Variety is increased* for the individual, rather than decreased as in the bureaucratic mode (Trist 1981, p. 9).[19]

The parallel stream of thought that had been developed in the form of the Human Relations school, whose practical proposals were picked up as job enrichment and job enlargement, was opposed vehemently by sociotechnical theorists as being too weak. These disputes have lost their fire today, when we can see that both schools were opposing Taylorism but neither were at that time making much headway against the logic of mass production.

The sociotechnical school obtained its first substantial application in the form of a series of innovations in Norwegian industry, conducted with Einar Thorsrud, and known as the Norwegian 'Industrial Democracy' programme.[20] These innovations spread to Sweden where they were taken up with rather greater gusto, as in the famous examples of Volvo work reorganisation experiments at Kalmar.[21] These experiences have been generalised by a group of researchers at the Stockholm Centre for Working Life, led by Bjorn Gustavsen.[22]

Parallel to the Anglo-American (and Scandinavian) developments that grew out of sociotechnical systems, a German industrial psychological approach emerged, termed Action Regulation Theory. Like sociotechnical systems, it was concerned with the design of jobs and the formulation of criteria defining 'good' jobs.[23]

One glaring failure of the classical sociotechnical tradition, as in the German Action Regulation Theory, was to overlook the quite different alternative in Japan in the form of the lean production system, and the implications that this would carry for job design in Europe. The Tavistock researchers were apparently unaware of what was happening at Toyota while they were investigating the emergence of teamwork in western countries. This is why in our exposition today we have to recognise three dominant paradigms, or models, of productive efficiency, rather than the dichotomy propounded by the sociotechnical school in its formative writings.

New production concepts in Europe

In Europe, partly in response to the Japanese challenge and partly in response to new competitive pressures and demands from trade unions for humanisation of work, observers were noting important shifts in organisation in the early 1980s. Industrial sociologists Kern and Schumann conducted a survey in core sectors of the German economy, in machine tools, automobiles and chemicals, and announced their discovery of 'new production concepts', meaning a form of organisation that broke with Taylorism (Kern & Schumann 1984; 1987). In follow-up surveys, they have confirmed their previous findings and extended their analysis to the electronics industry (Kern & Schumann 1988).

These conceptual innovations have been amply confirmed in empirical investigations. For example, work by Christel Lane has shown that German industry has taken up these concepts whereas French and British industry has been slower to do so because of the prevailing attachment to notions of large-scale activity, centralisation and rationalisation as supposed sources of competitive strength.[24]

Human-centred production systems

A European alternative to both mass production and lean production has been developed in the notion of human-centred production. This has now come to be called (rather inelegantly) the anthropocentric production system (APS). It is promoted in Europe for example, by the European Commission, as a genuine alternative to both the MPS and LPS.[25]

The notion of human-centredness in production systems stems from formulations first advanced by Howard Rosenbrock and by Mike Cooley in the UK.[26]

Both Rosenbrock and Cooley argued that the trend towards the 'unmanned factory', driven by distrust in human operators and a desire to automate the human element 'out of the control loop', was fundamentally misconceived. They knew from their practical experience that adjustments always have to be made to automatic settings depending on a range of circumstances; this was a negative criterion for maintaining the input of skilled operators. More positively, such operators represented a unique source of creativity, flexibility and innovativeness—but their contribution could be accommodated only by designing systems around their involvement. Hence the notion of 'human-centredness', or treating the skilled operator as central, and the technology as an extension of the operator's capabilities, complementing his or her skills rather than displacing them.

Human-centred Computer-Integrated Manufacturing

The idea of the STPS has received a new lease of life with the advent of programmable automation, leading to the concept of cellular manufacturing or, more generally, to human-centred cellular production.[27] The criteria of human-centredness in the context of the latest manufacturing technology, Computer-Integrated Manufacturing (CIM), are being refined in a series of studies carried out in Europe under the Esprit programme of the European Commission.[28]

Two demonstration production cells were established: at Rolls Royce in London (a computer numerically controlled (CNC) turning cell with two lathes), and at ITT Sealectro. The latter project involved the production of radio frequency connectors, using CNC equipment for turning, milling, heat treatment and assembly (Ainger 1988). The real value of these projects lies in their acting as test beds and feasibility demonstrations. As such, they give rise to a new problematic of the 'social shaping of technology' (Rauner, Rasmussen and Corbett 1988).[29]

The human-centred approach is starting to penetrate the literature on ergonomics and engineering design, in recognition of the fact that the notion of 'human-centredness' has to be refined into specific criteria governing the design process in a number of different contexts.[30]

The most striking feature to have emerged from these experiments so far, is not so much the development of a set of criteria for human-centredness, but a recognition that human-centred production systems have to be organised in semi-autonomous, or quasi self-sufficient cells. This is a powerful insight that links human-centredness to the developments in Cellular Manufacturing, which themselves have received a big fillip with the advent of CIM. Thus the circle closes, with the latest CIM cells making connection with the original notion of the 'semi-autonomous work group' introduced by sociotechnical researchers in the 1960s.

Dutch sociotechnical school: de Sitter

The most sophisticated current application of sociotechnical methods and principles to organisational renewal is the approach termed *Integral Organisational Renewal*. Because it was developed by a group of researchers in The Netherlands, it is now known as the Dutch sociotechnical school.[31]

The essential characteristic of the Dutch approach is that it takes the entire organisation as its point of reference, embedding the production system in the organisational constellation that also includes new product development, joint action with suppliers, logistics, relations with customers, and other facets of the innovative and integrated organisation. This is a point of view that we shall come across repeatedly in our discussions: it is a view of the enterprise *as a total system*, as opposed to the various partial approaches to production reform that ignore, say, new product development, or approaches to marketing that ignore manufacture and design. We shall see how these concepts of the total organisational system are applied when we look at best practice production systems in Chapter 3.

We may summarise the elements, or canons, of productive efficiency of the STPS as in Table 2.3.

COMPETING MODELS OF PRODUCTIVE EFFICIENCY

The abstract notions of 'production systems' exhibited here are not meant to represent world-historical ideas that march in some Hegelian order through history. They are meant, much more modestly, to capture the essential characteristics of the production decisions that individual firms make as they pursue their contrasting production strategies.

A firm which seeks to enhance its performance by further streamlining and rationalising tasks, by seeking further vertical integration of operations, by introducing computer systems to automate processes that are presently performed by skilled staff—such a firm is actually deploying a model of productive efficiency that we can call a 'mass production model'. It makes sense if the firm is a mass producer in a world where competitive success goes to those firms which can secure economies of scale and scope through giant structures, and can service mass markets with products which sell on the basis of low price. But if the world does not reward such a competitive strategy, then the model of productive efficiency that is derived from it is misplaced.

A firm which seeks to enhance its performance by linking tasks closely together, producing 'Just-In-Time' rather than 'Just-In-Case', by devolving responsibilities and authority to shop floor teams, by building quality assurance into jobs, and by building a production

Table 2.3 The sociotechnical production system

Organisational features:
- Customised production
  (competitive advantage based on price, quality, responsiveness and innovation)
- Flexibility of process
  (quick change-over; Just-In-Time)
- Functional flexibility of labour
  (multi-functional, semi-autonomous teams: production cells)
- Human-centred techno-organisational design

Outcomes:
- High quality, medium cost, innovative products
- Flexible specialisation of labour
- Low inventories and low buffer stocks
- Functional flexibility, continuous improvement
- Informed worker commitment to production goals

Inputs:
- High commitment, close customer and supplier relations
- High level of skills with intellectual content
- Team-based, overlapping coordination
- Management focus on strategic directions and facilitation of production
- High-trust industrial relations
- Organisational democracy as goal

system as a comprehensive technology—such a firm is deploying a model of productive efficiency that we can call a 'lean production model'. It makes sense if the firm is seeking to compete in a rapidly changing market where success goes to speed of innovation, market responsiveness and quality of product rather than low price. It calls for levels of worker commitment and input that might not be forthcoming unless the firm provides recognition and guarantees that develop more 'naturally' within what we are calling the sociotechnical system.

If a firm seeks to enhance its performance by seeking responsiveness through skilled and committed staff, working with tools and systems that extend their skills rather than displacing them, and tackles wasted activity through joint continuous improvement, then this firm is utilising a model of productive efficiency that we term a 'sociotechnical systems' model. It is grounded in what Walton (1985) and Kochan and Dyer (1992) call 'mutual commitment'. Such a firm will seek out networks of customers and suppliers, and it will structure its own internal operations as a network of 'factories within a factory' or as customer-centred cells. The essence of its approach will be to seek technologies and work systems that build on and extend the skills of its employees.

The decisions that firms make are concrete decisions taken in definite circumstances that never repeat themselves. To paraphrase the Greek philosophers, firms never step in the same market twice. But there are patterns discernible in the decisions that firms make, and this is what I am getting at in this notion of competing models of productive efficiency.[32]

But the really significant question is whether the STPS, with its bias towards skilled operators, can prove to be a viable competitor with firms which embrace the LPS, with its bias towards a modified Taylorism. I believe it can be, subject to a very important caveat.

It needs to be acknowledged that the scope of classical sociotechnical organisational design was, by today's standards, remarkably limited. The technical system was conceived as machinery and its spatiotemporal layout (e.g. Engelstad 1972; Rice 1958). The social system was deemed to comprise work or occupational roles in the production system proper; it virtually never sought to include technological design, new product development, marketing, accounting, nor any other of the numerous inter-related functions that make for successful enterprise. Indeed it is the strength of the Japanese lean production system that it does bring all these elements together into a coherent image or model of the successful enterprise.

This emphasis purely on production, at the expense of new product development, cost accounting and other necessary aspects of successful enterprise, is perhaps the most glaring weakness historically of sociotechnical theory. And it has cost companies dearly. Volvo, for example, perhaps the pre-eminent example in Europe of a company which has systematically sought to apply sociotechnical ideas in its car production divisions, has recently slipped badly, and in 1992 announced that it would close its two 'flagship' plants, at Kalmar and at Uddevalla. This meant that Volvo would henceforth be virtually indistinguishable from the other 'mass production' European vehicle producers, employing standard assembly line production techniques in a bid to stay abreast of Japanese competition. Berggren (1993) argues persuasively that

Volvo has abandoned its sociotechnical experiments without giving them a real chance (particularly in the case of Uddevalla) and that its real failure lay in the confinement of job redesign to factory production while new product development continued untouched in its exclusively linear, engineering-based mode. In this it is very different from the systematic integration that takes place between production, marketing and supplies in Japanese new product development.

The same ideas apply, with even greater force, to the design of manufacturing systems and the criteria used by engineers. No-one should underestimate the need of the engineering profession for such 'metaguides' to design, by which I mean criteria that stand outside of the design process but can inform it and engage with it. The depths to which such 'uninformed' design can sink are revealed in the relentless tendency to standardise manufacturing systems, reserving only the most mindless tasks for 'manual operations', and aiming to eliminate the 'human element' if at all possible. That this is still the typical approach was brought out in an important study conducted at Boston University, which surveyed the treatment of the 'human–machine' interface in current, standard engineering textbooks. This study revealed a shocking absence of even the most elementary considerations regarding human skill or creativity; textbooks uniformly equated the 'human factor' with sources of uncertainty and under-performance, and established the engineering goal as one of eliminating human factors as their top priority.[33]

Hence the salience to such engineers of a 'human-centred' design paradigm, to jolt thinking on to new and potentially more fruitful lines. This has happened in the familiar manufacturing case of CIM.[34] It is striking how it is now starting to make its appearance in 'human-centred' software engineering design and even in human-centred design of flight deck control systems in Boeing aircraft.[35] In this way the concept of human-centredness is diffusing; it can be expected to become a mainstream metaguide for engineering design as its advantages become apparent.

The competition between firms espousing different models of productive efficiency is likely to be intense. The challenge for European industry, and for firms such as those in Australia which seek to compete on equal terms with Japanese firms deploying the LPS, is to rise above their traditional narrow conceptions of production, and harness all the resources at their disposal. This means forming a 'production coalition' with their skilled workforce in order to achieve substantially higher levels of productivity and efficiency.[36]

Let us bring this discussion to a close by illustrating this competition in terms of a production 'space', and the differing positions that firms' strategies occupy in this space.[37]

GRAPHICAL REPRESENTATION: THE PRODUCTION SPACE

Utilising the standard state–space depiction of a dynamic, multidimensional process, we may picture production processes in abstract terms as movement in a space laid out along various production dimensions.[38]

Many such dimensions might be chosen, but three that are obviously relevant to our story, and which taken together cover most of the discretion available to firms, are:

- rate of product innovation;
- degree of task variation; and
- extent of labour responsibility.

We work on the assumption that these characteristics are under relatively independent management control (subject to negotiation). This feature is captured by the orthogonality of the axes in the linear space used to depict the production system.

The elements of the model are *production processes* and *production strategies*, within which we wish to capture the notion of the production paradigm. In this model, a firm's *production process* is depicted as an operating point along each of the production dimensions. For example, a firm might be operating at the following points: a medium degree of. product innovation, a medium level of process variability, and a medium-low level of labour responsibility. Leaving measurement issues to one side for the moment, we may depict such a production process as the point A, in Figure 2.1. This defines the unique conjunction of production decisions taken with regard to the issues we have identified as 'production dimensions' and which in our model define the production space.

By *production strategy* is meant a firm's preferred operating point along each production dimension. For example, the same firm might be seeking to achieve the following elements of strategy: a high degree of product innovation (to deal with rapid market fluctuations), a high level of task variation (to cope with process innovations), and a high level of labour responsibility (to break with Taylorism). These choices taken along each production dimension again define a unique point in the production space, depicted as point B. We can picture the firm's strategy as an attempt to shift its operating point from A to B.

We may use this model to depict in graphical terms the differences between production strategies employed within the MPS, LPS and STPS. Firms' strategies will tend to cluster in different regions of the production space, depending on the value-laden visions of productive efficiency they deploy. These regions may be taken to demarcate the entire production space, and are depicted as non-overlapping regions in Figure 2.1.

Firms whose strategies tend toward low product innovation (classical mass production), low task variation (production rigidity) and low levels of labour responsibility (classical Taylorism), will have strategy points that cluster in the MPS region (e.g. point A). Firms whose strategies tend toward higher product innovation (market responsiveness) and higher process variability, but whose task variation remains low (short-cycle production), while calling for higher levels of worker responsibility such as over quality assurance, will cluster in the LPS region. Firms like our example above, with point C, will cluster in the STPS region.

This model is used to illustrate the different sets of strategies employed by firms in practice. It also brings out other features. For example, it makes it clear that decisions taken along any of the production dimensions form a continuum, as does the production process and strategy chosen so that the allocation of any firm to one of the three paradigms, MPS, LPS or STPS, is somewhat arbitrary. This fuzziness of concepts used to make sense of real-world phenomena, is an unavoidable feature of the social and management sciences.[39]

We may readily see how the same model can be used to depict other facets of organisational life, such as new product development or software engineering. In these latter cases, the 'production dimensions' will be defined in terms of their specific activities (e.g. the degree of modularity and devolution of control in software engineering) and the criteria to be used will likewise reflect these activities.

CONCLUDING REMARKS

It has been my purpose in this chapter to present the elements of these competing and contending production paradigms, and to sketch at least a plausible picture of the historical processes through which they have arisen and what might be the course of their future

Figure 2.1 Production systems compared

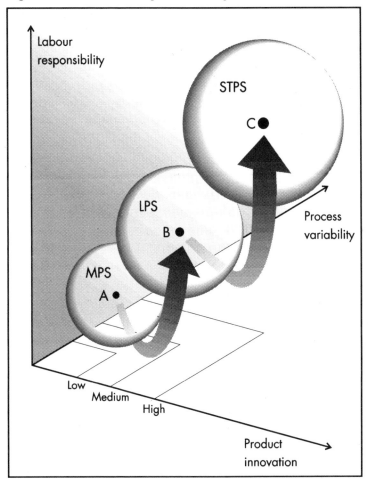

MPS   Mass Production System

LPS   Lean Production System

STPS Sociotechnical Production System

As market conditions become more turbulent a firm will attempt to shift its production from point A in the MPS region, through point B to point C in the STPS region.

evolution, bringing into play all the social, economic and institutional factors that bear on the variation and selection of production systems.

The sociotechnical production system model, or paradigm, of productive efficiency is not advocated here as a form of 'ideological commitment', nor as some form of categorical imperative that firms 'ought' to follow. Rather it is introduced as a set of criteria that are distilled from current best practices of firms which are successfully mobilising the skills, imagination and creativity of their workforces in structures which enhance and extend these skills, rather than constrain or cripple them. The vision I am offering here is of a design and production strategy that is linked to a firm's business strategy and market development strategy. The goal is to achieve congruence between these different facets of an organisation's operation, and thereby to lend some coherence to what is all too frequently a random and desperate search for alternatives in a sea of organisational uncertainty.

3

Teamwork and the new workplace culture

The lineaments of organisational best practice

In this chapter, I wish to delve deeper into what is meant by the term 'world best practice'. I take it to refer to the strategies, structures and processes employed by firms pursuing the model of the sociotechnical production system (STPS), variously described, for example, as 'high performance', 'high commitment', 'transformed' or simply as 'excellent'.[1]

With the liberation of firms from the mind-numbing shackles imposed by the decades of dominance of the mass production system (MPS), hundreds of firms in Japan, western countries and now the industrialising countries as well, are discovering the simple essentials of high-productivity, high-quality production.[2] Their insights are being captured and put to work by dozens of organisations that can influence the decisions of firms: unions, business associations, government agencies and even political parties, as well as toiling authors and consultants.

In a word, best practice organisations are lean in their war on waste and non-value-adding activity, while uncompromising in their pursuit of high quality, high productivity and timeliness of response. Above all, best practice companies are high-involvement organisations: they involve their staff in making decisions and in taking responsibility for dealing with variations in the production process, and for monitoring their own achievement of quality and production goals. Leanness combined with pursuit of high quality translates into cost-effectiveness. But, and this is fundamental, the reverse does not apply. So many firms which zero in on costs end up losing the game in terms of quality, productivity and timeliness,

51

and as they lose customers, and morale sags, they end up with increased costs as well. What a way to run a business!

BEST PRACTICE WORK ORGANISATIONS

What then can we learn from companies that achieve continuous improvements in productivity and quality?[3] The fundamental change to work systems is a break with the orthodoxy that sees efficiency stemming from a more and more minute division of labour. Such a view could only make sense from a perspective that saw productivity in terms of machines and humans as adjuncts of machines. Such an approach measures productivity in terms of throughput. It makes sense in a competitive environment that favours long-run replication of low-cost goods for mass markets. Its costs lie in the waste, the re-work, and the lack of coordination that is created by such a system, not to mention the worker alienation that companies all around the world have noted with concern.

The new production systems are emerging, as noted above, in manufacturing, process and service industries, in both the private and public sector. The new approach sees efficiency as stemming from the broadening of work responsibilities and the integration of tasks. It is adapted for a different competitive environment that favours higher quality, innovativeness, rapid response to market shifts and intelligent production. In place of the functional division of labour which ruled in the previous system, it places a premium on the functional integration of processes. In place of the technology of mass production dictating the work organisation, in the new approach there is a complementarity between collaborative work organisation and technology.

There is indeed an emerging international consensus on what constitutes 'best practice'. As an illustrative example, take the characterisation made by Boyer, in his presentation to an OECD conference held in Helsinki in December 1989. In this work, Boyer points out the ways in which 'best practice' firms today depart from MPS principles and practice. Best practice firms are conscious of:

- global optimisation of production flows (as opposed to piecemeal division of labour);
- total integration of research and development with production;
- new, close relations between producers and users;
- zero-defect strategies;
- fast response to market demands;

- decentralisation of production decisions;
- networking and joint ventures between producers;
- cooperative sub-contracting;
- building responsibility for maintenance, quality assurance and coordination into operators' jobs (i.e. multi-skilling);
- emphasis on training to maximise individual and collective competence;
- human resources policies to enhance commitment (such as more focused selection and career development policies); and
- labour–management cooperation.[4]

These twelve points could provide the basis for a handbook for 'best practice' restructuring in enterprises around the world, including Australia. Indeed, Boyer is not alone in advocating these measures, since a very similar set form the core of proposals being put forward by official and semi-official bodies in Europe, the OECD, and the European Union.[5]

We summarise the major elements of the new workplace culture in Table 3.1. This will provide the framework for our discussion of the emergent model of productive efficiency.

Table 3.1 The new workplace culture

Elements of the new culture:

- Job design involves self-managing, multifunctional teams
- Quality Assurance through process intent
- Product and process innovation
- Close relations with customers and suppliers
- Performance monitoring
- Skills formation
- Skills and performance-based pay
- New management tasks

TEAMWORK

The heart of the new work system is teamwork. This is grounded in a broadening of operator skills and responsibilities with a view to more and more activities and decisions being taken at the production level, compared with the present system where operators simply take orders handed down through a supervisory hierarchy. Fundamentally it involves a process of 're-engineering' the work flows so that groups of operators can take control of a series of tasks that produce a defined product or service.

As more and more decisions, responsibility and authority are vested in collaborative groups of operators (called teams), so the teams become more and more 'self-managing'. This simply means that they take over tasks that have traditionally been handled, according to the logic of the division of labour, by specialised staff such as 'production control', 'logistics', 'quality control' and 'maintenance' staff. Eventually the tasks of coordination and control traditionally exercised by supervisory staff are most efficiently exercised by team members themselves.[6]

World best practice teams have two prime features from which all else follows. They span several operations, giving them control over a well-defined sequence resulting in a finished product or service. This is their holistic feature, termed *process coherence*. And the technology they employ is adapted to their collaboration, and to the flow of product through its various phases within the team. This is called *cellular production*. It is worth pausing to look at these features before examining their implications.

Process coherence

Effective work teams are not created by arbitrarily identifying a group of operators, such as the operators of a group of functionally related machines. Even though some collaboration might be called for by such a group of machine operators, they have no clear focus on a finished product or service to give them a sense of identity. Their work is simply passed on to the operators of another machine, much as it is done under the usual arrangements.

For the same reason, an effective team cannot be created by arbitrarily dividing a sequence of tasks into two or three components, and calling them Team A, Team B, etc. An example might be dividing up a food production line into baking, moulding and wrapping processes, and calling operators assigned to each of these processes separate teams. Again, there is a limited degree of collaboration called for in such an approach, and to this extent such groups of operators can function as 'teams'. Such 'teams' would have a limited focus and limited sense of control over a finished product, in this case wrapped and packed food products, but could not be expected to exercise the initiative and responsibility that would emanate from a well-focused team.

Thus in multi-product or multi-service operations, teams can be product-focused or process-focused; the distinction is critical for effective team operation.[7] This is illustrated in Figure 3.1.

Effective work teams span a number of operations or processes, each of which is complementary to the others, in order to generate a clear focus on a given group of customers or group of finished products. There is no 'one best way' to allocate processes to an effective team.

Coherence gives the team its identity, and drives its sense of its own total performance. It is this in turn which motivates its attention to matters such as Quality Assurance, running repairs and maintenance, in order to achieve optimal performance.

Cellular production

Even if operators are brought together in a team spanning several processes, they will nevertheless lack coherence and identity if these processes are scattered across the plant. Yet the layout of most plants does not reflect a concern with team coherence. On the contrary, it generally reflects a focus on the functional division of labour, with similar operations all located together in the interests of functional uniformity. Such an arrangement makes sense only if operators are machine-adjuncts simply doing what they are told. As soon as they are expected to think about what they are doing, and to collaborate to effect better coordination between processes, then a different configuration is called for.

The new technical configuration, in which all the processes associated with a given team are located together (and preferably arranged in a U-shape, to emphasise the link between the beginning and the end of the sequence), is called a production cell. Cellular production is now recognised as world best practice in complementing work organisation with technical work configuration.

There are some striking implications arising from the adoption of cellular production. For one thing, it means reconfiguring machines so that they belong to individual, product-focused cells. While cells may share major pieces of plant and equipment, the concept calls for some dedication, and therefore duplication, of machines within cells. Hence machines are not utilised to their full; instead, it is people who are fully utilised. This is anathema to the previous approach based on a functional division of labour. Cellular production is not concerned to optimise 'machine utilisation'; it sees the machines as needing to be available when workers need them.

Another implication of cellular production is that sequential steps within a process are placed contiguously, wherever possible.

Figure 3.1 Team design: segmentation by product or process

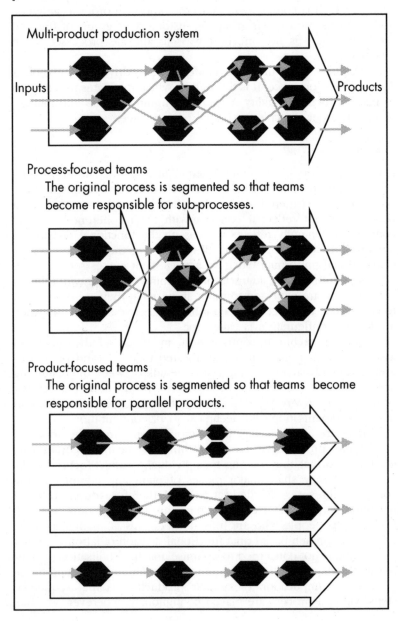

Multi-product production system

Inputs

Products

Process-focused teams
The original process is segmented so that teams become responsible for sub-processes.

Product-focused teams
The original process is segmented so that teams become responsible for parallel products.

The concept calls for physical relocation of plant and equipment that is widely scattered throughout a plant according to a functional layout. We shall see in the case of Bendix Mintex in Chapter 5 how reluctant firms can be to make this investment decision, but how in the end it is unavoidable.

The extraordinary organisational gains to be secured from cellular production arise from the new focus it gives to measuring performance in terms of overall product or service completion, rather than in terms of the individual efficiencies of separate processes. Thus complete orders are fulfilled by the one team, collaborating together thanks to the proximity of processes achieved with cellular layouts.

A second, equally significant gain lies in the capacity of production cells to switch rapidly from one product line to another, as called for by production orders. A third gain lies in the capacity to secure quality assurance at each step of the process as well as overall, in terms of the complete cycle of operations. These are the organisational gains that drive the productivity engine in the new workplace culture.

Secondary team features

Effective work teams which satisfy the two basic requirements of process coherence and cellular production have a number of features.

Firstly, traditional supervisory structures are clearly incompatible with an effective team whose members are exercising judgment and using their skills to make decisions. They must be allowed to coordinate their own activities. Any attempt to impose an external authority will only undermine their sense of responsibility and motivation, which is the very rationale for setting up the teams in the first place. Hence, there are no traditional supervisors in the new workplace culture. Coordination functions are taken over by the teams interacting with each other, under the guidance of team leaders. This is illustrated in Figure 3.2.

Secondly, effective teams have members who understand each other's tasks, and can take over such tasks as needed. In other words, the members of effective teams are multi-skilled. Effective teamwork is incompatible with narrow specialisation, which was the norm in the previous production system. Furthermore, team members take more responsibility for the overall completion of jobs, rather than mere performance of a given task. This means expanding skills and responsibilities to include such matters as machine

Figure 3.2 Hierarchical vs team-based coordination

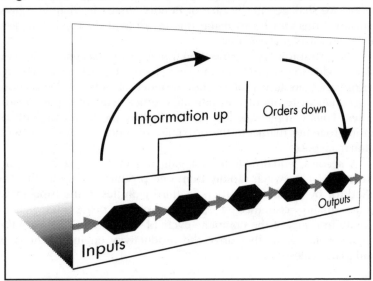

1. Vertical coordination through a hierarchy

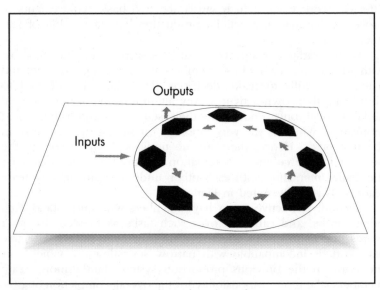

2. Horizontal coordination through teamwork

set-up and starting, machine trouble-shooting, quality assurance, and making corrections in response to observations. Since decisions taken impinge on other operators, such an approach calls for shop floor collaboration in place of the previous reliance on top-down supervision.

Thirdly, the process of acquiring skills is made the object of special attention through a well-articulated process of skill formation. This is a much broader notion than the previous idea of 'on the job training' (which normally meant watching someone else do a job before being expected to do it alone). Skill formation implies paying systematic attention to issues such as competency identification, skills acquisition, development of training modules, competency assessment, career paths formulation, and making links between skills and pay and linking both to vocational qualifications.

Fourthly, the team members need to acquire increasing levels of control over the flow of work through their production cell. This means taking over such functions as coordination, logistics, supply of raw materials, and so on. It also means acquiring control over matters traditionally the province of the supervisor, such as allocation of overtime and the exercise of discipline, and matters traditionally belonging to the personnel office, such as absenteeism, arranging for holidays and other breaks, and ultimately the putting on and putting off of team members. All of this represents a tendency towards self-management. Self-management in effective teams is not a single state, but rather an evolving spectrum of states with no clear beginning or end-point. What is called for is a controlled progression from one level of self-management to another.[8]

MANUFACTURING SYSTEMS DESIGN

The design of manufacturing systems has now been elevated to a 'technology' by leading engineering design firms such as Lucas and Bosch. They produce systems according to well-articulated design principles, many of which now routinely embody the sorts of ideas discussed above. For example, Lucas Engineering & Systems Ltd, a UK-based general manufacturing engineering consultancy, has produced a *Manufacturing Systems Handbook* which embodies ten principles of what is called 'lean production', explicitly contrasted with principles derived from 'mass production'. It is worth summarising these ten design principles, as follows.

1 Simplify and restructure the key production processes both in the office and out in the factory. Introduce new flexible team-based ownership of these processes according to natural work cell groupings. Then continue removing the non-value-added activities which are the unneeded legacy of the previous over-complex manufacturing system. Give particular attention to shedding superfluous work by indirect staff.

2 Delegate responsibility for the essential manufacturing control functions (such as scheduling, quality, maintenance and trouble shooting) to teams in the new simplified cell-based factory organisation. Provide them with simple operational tools, diagnostic and training aids, and visual control aids such as are embodied in the *kanban** material feed concept.

3 Make simplicity of operation the key criterion in the design of each cell.

4 For all machines or processes that may require tooling changes or operational reconfiguration, ensure very short changeover times through engineering design.

5 Use quick change capability to achieve Just-In-Time build of product mix in line with daily/weekly customer needs.

6 Use software systems like Materials Requirements Planning to support processes that are *kanban* or period flow control in nature and simple capacity overload analysis for cases where lot size scheduling is required.

7 Reduce the categories of service support functions, giving each a development or operational identity. Then create many small multidisciplinary teams to support these service functions and establish organisational mechanisms that encourage team approaches to problem solving.

8 Establish reliable performance measurements and institute team-based programs by which these measurements can be improved on a continuing basis against defined targets.

9 Introduce new technology—process control, robotics, computer numeric control (CNC) (rather than total computer integration) within the context of continuous improvement on a highly selected basis to improve specific performance measurements.

10 Design communication systems and training procedures/aids to be an integral part of any production process.[9]

---

* *Kanban* is a Japanese card system which authorises the production of components as they are needed by an associated assembly operation.

The interesting thing about this set of principles from our point of view is that it embodies as much of what I have called the STPS as of the LPS, while it explicitly distances itself from any link with the MPS. It is, in other words, a model of manufacturing design that reflects the tension between the two competing visions of pure 'lean production' and the sociotechnical approach.

Increasingly, it can be expected that the notions of LPS and STPS will be embodied in 'packages' like that produced by Lucas Engineering & Systems Ltd, and firms will be able to buy these solutions virtually 'off the shelf'. The danger will be once again that the process of involving and committing a skilled workforce will be lost sight of. It is the strength of the STPS that it keeps these issues continuously in view.

Let us continue to explore the implementation of the STPS in the context of self-managing teamwork, bearing in mind the claims of package suppliers such as engineering consultants.[10]

TEAMS: QUALITY ASSURANCE AND PROCESS INTENT

Effective teamwork is not an end in itself, but a means to achieving superior production results, such as quality improvement and assurance, timeliness and responsiveness. World best practice organisations focus all their activities on the attainment of these goals.

Take the case of Ford Australia. This company has developed a world best practice approach to quality assurance which is termed Process Intent. In place of supplying individual operators with lists of tasks and procedures, the Process Intent approach spells out the goals, or intent, of a process, in terms of measurable outcomes, and gives groups of operators the responsibility to take their own decisions, making local adaptations and variations in order to achieve these goals. This places quality assurance firmly in the hands of operators as a group, rather than seeing it as a specialised 'Quality Control' function to be executed after the fact. Firms take advantage of cybernetic notions of feedback to regulate and control their activities through the authority vested in operating staff.

An external manifestation of such an approach is the documentation of production procedures, highlighting the quality assurance checks that need to be made (under such headings as who, what, how) and the steps to be taken when variations are encountered. Such documentation is needed for a plant to achieve accreditation under international quality standards; such accreditation is coming to be seen as a necessary component of best practice.[11]

Quality and process documentation should not be a bureaucratic exercise, imposed on teams before they have even begun. Best practice firms recognise that there needs to be adequate foundational documentation. But they ensure that it is handed over eventually to project and production teams themselves, which will develop their own performance measures in coordination with quality professionals. Ultimately, teams have to have ownership of their own process documentation. The role of Quality Control staff at best practice plants shifts away from conducting on-line measurements to becoming the auditors of measurements conducted by operators themselves.

TEAMS: PRODUCT AND PROCESS INNOVATION

A world best practice organisation is not a static entity but one which is designed for maximum dynamic flexibility. Its responsiveness is reflected in rapid product and process innovation; indeed, the rapidity of innovation becomes a key competitive advantage of best practice organisations.

Product innovation refers to the design and development of new product lines, normally as variants of existing lines (and frequently prompted by feedback and intelligence gathered by production staff). Process innovation refers to the continuous improvement in production systems that a best practice organisation can expect from effective and intelligent teamwork.

In best practice organisations, self-managing teamwork is the organisational setting within which innovation takes place. Project teams are assembled for clearly defined purposes, bringing together members from a wide variety of backgrounds and ensuring that the needs of sales, marketing, production, or distribution are all taken into account. Operating teams at plant level are likewise geared to continuous improvement and to trialling of variants as part of their regular activities. Their efforts in this direction are captured and rewarded in their performance indicators. The thought given to innovation carries over into higher levels of quality in production.

TEAMS: RELATIONS WITH CUSTOMERS AND SUPPLIERS

Traditional organisations maintain a distance from their customers.

This is dictated by their competitive strategy which is one based on least-cost mass production and mass marketing; by definition, this is production-driven, rather than customer-driven. Henry Ford said it all when he enunciated his market strategy: 'You can have any colour you like, so long as it's black.'

In line with the principle of the functional division of labour, traditional organisations create specialist divisions to deal with customers ('sales') and their persuasion ('marketing'). Both divisions are divorced from production, and from distribution. All these divisions are faithfully reproduced within the corporate structures of most existing firms.

World best practice organisations are learning to take a different approach. Management increasingly is exercised through customer- or product-focused teams whose members come from sales, marketing, production, and distribution operations, as well as from such areas as quality control, new product development and product engineering. Such teams are designed to override bureaucratic rigidities in large organisations, and to bring the organisation back to its prime business activity which is generating business through satisfying customers.

Similarly, traditional organisations maintain a distance from their suppliers. In line with the principle of competitive tendering, suppliers (either internal, as in a vertically integrated operation, or external) are kept at arm's length. They are given as little information as possible (in the name of commercial confidentiality) and fierce bargaining takes place to drive down their supply prices. Again all this makes sense in a least-cost competitive strategy where collaborative teamwork is neither recognised nor sought.

World best organisations operate differently. They seek and insist on the closest possible relations with their suppliers, particularly in the matter of quality assurance. Again teams provide the setting for this new level of inter-organisational coordination. Their members work with suppliers to ensure that goods meet quality specifications, and that any problems emerging during production are dealt with and solved.

TEAMS: PERFORMANCE MONITORING

World best practice organisations are obsessive about their performance. They spend inordinate amounts of time and energy defining their performance, devising tools to measure it, actually measuring performance, and then taking action in response to the measured performance. Performance is taken to mean a range of measures, covering such matters as quality achievement, timeliness in responding to orders, and cost overheads. Thus the range of measures that are collected and analysed is much broader than traditional costs and variances.[12]

Again teams provide the setting for a radically different flow of information within the organisation (termed the 'information architecture'). In place of traditional practices where information is collected only to be passed 'up the line', and then forgotten, in the best practice organisation day-to-day performance data is collected by teams for their own use, and only later is a summary of their measures and responses taken passed to senior management where it is used for maintaining a strategic grasp of the organisation's overall trajectory.

TEAMS AND SKILLS FORMATION

The flexibility, adaptiveness and efficiency of a best practice organisation is based on the skills of team members. The traditional idea of task specialisation and the replacement of people with robots and hard-wired automation is anathema to such organisations. They seek the broadest mix of operating skills, combining practical competencies with theoretical knowledge. The competencies change with technologies and processes, but the knowledge provides a long-lasting framework within which intelligent decisions can be taken. From such a perspective, there is no end to the search for more efficient technologies, but always in the sense that they are tools for skilled workers to use.

In both manufacturing and services, the new production systems require a linkage between work and skill that was quite foreign to the formerly dominant mass production system. This has been documented most strikingly in industries where the previous approach has led firms to the brink of bankruptcy and they have saved themselves only by adopting a radically different approach to skills formation.[13]

In the OECD countries and in various sectors, the former job classification systems that divided processes into narrow tasks and linked jobs exclusively with machines, are being restructured to provide an explicit link with skill, a flexibility in use, and a notion of career path through the upward progression by workers as they acquire skills and experience. In advanced firms this process was accomplished in the late 1970s or 1980s, resulting in broad job definitions succeeding each other in a skills and payments progression. In Australia, the same process is occurring at a sectoral level rather than at the individual enterprise level, and is known as award restructuring.[14] Workers in the new production systems are expected by firms to make contributions to productivity enhancement through the understanding of the 'big picture', that is, how each operation is shaped by context and how contingencies can be accommodated within the overall process. This requires a novel approach to skill. In place of the narrow functionally specific skills of the formerly dominant mass production system, generic and adaptive skills are needed, the kind that are generally deemed to be 'knowledge'.[15]

Skills formation refers to the broad set of processes employed by best practice organisations through which skills in the workplace are defined, identified, acquired, assessed, and 'exchanged' for wage premiums through skills-based job classification systems and career paths. The notion of 'skills formation' is much broader than the traditional notion of 'training'.[16] Skills formation has an active component to it; it acknowledges that the process of knowledge acquisition occurs over time and builds on experience, in contrast to the 'empty vessel' notion that underlies 'training' and 'retraining'. The categories of skill formation are competence, performance criteria, and 'elements' that can be built up in modular fashion, as a wall can be built up from bricks. To be utilised, these competencies need to be assessed and evaluated against standards.

A model of the skills formation process

I have found it helpful to discuss the skills formation process in the form of a model that brings its various categories into direct relationship with one another.[17] The model I employ uses two basic constructs: the 'learning space' and the 'teaching space'. These are framed in the same state–space formulation used for the 'production space' given in Chapter 2.

The learning space

We start with a state–space formulation of a 'learning space'. The axes, or state variables, are the *competencies* relevant to any particular industrial agreement (or Award, in the Australian terminology). The values of the state variables are the 'levels' of competence attained, these levels corresponding to the levels spelt out in general in the industrial agreement. 'Skill' in this model is a point in the space, corresponding to a certain level reached in *each of the competencies* by a particular individual. 'Skill enhancement' is a transformation on the space, moving the original skill point to a location that is further from the origin (corresponding to the acquisition of higher levels in certain competences).

If skills acquisition occurs in one dimension only, then this will be termed 'upskilling' or vertical skills acquisition. If it occurs in more than one dimension, it will be referred to as 'multiskilling'. If competence is acquired in a dimension where there was no previous level of competence, this will be referred to as 'cross skilling'. Deskilling would be represented by a competence (i.e. a dimension of the skill space) being removed, through a change in organisation or technology or both.

The steel industry in Australia provides an example of this model of the learning space. Award restructuring has accommodated new production systems, and has created three skills streams for production workers, maintenance staff, and electricians. Six general job classification levels have been created, each succeeding the other in terms of higher levels of skill and responsibility, thereby creating career paths for all categories of worker. Some of the competencies relevant to the steel industry, over and above basic literacy and numeracy, are computer awareness/programming, metallurgy and advanced numeracy.

We can represent these competencies as the three axes of a 3-dimensional learning space, with each axis containing six divisions, corresponding to each level reached. (The space in this case is actually a lattice, with $3 \times 6 = 18$ points of intersection.) This is shown in Figure 3.3. A worker will already have a certain 'skill', chosen arbitrarily in Figure 3.3 as point A. This point represents a 'skill tally' as follows: computer awareness (level 2); metallurgy (level 1); advanced numeracy (level 1). The worker then undergoes training, and accumulates experience, so that he or she acquires, for the sake of argument, two further modules of computer awareness (to level 4), three further modules of metallurgy (to level 4), and two further modules of advanced numeracy (to level 3). This process of 'skills acquisition' or skills enhancement takes the worker to point B, corresponding to levels 4, 4, and 3 on each axis respectively. Point B is further from the origin than point A, showing that the worker at point B has greater skill than at point A. (This quantum could be measured, depending on the metric chosen for the space.)

Of course, where there are more than three competencies it is impossible to show the space graphically. However a single point in the space can still be visualised by setting up an array, with

Figure 3.3 Learning space: a steel industry example

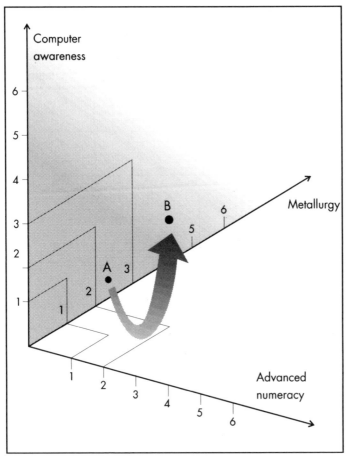

Skills acquisition is the process of moving from point A to point B

columns the competencies, and rows the levels. For the case of the steel example, the array is shown in Figure 3.4. Point A is now represented by the triplet (a_1, a_2, a_3). Point B is the triplet (b_1, b_2, b_3) where b_1 is 2 levels above a_1, b_2 is 3 levels above a_2, and b_3 is 2 levels above a_3. This corresponds to the process of skills acquisition given in the example. Representation in the array is not as neat as in a discrete space but it has to be used to make sense of skills

Figure 3.4 Learning array: a steel industry example

Levels	Computer awareness	Metallurgy	Advanced numeracy
6			
5			
4	b_1	b_2	
3			b_3
2	a_1		
1		a_2	a_3

$A \rightarrow B: (a1, a2, a3) \rightarrow (b1, b2, b3)$

transformations involving more than three competencies (which will normally be the case).

The 'learning space' model clarifies several matters immediately. Firstly, it illustrates the link between skills enhancement and wage premiums; it shows how a worker may progress from one 'level' in the restructured job classification system to a higher one by attaining the appropriate level (through training or experience) in *each of the competencies* defined by the award. Thus the worker in our example who is at point A will be in Level 1 of the award because he or she is at level 1 in two of the competences, viz metallurgy and advanced numeracy. As an extra level is acquired in each of these competencies, the worker can move to level 2 in the award, thus receiving a wage premium. At point B the worker has moved into level 3 of the award and by acquiring one further increment in advanced numeracy, can move to level 4 in the award.

Secondly, the 'learning space' model clarifies the notion of *assessment*, and in particular, *competency-based assessment*. Assessment is the process through which a worker may demonstrate that he or she has reached a certain level, or standard, of competence. It might be carried out by the employer, through challenge tests, or by an educational institution, through various assessment procedures, including exams, but also making allowance for experience. Assessment acquires an enhanced significance in the context of new production systems, because it will determine where a worker slots into an award classification, and hence will determine the worker's pay. In our example, the worker is assessed as starting at point A, and is assessed as ending at point B.

Thirdly, this model shows why assessment is in general carried out in terms of criteria of competence ('criteria-referenced assessment') rather than in terms of one person or group being assessed as superior to another ('norm-based assessment') which is the form familiar in educational settings.

The teaching space

In a similar way, we can construct a model of the activities of firms, and of the public education and training system, with regard to competency-based training, in terms of a 'teaching space'. In this case the axes, or state variables, are the subjects taught, and the values along each axis are the modules, or units, through which the teaching proceeds. There is no time built into this model, as it is assumed that learners complete modules at their own pace.

Points in this space represent 'entry points' and 'exit points' to and from training programmes. The exit points should normally carry some kind of *certification*. The entry points should normally carry some form of *credit transfer*, offering students credit for modules and/or courses previously completed. The linking of courses together in a network of credit transfer between exit points and entry points is termed *articulation*.

The Australian vehicle industry provides a case where the model of the teaching space may be applied. The restructuring of the vehicle industry award involves the development of an industry-wide training qualification, the Vehicle Industry Certificate. This qualification involves employees in undertaking study in 'properly accredited training modules covering core, process and enterprise knowledge'.[18] For the sake of this example, let us name these subjects as:

• core subjects (automotive manufacturing);

- process subjects (assembly, basic maintenance); and
- enterprise subjects (enterprise-specific procedures).

Each of these subjects contains a certain number of modules which can be displayed along each dimension of the teaching space, as shown in Figure 3.5. (In general there will be different numbers of modules per subject.) The origin represents a common 'entry point' into this teaching space, where no credit is claimed for previous work. Point A (a_1, a_2, a_3) represents an example of another entry point, in this case where credit is offered for previous courses completed or experience obtained on the job, at one automotive company or another. (Credit a_1 is given in core subject, credit a_2 for process subject etc.) Point B represents an exit point, where a qualification is obtained (in this case, the Vehicle Industry Certificate): it is awarded for completion of the specified modules b_1, b_2, b_3 in each of the subjects. Point C represents a further exit point, involving a higher level qualification after further modules are completed. Point C might represent, for example, a Vehicle Industry Higher Certificate. The higher certificate would be *well articulated* with the lower certificate if the modules in each course are comparable, so that credit for completing the lower certificate can be transferred across to the modules of the higher certificate.

As in the steel example, this vehicle industry case can be represented in array format, to cope with the problem that any more than three dimensions cannot be drawn graphically. The array corresponding to Figure 3.5 is given in Figure 3.6.

The teaching space of the model thus provides us with a convenient means of exhibiting the notions of multiple entry and exit points for training (as opposed to the single entry and exit points defined by juvenile apprenticeships in the traditional skills system), of modular training offerings, and of articulation between one set of qualifications and another.

Education and training systems should be motivated to move to modular format for delivery of their courses since the format clearly matches up with developments in skills acquisition associated with industrial skills formation. Subjects taught in modular format have the potential to marry up with competencies acquired on the job in modular progression.

Best practice skills formation
Best practice firms utilise the insights from this model of the skills formation process to construct systematic linkages between job classifications and competencies. These are what I term job classi-

Figure 3.5 Teaching space: vehicle industry example

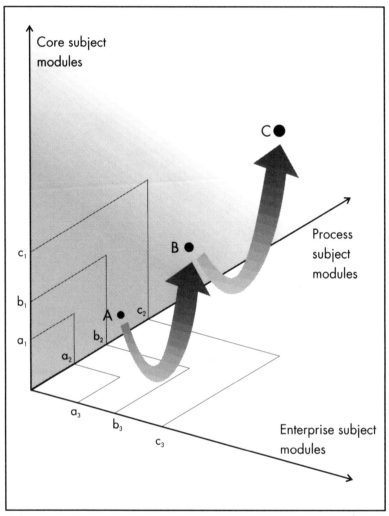

A (a_1, a_2, a_3) is an entry point

B (b_1, b_2, b_3) is an exit point corresponding to VIC

C (c_1, c_2, c_3) is an exit point corresponding to VIHC, with B as its entry point

Figure 3.6 Teaching array: vehicle industry example

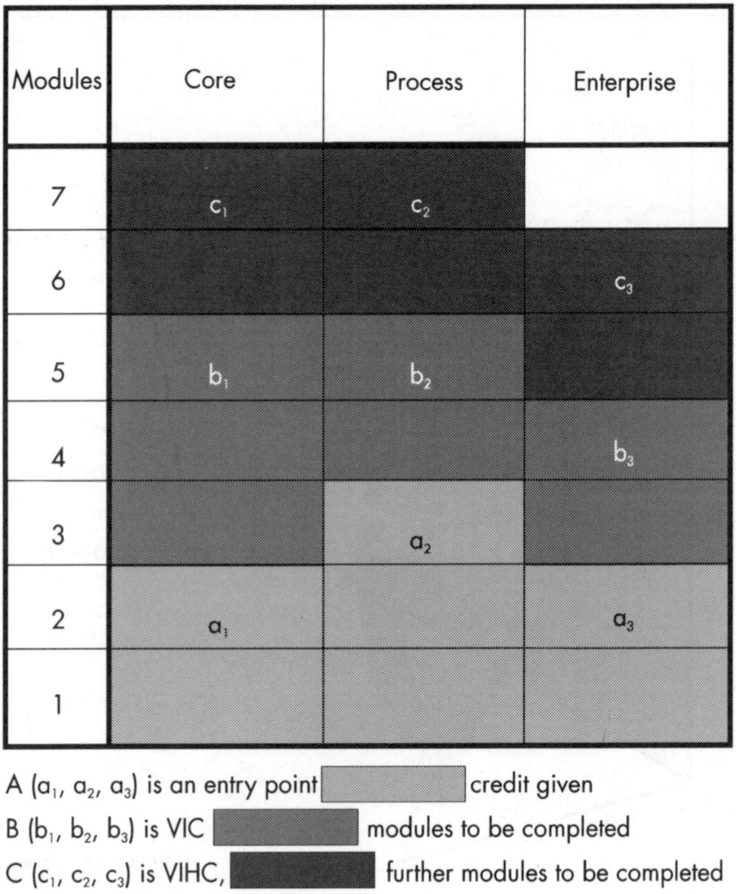

Modules	Core	Process	Enterprise
7	c_1	c_2	
6			c_3
5	b_1	b_2	
4			b_3
3		a_2	
2	a_1		a_3
1			

A (a_1, a_2, a_3) is an entry point [   ] credit given

B (b_1, b_2, b_3) is VIC [   ] modules to be completed

C (c_1, c_2, c_3) is VIHC, [   ] further modules to be completed

fication/competencies matrices, or arrays. They exhibit the competencies that need to be acquired to enable a worker to progress from one job classification to another and thereby pursue a career path. We shall meet such an example in the case of the insurance firm, Colonial Mutual in Chapter 6. The approach is illustrated in Figure 3.7.

In the case of Colonial Mutual, the model works as follows. Team members are expected to form skills both horizontally ('broadening') and vertically ('deepening'). They move up from one job classification level to another as they do so. Their skills become

Figure 3.7 Matrix of job classifications and competencies

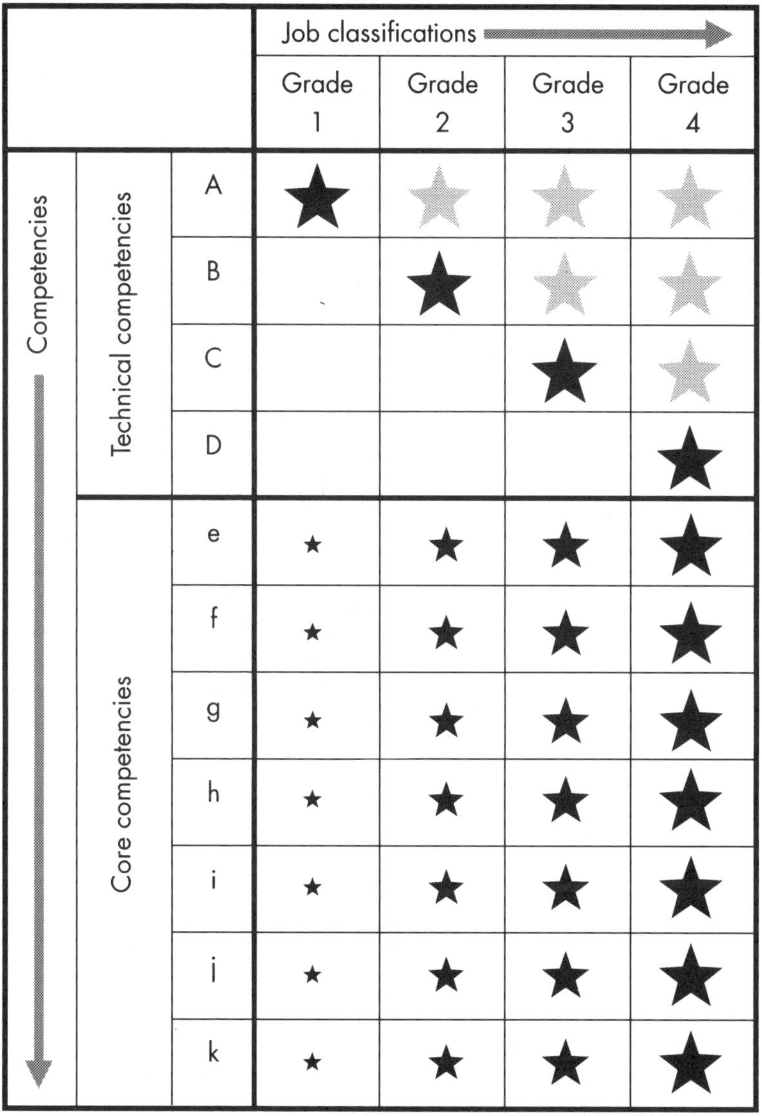

			Job classifications ➡			
			Grade 1	Grade 2	Grade 3	Grade 4
Competencies	Technical competencies	A	★	☆	☆	☆
		B		★	☆	☆
		C			★	☆
		D				★
	Core competencies	e	★	★	★	★
		f	★	★	★	★
		g	★	★	★	★
		h	★	★	★	★
		i	★	★	★	★
		j	★	★	★	★
		k	★	★	★	★

A worker can proceed from one job classification to higher classifications by achieving a spread of technical competencies and greater depth in a set of core competencies.

73

broader as they acquire more and more 'technical competencies' (in this case, skills to perform transactions related to new business, claims, renewals, and changes to insurance policies). Their skills become deeper as they acquire more and more advanced 'core competencies' such as knowledge of the insurance industry and its procedures, company knowledge, teamworking, computer literacy, and so on. (We shall see in Chapter 6 how Colonial Mutual have negotiated the details of implementation of this model of skills formation.) Once there is a systematic approach to the formation of skills in an enterprise, the issue of rewards and motivation quite properly presents itself.

TEAMS: SKILLS- AND PERFORMANCE-BASED PAY

Pay remains the principal motivator, and sends strong messages about how the firm regards its employees. If senior management are talking in terms of cooperation and continuous improvement while keeping all employees on individual incentive payments, they are unlikely to find their message being taken seriously. However, changes to pay systems are notoriously difficult to effect. Most organisations find that they can cope with skills-based pay or performance-based pay but rarely with the two together, at least at first. The innovative organisation aims to move in the direction of establishing a link between people's accomplishments and what they find in their pay packets.

Skills-based pay

Pay can be linked with skills through broad-banded job classification systems where successive classifications carry higher or broader competencies, and attract pay premiums. This is the approach followed in the restructuring of Australian awards such as in the new Metal Industry Award.

Skills-based pay needs to be contrasted with seniority-based pay which rewards employees for years of service irrespective of skill or performance, and with payment for work performed irrespective of the skill the worker brought to the job or the quality of the performance in completing the job.

For the organisation, a move to skills-based pay means taking on board a number of important issues.

74

- Employees need to be encouraged to acquire extra skills, for example through granting study leave.
- Employees acquiring extra skills and qualifying for extra pay need to be provided with appropriate positions. Firms which link pay with skills and then deny employees positions at the higher levels of responsibility are inviting a backlash.
- Job structures need to be based on competence, weeding out all job descriptions which are couched in terms of machinery operation or task without any reference to the skill or competence needed.
- Fair procedures need to be put in place to enable employees to make the transition from one skill-based pay category to the next. Different approaches are possible, involving weighting systems (where competencies acquired are accorded points which accumulate in the employee's 'skills account'), modular competency acquisition and assessment systems (where classifications are defined in terms of certain numbers of modules attained), and peer review systems where competency modules, experience, on-the-job performance and other factors are taken into account.
- Appeal procedures need to be established, where employees feel that they may have been unfairly treated.
- Transitional arrangements to the new system have to be thought through. Some firms design perfect systems then trip at the last gate where they make the mistake of assigning experienced employees to low classification levels, thus creating dissension and resistance where there might otherwise have been support. Transition arrangements need to be designed to ensure smooth functioning for the future, rather than getting everyone in the right classification from day one. If it starts smoothly, the new system will allow the smart employees to rise quickly, without necessarily penalising long-serving employees who may be unwilling to plunge into the new system but are still prepared to serve in the way they know and understand.

Skills-based pay systems thus place on the negotiation agenda novel issues such as competency assessment procedures, appeal mechanisms, and skills weighting and valuation techniques. But the reward for the organisation is greater commitment on the part of employees, and the facilitation of further organisational and technological innovation which will be expected to enhance productivity and efficiency.

Performance-based pay

Performance-based pay seeks to harness the wages system to the quality and efficiency of employee performance, on either an individual basis or, more commonly, a team basis. Performance-based pay is generally taken to mean something broader than the offering of individual incentives based on individual output (which frustrates any kind of group activity or cooperation between workers) or the offering of end-of-year bonuses. 'Performance' is the term used rather than 'productivity', because what is being rewarded is quality and efficiency of work (conformance to quality standards, timeliness of response) rather than mere quantitative output. (The weakness of most incentive systems is that they encourage quantity of output at the expense of quality.)

Performance-based pay can be calculated according to a fixed formula (with pay premiums linked to defined achievements). We shall see in Chapter 6 how the insurance firm Colonial Mutual has linked its skills-based pay system to this form of team-based performance reward. Alternatively, the bonus can be calculated as a specified share of a designated financial aggregate, such as 'value-added' or, alternatively, profit. The latter system constitutes a form of 'sharing' in the results; sharing in value-added is termed gainsharing, while sharing in profits is called, simply, profit-sharing.

Organisations successfully utilise either approach. In many organisations, individual 'performance increments' are negotiated in accordance with regular reviews, which might be conducted annually. In general, such performance increments are best negotiated at the individual level. They are difficult to fit into some award structures which have sought to exclude such increments through suspicion that they would be used to undermine worker solidarity and encourage favouritism. A well-planned and executed model should be able to avoid such charges.

Gainsharing systems are ideally adapted to the reward of groups or teams. The team is encouraged to compute the value its activities have added, and then members are allocated a share or proportion (say, twenty per cent) of this aggregate.

In Australia, a highly successful form of gainsharing system, called the *Common Interest Programme*, has been installed by companies over the past two decades. We shall examine a particularly clear example of this system, and how it has accommodated subsequent changes to work organisation, in our study of CIG Gas Cylinders in Chapter 10.

TEAMS: NEW MANAGEMENT TASKS

In the best practice organisation, management responsibilities are markedly different from those exercised in the 'command and control' model espoused in the traditional organisation. As teams become genuinely self-managing, they take over many of the disciplinary and coordination functions that were necessary in a hierarchical system. The consequent effects on the roles of professional staff positions, on middle level supervisory positions and on senior management positions, are far-reaching.[19] It is not that these roles are eliminated. In the best practice organisation, there is still a need for professional expertise, for coordination, and for strategic direction. But these functions are no longer seen as controls. Rather, they are seen as services provided to self-managing teams.

Thus teams take over traditional maintenance and quality assurance tasks. But they need professional maintenance workshops to conduct preventive maintenance programmes, and professional quality control laboratories to conduct audits and regulatory measurements.

Teams take over the coordination of tasks among their own members. But they need team leaders to ensure that this coordination is conducted efficiently. And they need clerical and administrative support in circulating production and logistics information which is critical to their decision-making. This is how teams stay on target and make corrections as they veer off-target.

Senior management is left with the core responsibilities for maintaining a strategic direction for the organisation as a whole, and for keeping the various parts working well together. At the Ford Plastics plant, for example, senior plant management are assigned 'blocker remover' roles, to work with project teams and assist them to overcome obstacles created by the previous hierarchical structures. The products produced have to sell. The technologies employed have to work. The activities engaged in have to be value-adding and productive. Overall organisational performance has to be monitored, and warning signs of future problems detected and actions initiated. These are the tasks of senior management in the best practice organisation.

THE DESIGN OF TEAMWORK STRUCTURES

Let me summarise my approach to the design of teamwork structures through investigating general criteria that such structures should possess. I have developed six criteria which may be used in the design of product-focused teams. These summarise the sociotechnical considerations that should feed into the allocation of staff to teams. The six criteria (Six Cs) are as follows:

Contiguity

All team members should work within sight of each other, in direct communication with each other, and in such a way that sequential production processes are completed by contiguously placed workers. This criterion is introduced to enhance communication within the team, and to underpin the focus on a finished product or process.

Complementarity

The team should span a number of operations which follow each other in sequence, so that the activities of team members complement each other, and give the team as a whole a complexity that individual departments do not have. This criterion is designed to ensure that the team controls a complex of operations and is able to make significant decisions in terms of allocating its own members to operations to ensure smooth production.

Closure

The team should have control over a sequence of operations that result in the production of a complete product or process. This criterion is drawn from the literature on industrial psychology, to give team members a sense of satisfaction in completing a whole task rather than simply acting as a cog in a larger wheel. Closure also has the practical effect of providing team members with tools for testing quality over a whole sequence of operations, and for testing quality of a 'finished' product.

Continuity

Teams or cells should be arranged in such a way that there exists a demonstrable flow of product through the team operation, again emphasising interdependence and the integrity of the team's responsibilities.

78

Coherence

The team should have a clear identity or focus, such as the responsibility for producing a finished product or group of products, or dealing with a designated group of customers.

Containment

The team should span as many functions as are needed to ensure its smooth running. Such functions include running repairs and maintenance, quality assurance, process adjustment, start-up and shut-down, and so on. This criterion complements that of closure. Closure concerns the span of operations or processes covered by the team; containment concerns the span of skills or competencies needed within the team to effect its operations.

Teams constructed according to these criteria, which generalise the experience of firms that are engaging successfully in workplace reform, have the best chance of proving their worth in terms of productivity, efficiency and employee morale. But there remains a further factor in determining whether they will prove to be viable and sustainable organisational innovations, namely the nature of the relations between teams (or cells, or 'clusters') and the organisation itself. The old hierarchical model has to go. But what is to take its place? Here we find some of the most interesting and innovative ideas in recent management literature, such as 'cluster' organisations and 'spider's web' organisations.[20]

A TEAM-BASED ORGANISATIONAL MODEL: DISC

In my work and research, I have found it most convenient to depict the new organisational structures by starting with the service or production cells themselves. We make them, rather than a hierarchical reporting relationship, the foundation of an organisational model. Each cell will be directed towards its own activities or its own client group, and will be responsible for managing its own internal affairs. Local coordination between cells can also be managed by them, through a variety of ad hoc measures including overlap of functions and face-to-face coordination. This aspect of the model is depicted in Figure 3.8.

To achieve organisational coherence and integrity, there is a need for one or more global coordinating agencies (including various professional activities such as accounting and middle management coordination). Let us depict them as 'coordinating cells' whose activities span all of the production cells. Because of the dynamic property of the production cells (for example, their variable number, depending on the client base of the organisation, and their variable size, depending on the workload of the groups that constitute them), and the integrated nature of the organisation which is based on them, I propose that we name this organisational model the DISC structure, since it is based on Dynamic Integrated Service Cells, where services are interpreted in the widest sense (i.e. they could be manufacturing services). Figure 3.8 depicts the DISC organisational form.[21]

This organisational model has several features which are worth attending to. Firstly, the basic organisational unit is the self-managing team, or cell. This is in stark contrast with the dominant existing organisational model in which the organisational unit is a group of discrete workers doing separate tasks under the control of a supervisor. Thus much of the coordination that needs to be carried out in the dominant model through supervision and management hierarchies is conducted through face-to-face cooperation and coordination within the work cell itself. The key to cooperation within the cell is the integration of functions facilitated by the use of information technology.

Secondly, the multifunctionality of the service cells dispenses with the need for traditional divisional structures within firms, for example, for separate marketing, advertising and 'customer relations' divisions that grew out of the previous functional division of labour. This multifunctionality is what enables cells to develop their strong customer focus and to monitor their own quality of service.

Thirdly, coordination between cells is provided for through both local and global channels. Local coordination between service cells is provided for by overlapping membership between cells and by direct face-to-face negotiations. This is direct coordination and management of local interfaces, as distinct from the traditional model which depends exclusively on a hierarchical structure for such coordination. Direct bilateral management of interfaces promises to be much more efficient. This organisational innovation recalls Likert's discussion of 'linking pins' between groups within an organisation—except that Likert confined his consideration to links between superordinate and subordinate groups, rather than the laterally linked service cells depicted in the diagram.[22]

Fourthly, global coordination between cells is provided by the existence of support units offering technical, legal or accounting services that are shared in common by all cells. In the case of

Figure 3.8 DISC organisational model

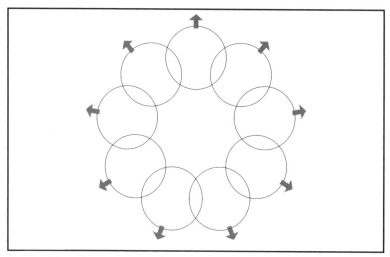

1. Local (overlapping) coordination
Cells of operators with product/customer focus e.g. regional
   groupings

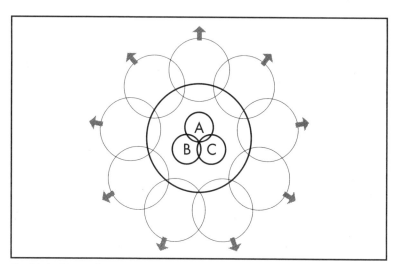

2. Global coordination
A, B, C: global coordinating and support units

manufacturing cells, these technical services might include such matters as preventive maintenance, quality control laboratory facilities, technical support and documentation, and logistics support. In the case of service cells, the support services might include computing and software support, technical support (e.g. underwriting and policy expertise in the case of insurance), as well as global accounting and performance measures aggregation services.

The DISC model is not prescriptive; it does not specify a particular form of relationship within work teams other than the fact that they should exploit cooperative group dynamics; it does not specify the number or size of the cells. It specifies only that the operating activities of the organisation will be conducted through self-managing teams, and that coordination mechanisms of both a local and global character will have to be established.

An important latent property of this model is its recursive character: the same formal designation can be applied to any level of the organisation. Thus the overlapping DISCs can represent, at the corporate level, overlapping market-focused business units that bring together representatives of production, marketing, sales, supply, logistics, new product development, and finance—all functions kept quite separate in the traditional corporate hierarchy. Any one of these business unit DISCs can then be disaggregated to its production level, where the production is actually accomplished by product-focused teams.

Recursivity is a powerful property of organisational models. (It is one of the reasons for the popularity and longevity of the hierarchical model itself.) We shall return to this issue in the final chapter.[23]

DISCs and Theory Y

The DISC model is formulated in response to the concern, expressed for example by Douglas McGregor in his 1960 classic *The Human Side of Enterprise*, that traditional approaches to depicting organisational life (i.e. the familiar organisation chart) constitute, through their rigidity and focus on individual lines of accountability and control, a serious obstacle to organisational innovation and use of the full potential of information technology.

It was McGregor's 1960 book that introduced the world to Theory X and Theory Y. His approach was ingenious. Look at the world of work and organisation, he said. See how it is structured, with long lines of supervision, control and command. It must be based on a theory of human nature that depicts people as stupid, lazy, recalcitrant and malevolent. This he called 'Theory X'. Yet the experimental evidence does not seem to support this depiction. Basing himself on Lewin's group dynamics, and on the behaviour of groups outside the work setting (as in laboratory team settings, community and family), McGregor argued that a more realistic depiction of people's behaviour was to see them as collaborative, responsible and well-meaning. This is Theory Y. Now for the crunch. Why isn't Theory Y behaviour more readily observable in industry? Because, argued McGregor, the structures based on Theory X assumptions *prevent Theory Y behaviour from manifesting itself.*

The connection with the manner of depiction of an organisation is immediate. McGregor noted that the form in which organisation charts are drawn has an important bearing on the way that people within the organisation see their role. He strongly advocated reliance on teamwork as a means of improving coordination and morale. He foresaw that organisations attempting to operate more complex systems would be faced with mounting costs of coordination if they adhered to their traditional hierarchical reporting structures.

McGregor was not overly sanguine concerning the prospects for a rapid transition to teamwork as the basis for organisational innovation, nor for organisational models to shift from a conception 'of an organization as a pattern of individual relationships to one of a pattern of relationships among groups' (McGregor 1960, p. 242). However, in optimistic mood, he conjectured that:

> It is probable that one day we shall begin to draw organization charts as a series of linked groups rather than as a hierarchical structure of individual 'reporting' relationships (McGregor 1960, p. 175).

I claim that the DISC organisational model embodies McGregor's aspirations as espoused in Theory Y. It is the appropriate depiction for organisations that are seeking to set a new standard of quality and efficiency in their production systems. Its superiority will be demonstrated wherever organisations deal with a well-defined customer or client base, and provide them with a reasonably complex level of service calling for interaction between specialised staff.[24]

In a precise sense, then, the DISC model can be said to form a new organisational paradigm for the new production systems in the era of information technology. It is paradigmatic in the generality of its likely application, in the standard of efficiency it will set for firms in sectors where it has been taken up, in the potential for efficiency gains to be registered in sectors where it has not yet been taken up, and in its comprehensive restructuring of present organisational forms. The model can be seen to form a paradigm, or template, which firms will have to emulate if they are to prosper. It is an organisational depiction of McGregor's Theory Y in action.

This discussion takes us to the issue of the process by which new organisational forms, or paradigms, diffuse through the entire economy. It involves strategies of organisational change and organisational learning, as well as more evolutionary concepts like the appearance of small firms embodying the new forms and ousting the old in a process of commercial selection. This is the reality of the global battle that is currently taking place between competing models of productive efficiency.

4

Sociotechnical organisational change
Technological and organisational co-evolution

Behind the rhetoric of 'world best practice', or 'excellence', there lies a struggle over the form of organisation that will emerge to power industrial development into the twenty-first century. The winners in this competitive battle will be the organisations most able to adapt to changing conditions. This is not the first time that there has been such a struggle between competing paradigms or models of organisation. Indeed, according to Perez and Freeman, it is the fifth such upheaval since the Industrial Revolution. They have identified four previous such shifts, associated sequentially with the rise of mass production and the 'emergence of oil-based energy systems (fourth shift); the rise of large corporations and the development of new materials such as steel and new energy technologies such as electric power systems (third shift); the emergence of steam power and the development of new transport systems (second shift); and the emergence of mechanisation following the invention of the factory organisation of production (first shift, equated with the Industrial Revolution).[1]

Thus Perez and Freeman have developed an approach to the current upheavals in industry associated with the introduction of information technology (IT), that looks for counterparts in similar periods of upheaval in the past. In my work I have found this framework to be of compelling interest. I have adapted it to construct a co-evolutionary model of techno-organisational change, bringing the focus back to the complementary changes in technology and organisation which succeed each other and which open and foreclose possibilities for each other. It is worth spending a moment to sketch the outlines of this model, before looking in historical and comparative terms at the co-evolutionary process itself.

TECHNO-ORGANISATIONAL CO-EVOLUTION

Competing paradigms emerge through a process of techno-organisational co-evolution. By this phrase, I mean a process in which organisational features change in tune with technological configurations, and vice versa, technological changes are introduced as and when organisational possibilities permit. In practice, it works as follows. A certain change in technology may be contemplated (for example, linking CAD with CAM (computer aided design with computer aided manufacturing), or more prosaically, linking packing operations with manufacturing through a conveyor system). This change creates a 'space' for an organisational change, namely a linking of packing and manufacturing operations within a common team. Out of a range of options, a shift in organisation is effected, such as towards employee involvement teams or pilot self-managing teams.

This organisational change in itself creates a range of possibilities for further technological change, such as a change in configuration towards a cellular arrangement. This in turn creates the possibility for a further shift in organisation, such as towards a more broadly based teamwork arrangement. As more business systems are brought within the ambit of a team, so a further technological change may be effected, bringing into the cell the machines, equipment or software needed to run these new systems. And so the process goes on, with a shift in organisation creating the need, or possibility, for a change in technology, and likewise a change in technology creating space for a shift in organisation.[2]

Let us spend a moment looking at the five paradigm shifts, since the approach will provide a perspective on the struggle between competing paradigms in the present period.

First paradigm shift

The first paradigm shift occurred with what used to be called the Industrial Revolution, in the last quarter of the eighteenth century. The change in techno-economic base was fundamentally a shift from a 'putting out' system of cottage-based production using manual labour, to a factory-based system that enabled new factory masters to exercise greater control over the quality and cost of production and to discipline a workforce that was largely recruited from unskilled sectors including women and children. The first factories, particularly textile mills in England, were thus born in a climate of extreme social unrest and violence. They were fought by skilled workers in a guerrilla campaign that culminated in the Luddite rebellion of 1819–20. The defeat of the Luddites (in what amounted to a civil war involving the mobilisation of an enormous army) provided the setting for the expansion of the factory system, and for enormous gains to be made in productivity through control over the labour process, through extending the division of labour, and through mechanisation. This was the context in which innovations such as water-powered machinery and canal navigation for freight transport could be made.

Such an account, by adopting the perspective that factories were above all a social and organisational innovation, and as such paved the way for subsequent technical innovations, therefore reverses the conventional view of the Industrial Revolution as being sparked by technical progress.[3]

Second paradigm shift

The new system quickly established a new competitive advantage based on cost advantages accruing through centralised production, division of labour, and mechanisation. It spread to other sectors beyond textiles, ousting domestic production in one sector after another. But as it became pervasive, its productive limitations became manifest, and a series of innovations triggered by the attempt to overcome them ushered in the second paradigm shift in the 1830s. These involved a technical revolution in energy supply, with Watt's steam engine having a dramatic and immediate effect. It liberated factories from their dependence on a source of flowing water, and this led in turn to further dissemination of mechanisation and the location of factories within existing communities, stimulating rapid industrial urbanisation.

Accompanying this was a revolution in materials, focused on iron but also pottery, and in transport, involving iron railways and steam locomotion.

Productivity soared with these innovations, leading to a broader-based regime of accumulation, and the production of wage goods for the new working class from the new factories. The railways and the fledgling postal service created the need for non-government bureaucracies to regulate their operations; these organisations looked to the army and the church for their models of hierarchical efficiency.

This period also saw the triumph of an industrial mode of regulation, overthrowing mercantilist and agrarian protection (through the battle over the Corn Laws) and basing commercial activity on the foundations of the joint-stock company (itself modelled on the chartered enterprises founded by royal decree to administer colonial trade with such outposts as Hudson Bay and the East Indies). It also saw the rise of the first skilled workers' 'combinations' (trade unions) and their struggles to obtain legitimacy after the debacle of Luddism. The early attempts to organise workers were along class lines in the Grand National Union and Chartist groups, but with their collapse skilled groups sought, and in many cases succeeded, in reasserting control over their labour process in the new context of mechanised production.[4]

Third paradigm shift

During the period of the second paradigm there was much more systematic attention being paid to innovation. Some of the inventions became so important that they ushered in a wave of investment associated with the third paradigm shift in the last decades of the nineteenth century. The technical basis of the shift was the introduction of electric power and its supply to whole industrial and urban regions through articulated networks: these were the first examples of complex technological systems that have become such a feature of the twentieth century (Hughes 1989). There were related technical innovations in the form of steel and chemicals, producing unheard of gains in productivity and potential (such as in the construction of the first steel-plated ships and the first steel-based buildings, or skyscrapers). It was this paradigm that ushered in the notion of modernism as a distinct cultural movement that identified with the vigour and dynamism of machinery.

The regime of accumulation of the third paradigm saw manufacturing become the driving economic force of the world's emergent industrial powers: Britain, Germany and the USA. Giant corporations emerged, particularly in the USA after the defeat of the South in the Civil War, based on vertical integration of separate, formerly market-coordinated activities. It also saw the spread of unionism to unskilled workers, and a mode of regulation that included pervasive financial innovations such as stock exchanges and private banks, backed by emergent central banks.

The third paradigm saw major technical innovations involving the standardisation of products, labour and processes. During this period, these innovations developed in the form of interchangeability of parts (the 'American system of manufacture'), the standardisation of labour processes into basic constituent units (through the work of Frederick Winslow Taylor and his disciples), and finally the standardisation of process by the introduction of moving conveyor lines for assembly. It was the coming together of these innovations in the first assembly line that really signalled the shift to a fourth paradigm, based on mass production.

Fourth paradigm shift

If any date and place can be taken as indicating the start of the modern era, it is surely 1913 at Highland Park, Michigan, when the first Model T cars rolled off Henry Ford's first assembly line. The processes of standardisation came together in the system we now call mass production (Hounshell 1984), which ushered in the biggest paradigm shift of any to that date—so significant in fact that Piore and Sabel call it an 'industrial divide', or parting of the ways between craft- and custom-based production and mass production (Piore & Sabel 1984). Standardisation of product, process and labour was soon matched by standardisation of accounting techniques in the form of standardised labour costing and accounting procedures such as 'Return on Investment' calculations (Johnson & Kaplan 1987).

Mass production—or what should more accurately be called standardised production—became pervasive because of the significant cost advantages reaped by returns to scale and by the use of unskilled detail labour on assembly lines. These twin advantages seriously undermined the competitive strength of production by batch and bespoke activities. The new mass methods, implanted during the First World War, set a new industry standard and new model of productive efficiency. This was to have major ramifications for workplace and business organisation, as we have traced in Chapter 2.

But as we have seen above, it soon became apparent that the advantages of mass production depended on certain conditions obtaining beyond the sphere of production itself. The gains of mass production could be reaped only by the creation of mass markets leading to mass consumption, which required standardisation of consumer taste (exemplified in Henry Ford's remark that his customers could have any colour they liked in a Model T as long as it was black) and the payment of high wages to underpin purchasing power. This was the new 'regime of accumulation' required by the emergent production paradigm. But efforts made in this direction (for example by Henry Ford himself, through his famous $5 per day, relatively high, pay rate) were not enough to create a new regime of accumulation in the 1920s, and the whole edifice came crashing down in the Depression. This provided the lesson that capitalism could not be sustained in the absence of an accommodative social and economic framework.

After painful recovery, largely through the war effort, mass production and mass consumption took off in tandem only in the post-war period, thanks to a combination of factors such as the institutionalisation of collective bargaining allowing wages to keep pace with productivity, to Keynesian macroeconomic regulation of the business cycle, and to social security systems and the welfare state which upheld purchasing power. This was complemented by an international mode of regulation involving new global institutions (the International Monetary Fund and the World Bank promoted fixed exchange rates under the Bretton Woods system). In addition, a liberal trade regime gave manufacturers in countries with large metropolitan populations access to each other's markets and to the Third World. This whole system is what is now called Fordism. Its heyday was the 'golden era' from 1945 to 1968 (Marglin et al. 1989).

The Fordist system stamped its image of standardisation not just on manufacturing, but on wider sectors of service provision and in public utilities. Indeed as the 'golden years' wore on, the major Fordist innovations occurred in service sectors such as fast-food retailing and supermarkets which extended Taylorism from the factory to the retail outlet. In turn, the mass unions which grew up in the wake of mass production took on the standardised features of the system of which they were part. Industrial relations bargaining took on an ever more standardised format, with collective bargaining agreements adopting Taylorist job classification systems and narrowing the agenda of issues susceptible to negotiation. The rigidity of mass production made it intolerant of variation or workplace initiative.

This highly compressed account of 250 years of industrial history is designed to bring out certain fundamental points. Firstly, each paradigm shift was prompted by severe restrictions to production and expansion imposed by the structure of the previous regime. Secondly, each shift required a carrier technology and organisation that became pervasive, due to cheapness and abundance of supply. Finally, each transition was painful, involving major social upheavals as the former sociotechnical framework gave way and the new one emerged. Our account culminates in the claim that the decline of the Fordist system, and the prolonged labour pains of the emergent fifth paradigm, is fundamentally the source of the instabilities evident in the world economic and financial system over the past fifteen years.

Fifth paradigm shift

Perez and Freeman argue that microelectronics and information technology generally, are having pervasive effects through the economy that are entirely analogous to the previous paradigm shifts. The point of the analysis is to focus on the complementary organisational shifts that are opened up by these technological innovations, which in turn put competitive pressure on the techno-organisational arrangements typical of the fourth paradigm era.

At the technoeconomic level, the rigid systems of Taylorist work organisation and deskilling associated with early automation proved to be increasingly less able to cope with shifting markets and the product and process flexibility they called for. New technologies based on microelectronics offered unheard of flexibility through programmability, but these gains could not be reaped within Taylorist work structures (Jaikumar 1986). The drive for productivity enhancement along the old lines proved increasingly illusory (Skinner 1986). In some cases these efforts ran up against human and physiological limits, as evident in widespread worker alienation, absenteeism, and injuries caused by repetitive work.

The new technologies called for task integration and group work and multiskilling, if their possibilities were to be tapped. None of these were compatible with Taylorism. In Japan, the large producers quietly abandoned the Taylorist ethic, producing a new intermediate variant called Toyotism (Kaplinsky 1988) or, as has now become standard, the 'lean production system' (Womack et al. 1990). Small producers could afford the low capital costs of programmable microelectronic equipment, and increasingly made inroads into high-tech markets through networking in cooperative clusters of small companies employing highly skilled workers. Thus there emerged new 'industrial districts', such as Emilia-Romagna in Italy, Baden Wuertemberg in Germany (Sabel 1989), and the Tokyo–Osaka small firms axis in Japan (Friedman 1989), all of which have become prosperous and all of which are based on cooperative small firm networks rather than on mass production. Thus the Fordist technoeconomic base proved unable to respond to opportunities available to production systems that were not bound by its rigidities. These are the arguments taken up in the business press which have informed our discussion in Chapters 2 and 3.

THE NOTION OF PARADIGM SHIFTS

The literature on paradigm shifts, and associated notions of 'flexible specialisation' and 'new production concepts', has met with a mixed reception. It draws on three major strands of thought.

Firstly, there is a Schumpeterian source in the notion of long waves in economic development, deriving from Kondratiev's original notion but emphasising the role of innovation and the diffusion of technical developments. This source has been captured in the notion of a 'national system of innovation'.[5]

Secondly, there is the economic dimension, linking technological waves of innovation with changes in investment and ultimately consumption, mediated through government macroeconomic strategies. This is the specific context in which Perez and Freeman place their work, as a critique of the absence of such considerations in mainstream Keynesian economics (Perez & Freeman 1988).

Thirdly, there is a source in the notion of 'paradigm shift', as introduced by Kuhn in his discussion of change in scientific theory (Kuhn 1970). The terminology of paradigm shift derives from the work of Thomas Kuhn on shifts in 'scientific paradigms' being able to account for the successive series of conceptual revolutions which constitute the history of science. Since then, the concept of paradigm shift has become very popular as a means of explaining or accounting for ruptures in practice and theory in other areas of human activity, such as technology, law and politics.[6]

ECONOMIC FACTORS IN DIFFUSION OF A NEW PARADIGM

Two issues stand out as of primary concern. The first is the economic mechanisms that underlie diffusion of a new paradigm. Perez and Freeman are at pains to point to the fact that in each of the five shifts, the new technology (and, I would argue, the organisational form) constitutes a range of new 'best practices' that other firms ignore at their peril. Perez and Freeman spell this out in the form of three conditions that must be met by any genuine 'leading edge' technology:

- it must be capable of being utilised in almost all sectors and affect almost all products and services;
- it must be cheaper than the technology it is supplanting; and
- it must have abundant sources of raw materials.

These are the conditions governing the economic sources of an 'upswing' in investment driven by the new 'lead' technology in each of the five epochs. It is clear that the conditions are obviously satisfied by microelectronics and IT generally in the current period of restructuring. They were clearly satisfied by oil and mass production in the early decades of this century. With further argument and demonstration, one can show that they were satisfied by steel, electric power systems and integrated firms in the third epoch, by the steam engine, railways and the joint stock company in the second epoch, and by mechanisation and factory organisation at the beginning of the Industrial Revolution.

In each case it is not a question of appealing to some form of technological determinism. Rather it is a matter of demonstrating how one set of lead technologies and organisational forms oust another by becoming a 'best practice' that other firms and sectors must match, or go out of business. This is the driving force of techno-organisational diffusion which underpins the notion of 'competing models of productive efficiency' discussed in Chapter 2. It is in this sense that I describe emerging organisational forms that can exploit the flexibility of IT, through programmability, in the current period as potentially ousting those which cannot exploit these forms of flexibility. Empirical work supports this thesis, as we have seen.[7]

The sweep of history covered by the 'paradigm shift' literature has of course attracted its critics, some of them quite vociferous.[8] For my part, I believe it provides us with a useful handle on the present upheavals, informed by similar upheavals in the past, leading us to focus on the 'mismatch' between social and organisational structures that made sense in the era of mass production, and the structures that facilitate organisational flexibility, responsiveness and adaptability in the current period. In my view, it makes sense to characterise these upheavals as 'triggered' by IT, with its propensity to favour new forms of organisation based on integration over previously dominant forms of organisation based on division of labour and fragmentation of tasks—without in any way claiming that the changes were 'caused' by IT.

It bears repetition that this account is not in any sense 'technologically determinist', even though it is placing technological (and organisational) changes at the centre of analysis. The point is to establish that once a certain techno-organisational form acquires the characteristic of 'best practice', it is able to drive out other forms through firms adopting it in order to stay up with the competition. The process of co-evolution brings out the mutual inter-dependence of technology and organisation.

What the 'paradigm shift' literature does not specify is *how* the shift is to be accomplished by firms. Here a range of options present themselves, and take us into the literature on organisational change. It is the concern with change and its strategies which is the thread that weaves itself throughout the rest of this volume.

THE ADOPTION OF NEW ORGANISATIONAL FORMS

The diffusion of new organisational forms requires one of two organisational processes: either new organisations embodying the new forms are created, or existing organisations are transformed. In the 'population ecology' model of organisational populations, the emphasis is on the former.[9] But undoubtedly the most significant avenue for diffusion of new forms is via the transformation of existing organisations.[10] This is where we enter the contested terrain of 'organisational change'.

How do best practice organisations become so good? What kind of transitional strategies do they pursue in transforming themselves? How do they deal with the fact that people inevitably have a stake in the old structures and systems that need to be replaced?

There is a school of thought that sees best practice in terms of incremental, 'bottom-up' change that is essentially participative in character. There is a contrasting school of thought, or school of deeds, that sees change in terms of top-down transformation imposed autocratically by hard-driving chief executives. The danger with the first approach is that it is liable to drift; it lacks leadership and strategic direction. There is little future for a participative organisation that is losing its markets and falling behind technologically. The danger with the second approach is that while it smashes resistance and sets a breakneck pace for change while keeping a strategic eye on the organisation's environment, it fails in the long run to generate sustainable change. The idea of people taking responsibility for their own actions is contradicted by the terms of the change process itself. The top-down approach runs the risk of destroying the roots from which a future viable organisation will grow.

Discussion of this issue needs to start with recognition of a sobering fact. Most programmes of organisational change end up as failures. The few successes, such as in the companies discussed in this book, highlight the factors that need to be taken into account if a change programme is to be successful. After all, a major change programme is probably the largest single undertaking that most people will have to endure in their working lives. There is little point in blaming them for demonstrating 'resistance to change' if senior managers, unions and middle managers do not make the effort to reassure people whose jobs, skills or careers can be radically affected, even destroyed, by the change.

Take the case of Ford Australia as a typical example. As in most cases of workplace reform currently underway in Australia, promotion of change at Ford has come from senior managers and from forward-thinking union delegates and shop floor workers, while resistance has come from those who see themselves having something to lose, such as middle-level managers and supervisors. The Ford submission to a Senate inquiry on technological change made some interesting observations on the process of change.

> Changing the culture of an organisation is obviously complex, and necessitates action on many different fronts. Success requires appealing not only to the intellect but also to the emotions in order to change people's behavioural habits.
>
> We have learned that conservatism dies hard. Each interest group in the organisation has to be addressed with specifically tailored actions. These interest groups include senior management, middle management and supervisors, union representatives and union officials (in their capacities as worker representatives), and operators themselves. Of these, we have found that it is the middle levels of management, and supervisors, that present the biggest challenge. This includes technical people, who have a vested interest in no change, because the team approach meant that they had to share power with people they considered to be 'non-experts'. Involving unions and their representatives from the beginning helps to ensure their commitment.
>
> We found that it is better to start small, with pilot programs in limited areas giving concrete form to the proposed changes, and expand after some demonstrated successes. This 'organic' form of growth is both more manageable and more successful than attempting to institute an overall, company-wide program at a single point of time (Australia. Parliament. Senate. Standing Committee on Industry Science and Technology 1990, Submission 28, p. 6).

This is a good description of the philosophy that has guided the change process at the Ford Plastics plant since 1990, and at Ford more generally through the latter half of the 1980s. It also conforms to the best examples of successful organisational change reported in the literature.

For example, a widely discussed study by Michael Beer and associates at the Harvard Business School, 'Why change programs don't produce change', makes very similar points to those made by Ford (Beer et al. 1990). Beer and colleagues argue that top-down management-driven programmes rarely engage with the specifics of work, which is where change has to occur if abstractions like 'quality', 'performance' and 'excellence' are to mean anything. Beer et al. also argue for a species of 'organic' change, starting at plant level and working up to the top executive levels. As they put it:

> The general (plant) managers did not focus on formal structures and systems; they created ad hoc organisational arrangements to solve concrete business problems. By aligning employee roles, responsibilities and relationships to address the organisation's most important competitive task—a process we call 'task alignment'—they focused energy for change on the work itself, not on abstractions such as 'participation' or 'culture' (Beer et al. 1990, p. 159).

The model of change developed at the Ford Plastics plant takes this further in that its focus on quality enhancement by work area teams provides a new and challenging context for managers themselves. This 'yeast effect' of the shop floor changes, working their way through the body of the organisation to the top management, is one of the most striking features of the change process at Ford. The quality-conscious teams require, indeed demand, the cooperation, facilitation and timely intervention of senior management in order to get things done. Management in turn responds to this pressure, seeing itself in a novel 'problem solving' light, which comes to take the place of the traditional focus on 'command and control'. The shift in management perspectives and practices brought about by the structural changes at Ford has been far more profound than would have been possible through mere exhortation or 'change management' from the top.

RESISTANCE TO CHANGE?

The model of change proposed by Beer et al. is superior to much that is on offer from the Organisational Development school of thought, which raises 'participation' to a lofty ideal, but then seems to locate all obstacles to change in people's apparently irrational 'resistance'. If people are going to lose their jobs as a result of the changes, then their resistance is anything but irrational.

Organisations that are serious about change spend a lot of time and energy in determining who will be the winners and losers, and then in making offers to accommodate the losers, either to compensate them or to involve them in the changes. It is middle level management positions, particularly those of supervisors, who are most threatened by the shift to teamwork. They are therefore the most obvious source of 'resistance' to any planned change. An intelligent change programme will therefore target these supervisors to offer them training first in understanding what the changes are all about, and then in offering them a role in the new workplace culture. They might wish to adapt and become a team leader; they might wish to apply their experience through becoming a trainer or facilitator. They may even be happy to become an ordinary team member. If after gaining some insight into the new culture they find that it doesn't appeal, then a wise company will offer them an exit with dignity.

This was precisely the strategy followed by Colonial Mutual in its shift to self-managing teams in the insurance industry. Many of the old-style supervisors were only too happy to discard the surveillance and control functions they had to exercise in the old regime, and readily adapted to being highly-motivated team leaders. Others provided assistance in the newly formed professional consultancy team formed to back up the front-line customer service teams. Others quietly left, with dignity.

These strategies are anticipated by the insights of Frederick Herzberg, who in the 1960s insisted that employee motivation could not be achieved by any number of 'self-actualisation' programmes, if basic security issues were not attended to first. Herzberg called these the 'hygiene factors': they include employment security, wages, preservation of skills, and above all, a sense of dignity and worth. It seems obvious in retrospect. How could a change programme which flouted such concerns possibly succeed?

LEGITIMATING CHANGE

A change programme that pays due regard to people's security and motivation may still fail, for want of legitimacy in the eyes of the people who have to make it work. A programme that is foisted on people without adequate explanation will not be supported.

The extraordinary feature of strategies associated with

Organisational Development and associated accounts of the process of organisational change, is that they lack provision for legitimacy; they lack any form of constitutional foundation in the form of rules or principles that are agreed in advance with those who are about to undergo the change. This is even more remarkable when one considers that most of these accounts emanate from the USA where a concern with legitimacy and constitutional proprieties pervades the body politic. But in the organisational sphere, the same concerns are conspicuous by their absence.

Take the case of the influential account developed by Beer et al. mentioned above. While it attends fully to the structural and motivational features of change, it is strangely silent on the question of legitimacy. This is where industrial relations can make its contribution to the change process.

The model of change employed at the Ford Plastics plant, for example, is richer than that provided by such business theorists as Beer and colleagues, or at least more relevant to Australian conditions, in that it takes fully into account the industrial relations framework through which change must be negotiated. At Ford, industrial relations is the ever-present but never intrusive context within which the moves towards expanded job definitions, multi-skilling, teamwork and all the other changes are proceeding. The plant management have grasped the opportunities presented to them by award restructuring within the guidelines (constraints) laid down by their own corporate management and the industry-wide negotiations.

Industrial relations agreements are seen as providing for all parties the 'rules of change' in a process of organisational transformation. This is the sense in which one can claim that industrial relations provides the constitutional foundations for change, spelling out the rights and responsibilities of the parties and the appeal mechanisms in the case of grievances.

The case of the Australian Taxation Office provides another telling example of change that is 'legitimated' by a comprehensive, negotiated 'Modernisation Agreement'. Such an agreement spells out the rights and responsibilities of the parties, allocating the functions and duties of representatives and of change process committees. It provides for consultative processes and for avenues of appeal. The hidden sub-text of such an agreement is that it underscores commitment and cooperation. The workforce is saying: if you respect these 'rules of change', then we will cooperate, and indeed work hard, to make the change a success.

At the Centre for Corporate Change in the University of New

South Wales, my colleagues Professor Dunphy and Dr Stace have been working on these same issues, but from a somewhat different perspective. In their book, *Under New Management*, Dunphy and Stace (1990) review the change strategies of thirteen service organisations in Australia. In the process, they throw a lot of well-aimed cold water on the pretensions of Organisation Development consultants who insist on organisational change as a cooperative, incremental, participative process (usually, however, ignoring the union) more or less as an 'ethical imperative'.

Dunphy and Stace take a robust approach, arguing that real organisations adopt change strategies in keeping with the extent to which they 'match' their environment. In some cases of good prior fit, continuous adjustment will be adequate; in other cases, where the organisation has been allowed to drift, there will be a need for total organisational transformation driven through by authoritarian, coercive means. Depending on the context, the appropriate strategy might be 'modular transformation', or 'total transformation', and the style might be 'collaborative' or 'directive'.[11]

Of course this graduated approach to the analysis of change is sensible. Firms that are already approaching 'best practice' conceive their change strategies in ways that are very different from those that wish to become best practice firms but are still mired in old forms and procedures. But of course these are analytical categories; they do not specify *how change is to be accomplished*. I have found in my own case studies that firms make strategic choices in terms that reflect their immediate market and technological options, and cast around for whatever methods are available. It is not as if a group of senior managers make an informed choice between, say, *developmental transition* and *task-focused transition*. If the company is a typical staid, conservative and relatively rigid enterprise, the senior management task is to get it moving, through unshackling the resources that are being dammed up by the present structures and processes, and to do so in any way that they can.

The choices I see firms making are between change that is foisted on them by external events, such as industrial relations developments, or change induced by the need to catch up with new technologies, new products, new processes, or new ideas. Rarely is change thought through in advance and conceived to achieve a particular strategic goal. What is outstanding about the firms whose stories we consider in Part 2 of this volume, is that they have succeeded in rising above the swirl of events to gain a perspective on their present position and its relation to their desired position at some future date. This is the essential feature that I would highlight in 'best practice'.

We are left with the question: how do organisations go about 'directive change'? To call it this is not to provide a strategy. To actually probe beneath the words, we have to ask ourselves what leadership and involvement actually mean, and how best practice firms can combine the two in transforming themselves.

In my experience, the twin keys to successful organisational change are *leadership* and *involvement*. In the first place, *leadership is necessary and irreplaceable*. It is needed to generate the overall strategic direction of change, the goals of the process, and the resources to be invested in it. Within this framework, which is public and accessible, the organisation's members can be encouraged to take over the process of change for themselves. The tools used are many and varied. There are consultative committees, at both corporate and plant level. There are project teams that work with engineers on the technological and organisational details of change. There are group briefings held regularly to keep everyone informed, and there are private counselling sessions to answer people's individual queries and respond to their fears.

The theory of change espoused here is that change works best, resulting in sustainable new structures, when it involves those who have a stake in the outcome. By contributing to the change process, they are making their own personal commitment to its successful implementation. The process of change may be slower than in the top-down, crash-through variety, but its long-term results are far more secure and flexible in the face of unexpected developments.

But people will only cooperate in change if they are convinced that it is in their interests to do so. The framework for change established at the outset is designed to meet their initial fears and concerns. Guarantees have to be given concerning such basic issues as employment, salaries, and skills. Without these guarantees, people are given no incentive to cooperate with the change, and indeed are given every incentive to fear the worst, and oppose everything. All too often, their fears are rational and well-grounded; they will lose something in the change. The essential point—and this is where leadership is irreplaceable—is to be able to demonstrate that individual losses (such as supervisor positions) can be outweighed by overall gains, and that even for individuals who are displaced, there will be positions available if they wish to take advantage of the new opportunities.

The case studies presented below provide us with real examples, indeed with virtual laboratories, where the specifics of issues such as leadership and involvement can be probed. They are not simple or straightforward issues. My (somewhat cryptic) characterisation, based on the insights gained in these studies, would be that leadership is the capacity to offer people involvement on their own terms, subordinating their individual interests to that of the organisation as a whole, while involvement is the process of allowing people to exercise leadership over themselves and their colleagues, within certain prescribed areas of responsibility. Thus leadership entails involvement, while involvement calls for leadership. It is my task to show how this works in the setting of the examples discussed below.

WORKPLACE INNOVATION AND THE LEARNING ORGANISATION

Nothing is given in advance and nothing is determined in the battle for the fifth paradigm production organisation. It is one thing to characterise choices in clear terms, as between the three paradigms or models of MPS, LPS and STPS. In the real world nothing is ever presented as simply as this.

In reality, firms grope their way to a form of organisation that complements the environment they operate in and the technology they employ. The process of techno-organisational co-evolution that they are engaged in proceeds through a series of choices. Firms can use criteria to guide their choices, but in any case they will not be free agents. For example, unions will have their own agenda, as will public agencies, not to mention other competitors.

Successful firms that achieve superior performance are now characterised as 'learning organisations'. By this phrase is meant the process through which firms probe their environment, testing and experimenting with strategies and structures until they find one which is best adapted to the firm's circumstances. They then institutionalise these strategies and structures in the firm's routines, its procedures, its structures, so that they become part of its 'culture'.[12]

But we are getting ahead of our story. Firstly, we must look at how real organisations change their structures and processes, in all the complexity of real, turbulent conditions. In these conditions, firms grope their way forward, experimenting first with this then with that strategy, seeking an accommodation with market forces and technologies that cannot be predicted and which constantly threaten to blow the firm's strategy off course. In these conditions, the robustness of firms which can call on the skills of their employees emerges as a striking competitive advantage.

Part 2

Workplace reform in Australia: case studies

5

Cellular manufacturing
Bendix Mintex

It is now widely recognised that best practice in manufacturing involves devolution of production authority to largely autonomous teams of operators responsible for complete manufacturing cycles or groups of products. These are termed manufacturing cells, or 'factories within a factory'. They are the central feature of the emergent 'focused factory'.[1]

Manufacturing cells represent an organisational innovation of the first importance. As discussed in Chapter 3, a cell consists of a group of machines and processes laid out in such a way that a self-contained team of operators can produce a whole product or series of products. The term 'cell' is defined as an organisational structure in which a social innovation (teamwork) is combined with a technical innovation (cellular arrangement of machines) to produce a genuine 'sociotechnical' transformation of work. The cell replaces traditional 'functional layout' where tasks are grouped and products and components move backwards and forwards between these functional areas during the production process.

The manufacturing cell innovation lays the foundation for the following features of 'best practice' manufacturing.[2]

- The cell produces a whole product, end product or component, thus enabling the team members to cooperate in its production with a sense of accomplishment and control over outcomes that is not possible in traditional functional layouts.
- Batch sizes can be drastically reduced, approaching the ideal of 'flow production'. This makes production much more flexible,

switching between one product line and another as needed (subject to the technical constraint of die changes).

- Flow production encourages the introduction of Just-In-Time manufacturing principles, linking suppliers to final producers, and offering much improved market responsiveness.
- Control by the team over the end product enables them to institute quality assurance techniques under their own management, thus laying the foundation for Total Quality Management (TQM) and 'first time right' quality production.
- Alienating modes of work are dispensed with and operators develop a sense of pride and ownership in their task that derives from, and is directly related to, the control and responsibility that they exercise.

The question to be faced in any consideration of such a profound workplace innovation is: how do firms go about implementing such a transformation? How do they shift from their present rigid structures to such a radically new organisation of work?

The automotive components supplier, Bendix Mintex, provides an excellent case study on this issue. Bendix Mintex, a medium-sized automotive components supplier situated in Ballarat, Victoria, is one of the first organisations in Australia to design, install and operate a genuine world-class manufacturing cell. Bendix Mintex has moved to produce its brake linings and other friction products entirely through five manufacturing cells, making the transition over a twelve month period from mid-1992 to mid-1993. At the time of our study (September to November 1992) the first two cells were installed and entering successful production.[3]

At Bendix Mintex, the cells installed are responsible for the production of brake linings and other friction products that go into cars. In each cell, a single production flow on conveyors has been installed to link the moulding, painting and finishing processes, all arranged in a U-shape, with quality inspection and finishing placed at the focus of the U. The first cell comprises fifteen people per shift, and covers high-volume production of moulded friction materials. The cell brings together steps which were previously scattered through the plant: moulding, powder painting, grinding, clipping and packing. The second cell produces similar products at lower volumes per run; it comprises thirteen operators per shift. The two cells share some facilities, and occasionally swap team members.

Bendix Mintex is now starting to achieve the productivity, quality and cost results that are advertised as flowing from the 'reinvented factory'. One of the striking things is the way that the appearance of the factory has been transformed with the introduction of the two manufacturing cells. At our first visit, prior to its introduction, the factory had the traditional functional layout, with rows of moulding ovens followed by batteries of grinders, then by rows of powder painting ovens, and so on. It was gloomy, frenetic and struggling against an overwhelming tide of inventory stacked in carts all over the floor. An idea of what it looked like is conveyed in Figure 5.1.

The cell has introduced cleanliness, order and a sense of purpose. Gone is the inventory problem, as finished batches are inspected and whisked away to warehouses or delivered to car plants. The conveyor lines carrying partially finished mini-batches of product give a clear sense of the stages of production and emphasise the collaborative efforts of operators within the cell. A picture of the operating cell, taken in late October 1992, is shown on page 108.

Along with the old functional division of labour, Bendix Mintex has dispensed with the traditional supervisory structure and introduced team leaders in place of supervisors and leading hands. These team leaders are working members of their teams. Since the introduction of the cells, they have experienced a quantum leap in enthusiasm and morale.

This latest episode in the programme of workplace reform at Bendix Mintex has attracted government recognition and support through the Australian Best Practice Demonstration programme.[4]

The company is already achieving export levels of 20 per cent of its output, and it plans to raise this figure to 40 per cent in the next five years, targeting the Asia Pacific region. The close link between workplace reform and business strategy is therefore underlined.

The story of Bendix Mintex is particularly interesting because of the twists and turns taken along the way to best practice manufacturing. The cellular manufacturing innovation at the Bendix Mintex plant follows two previous attempts to introduce teamwork which ended in failure and frustration. The previous efforts were carried out without technical changes to processes; they operated purely within the social region of the sociotechnical continuum. Other attempts were made using purely technical changes, without social innovations.

Thus Bendix Mintex has in the past displayed a kind of 'organisational schizophrenia', emphasising either social or technical innovations but rarely the two together; in this it was no worse nor

Bendix Mintex pad moulding plant before (*above*) and after (*below*)

better than countless other Australian manufacturing plants. But the introduction of cellular manufacturing has 'cured' this organisational schizophrenia, emphasising a balance between social and technical innovation and paving the way to serious improvements in productivity, quality achievement and staff morale.

Unions have played an important role in the workplace reform process at Bendix Mintex. Union delegates have made their contribution to the participative process of work redesign. Bob Jackman, the Managing Director of Bendix Mintex at Ballarat, has gone on the record to state that: 'It is my opinion that any attempt to introduce workplace reform without establishing the foundations of good employee relations and union cooperation will have a limited chance of success' (Australian Trade Commission 1992).

Bendix Mintex: organisational background

Bendix Mintex is Australia's largest manufacturer of automotive and industrial friction materials. Its main products are disc pads and blocks that are used in brakes and clutches, as well as friction materials for industrial application. It supplies direct to automotive manufacturers as well as to a large 'after sales' market for spare parts and kits. Most passenger vehicles built in Australia use Bendix Mintex products. Its head office, manufacturing plant, sales and distribution centre are all located at Ballarat, Victoria, where 600 staff are employed.

Bendix Mintex was founded at Ballarat as a small operation employing 30 people in 1955. It was established as Mintex Ltd by the UK firm British Belting and Asbestos, to supply moulded linings of friction material for which the trade name was Mintex, to specialist brake shops in Australia. (The parent company was founded in Yorkshire in the nineteenth century to supply belting for factories, in the days before electric motors when machines had to be driven by belts coming off a prime mover.)

As the car market in Australia expanded, so Mintex's fortunes improved. In 1963 it attracted a takeover offer from the US automotive firm Bendix Corporation; following negotiations with the parent company, Bendix acquired 51 per cent of the Ballarat operation, establishing a new entity named Bendix Mintex. Elsewhere, the two multinational giants continued to compete head to head. Indeed, Australia remains the only part of the world where they collaborate.

In 1965, Bendix Mintex began manufacturing disc pads and won its first original equipment contract with General Motors Holden. This was followed in 1967 by an original equipment order to supply the Chrysler Valiant with disc pads. Further inroads into the original equipment market followed.

In 1970, Bendix Mintex expanded its range of products to include clutch facings, with the acquisition of the firm HK Porter Australia. This brought rights to manufacture another brand of clutch facings ('Thermoid'), and further contracts in the original equipment manufacturer market. Vertical integration followed in the late 1970s, with Bendix Mintex acquiring the capacity to manufacture its own metal backing plates for friction products and presses for the moulded products. This highly skilled toolroom and maintenance shop provided Bendix Mintex with great flexibility, underpinning its market strategy of serving a number of parallel niche markets simultaneously. In line with current best practice thinking, this same metal backing plate operation, which is being kept separate from the formation of disc pad manufacturing cells, is being encouraged to operate as a separate business unit, seeking orders from outside Bendix Mintex. Thus the wheel turns, from vertical integration in the 1970s to vertical disintegration in the 1990s.

Early on Bendix Mintex recognised that its future lay beyond the relatively small Australian automotive market. In 1975 efforts were made to promote sales in the South-East Asian region through a Bendix distributor located in Singapore and this grew to a wholly-owned sales office in 1979. Exports to South-East Asia have built up steadily ever since.

In 1983, the Bendix Corporation was taken over by Allied Signal Inc. of the USA. This led to no immediate changes at Bendix Mintex which continues to be jointly owned by 51 per cent American and 49 per cent British interests.

The market strategy chosen by Bendix Mintex is to be a universal supplier: it is prepared to produce friction materials for any make of car. Its installed technology has been designed to support such a broad-spectrum strategy. In turn, this has provided a favourable environment for the present shift towards cellular manufacturing.

In the 1980s, Bendix Mintex came under the same pressures experienced by the automotive industry generally in Australia. Restructuring has been actively encouraged under the Button Plan, launched in 1984 and updated in 1989 and again in 1991.[5]

Cost pressures experienced by automotive manufacturers have been passed on in magnified form to components suppliers. According to evidence supplied to the Industry Commission, 'most vehicle assemblers are now demanding productivity gains sufficient to achieve real price reductions of around five per cent per annum as a condition of longer term supply contracts, although the extent of productivity offsets negotiated varies from vendor to vendor' (Industry Commission 1991, pp. 29–30). Bendix Mintex has certainly been feeling this cost pressure, along with demands from manufacturers for Just-In-Time deliveries and for improved levels of quality assurance. This is the extremely competitive environment faced by Bendix Mintex in the 1990s, and it is driving the company's relentless search for greater levels of productive efficiency.

INSTALLATION OF A MANUFACTURING CELL

Traditional batch production, which is actually far more common than production using assembly lines, is based on functional groupings of machines. At Bendix Mintex, for example, the layout until recently has been along such functional lines. In one part of the plant, all the moulding of friction materials was carried out in batteries of ovens. Operators would stand before these batteries, weighing out mixtures and inserting them in moulds to go in the ovens. They simply worked to order, with little idea of, or interest in, what would happen to the moulds after they were taken off to the next process. Prior to this operation, another part of the plant was responsible for producing the mixtures by blending materials in hoppers, and in another part again, metal backing plates were produced by casting hot metal in dies fashioned elsewhere in the Bendix Mintex toolroom. After moulding, other sections of the plant would be responsible for painting (powder coating and oven drying); another section would be responsible for grinding and finishing; and another section again for packing. Quality control was formerly a separate activity. This was altogether a very wasteful system: scrap rates were sometimes very high (running at six or seven per cent, or higher).

Orders would be received at the plant and would be made up as a batch, sometimes involving a run of thousands of parts. A batch of product would move through the various functional processes, following its own zig-zag course depending on the operations needed and the sequence in which they could be performed.

At Bendix Mintex, the path followed by actual batches was extremely convoluted, reflecting this functional organisation of production. The path of one such batch is shown in Figure 5.1.

111

Figure 5.1 Bendix Mintex batch path — before

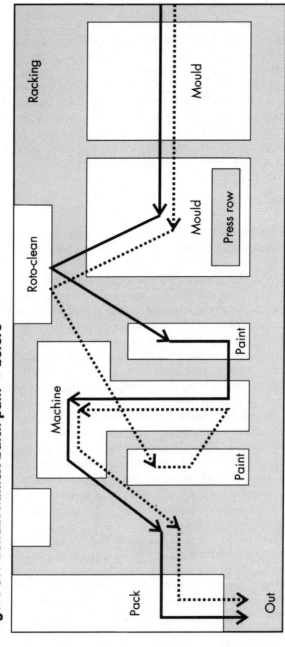

The existing layout/team structure/logistics has resulted in: complex work flows
                                                                 lots of WIP
                                                                 high finished goods stock
                                                                 cramped, hot, noisy working conditions,

Source: IE Management Consultants/Bendix Mintex

The path followed by the batches is complex, and gives no group of workers any sense of ownership of a particular batch. Often when quality inspection got to check a batch, it was weeks since the actual operations had been carried out, and if faults had to be rectified, it was virtually impossible to trace back to where they might have occurred.

Cellular manufacturing reorganises this functional division of tasks into one which is based on the capacity of groups or cells to produce a given family of products. The idea is that each cell contains machines and processes sufficient to produce a single product or family of products, with the operators acting as a team. In this sense, the cell constitutes an autonomous group of processes, and the operators likewise constitute an autonomous group.

TECHNICAL REDESIGN PROJECT

Through the 1980s, efforts at Bendix Mintex to reform operations focused on the introduction of TQM principles and the introduction of self-managing teams. An early attempt to introduce teams in disc pad production was aborted when it was clear that inadequate training had been provided. After a consultant was brought in and provided extensive training for supervisors on their new role as well as for some shop floor operators, a second effort was made to move towards semi-autonomous work groups. Because the company at this stage was not convinced of the need to complement the job redesign initiatives with technological changes in layout, the newly-formed teams ended up being scattered through the plant in line with the former functional division of labour. This initiative too petered out, leaving some bitterness in its wake.

By mid-1991, Bendix Mintex senior management had come to recognise that the purely 'social' approach to team formation was not succeeding, and faced up to the necessity to introduce technical changes in the layout of the plant to support and underpin team-working. This meant moving towards cellular manufacturing. It also meant calling for substantial investment.

The company's parents were apprised of the situation, and an investment package was put together and finally approved. The package was termed the Technical Redesign Project and it was costed at $5.2 million.[6]

At this point, the Federal government had announced its Best Practice Demonstration Programme, offering firms assistance with initiatives designed to bring them abreast of world best practice in both manufacturing and services. Bendix Mintex approached the programme's Steering Committee with a submission seeking assistance with its Technical Redesign Project on the grounds that its aspirations were to achieve best practice, and that the changes were being pursued in a participative manner.

Bendix Mintex was one of the successful companies and (like other grantees) received funding of around $0.5 million to assist with consultancy and contract engineering expenses, as well as with some of the non-capital expenses (covering such matters as relocation of plant and services, benchmarking expenses, and incidentals). This underlines the role of government in assisting firms to make the transition towards workplace innovation.

The Bendix Mintex Teams Steering Group deliberated long and hard over the strategy for technical redesign. Eventually it was decided to focus on changing the physical layout in Plant A, where the company's 'bread and butter' products are produced. An all-day workshop was staged by the Teams Steering Group in January 1992, and benchmarks were set for the approaching technical redesign. It was decided that cellular manufacturing would be initiated with a pilot cell or cells in the disc pad production area.

A project brief was prepared for consulting engineers, and the contract was awarded to a leading firm with extensive experience in introducing cellular manufacturing systems. This firm expressed their willingness to work with a local project team. The team started out with twelve members, but eventually settled as a core of five staff working full-time under the direction of the consulting firm.

This was an interesting and novel arrangement in itself. It represented a departure from the traditional form of engineering consulting, where the technical evaluation and recommendations are made by an outside consulting team, which then frequently implements its own recommendations; the company's technical staff are then expected to pick up a finished process and make it work. The Bendix Mintex arrangement was informed by notions of organisational learning, with consulting engineers bringing their expertise and knowledge of other systems to bear on the problem, and in the process, passing on this expertise to the full-time project team which conducted the detailed evaluation under the consultants' supervision. This arrangement allows the client firm to acquire maximum benefit from the experience, and build up a store of knowledge of its own procedures that is invaluable in making the new cellular arrangements work.

A well-defined project plan was prepared by the consulting

engineers in consultation with the Project Team. It envisaged a five stage process. The first stage was to define the overall cell structure and design the pilot cell, and was embarked on in earnest in February and March 1992. Stage 2 was the implementation of the pilot cell; stage 3 was the implementation of remaining cells in the disc pad process, perfecting their operation as the process unfolded; stage 4 was envisaged as being the installation of cellular manufacturing across the whole site; and stage 5 was to be one of continuous improvement and cell team development. In the event, stage 2 encompassed the implementation of two pilot cells. Stage 3 was envisaged as being completed during the first six months of 1993.

This project plan is of great organisational significance in itself. It constitutes a founding article of what is understood to be a complex process of sociotechnical change. It brings out into the open the commitment to bring the whole of the plant into cellular manufacturing within a certain time period which is synchronised with the capital investment programme. The pilot projects are seen as first steps on a committed journey.

This is a very different approach from one which views pilot projects as 'experiments' which will be 'evaluated' prior to any decision being taken to proceed. Such an approach nearly always ends up with the pilot being isolated, indeed quarantined, from the rest of the operation which takes steps to build up its 'resistance' to the infecting innovation. Under such a scenario the innovators end up losing their enthusiasm, the pilot eventually collapses, and workplace reform is set back by years. At Bendix Mintex this common mistake was avoided, and maximum support for the change was sought from the open and explicit commitments being made.

The project team played an important role throughout the planning process. As well as working with the consultant engineers, team members liaised constantly with their peers in the plant. They took upon themselves responsibility for providing briefings to shop floor staff, for issuing newsletters, and for keeping management and unions informed of progress through the Steering Committee.

Project team members also participated in 'benchmarking' visits to other plants where the consulting engineers had previously worked, seeing for themselves what cellular manufacturing arrangements looked like. This external perspective was another important factor which has contributed to the success of the cellular initiatives.

Project design and implementation

The design of the cellular arrangements began with an exhaustive collection of base data which examined every aspect of current operations. Process flows were plotted in detail, with a view to identifying bottlenecks, frequencies, and the range of processes, products and equipment involved. In some instances, stock was found to follow a winding four kilometre journey through various processes before ending up in the warehouse. High levels of work in progress were documented, excessive levels of materials handling, and long lead times—the object of the new cellular arrangements was to improve all these aspects.

The basic principles of cellular manufacturing were identified by the consulting engineers as involving simple, direct routing between operations and close spacing of operations with clear sight lines for operators to see each other and to see the current state of work in progress.

The consulting engineers developed an 'ideal' structure for manufacturing cells, involving single products using the processes of moulding, painting, machining and packing. In practice it was recognised that products would have to be grouped together (since there are over 1800 of them) enabling teams to focus on a group of similar products with a similar processing sequence. Cell design options were canvassed. Defining cells in terms of specific processes was considered and dismissed as a logistics nightmare. Defining them in terms of volume of production was also canvassed (e.g. high volume, medium volume and low volume cells), together with an original equipment cell; on its own, this arrangement would lead to excessive equipment duplication and make load balancing difficult. A third option involving cell definition by friction material used (i.e. a variant of the process approach) was also considered and discarded.

In the end, an approach to cell definition that involved consideration of both process and product was adopted. In the main, the major focus of each cell would be a family of products (defined partly in terms of their volume) and there would be some sharing of resources and equipment between cells.

From these considerations, the consulting engineers recommended a five cell structure as the model for the disc pad operation. Cell 1 would focus on high volume powder painted kits involving around 100 different products, while Cell 2 would focus on medium volume powder painted kits in smaller production runs. Cell 3 would focus on very small production runs of powder painted kits, catering for up to 968 products. Cells 4 and 5 would cover wet painted products; Cell 4 would focus on operations tailored to the

116

unique requirements of original equipment manufacturers, while Cell 5 would deal with the rest.

Cells 1 and 2 (set up first) would have their own moulding ovens, they would share powder painting facilities, and they would have their own machining and packing operations. Each cell would enable a clear U-shaped product flow to be followed, with small batches moving in trays around a conveyor system on elevated rollers.

The planned layout suggested by the consulting engineers is shown in Figure 5.2.

Each cell was designed so that eventually it could be looked upon as a mini-business. It was stressed by the consultants and project team members that each cell would therefore need its own work area, facilities, equipment and operating procedures. This is what had signally been lacking in the previous 'social only' approach to teamworking. The failure of this experience was uppermost in the minds of project team members.

These cell definitions were arrived at during a period of intense discussion. Successive drafts were posted up on notice boards and subjected to thorough plant-wide debate. In all, there were six versions before the final model was settled on.

There is an important organisational point at stake here. What might appear to be an over-long process of consultation and participation in fine tuning the cell proposals was followed by rapid implementation once the decision to proceed was taken. This is the strength of participative change of the kind being carried through at Bendix Mintex. It contrasts with the crash-through approach, where decision-making is rapid but implementation is slow and costly as numerous details not previously considered come to light and resistance to the whole process has to be overcome.

Logistics

Cell design proceeded in tandem with an approach to the scheduling of work which was envisaged as changing from the 'production push' approach that was prevalent, to a 'demand–pull' approach combined with Just-In-Time. It was envisaged that cells would react to demand generated by the stock levels in warehouses or to orders for original equipment supply. The consultants expressed the view that the existing information flow system at Bendix Mintex was complex and difficult to follow. Because of long lead times, there was little relation between forecasts and actual demand, resulting in high levels of stock and work in progress.

Figure 5.2: The actual cell structure

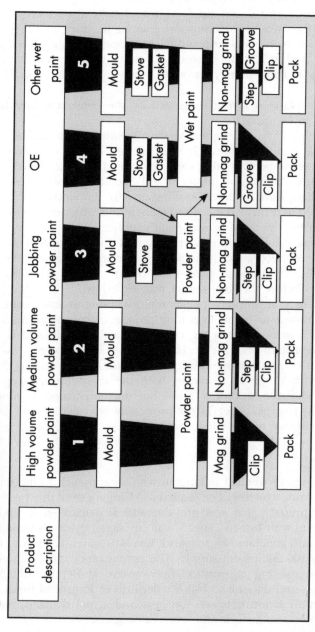

This structure creates focused cells by grouping products with a similar process sequence.
Source: IE Management Consultants/Bendix Mintex

The consultants recommended a simple two-piece *kanban* Just-In-Time card system to link stock levels in the warehouse with production by the cells. Production of a small batch would be authorised by a card, half of which would go to the backing plate production section (assumed to be kept separate from the cells) and half to the relevant cell. The two pieces of the card would be reunited when the backing plates were combined with friction materials in the cells, and the card would then return to the warehouse. The existing complex Materials Requirements Planning system could be replaced by a much simpler 'make to order' system involving a display area at the focus of the cell where the orders, and their *kanban* cards, would be displayed. In practice, this has proven to be one of the most difficult aspects of the cellular system to implement. At the time of our study, the pilot cells were not in control of their logistics, creating a situation of high stress for cell members and particularly cell leaders who had to cope with arbitrary changes in work schedules.[7]

Cell performance measurement

The critical difference between teamworking in manufacturing cells and traditional supervised systems, lies in the capacity of the cellular team members to monitor their own performance and make adjustments as appropriate. This means collecting data, evaluating it, and acting on it. Performance measurement is thus central to successful team operation.

The project team and consulting engineers developed a strong critique of the prevailing system of performance measurement at Bendix Mintex. They identified a vast array of indicators that had grown up in a haphazard fashion, without any coherence or 'discipline', which only became available in some cases six weeks late, and which were usually designed to be fed up to senior management without having any impact on the team members themselves.

What was recommended was a complete overhaul of the performance measurement system, oriented towards the needs of team members working in cells. There would be a daily Team Operations Report, from which a daily management summary would be extracted, to be assessed at daily team reviews and used in the formulation of action plans. Core indicators were identified as relating to productivity, scrap rate, lead time, downtime, work in progress, and cost per disc; care was taken to devise measures for each of these in such a way that the measures were seen to be under team members' control. A proposal for shop floor data flow was then formulated, assigning responsibility for the collection of relevant data, and specifying its purpose and the sort of actions that would depend on it.

Much of the performance measurement would inevitably relate to the quality of work being produced, and so the introduction of cellular arrangements entailed a similar overhaul of quality assurance procedures.

Quality control

Prior to the operation of cellular manufacturing, Bendix Mintex employed traditional QC inspectors operating in a traditionally separate QC mode, that is, quality was checked rather than built into the product.

At the time of the establishment of the cells, an 'intermediate' form of quality assurance (QA) was attempted, to try to build some QA responsibilities into the work of the cell team members. That this has borne fruit is attested by the dramatic improvements in the scrap rate recorded so far.

Work is performed in this 'intermediate' phase according to a series of 'Process Control Plans' which have been developed for each individual process, as seen in Figure 5.3.

A Process Control Plan chart spells out the 'Process Intent', that is, the goal of the process (such as attaching the correct clip to the disc pad), and if necessary, its purpose.[8]

The specification and standard of acceptance for each process is then spelt out, and the methods to be used, and *who is to use them*, are then specified. In the case of the disc pad clip, all controls are specified as being performed by QC examiners. Because so much of the QA process is specified externally and is performed by separate QC examiners, it can only be described as an intermediate form of QA within the cell.

As confidence with cellular manufacturing grows, so the responsibility for QA is embedded more and more securely within the cell's team members. Bendix Mintex has now established the Cell 1 and 2 'Performance Project', which has resulted in the development of a radically different QA approach, termed the 'Quality System Improvement Proposal'. This entailed redesigning the quality system from the bottom up, and placing most of the responsibility for ensuring quality in front line operators, working from redesigned and simplified charts. The job of QC inspectors changes from doing the measuring and checking, to auditing operators' set ups and

Figure 5.3 Bendix Mintex process control plan

PROCESS CONTROL PLAN

PRODUCT ....DISC. PAD........ PROCESS ....CLIPPING........ DRG. ISSUE....01.... P.C.P. No. ...... PAD – 17

Use with current product drawing   No changes without Q.A. and Product Engineering approval

DOWN STREAM PROCESSES AFFECTED	CHARACTERISTIC TO BE CONTROLLED (Product characteristic whenever possible)	SPEC & STANDARD OF ACCEPTANCE	CONTROL				
			FIRST OFF		LINE CHECK		
			METHOD	BY WHOM	METHOD	BY WHOM	
CLIPPING → CUSTOMER	PROCESS INTENT:– To securely attach the correct clip to the disc pad. PURPOSE:– Wear indicator. To retain product in caliper.						
	① Ensure clip conforms to that specified on the product drawing.	PRODUCT DRAWING	CROSS REFERENCE CLIP WITH PRODUCT DRAWING	QC EXAMINER	VISUALLY CHECK AGAINST FIRST OFF. FREQUENCY:– HOURLY	QC EXAMINER	
	② Wear indicator.	VISUAL	MANUALLY CHECK FOR MOVEMENT	QC EXAMINER	MANUALLY CHECK FOR MOVEMENT FREQUENCY:– HOURLY	QC EXAMINER	
	③ Depth	PRODUCT DRAWING	CALIPER	QC EXAMINER	CALIPER FREQUENCY:– HOURLY	QC EXAMINER	
	④ Ensure clip is on the correct side.	VISUAL	VISUALLY CHECK ON PRODUCT DRAWING	QC EXAMINER	VISUALLY CHECK AGAINST FIRST OFF FREQUENCY:– HOURLY	QC EXAMINER	
	② Ensure clips are secure.						

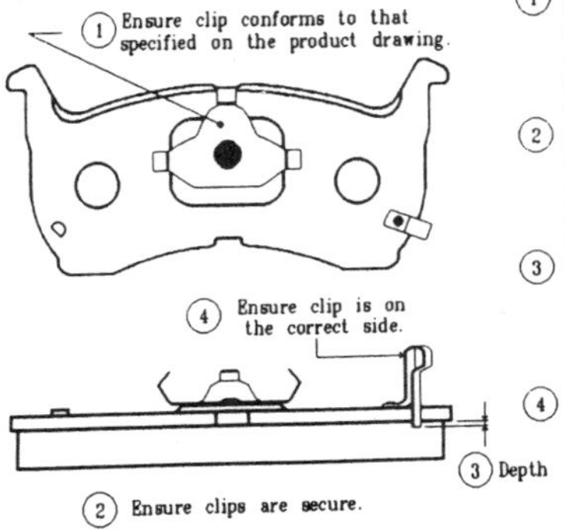

NOTE:– Retain first off sample for future reference.

RECORD RESULTS ON THE QC PROCESS CONTROL CARD

Change	By	App.	Date	Planned By	Release Date
Change			22–7–01	Alan Lyall	22–7–01

Iss.	Date	Change	By	App.	Iss.	Date
01	22–7–01		ALL	ALL		

measures. QC operatives would continue to perform specialised tests such as measuring the specific gravity of pads at moulding. The basic philosophy behind the new approach is to make it 'easy to do it correctly'. It is recognised that to achieve this, operators must have all the information they need at the machine.

Two kinds of documentation have been developed, and these were being trialled with the cells at the time of our study. One part stays at the process; this is the redesigned Process Control Plan. The other travels with a batch; this is a redesigned Production Record Sheet and a travelling Process Card. Both documents are tailored to the needs of specific processes.

An example of the new approach putting more responsibility back with the operators is shown in Figure 5.4 in a Process Control Plan for Pad Moulding.

The newer Process Control Plan again spells out the purpose of the process (not using the term 'Process Intent', which was found to be cumbersome), for example, 'To form the friction material to the correct shape and density and bond securely to the backing plate'. The relevant process and quality controls are then specified, for each of five stages in the production process: preparing for set up, setting up the process itself, first checking the unit produced, checking after each sequence of 30 units, and checking the last unit of the batch.

At each step, the document specifies when the action is required, who is responsible, what needs to be done, and how the actions are to be performed. Almost all of the actions are to be carried out by operators and setters themselves, rather than by QC personnel. QC staff thus move to play more of a quality audit role than one of direct product inspection.

The redesigned Process Control Plan sheets provide an invaluable training guide for new operators, as well as providing an on-the-spot reference for operators already familiar with the overall process. For good measure, the document reminds operators of the downstream processes affected by their actions—the 'internal customers' who have to live with the results of their quality assurance procedures.

The travelling documentation complements the Process Control Plan. A Process Card is a permanent laminated card that lists the process routing, tooling and specifications to be used, calling up the relevant documents on its journey. The Production Record Sheet is a single sheet of paper that sets out check lists for each batch that is to go through the process, requiring a response from setters

Figure 5.4 Bendix Mintex process control plan for pad moulding

Purpose of the Process: To fuse the friction material to the correct shape and density and bond securely to the backing plate.

Process Notes
1. No changes to this plan without QA approval.
2. Record results on the Production Record

Process and Quality Controls

When Action Is Required	Who Is Responsible	What Needs To Be Done	How To Do The Actions
Prepare For Set Up	Setter	Confirm batch is ready to start.	Check that tooling and components are available. Mark off check list on Production Record Sheet.
Set Up	Setter	Set temperature, pressure and mould cycle.	Set to targets on Routing Card. Use press computer where available
		Set cavity depth	Set to target depth on Routing Card
	Operator	Product and Component Traceability.	Record the backing plate part and run number, mix type and number, and backing layer type and mix number. Sign off Record Sheet.
		Audit preparation.	Check setter's preparation check list against the Routing Card, fill in Operator Audit check list on the Record Sheet
		Measure Temperature.	Check die surface temperature with digital thermometer until it is in the specification on the Routing Card.
First Off Check	Operator	Pad Thickness.	Measure minimum and maximum pad thickness with a dial thickness gauge and record on the Record Sheet.
		Pad Construction.	Compare pad to diagram on Routing Card and mark off check list on Record Sheet.
		Visual Inspection.	Check whole lift of pads for visual defects as shown in diagram. Samples of faults and standards are kept at the moulding QC area. Record all faults on Record Sheet with actions required to control or prevent them
		Backing Plate Flatness And Condition.	Check flatness with small steel ruler, there should be no obvious gaps. Visually check plate for damage from mould tooling.
	Quality Control	Audit Set Up.	Check set up to Routing Card, fill in check list on Record Sheet.
		Audit First Off Checks.	Check Operator's measurements and check lists are done and correct
		Pad Density.	Measure and record specific gravity (SG) of 3 pads to test method BBE2-1.
Line Checks Each 30 lifts & 1st lift after break	Operator	Die Temperature	Measure with digital thermometer and record
		Weighing, Spreading, Density	Compare whole lift to spigot appearance boundary samples. Comment on Record Sheet if faults are found, with corrective action to prevent them.
		Visual Inspection	Use same method as First Off visual inspection
Last Off	Operator & Setter	Tooling Check	If tooling has caused problems during batch, label with a DIO N01 (SI) sticker and fill out Fault Action Request

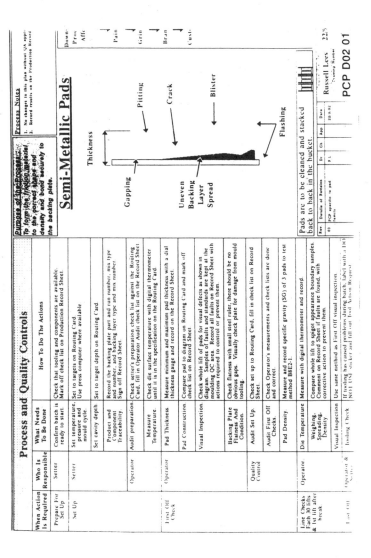

Semi-Metallic Pads — Thickness, Gapping, Pitting, Crack, Uneven Backing Layer Spread, Blister, Flashing

Pads are to be cleaned and stacked back in the bucket.

Rev	Details of Revision	Di	Ch	App	Date
03	PCP specific to pad family	P.L.			22-5-92

Russell Lees

PCP D02 01

and operators as well as a QC audit as the batch is progressively completed. Again this Production Record Sheet emphasises the quality checks to be adhered to throughout the process (in the case of disc pads, moulding preparation, moulding set up, moulding first off, moulding line checks, painting, grinding and release to kit assembly). A Process Log at the conclusion notes the batch details and any scrap recorded.

It is anticipated by the quality engineers who have devised this system that it will 'provide a workable system that complies with the requirements of the quality system standards, and gives a lot of extra process and quality control with a minimum of extra time and paperwork'. This is indeed a proposal for a 'best practice' quality assurance system.

Technical upgrading

In addition to investments in cell layout, the opportunity has been taken to invest in the technical upgrading of processes in the disc pad operations area. Again a number of organisational options presented themselves. The usual method of introducing technical upgrades is for technical engineering staff to make the assessments, order the equipment, undertake the installation, and then to 'train' shop floor operatives in the new procedures.

Consistent with the participative approach to workplace redesign at Bendix Mintex, the technical redesign project team has been actively involved in formulating and assessing options available for technical upgrading. Since new work procedures are being designed and implemented at the same time, the necessity to interface technical changes with organisational changes has been underlined and, in this case, acted on.[9]

The case of material handling upgrading provides a good example of how the project team went about its technical tasks. The prevailing system involved batch production utilising steel baskets, with electric pallet trucks and basket tippers moving the material through the factory from one process area to another. This system was cumbersome and resulted in long delivery lead times, high inventory levels, damaged stock and inaccuracy in meeting production orders. The adoption of cellular manufacturing provided the opportunity for the total replacement of this system with a programmable materials handling system under operator control. The new system chosen consists of a series of roller conveyors. Disc pads are moved along these conveyors in plastic containers holding 300 pieces each. The new system has been ergonomically designed so that there is little lifting needed and equipment is positioned so it does not impose a barrier to 'social relations' in the plant. The materials handling system runs down the side of the presses. It is a dual system so that baskets can be moved from the mobile system to the waiting system until the orders have been filled. Once the order is completed, the basket is relaunched on the mobile system and travels down the straight of the U towards the paint line which is positioned on the opposite long side of the U. Here the baskets leave the system, go through the paint machine and back onto the materials handling system. From here the parts are conveyed to the grinding and machining areas before finally moving on to the wrapping and packaging area.

The conveyor system has been welcomed by staff, as it makes the movement of stock easier, more accountable and reduces scrap due to damage inflicted in transit. Most staff were pleased that the system was not too imposing and did not prevent social interaction.

Cell leadership

The consulting engineers had little to say on the question of leadership and supervision, other than acknowledging the importance of 'employee empowerment', 'harmonisation', and the achievement of 'quality through people'. The transition to teamworking was not envisaged as requiring any special prior training. As it turned out, this was a major miscalculation on the part of the consultants.

Team leadership within the cells turned out be a major issue of debate, with the project team and plant management adopting sharply conflicting positions. Surprisingly, it was the project team who were pushing hardest for recommendations that the new teams have a team leader. Plant management were not totally convinced, believing that team leaders would eventually become glorified supervisors or leading hands. Debates between management and the project team lasted close to two months before a compromise solution was reached.

The intermediate structure that was suggested and adopted involved having a cell leader responsible to the team and to the shift coordinator. The role was seen as one of taking the team towards independence as quickly as could be effectively achieved. After this, the position could become redundant or move to a rotational system. The team leaders were to assist and work with the teams to formulate plans, negotiate work targets and the allocation of resources to ensure that the team could meet its production schedules.

As it turns out, the project team was undoubtedly correct in calling for an interim team leader position; there would have been chaos if teams had moved to 'self-management' straight away in the new conditions.

CELL IMPLEMENTATION

The first cell was established in July 1992 after a two-week period of reorganising, shifting presses and the paint line, and setting up the new conveyor system. The process resulted in minimal dislocation and the plant managed to stay ahead in terms of production planning. The first cell is a high volume category A popular piece manufacturing unit. This cell makes up to 100 different part numbers all in straight sets involving six different set ups.

The cell team consists of fifteen members operating in each team over three shifts. The cell's equipment includes ten 200-tonnage moulding presses; ten 150-tonnage moulding presses and five 76-tonnage moulding presses. It has an automatic grinder and shares a powder paint line and a shrink-wrap machine with the second cell. The cell is designed in a typical U shape with the middle of the cell kept free for the kanban board, performance indicator board and for staff meetings. The team working in Cell 1 identify their products through the use of blue coloured storage containers. At the top of the U the cell operators check a kanban card specifying the friction products to be matched to the backing plates and then they start production. When the product is complete, it awaits delivery to the warehouse.

One of the benefits flowing from the cellular manufacturing approach that has been adopted at Bendix Mintex is that staff felt happier that they could now identify the production process and see the development of the whole product. Being able to see what everyone else was doing was rated as an important aspect of working in the cell by team members. Other benefits relayed to us included staff being able to perform a variety of tasks and having some control over their scheduling of tasks which was allocated at weekly team meetings. This meeting also provided staff with a forum where they could suggest improvements to quality and to reduce scrap rates, as well as with a chance to air grievances. This usually took the form of asking other team members to 'pull their weight'.

Cell 1

Cell 1 overall had been improving, although at the time of our visit the plant was in a state of crisis, having to fill back orders and build up stock. This situation had arisen as a result of the 'logistics' system being in a state of transition. Daily and weekly performance measures were being logged by Cell 1. Dramatic improvements had been registered in cycle time which had been reduced from an average of 21 days to 3.2 days (against a target of 2 days). It takes, on average, around three-quarters of a day to actually fill orders; the remainder of the time goes in production planning and the receipt of backing plates. The cell was being badly let down by the support departments. The productivity measure was also steadily increasing from its base of 50 to the target of 60. Scrap rates had also fallen dramatically, indicating a significant improvement in the achievement of quality targets. Work in progress had also been considerably reduced. Thus the cell is starting to meet the ambitious work improvement targets that were envisaged for it by the project team and consultant engineers. It is worth noting that these improvements had been registered under the most trying circumstances involving increased overtime to get through backlogs, minimal team training, lack of support systems and little team leader training.

One source of annoyance expressed was that because batch sizes were so small (in lots of only 300), too much time was being wasted performing set ups and die changes. Rapid switching from one product to another of course is seen as one of the advantages of cellular manufacturing—but during our visit it was clearly disrupting the rhythm of production to a significant degree. Balancing the needs for flexibility with production rhythm is clearly one of the issues that work improvement teams will have to focus on in future.

Cell 2

Cell 2 was implemented a month after Cell 1. It produces a combination of straight components and part sets in smaller volumes. This cell produces 300 different part numbers, 50 per cent of these being straight sets, the remainder being part sets, that is, two inners and one outer or a two part set or three part set. It operates the same types of presses found in Cell 1 and the common side that it shares with Cell 1 is taken up by the paint powder line. Cell 2 has thirteen people and its experiences replicate those of Cell 1. Most team members enjoy the job rotation and the satisfaction of being able to identify with the end product. Some dissatisfaction was expressed concerning the competition that is starting to emerge between cells. It was also thought that the cells did not get the assistance that they required in the form of team training.

Cell 2 performance figures also indicate a trend which the company would find encouraging. Although more work needs to be put into improving the productivity figures, other figures relating to scrap already show an improvement. The team believed that with more support and focus their efforts would start producing better results. Once again the most frustrating experience was the difficulties encountered on the logistics side of the operation. Members of the cell team were resentful that the pressure was on due to poor planning and shortsighted production decisions. This had left the teams with a huge backlog of work, and the necessity to work heavy overtime which most staff found draining.

The two cells were already starting to develop close ties with each other, sharing staff to put the disc pads through the paint machine and also sharing the moulding process control staff. This is a small group of maintenance and quality assurance staff who have been assigned from their traditional production departments and broken into smaller teams to assist the cells with minor maintenance and quality issues. This is an innovative aspect of cellular manufacturing, as these staff have taken it upon themselves to demonstrate to the teams how to fix minor problems and become more responsible for quality. Already this is having positive effects, as seen in the performance figures for scrap rate and downtime.

Cellular manufacturing consolidation

Bendix Mintex management noticed about a month after the two cells had been operating that issues which had previously been hidden emerged as a result of the sensitivity of the system. This is a common experience as organisations move in the direction of lean, value-adding sociotechnical production methods. In response to the emergence of these hidden problems, four 'special issue' teams have been established, made up of management, engineering staff and shop floor staff, to investigate ways to resolve these issues. The teams established so far include:

Housekeeping group

This group is responsible for the safety and the cleanliness of the plant as well as the painting and signposting of the factory.

Equipment reliability and scrap reduction group
This group had been one of the most successful in implementing new approaches to scrap reduction. It has staged a brief team course for staff to make them aware of ways to reduce waste.

Training team
At the time of our visit, very little team training had occurred for the cell groups. The human resources manager was on a study mission to Europe looking at other facilities and training modules. Cell teams were not at the point where they had the confidence to take care of all the issues. The movement to cells has demonstrated to management the level of inter-dependence that the teams have, and the necessity to anticipate this inter-dependence with adequate training.

Logistics group
This group had the toughest task and were working on several projects. The major one has been the implementation of an information system that is compatible with techniques associated with cellular manufacturing. They were also designing charts and diagrams to build robustness into the quality systems and were working on the implementation of new simplified measures so that cells could become aware of their own performance.

This programme had just started and the other teams were hoping to be able to achieve the same success as the equipment reliability and scrap reduction group.

CONCLUDING REMARKS

Bendix Mintex is a company in Australia that has firmly committed itself to the attainment of a sociotechnical production system through a process of sociotechnical organisational change. The team-based cellular manufacturing form of organisation it has elected to install, and the negotiated, participative strategy it has pursued, with its advances as well as its setbacks, provide an exemplary case of workplace reform. It shows clearly the complementary character of organisational and technological change in overcoming what I called above its 'organisational schizophrenia'.

The continuous improvement anticipated as being one of the effects of the move to cellular manufacturing is starting to manifest itself. Bendix Mintex has learnt the hard way that sociotechnical workplace innovation calls for innovations at both the social and technical ends of the spectrum, and that changes in one entail complementary changes in the other.

The strategy of bringing in outside consultants for both the social as well as the technical innovations, and then internalising their teachings, is a classic case of organisational learning. As the process of techno-organisational change proceeds, an institutional memory is being created at Bendix Mintex that will provide a solid foundation for organisational learning and further improvement in years to come.

6

Team-based client-centred service cells

Colonial Mutual

Best practice in the services sector is now widely recognised as following manufacturing in the establishment of self-contained, autonomous operating cells as their basic organisational unit. These client-centred customer service cells are possible because of the revolutionary effects of information technology. This allows each member of the cell to have access to a common database of files on each current customer and to work as a group in servicing these customers' needs. Such an approach puts paid to the white-collar factories that many large, bureaucratic service organisations had become.

This organisational innovation in the services sector has the same team-based, value-adding approach pioneered in the lean production system and perfected in the sociotechnical production system. The starting point in the case of services is the achievement of a customer focus and the construction of a service delivery system. This allows operators to control the quality of their interaction with clients while obtaining feedback on their group performance. Technology in this model is used to extend the capacities of the front-line service deliverer, rather than for purposes of monitoring, surveillance, or the rigidification of activities through automation.

These client-centred customer service cells, or one-stop shops as they are known from the fact that the cell members can handle all the affairs and transactions of a given customer group, are appearing throughout the services sector. They can be found in utilities organisations such as gas, electricity, water and telephone companies; they can be found in the financial services sector, such as in insurance offices and building societies, and eventually they will make their appearance in banks. Thus a common model of organisational innovation is diffusing through the services sector.

CLIENT-CENTRED SERVICE CELLS IN COLONIAL MUTUAL

High above Collins Street in Melbourne is one of Australia's best known life assurance companies, the Colonial Mutual Life Assurance Society Ltd. One of its group of companies has made the transition to client-centred customer service cells, in one of the most interesting workplace innovation programmes of recent years. The firm Colonial Mutual Life Australia changed the operation of its Client Services Division (CSD) to quasi self-managing teams during 1991–92.[1]

Within the CSD, each team consists of 15 to 25 clerical workers performing tasks and procedures that complement each other and on which they can cooperate. They are seated at computer workstations in groups of four. Through their terminals, they can access any aspect of a customer's policy, whether the matter being dealt with involves new business, some kind of alteration, a renewal, or dealing with a claim. The team members continue to specialise in some aspect of this policy processing and maintenance work, but they now complement each other and are becoming multi-skilled through teaching and learning from each other. Above all, the team members are being allowed to work out for themselves how they allocate tasks and functions—in other words, they are on the way to becoming self-managing.

The one-stop units differ radically in their organisation from the rigidly separated departments from which they grew. Like most insurance companies, Colonial Mutual sought efficiency in the past through an extreme functional division of labour, with each aspect of business dealt with in one department and then broken down into several quite distinct and separate steps. For example, someone would be responsible for dealing with address changes to policies, and with nothing else. The result was frustration for both customers and staff: for the customers because they never knew who was dealing with their business or claim, or where in the maze of departments and sections it had reached, and for the staff because they never controlled a complete process, never saw the end result of their efforts, nor saw the customer as a whole person with a set of inter-related needs and concerns. For the organisation, it meant inefficiencies through duplication of effort, lost files, and a constant waste of time and energy in retrieving what was lost or delayed because of the organisational structure.

Using a one-stop operation dramatically overcame these barriers. Clerical operators in the one-stop units process the same kinds of business, but instead of sending queries off to another department, they now ask their colleagues at the next desk for the relevant information. Customer enquiries are dealt with while the customer is on the line; relevant information is called up at the one-stop operator's terminal from the different computer files, and again if a matter is in process, a quick check around the room tells the operator where it has reached, and this information can be passed on to the customer straight away. The one-stop units thus achieve customer focus and quality assurance through a combination of task integration and teamwork facilitated by the new information technology.

Even in the few months of the one-stop units' operation, quite dramatic improvements in measured turnaround times have been recorded. But more important even than these quantitative improvements in workflow has been the uplift in staff morale, the reward of being able to follow through on queries and assignments, the satisfaction of being able to deal with a customer as a person rather than in fragments (as an 'address change' or a 'disability claim'). Staff members recounted their stories of this new sense of liberation. And they have unleashed a stream of improvements in the first few months. Just by sitting next to each other and comparing notes, they have discovered many duplications in procedure that can be eliminated, and have abolished forms and paperwork that were invented in the days of inter-departmental queries, but which become unnecessary and indeed an obstacle in the new conditions of one-stop operation. Thus they are engaging directly in a practical example of business process re-engineering.[2]

The CSD at Colonial Mutual was committed to changing its entire operation, involving around 400-plus staff, to the one-stop organisational form by the end of 1993. There are twelve one-stop teams, formally called Client Service Units, located on three floors of the Colonial Mutual building in Collins Street. Each deals with the affairs of a defined customer group. The teams include as many policy processing functions within them as possible, including underwriting (or the risk assessment component of offering policies covering death or disability benefits).

The teams are backed by a range of support operations to cover general functions such as training and technical advice. There is a Professional Support Unit of around a dozen professional staff who give advice and support in such matters as computer systems operation, underwriting, and training; they also provide a convenient locus for assessment and review which is being completely overhauled along with the move to one-stop operation. A Global Administration and Accounting Unit was also formed and a Personnel Division.

Intensive planning was undertaken by the CSD to facilitate this organisational revolution in the move to one-stop operation. The whole transition is envisaged as taking five years, from preliminary planning to perfection of all the infrastructural support for the cells.[3] Project teams have been formed on all aspects of the new system's operation, such as in supportive human resources strategies, in a determined effort to avoid the fragmentation of responsibilities that has undermined similar initiatives in the past. Particularly in the area of human resources strategy, new forms of skill-based job classification systems, new systems of career progression, new approaches to training and skills assessment, are all being developed. This is in the context of a general shift to Total Quality Management (TQM) and greater customer focus on the part of Colonial Mutual.

The Finance Sector Union, which covers clerical staff at Colonial Mutual, has been a strong supporter of these innovations. Initially suspicious that one-stop units might become a means for intensified surveillance and control of their members, the union was in the end convinced of the soundness of such a skills-based strategy, and supported the introduction of the units and the application by the company for government assistance through the Australian Best Practice Demonstration Programme. The entire organisational change to self-managing teamwork was covered by an agreement reached between Colonial Mutual and the union in September 1992.

CLIENT-CENTRED SERVICE CELLS IN THE WORLD INSURANCE INDUSTRY

Similar moves towards self-managing teams equipped with information technology are reported in the insurance industry around the world. In the USA, the life insurance company Shenandoah (of Roanoke, Virginia) has introduced self-managing teams as a major change in its operating procedures. According to John Myers, the company's second vice-president in charge of human resources, Shenandoah spent millions in the 1980s installing computer systems but seeing little or no gains from this in terms of efficiency. They then abandoned the old concept of 'jobs'. 'We combined seventeen different jobs into one team operation and each member of the team is currently learning all seventeen of these jobs. Now when a piece of paper comes into the organization, it touches one set of hands and one set of hands only.'[4]

The number of people has not increased, and the technology has not changed. Each team is made up of six members, two each from premium accounting, policy issue (i.e. new business) and policyholders' service departments. Each team services a geographic area. The teams are self-managing to the degree that they take care of work assignment, setting holiday schedules, designing office layout, training one another, selecting team members, interfacing with other units, and administering their own team discipline. The teams have access to an advisory and counselling unit made up of former department managers and supervisors. Team members are paid for the skills they acquire; each time a team member learns one of the designated skills, his or her pay increases. Certification that the person has acquired the extra skill is by peer review. Thus, apart from the size of the teams, the Shenandoah concept appears to be very similar to that of the CSD at Colonial Mutual.

Another insurance company in the USA reported as going down this road is Mutual Benefit Life. Like other insurance companies, its new business section was getting bogged down in the maze of clerical functional divisions and bureaucratic paper chains created by its segmented structure. Under the stimulus of a new company president, existing job definitions and departmental boundaries were swept away and a single new clerical position of 'case manager' was created. Case managers are given total responsibility for an application from the time it is received to the time a policy is issued (Hammer 1990). Case managers are assisted in performing all the tasks associated with an insurance application, through being able to run an 'expert system' on personal computer workstations and to connect with automated systems on a mainframe. The technology and the work design mean that case applications jobs are now focused on the customer, and on outcomes, rather than on some particular task. Layers of supervisory management have been eliminated. Personnel practices also had to change. The company's job-rating scheme could not accommodate the case manager position, which carried a lot of responsibility but no direct 'reports' (i.e. people reporting to the position). New job-rating schemes and payment systems therefore had to be devised. Mutual Benefit Life has also re-engineered the relationship with its field agents, through its Quality Partnership Programme (King 1990). This offers improved financial benefits as well as partnership status in the organisation.

Yet another US insurance company to move in this direction is Northwestern Mutual Life. It has experimented with self-managing work teams in its policy change division, and it reports that the concept is working. Significant changes have also been implemented by the insurance company Aid Association for Lutherans, which is developing the self-managing work team concept in its insurance product services division (approximately 450 employees) and field administration services (covering around 50 employees). These changes have reportedly necessitated new human resources management approaches and systems which are similar to those being implemented by Colonial Mutual.

Thus Colonial Mutual is clearly not alone in embarking on a one-stop shop team-based service operation. It is part of a discernible world-wide trend in the insurance sector, and indeed, for the services sector generally.

A COMMON MODEL FOR THE SERVICES SECTOR

A pattern is already becoming apparent. Service organisations that deal with customer transactions are ideally placed to radically transform the bureaucratic, hierarchical and functional division of labour systems that they have inherited.[5] Teamwork allows them to re-integrate tasks that were previously fragmented into coherent wholes, with team members performing complementary parts of the processes. This is what lays the foundation for quality of service, since a process can be followed through by the team as a whole from initiation to completion. Information technology allows these service organisations to provide operators with a composite picture of a customer's affairs or transactions, whereas such records were held in rigidly separate compartments in paper-based systems and systems built around large, centralised mainframe computers. This provides the technical foundation of customer focus.

The organisational model for the coordination of such client-centred service cells is provided by the DISC model, as discussed in Chapter 3. The client-centred cells form overlapping discs, with local coordination provided by face-to-face interaction, and global coordination provided by specialist consultancy service units.

This striking convergence is surely only in its infancy. It holds out the prospect of the overthrow of the functionalist division of labour within the service sector that has turned so many service organisations into 'assembly lines', building up processes through the repetitive performance of simple tasks, with all the inefficiencies and frustrations this entails. When combined with interactive expert systems, the new paradigm can be expected to sweep through government departments such as social security and health insurance, banks and investment houses, travel agencies, and other service organisations. The insurance industry itself is likely to be utterly transformed, at least in the sectors dealing with complex products and value-adding activity. In this sense, Colonial Mutual is gaining a competitive advantage by being first with an innovation that is likely to force other companies to emulate it or lose business. Thus we are witnessing first hand the process of diffusion of an important organisational innovation in the services sector in a space opened up by the technological innovation of computer-based systems.

COLONIAL MUTUAL: COMMERCIAL AND ORGANISATIONAL BACKGROUND

Colonial Mutual is one of the oldest and best known of Australian companies. It was founded as a life assurance office in Melbourne in 1873 by the talented and energetic T. Jacques Martin. The first balance sheet produced in 1874 showed total funds of 2864 pounds; total assets of 3934 pounds; and business in force of 117 501 pounds. Within less than ten years, branches had been established in every state (then still separate colonies) as well as in Britain, Fiji, South Africa and New Zealand. Colonial Mutual was one of the first Australian multinationals.

Colonial Mutual grew comfortably, offering life policies as its staple business. In 1907, it was the first insurance company in Australia to issue personal accident policies and then in 1909, the first to write industrial business as well. The first superannuation fund was underwritten in 1917. In 1927, Colonial Mutual pioneered in Australia the concept of life insurance with premiums paid by payroll deduction (now called group schemes). Thus its early years were marked by substantial product innovation. Up to the 1980s, Colonial Mutual quietly expanded its core business and enjoyed a conservative and profitable existence. In the era of financial deregulation in the 1980s, it developed new products.

By 1990, the Colonial Mutual group worldwide had funds under management of $A11.4 billion, and a premium income of $A1475 million. Its business spanned Australia, Britain, New Zealand, Fiji and, through a joint venture with Jardine in Hong Kong, the rest of the Asia Pacific region. (Colonial Mutual withdrew from South Africa in 1986.) This constellation of activities is extended by a market sharing agreement with Japan's Meiji Life and affiliation with the Swiss Life employee benefits association.

Life insurance is still Colonial Mutual's major business although general insurance is also important, while superannuation is a fast-growing area, conducted through the Jacques Martin Group (which in turn consists of separate businesses such as Jacques Martin, Jacques Martin Hewitt International, offering employee benefit consulting services, and Co-Cam Computer Group). Colonial Mutual Investment Management Ltd is involved in wholesale financial services, offering funds management for corporate clients and for the assets of the Colonial Mutual group in Australia. Worldwide the Colonial Mutual group employs 3148 administrative staff, and 3415 tied agents in the field.

Colonial Mutual is still the largest business division within the Colonial Mutual group, with funds under management of just over $6 billion, and life insurance premium income of $899 million in 1990. This makes Colonial Mutual the fourth largest life insurance office in Australia, with around 5 to 6 per cent of the market; it is considerably smaller than the largest offices, AMP and National Mutual. Colonial Mutual has recently merged with Scottish Australia Financial Management Ltd.

FINANCIAL DEREGULATION AND CHANGES IN THE INSURANCE INDUSTRY

The radical move to establish a new form of organisation using one-stop units traces its origins to the turbulent history of insurance in the 1980s under the impact of financial deregulation, to the succession of changes at Colonial Mutual itself involving decentralisation followed closely by an ill-fated recentralisation, and to the declining staff morale and efficiency evident in the factory-like functional division of labour that prevailed (as it did at most other insurance companies) in the late 1980s.

Traditional life insurance policies have been the bread and butter of firms like Colonial Mutual for well over 100 years. With the differentiation of the market in the 1980s, firms have felt competitive pressures to offer more sophisticated products and coverage for various forms of disabilities, and to link policies with various forms of investment. New developments have been industry superannuation, resulting in huge market growth for the insurance industry, and the development of financial services products (such as rollover funds, lump sum and other 'single premium' products). The major areas of business expansion are currently deferred annuity products, disability products, fund superannuation business, and regular premium business in the aftermath of the 1987 Stock Market crash. Further changes are being introduced as legislation changes, for example, in the area of superannuation, and due to growing pressure for disclosure requirements for consumer protection to correct some of the abuses perpetrated in over-zealous selling of policies in the 1980s.

ORGANISATIONAL RESPONSES OF COLONIAL MUTUAL

The standard, traditional organisational response of Colonial Mutual to this burst of product proliferation was to set up new, parallel structures for each new product or class of products as they were developed. Such a strategy can best be described as reactive, following the familiar organisational model of the divisionalised firm. Thus large fund superannuation business was hived off to the new Jacques Martin subsidiary which grew fast and has already overtaken traditional life insurance as a volume business. (Colonial Mutual continues to handle small fund superannuation and individual superannuation products.)

Within Colonial Mutual itself, the development of new products resulted in the proliferation of computer-based systems, with minimal overlap or integration between them. Financial services business, for example, was allocated to a separate department within the CSD, dating from 1986/87, due to its rapid growth. Each new life insurance 'product' is supported by its own computer system or software package. This accentuated the tendency within the life division to organise work along strictly functional lines, with employees expected to work in one system only and with each system kept quite separate from the others.

Under these conditions of increasing centralisation of systems on mainframe computers and parallel proliferation of product-based systems, the search for new sources of efficiency became an overriding preoccupation with Colonial Mutual and other insurance companies. In parallel with their counterparts in manufacturing who sought to overcome inefficiencies caused by their fragmented work structures (Skinner 1986), the insurance companies sought efficiency through 'restructuring' and further intensification of computer processing applied to their existing functional division of tasks. The restructuring involved, at different times, elements of concentration, decentralisation and recentralisation. These are the organisational transitions that provide the backdrop to the successful implementation of client-centred service cells at Colonial Mutual.

Concentration

A scattered series of departments dealing with various aspects of policyholder affairs were brought together in a single divisional structure in 1978, to form the Policyholder Services Division. This was driven partly by the search for efficiency, and partly by the drive to concentration that accompanied the introduction of mainframe computer processing into insurance operations. In response to perceived inadequacies in the tightly centralised structure prevailing at the time, the division initiated the devolution of a majority of tasks to state branches of Colonial Mutual.

Decentralisation

The state branches were already responsible for servicing claims, for conducting initial underwriting, for performing alterations to policies (again confined to non-complex aspects) and for interfacing with policyholders, while the Principal Office in Melbourne carried out all complex alterations, re-insurance and underwriting, renewals and conservation of policies. Alterations, conservation and, finally, renewals were all transferred to state branches between 1978 and 1982; these transfers of responsibility meant that duplication of underwriting activity could also be eliminated. By 1984 only a small specialist and monitoring team was left with the oversight of policyholder affairs at the Principal Office. This brought Colonial Mutual into line with the decentralising tendencies of other insurance companies.

Over this period, staff numbers within the Policyholder Services Division were also diminishing, from 360 in June 1978 down to 218 in June 1984; these were declining as a result of more intensive use of computer systems and the intensified use of job evaluation to squeeze extra productivity out of the existing work organisation systems.

Recentralisation

In 1984 it was decided to recentralise almost all of these operations in Melbourne. This decision, which was to have severe consequences for efficiency, was apparently taken solely on the grounds of cost; the decentralisation accomplished over the previous six years was viewed by a new management team at Melbourne as duplicating overheads and devolving too much control. Memos were written at this time canvassing methods for reducing costs, including withdrawing services to policyholders (seen as counter-productive), automation (seen as coming anyway), or restructuring. Restructuring was interpreted purely in terms of variants of centralisation (rather than work reorganisation); recentralising all activities in Melbourne was seen as optimising savings opportunities. This amounted in practice to reducing staff numbers, particularly of expensive professionals such as underwriters. It also fitted in with plans to install larger mainframe computer systems.

The recentralisation was a disaster for Colonial Mutual. As it took place in 1984 and 1985, large-scale retrenchments occurred at every state branch, with very few staff accepting the offer of a transfer to Melbourne. Of the twenty or so who came, only four remained by 1986. Thus there was virtually a 100 per cent staff turnover within two years. To take the place of experienced staff, large-scale recruiting was initiated in 1985 and 1986, focusing generally on unskilled young people coming straight from school. They received basic keyboard training and were put onto repetitive simple tasks, such as change of address or elements of procedures such as renewals or new business. This placed the skilled staff at Melbourne under great pressure; they were caught up either holding together the administration with its largely untrained workforce, or trying to cope with the introduction of a new computer-based system.

The latest system at that time was Lifedata II; as with most large new systems introduced at that time, it was found to have bugs that needed ironing out as well as financial records that were in backlog. Indeed, by late 1985, backlogs of work had reached 20 000 hours; mistakes, due to lack of skill, were common. Staff who found themselves tied to repetitive tasks were leaving, no doubt through boredom or frustration; turnover was running at the high level of 40 per cent per annum.

The combination of an organisational centralisation with all its attendant headaches, together with the introduction of a new and complex product system, was taking its toll. Colonial Mutual was in serious trouble. It took three years for the situation to settle down and stabilise, as skills were acquired, quality controls were gradually brought in, work measurement was introduced, and staff turnover was reduced to twenty per cent. Lifedata III was reorganised for a total expenditure of $4 million, and then was introduced without further problems. Just to survive, organisation was along what were described as military style functional units, that is, along a strictly functional division of labour with bootstrap efforts to get on top of the chaotic conditions created by the recentralisation.

This was the organisational structure existing by the late 1980s. It provided fertile ground for a new manager to infuse new life by introducing radical ideas. Clearly the organisational strategy of keeping products and systems in separate compartments, and taxing staff to squeeze the last drops of productivity out of narrowly defined tasks, had been taken as far as it could go. Another approach which sought efficiency gains not in terms of individual tasks but in terms of overall, integrated processes, was clearly an option to be considered. This is where the one-stop operation makes its entrance.

THE MOVE TO SELF-MANAGING TEAMS

The work of the Client Services Division (CSD) of Colonial Mutual involves the reception and maintenance of insurance policies, the processing of claims, and all liaison work with clients and agents in the field. It does not handle money or issue cheques which is done by the Accounts Division.

In new business, policy proposals are received from agents and are processed according to their complexity and requirements. Those without any death or disability cover (called 'pures' by the clerical staff) are processed most simply, while those involving death or disability cover (called 'non-pures'!) are subjected to underwriting analysis. If documents have to be checked, or new information sought, the proposals are placed in 'suspense'. Maintenance of policies involves collecting premiums (by payroll deductions, direct payment by cheque or cash, or direct debit payment, termed 'bank transfer'), handling customer enquiries, communications, making alterations and amendments (such as change of address), and dealing with lapses, cancellations and surrenders (termed, optimistically, 'conservation', presumably to set staff the challenge of 'saving' policies which lapse or terminate). Claims can involve dealing with the simple maturity of a policy, responding to a death, or evaluating a disability; these all have to be processed, checked and orders issued to draw cheques.

Employers involved in group schemes have their own procedures to be attended to, as do superannuation fund affairs. Single premium products (such as rollover funds, annuities and insurance

142

bonds) are handled separately within the financial services department. A recent further addition has been the assignment of a small group of staff to maintain policies sold through financial institutions such as credit unions and building societies; this is referred to as 'financial institutions' business. This is the nature of Colonial Mutual's business. The critical issue concerns the way this is organised.

Prior to the one-stop units being established, CSD dealt with all this work through nine functional departments, covering seven processes (new business, claims, investment accounts, group business, policy administration, alterations, bank transfer/conservation) and two general services, underwriting and customer services enquiries. Within these departments, the work was broken down into around 50 separate operations, each responsible for an aspect of processing policies or providing group support such as word processing, mail centre, records and the all-important customer services centre, which handled enquiries and complaints. These tasks were further broken down into around 300 elemental procedures, some of which were performed by individuals in endless repetition. There was further division of tasks outside of the customer services area.

Overall, Colonial Mutual has a traditional corporate divisional structure. Apart from CSD, which accounts for 400-plus staff, there are divisions concerned with accounting, actuarial, marketing, sales, personnel, information services, and general management. Thus the CSD is embedded in a traditional corporate structure, more or less in the same way that innovative manufacturing divisions are frequently hampered by traditional structures covering sales and logistics that inhibit innovations. This is precisely one of the critical factors involved in the survival of the CSD innovations.

ORIGINS OF THE ONE-STOP CONCEPT

In April 1990, a new manager was appointed to head CSD (or Policyholder Services Division as it was then known). He was given a brief to spark new life into the division, in line with the shift towards a focus on the *quality of customer service*. Initial steps taken were conventional enough—the elaboration of a mission statement with 'core values', 'key result areas' and so on. This was greeted by staff with the usual indifference—after all it looked like just another management fad.

However, things started to change with the emergent focus on one-stop operations. A 'strategic directions' conference in May 1990 debated the future of the group and the merits of one-stop operations in so far as information could be obtained about them. There was a reluctance and a hesitancy about going down a radically new organisational road; on the other hand, it wasn't difficult to see that the existing arrangements had their deficiencies. Eventually the conference came up with a set of agreed actions: to implement one-stop processing and client-based servicing, to develop a human resources strategy to go with it, as well as information technology, and to progressively introduce quality management techniques such that planned, continuous improvement would become an integral part of the division's work. Once the decision to proceed had been taken, a one-stop project manager was appointed who had had experience of such operations in both Britain and Australia. Four months later, a second strategic planning group conference was held over a weekend in September 1990. This adopted strategies and plans for 1991 to introduce 'one-stop processing', as opposed to what the conference notes called 'an assembly line policy based service', starting with pilot units in the second quarter of 1991. Thus the die was cast for a radically new organisational direction.

PLANNED IMPLEMENTATION

Pilot one-stop units within Colonial Mutual were planned to cover typical areas of work within the Client Services Division. These were envisaged as covering particular geographical areas and product lines, such as South Australian personal insurance business as well as the small volume of business sold through financial institutions.

Further units were to be added later in the year, the exact timing to depend on experience with the pilot operations. In the meantime, work would be done in systems development, job design, training and so on to support these units. It was further resolved to change human resource management practices to support TQM and one-stop processing. As a planning tool, it was decided to undertake a staff survey to determine staff wishes and aspirations. It was tentatively agreed that a new strategy would entail new job grading and salary structures based on skills and performance, offering an attractive career path for high performers, and reducing the levels of management (currently six or seven on average). Thus CSD embarked on a comprehensive programme of change.

In the event, these plans have been followed more or less as envisaged. A core management team was formed under the direction of the one-stop project manager, bringing together Colonial Mutual's expertise in insurance products, in personnel and human resources, in computer systems, in accommodation arrangements, and in other technical topics. Project teams were formed to oversee the detailed planning for the new one-stop regime.

A decision was taken early on to move ahead rapidly through pilot programmes, in a deliberate strategy of learning by doing. The pilots were not conceived as test runs to see if one-stop operation was a good idea. Rather, the decision was taken to move the whole of CSD onto a new one-stop footing, but to do so in single, graduated steps. This was a critical and important decision; it gave the planning teams a clear focus for their activities, and built in a sense of momentum that might otherwise have been lacking. It was a strategy that carried a high degree of risk—for if too many mistakes were made in the early pilots, the whole approach stood to lose credibility. In the event, the transition phase has been handled with great skill. At the time of our first study, when the pilot unit had been in operation for only two months, already there seemed to be an air of certainty about the achievement of the goal. There was a sense of wonderment that the old system could ever have worked at all (allowing for the fact that people are still required to work within this system until the transition is completed).

Staff were carried along with these proposals through regular briefings. (It would be stretching terms to say that they were consulted.) The organisational environment at Colonial Mutual would not have allowed such a radical step as genuine staff consultation although senior managers well understood that the direction they were moving in entailed consultation along the way and was likely to generate a very different, open and participative kind of organisational structure as the process unfolded. Unions were briefed, and eventually the Finance Sector Union reached an agreement with Colonial Mutual on workplace reform and the one-stop project, ratified in September 1991.

HOW THE ONE-STOP UNIT WORKS

The pilot one-stop operation, set up in 1991, provided in one unit all functions to personal customers in South Australia and the Northern Territory who were previously supplied through fifteen separate departments. It serves as a model for the subsequent units. It numbers some twenty employees, who are grouped into four process functions: new business, alterations, renewals and claims (although they continue to keep their functional appelations and responsibilities). There is a supervisor or team leader in charge of the whole unit (but acting in a very different way from traditional supervision, as discussed below).

The unit is supported by a range of technical and professional staff who provide general services shared by all the customer units. There is a support team of senior staff who provide professional support in such areas as system operation, underwriting, launch of new products, training, coordination of TQM projects, as well as assessment. It is largely staffed from former supervisors and managers who have been or are to be transferred by the move to the one-stop operation. The support group is headed by a supervisor/manager.

In addition, there is a Global Administration and Accounting Unit, designed to support the tasks and activities of each of the Client Service Units. As its name implies, this global unit performs functions common to all units, such as accounting and administration. The accounting function will be responsible for all reconciliations performed in CSD, such as daily and monthly ledger and cash flow reconciliations, monthly budget analysis, and assisting line management to respond to audit issues. The main focus of the administration function will be the preparation and distribution of reports generated by the various computer systems. It will also include the control of group certificates, annual statements, work measurement statistics and performance reports for all CSD employees.

THE ORGANISATIONAL MODEL BEING DEVELOPED BY COLONIAL MUTUAL

The Colonial Mutual pilot experiments with one-stop units approaches the ideal form of organisation depicted in Chapter 3 as the DISC model. The discs constituting the model are genuine teams that are quasi self-managing; they have functional overlap, giving them a form of linkage that traditional structures do not permit; but above all they have a system of coordinating cells in the form of the Personnel Division, the Professional Support Unit and the Global Administration and Accounting Unit, which are genuine coordinating team-based entities rather than traditional supervisory or control structures. The Colonial Mutual form of the DISC model is shown in Figure 6.1.

It is this pattern of coordination that is such a striking feature of the CSD's model of a one-stop operation. Coordination via a

Figure 6.1 DISC organisational structure

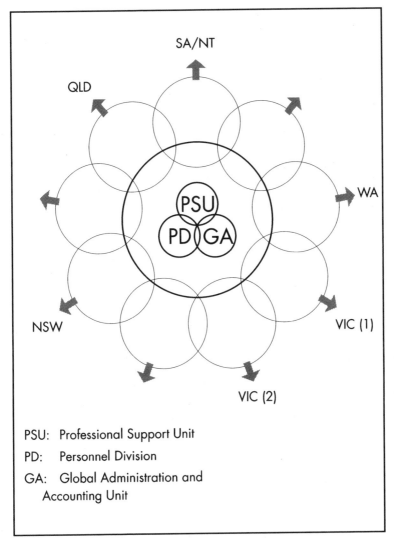

PSU: Professional Support Unit
PD: Personnel Division
GA: Global Administration and
    Accounting Unit

Colonial Mutual's Client Service Division, Melbourne, 1991–93
Cells of clerical operators are focused on regional groupings of
policy-holders, with global coordination provided by professional
support units

support team rather than via a supervisory hierarchy is of the essence in the 'new production systems' in the case of services. It also reinforces the culture of teamwork. In this way it provides a role for professional and former supervisory staff to support and reinforce the new self-managing team structure rather than, as so often happens, seeking to undermine it.

Self-generated continuous improvement

Within the first two months of the pilot unit's operation, there was an avalanche of new ideas and questioning of the old ways of doing things. Colonial Mutual staff called this phenomenon 'self initiated TQM'. One avenue explored by staff concerned the link between new business and bank transfers, where the bank details were checked twice over. In the one-stop operation this duplication was quickly discovered and eliminated. This experience also brought home to new business operators the importance of getting details right the first time.

The team members themselves enthusiastically report examples of such improvements in their presentations. During the study, we witnessed one of the first of such presentations to state managers; it was received very well. (Team members have since made a similar presentation to the board of Colonial Mutual—an unprecedented occurrence in the annals of the company, and a further demonstration of the changes unleashed by one-stop operation.)

Some systems were tried and found not to work. An example concerned the posting of policy documents. The 'problem proposals' (requiring further analysis) and posting of policy documents were left until all other business was issued, particularly during reps' pay week (agents or representatives in the field are paid every second week). This led to backlogs, so it was varied to allow for entry of proposals in the morning and the issue of policies in the afternoon; the new arrangement was found to work much better.

Coordination and supervision

Traditional supervision, in the form of command and control functions, has been dispensed with in the one-stop unit. There is a unit manager who plays a very important role in keeping the unit's sense of its coherence and development very much to the fore. Most of the decisions regarding allocation of tasks and personnel matters which have traditionally been handled by supervisors, are now self-administered by the team members. In this sense they have become quasi self-managing, perhaps faster than anyone expected. Much of the coordination function which has also been performed by supervision in the traditional hierarchical structure, has been absorbed by the interaction between team members themselves, and by the operation of the Professional Support Unit. In this way, a new organisational model is being forged in CSD, as a radical alternative to coordination through hierarchy.

The team leader has come to play a role that can be characterised more in terms of leadership than control. In the terms used by Senge (1990), the unit manager has the task of building the features of the team as a learning organisation. In the terms used by Kotter (1990), the unit manager as leader is involved in setting directions (rather than planning and budgeting), in aligning people (as opposed to organising and staffing) and in motivating people (rather than controlling and problem-solving). All these functions are evident in the emergent role of the unit manager.

An interesting question concerns existing supervisors within CSD. In other organisations which make a radical break with traditional patterns of coordination and where existing supervisors become redundant, the process of change has often been bloody, with middle management fighting it and sabotaging it all the way. As far as we could tell, this has not been the case at Colonial Mutual. Existing supervisors appear to have welcomed the move towards a one-stop operation, and are eagerly volunteering to play a new role either as team members (where their experience is valued), as unit managers of the pilot operations or as members of the Professional Support Unit. Colonial Mutual is accommodating them in all three directions. There have been no pitched battles and no forced terminations.

The Professional Support Unit

The Professional Support Unit attached to all the one-stop units is designed to play a coordinating and facilitating role. It was established in April 1991 and at the time of our study was still in the process of recruiting its members. It was to have a full complement of eleven staff, all of whom were to be expert professionals in each of the existing seven areas of CSD operations: investment accounts, traditional policy alterations, new business, underwriting, claims, group services, and financial services. It is these professionals who constitute the primary resource in the writing of the procedure manuals for all the existing operations, and for carrying out the training of one-stop clerical staff as they broaden their competencies and become multi-skilled. By 1992, the majority of their time was spent on training.

In the transitional phase, the Professional Support Unit played an important role as an intermediary between the one-stop units and the conventional departments which remained. Also in this transitional phase it functioned as the collector and disseminator of 'best practice' standards and procedures which might be developed in one unit but would be of interest to all other units.

The Professional Support Unit is an organisational innovation of the first importance; it provides for a form of coordination of teams which does not depend on a management hierarchy. It is the embodiment of an institutional memory, and as such represents an important step towards the CSD becoming a genuine 'learning organisation'.

Global administration and accounting unit

As mentioned above, the one-stop units are also to be serviced and coordinated by a 'global unit' carrying out functions which are common to all units and which would otherwise distract them from their customer focus. These include such personnel matters as the issuing of group certificates for tax purposes and annual statements, as well as common tasks such as collection and dissemination of work measurement statistics, staff opinion surveys and performance reports.

Accommodation and environment

An important factor in the success so far of the pilot one-stop unit has been the attractive environment and accommodation it has enjoyed. The pilot unit on the 15th floor at Colonial Mutual Principal Office had a quite different feel to it from other offices in the building, and particularly from the floors where CSD operations were still conducted in the existing set-up. The space has an openness to it which encourages team members to walk around; it is light and airy; and the workstations are arranged in clusters of four that provide people with a sense of 'home' that is also shared with others.

Other innovations have involved dispensing with colour coding which in Colonial Mutual previously defined status (for example, only managers sat on red chairs). The elimination of this colour coding had great symbolic value for CSD staff.

These remarkable features have not been bought with hugely expensive outlays in office design that is becoming fashionable in some offices. Nor has it been achieved by giving the pilot unit more space per person than existing operations. Indeed it has been given a lower space per person ratio (ten square metres per person, as opposed to eleven or twelve in other departments) but it has used this allocation more imaginatively.

Boundaries of the one-stop unit

Outside the one-stop unit, there are structures that demand to be accommodated. There are the job classification and pay structures being developed across the whole of the insurance industry through award restructuring, and there are other divisions of Colonial Mutual to be satisfied, as well as clients and agents. This is a hazardous environment in which CSD is navigating its uncertain course.

Relations with clients are shared across several Colonial Mutual divisions. In particular, all financial transactions (receipt of funds, drawing of cheques to meet claims or obligations) are carried out through the Accounts Division. Here our study found that there is little sympathy for or understanding of one-stop operations. As far as accounts personnel are concerned, it is their job to check the moneys receivable or payable, and to double-check authorisations which have been made by operators in CSD. One-stop operation complicates their lives in sharing tasks around that were previously 'signed off' by a named supervisor.

All paperwork generated by a claim or by new business has to be passed to Accounts, where it is checked and filed. This places a new perspective on one-stop operations. The work of the teams is still being checked at the point of transactions. The culture of teamwork is confined at this stage only to CSD, and then only to a small group within CSD who have actually experienced teamwork or have participated in its planning. In other words, the hold of teamwork within Colonial Mutual is still very tenuous.

At the time of our study, there appeared to be no plans to spread the concepts of teamwork into other Colonial Mutual divisions. This could create a major problem for CSD if it ends up becoming an island of innovation in a sea of conservatism; its prospects for survival under such conditions would be slim indeed.

TRANSITIONAL STRATEGY

The one-stop operations were established without any changes to operators' job classifications or pay levels. This was partly because a transitional strategy had not yet been settled on, and partly because Colonial Mutual had imposed a salary freeze on all staff until July 1992 (for reasons quite separate from the one-stop innovation).

However the transitional question was far from being ignored. It was recognised that elsewhere in industry it is problematic to transfer workers habituated to a Taylorist, fragmented job system, to a skills-based, career-track, work organisation system with expanded responsibilities. Some organisations have made fatal errors in the transitional step, such as framing the criteria so strictly that employees with long experience but few formal qualifications end up being classified at the same level as raw recruits who happen to have come to the job straight from school; such approaches foment great unrest and hostility, and understandably so.

At CSD, the question was tackled in such a way that generous allowances would be made for experience, and periods of grace accorded existing employees to allow them to acquire the skills modules that correspond to their claimed level of competence.

The form that the human resources support system has taken is very much along the model of the skills formation process presented in Chapter 3. The model eventually developed was based on the recognition of three factors essential for successful and sustainable teamwork:

- a broadening of operational skills to enable a member to offer a range of skills to the team;
- increasing expertise (deepening of skills) to enable the team to become more efficient and responsive; and
- acceptance of responsibility for 'leadership' in team support work.

Total multiskilling, where *everyone* in the team can do *everything*, was deemed to be neither desirable nor efficient. This is in line with best practice thinking, which sees teams themselves as powerful instruments of organisational learning; this implies that each team should contain members with a mix of skills and experience.

Eventually a skills-based classification structure for jobs was devised, providing for four successive levels for unit members, up to a fifth for team leader, and crossing two specialist classifications for staff in the support group, and a final senior classification for the manager of the support group.

For the team members in units, progression through the classification structure is linked to the acquisition of mixes of competencies that reflect the broadening and deepening principles. Generic skills that could be acquired at successively deeper levels spanned the gamut of product and industry knowledge, customer service, team operation, and TQM principles. Technical skills that could be acquired sequentially, in a cross-functional broadening process, included new business, renewals, alterations and claims.

Progression from grade to grade takes place through a procedure that has been negotiated and agreed with the union. (This is another example of the intermingling of human resources management issues and industrial relations.) Unit members can build up their skills as they complete various training modules and submit to various tests; this is the competency assessment component. Once a person acquires the skills laid down as being needed for advancement, he or she can request progression to the next level. The team member is then interviewed by a panel consisting of the team leader, another team member and a representative of the Personnel Department (that is, peer review). If the interview is satisfactory, the team member is then promoted to the next level. This creates a sense of occasion, and provides an opportunity for teams to develop their own rites of passage as their members progress. On the other hand, if a person fails to be approved and disputes the panel's ruling, then various appeal mechanisms are provided.

A team performance bonus scheme was negotiated as a further element in 1992, to begin operation in 1993. Teams are given responsibility for areas they control and the system pays a bonus to a team which improves on current performance across three broad areas: profit, customer satisfaction and process improvement. As the system is also about improving overall performance, a share of each team's bonus is earned through the team members' ability and willingness to improve the performance of other teams. This is the model of personnel and skills formation systems in best practice organisations.

BUSINESS PERFORMANCE MEASURES

By the end of 1992, CSD had in place a comprehensive set of measures of team performance, covering administration profit, customer satisfaction, sound business practice, growth, cost control, productivity, waste reduction, cycle times, people empowerment, appropriate systems, successful projects, and quality management.

Measures of customer satisfaction, for example, were compiled from distributors' competitor ratings, distributor administration feedback, policyholder satisfaction, policyholder complaints, and sales management satisfaction.

Measurement of cycle times has been possible only with the introduction of teamwork (because under the previous bureaucratic system the existence of cycles was barely perceived). Measured rates show steady improvement across CSD over the two years to December 1992, as shown in Figure 6.2.

By the end of 1992, just on 80 per cent of transactions were being completed within the target time frame (specified as one day, three days, one week, two weeks or a target at greater than two weeks, depending on the transaction's complexity). This compares with only 30 per cent of transactions being completed within objectives in the early months of 1991, when the move to teamwork was just beginning.

Thus the quantitative measures of quality, timeliness and efficiency of work are starting to demonstrate the efficacy of the CSD reforms to its work systems.

CONCLUDING REMARKS

Colonial Mutual has embarked on a fascinating experiment with one-stop operations in its Client Services Division. So far the acceptance has been overwhelming—staff have voted strongly with their feet to participate in the new working systems. Although the experiment is still in its infancy, there are positive results registered so far. The supporting development strategies for job classifications, skills formation, career progression, and skills- and performance-based pay, have been negotiated and are working well. Measurement of the efficiency of integrated task structures is demonstrating clear improvements over the previous organisational model, and considerable further gains in productivity are expected.

The experiment has as yet had little impact outside CSD. Guidelines for the transition have been developed in conjunction with the Finance Sector Union and performance agreements with other departments of Colonial Mutual are being developed. The board of Colonial Mutual has given the strategy their approval. But as yet, there is little discernible impact of the new organisational structures on other divisions. It has to be seen as a limited experience to date,

Figure 6.2 Transaction processing

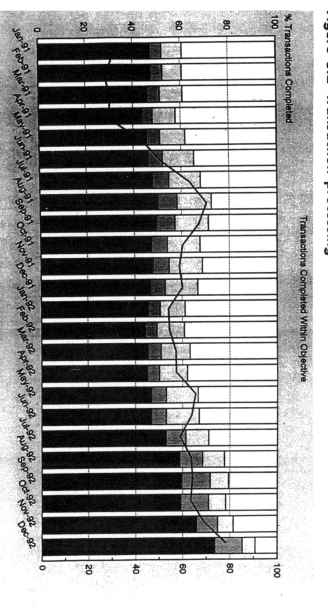

and one moreover which has to prove itself to an incoming management team.

Yet, as argued above, it has enormous potential. It is a step towards the development of a totally new organisational structure; it is applicable to other insurance companies and indeed other service sectors, and it has clear parallels with the best practice in new developments in the manufacturing sector. It is sociotechnical innovation in the best sense, in the way that it combines social innovation (self-managing teamwork) with technological innovation (computer workstations and a common customer database) in a workplace innovation that is greater than the sum of the two.

Three issues appear to be central to the success of the one-stop operation. Firstly, the team has successfully integrated tasks that were previously fragmented by placing them all within the scope and responsibility of the team and the operators within it, and by equipping team members with computer terminals that allow them to build up composite pictures of a customer's affairs. Previously, operators were restricted to accessing only the computer systems connected with their particular function.

Secondly, the team is more than a group of operators doing similar things. The tasks being completed complement each other, and taken together, allow team members to complete whole tasks in cooperative fashion, in such a way that all members have a picture of the process in its entirety. This is what is referred to in the organisational literature as closure, and it is one of the defining characteristics of jobs that are both satisfying and efficient. The teams can thus be described as being multi-functional rather than operating as aggregations of uni-functional staff.

Thirdly, the team is approaching a degree of self-management in such matters as the allocation of tasks, and the manner of response to customer queries. Through interaction, cooperation is being forged. It is also pioneering a novel form of coordination through the role of the Professional Support Unit and the Global Administrative and Accounting Unit, which offers professional support and facilitation as well as a convenient locus of skill and performance assessment for team members. This allows for coordination of units by overlap of function, rather than through the traditional hierarchical structure.

These three features capture the essential innovativeness of the one-stop operation. Together they account for three observable and, in principle, quantifiable improvements:

• they enable team members to generate a clear focus on the needs of customers (prevented in the preceding system by the fragmentation of tasks which meant dealing with only one aspect of the customer's concerns);

- they provide the foundation for a clear focus on quality, given the condition of closure (prevented in the preceding system by an inability on the part of operators to exercise responsibility over a process in its entirety); and
- they generate a high level of staff morale, which translates into greater levels of productivity and efficiency.

All these features are clearly observable in the Colonial Mutual experience. It amounts to the formulation of a new model of service organisation, which we have characterised in terms of overlapping Dynamic Integrated Service Cells, or DISC. This is the emergent 'best practice' organisational form which is currently diffusing through the service sector.

7

Quality assurance through process intent

Ford Plastics

The commitment to enhance quality standards in manufacturing industry is widely seen as driving the revitalisation of firms and even entire sectors that appeared destined for destruction. A multitude of quality practices and practitioners have arisen to feed off this drive. Many of them are genuine, and are proving to be of enormous benefit to the firms that adopt them. But an alarming number are false prophets, preaching that firms can have 'the gain without the pain'— in this case, without suffering the pain of fundamental restructuring of outmoded work organisation systems. Yet if quality assurance is simply grafted on to the traditional Taylorist work organisation, in line with the prevailing functional division of labour, it becomes simply another 'division' within the firm, and its procedures simply another source of discipline and control over the workforce. The sought-for breakthroughs in productivity and efficiency will be a long time coming.

A very different model is being pursued at a manufacturing plant in Melbourne where quality of work and productive efficiency are being enhanced, not through resorting to rhetorical exhortation, nor by purchasing a Total Quality Management system off the shelf, but by painstaking negotiated reconstruction of jobs on the shop floor to build greater responsibility and involvement directly into the performance of work. Previously fragmented tasks are being re-integrated; previously separate jobs are being combined into teamwork; and production authority is being devolved to teams from previous tight supervision structures. The strategy followed has utilised employee involvement teams, followed by work area quality teams, and is now engaging directly with the establishment of on-line quasi self-managing teams for mainstream production activities.

The plant is the Ford Plastics plant, located in the Ford Motor Company Australia Ltd complex at Broadmeadows, Melbourne. The quality enhancement model being pursued is called 'process intent'. It is so-named because in place of operators simply receiving instructions as to what to do, they are given information regarding the goal or 'intent' of the process they are engaged in, and are expected to exercise some discretion in how they achieve that goal. Let us look at an instance of its operation, bearing in mind the difficulties involved in making what appear to be minor changes in the industrial setting of car manufacture.

PROBLEM SOLVING AT THE FORD PLASTICS PLANT

In June 1989, a group of employees at the Ford Plastics plant were presented with a problem. Operators making the plastic casing that would fit around car heaters and air-conditioners were having difficulty in fitting certain kinds of vacuum loom clips into the holes that had been drilled for them. The operators were required to insert around 200 of these clips into the holes every hour. The holes were too small, and the operators had to force the clip each time. The extra pressure they had to exert gave them sore thumbs after only two or three hours work. A few days of this kind of work, and they were becoming candidates for repetitive strain injury.

The group of employees that looked at the problem was a self-selected team that came from all over the Plastics plant. There were two from the production lines, two from engineering, a production supervisor, a manufacturing manager, a maintenance fitter, and a cleaner. They called themselves 'Chain Reaction', and they had come together as one of Ford's Employee Involvement teams, one of 25 operating at the plant. They were looking for problems to solve, and here was a good one. The group members tackled this challenge by developing an overall strategy, starting with measurement of the size of the problem, and consideration of various options, and testing and validation of a solution. The group first identified the sections in the plant that might be able to help, such as Quality Assurance or Product Engineering. With technical assistance, they then obtained measurements of the force that had to be applied by operators to squeeze the clips into the holes; it turned out to range from 84 to 168 newton, averaging around 120 newton, which is a considerable effort. This provided them with a benchmark against which to measure improvements.

They then went on to look for the underlying cause of the problem and soon found that the specifications for the size of the hole used by Ford and by the clip manufacturer were different; Ford had specified a hole size 6.05 mm to 6.65 mm while the clip manufacturer recommended a hole of 7.00 mm. It was this discrepancy that was the source of the difficulty. They then thought about short-term and long-term solutions. A short-term option was to have larger holes drilled in the casing, to enable the clips to be fitted more easily. This was something which could be effected by the operators without changes to work practices, and when tested, it was found to work reasonably well. Measurement of the effort required by operators showed that it had been reduced by 30 per cent, to an average of 83 newton.

The group then tackled the longer term issue, of the discrepancy between specifications. They considered various options, such as reducing the size of the clips or altering their shape (too complicated); using a power tool to insert clips (difficult to design); using a lubricant (minimal effect) or rotating operators (merely distributing the injury). In this way, they selected from their list of seven technical options, the solution of enlarging the holes at Ford to coincide with the specification being used by the clip manufacturer. (Obviously, in the longer term, Ford engineers would have to attend to the specification discrepancy at source.)

The group then devised a checklist of actions needed to implement this solution, and drew up a formal proposal seeking approval to have the necessary changes made. This involved the group members in making a presentation to the plant's Employee Involvement Steering Committee which consisted of their peers as well as management representatives, and winning their support for the plan proposed. Their recommendations were accepted. They then proceeded to liaise with the relevant Ford staff to have appropriation requests drawn up, and with the supervisor of the heater assembly area to 'sign off' the changes they were recommending. This done, the section changed its procedures, and larger holes were drilled routinely to accommodate the specified clips.

Not content with seeing their solution implemented, the Chain Reaction group followed up with checks on the results of their efforts. They had measurements made of the size of the holes in the casing to confirm that it was now meeting the clipmaker's specifications. They had measurements made of the force exerted by operators under the new conditions, and found that on average it now took only 46 newton to insert the clips. This was a 60 per cent reduction in effort, and provided work rates were not increased, it eliminated any concern over repetitive strain injury. The whole episode had taken around two months.

This was just one of the problems tackled and solved by Chain Reaction in the course of 1989. Problems like this may seem small, as indeed they are. But they are the kinds of problems that nag at workers and reduce their effectiveness; in the past they might have waited years to be fixed if they were ever attended to, and in the meantime allowed cynicism and contempt to breed, as well as occupational injury and disease. These Employee Involvement groups have won widespread support within Ford plants by tackling practical problems in such a thorough way. In these cases it was not senior management, engineers or external consultants fixing the problem but groups of operators themselves. This is what is meant by incremental innovation, or continuous improvement, and it is the key to competitive success in the 1990s.

The Ford Plastics plant, which supplies plastic components to all of Ford's current vehicle models, is now a veritable laboratory of workplace reform. Under the leadership of the plant manager who took over the reins early in 1990, the plant has been encouraging a drive for quality enhancement that starts with workplace change and worker involvement, through Employee Involvement teams like 'Chain Reaction', and more recently through 'Q1' quality improvement teams systematically analysing production systems and seeking improvements in the quality of the plant's output. The next step, which is currently underway, is to reorganise production so that it is carried out by a series of work area teams. These will be virtually self-managing, and will take over from the current top-down supervisory structures that have grown up in the post-war period in the Plastics plant as they have throughout Australian industry. It is envisaged that areas of the plant will be operating as full team-based manufacturing cells in the mid-1990s.

The striking feature of this approach is not so much the effect it has on workers, which is dramatic enough, but the effect it has on management. Productive workers cooperating in teams demand an improved quality of management to ensure that materials arrive on time and in good order. Their demands work through the body of the firm, raising the quality of management performance, in the same way that yeast works through dough to make it rise. This 'yeast effect' of teamwork and process intent is one of the most significant yet least recognised features of the new production systems. Breadmaking might be far from the concerns of the Ford Plastics plant, but because of this propagation effect, its approach to organisational innovation could with justice be called a 'yeast effect' strategy.[1]

FORD PLASTICS: ORGANISATIONAL BACKGROUND

Ford Australia has been producing plastic components (such as fuel tanks, bumper bars, steering wheels and dashboard assemblies) for its own vehicles for twenty years. The Plastics plant employs just over 500 staff and produces components and sub-assemblies for the rest of the Ford company, to the value of around $120 million per year. The plant has operated since 1971, and is equipped with injection and compression moulding facilities, to which have been added extrusion and blow moulding (for example, of fuel tanks, a process pioneered by Ford Australia). The plant's operations are linked to the assembly complex through Just-In-Time delivery arrangements, with delivery trucks shuttling back and forth between the plants every twenty minutes.

Efforts being taken to drive the Australian automotive industry towards greater levels of productivity and efficiency form the organisational context within which the Plastics plant is operating. Microeconomic reform within the industry is proceeding through comprehensive adjustments to job classifications, skills formation and wages, a process known as award restructuring, amid broader efforts to overcome the past intransigence between capital and labour in this industry. These have been fostered nationally through such initiatives as the Button industry plans, the formation of the tripartite Automotive Industry Authority, the tripartite overseas mission of 1988 which looked at current best practices in Japan, USA, Germany and Sweden, the restructuring of vehicle industry awards and the development of the Vehicle Industry Certificate as a skills benchmark for process workers and, at the end of 1990, an unprecedented intervention by all the industry unions offering cooperation with restructuring in return for guarantees from the companies regarding continued operation, investment and skills enhancement.[2]

Ford generally has been acknowledged as a leader in organisational change and employee involvement at the micro level through the latter half of the 1980s. A study conducted at Ford in 1988 found that employee involvement had been backed substantially by Ford management over a sustained period, and that it resulted in real, if modest, gains for the workers involved (Lever-Tracy 1990). In contrast to many similar programmes launched in manufacturing industry, where the commitment is at best superficial, Ford has been successful in attracting worker participation and union support for its efforts.

The Ford Employee Involvement programme began on a pilot basis in Sydney in 1983, and since then has been taken up in all the company's plants. By the end of 1988 there were a total of 310 such groups in Ford, covering around 3500 workers. The Plastics plant has a number of functioning groups, with colourful names such as 'Chain Reaction', 'Divided Nations' and 'Troubleshooters'. The groups perform a serious function, solving a myriad of small but niggling technical problems; more to the point, these groups have acted as a catalyst to change the industrial culture at Ford, paving the way to more comprehensive employee involvement.

At the Plastics plant the next step has involved the promotion of first class quality with the formation of Q1 teams, named after the Ford Q1 quality programme which operates world-wide. The Q1 teams are cross-functional groupings of staff, drawn from areas such as engineering, manufacturing supervision, scheduling, materials, and shop floor workers. The teams are mandated to address all the quality issues they can find in the processes they are involved with, according to a charter developed and promulgated by the plant management.

The Q1 teams have taken the Ford Employee Involvement programme a significant step further, in that they call for systematic analysis of operations and intervention to improve them, with measurement of the results. The Q1 Polyurethane team, for example, has been operating since mid-1990, meeting for around an hour each week. It has systematically investigated the quality characteristics of steering wheel production, identifying operational limits and procedures for monitoring compliance. The team entered into negotiations with its 'customer', namely the Instrument Panel group and its Q1 team, to smooth out production flow problems, and opened similar discussions with its upstream supplier at Ford.

At the time of the study, in 1991 and 1992, the Plastics plant was embarking on a further development in work organisation, towards self-managing production teams. This represents a quantum shift in worker involvement, offering the possibility of substantial productivity gains as the structured irrationalities of the former system of command and control are dismantled. But a move towards fully-fledged teamwork also carries substantial industrial relations implications. Demarcation issues come to the fore, such as the perennial issue of preventive maintenance, the issue of quality assurance, and most significantly, the role of supervision. At the time of the study, the Plastics plant was wrestling with these problems. But a mandate for change existed within the recent industry-wide industrial relations negotiations.

INDUSTRIAL RELATIONS FRAMEWORK

In the Structural Efficiency agreement reached between Ford and the vehicle industry unions in September 1989, the introduction of teamwork was identified as a special matter (Australian Industrial Relations Commission 1989b). It had previously been highlighted in the report of the tripartite study mission overseas, where the recommendation was made to proceed to teamwork, initially on a pilot basis (Federal Chamber of Automotive Industries/Federation of Vehicle Industry Unions 1989). In the event, Ford was prepared to make the running on this issue, and the Plastics plant has picked up the prime responsibility for introducing such a new way of working.

The 1989 agreement identified the key issues to be addressed in the development and piloting of the team concept. These included such matters as the role and responsibility of the team leader, the common objectives of the team concerning quality, safety and production, the multi-skilling of team members, the provision of guidance and training, and the exercise of discipline on each other by team members (for example, over punctuality and attendance). In line with this clause in the Ford–Vehicle Builders Employees Federation agreement, the Plastics plant established a planning group to develop a more detailed charter for teams.

At the time of the study, only a few work areas had experimented with full teamwork. One of these was the paint shop, which made the transition from Q1 team to work area team status early in 1991. Workers in the paint shop are now completely responsible for monitoring the quality of their own performance. Whereas previously operators were expected to let defective bumper bars go through to be picked up by Quality Control inspectors at the end of the process, now the team members perform this role themselves in the 'process intent' manner spelt out by the plant manager, Tom Pettigrew, in his earlier career at Ford (Pettigrew 1983). Every morning the team holds a meeting to review the activities of the day before, discussing any difficulties that may have arisen. Six indicators of quality are being measured and recorded: getting things right first time, facility uptime, area labour cost (that is, number of direct workers), area scrap cost, process capability and area supplies cost. The aim is to move to a state where the team is responsible for monitoring its own costs and revenues (according to imputed prices for its products accepted by the downstream 'customer'), and hence, its own added value.

This organisational innovation can be seen to represent a significant departure in human resources management, and one which is integrated with production strategy. The innovation has been achieved by strategic management intervention within the constitutional framework laid down by a significant industrial relations reform, namely award restructuring. The Plastics plant has been able to restructure its former Taylorist work organisation systems in line with the margin for change negotiated between the parties nationally. Award restructuring has proceeded in accordance with the Structural Efficiency Principle laid down by the Australian Industrial Relations Commission in its National Wage Case decision of August 1989 (Australian Industrial Relations Commission 1989a). Within days of this decision being handed down, the Vehicle Builders Employees Federation applied to the Commission to vary the Ford Australia Vehicle Award, presenting an innovative agreement with Ford as evidence of goodwill. This agreement established a new classification structure for process workers, defining a new career path for them. It established a new training strategy, to culminate in a new industry-wide qualification: the Vehicle Industry Certificate. It provided for the expansion of job roles, covering such matters as incidental maintenance. Also, as noted above, it provided for the piloting of teamwork.

To support the moves towards teamwork, Ford has also been leading the way in the enhancement of skills formation through the Vehicle Industry Certificate.[3] A massive skills audit exercise has been conducted over a two year period, in conjunction with a facilitator from Gordon College, Geelong. Competency levels of employees were determined by review panels in an exhaustive exercise to determine where credits should be given and where further training would be required. The Certificate has now been introduced within Ford, offering employees wage premiums when they acquire the skill and knowledge points (up to twenty) spelt out in the competency standards. Ford and the union took their work relating to the Certificate to the Industrial Relations Commission for ratification in June 1991, and it is now being implemented throughout the company (Australian Industrial Relations Commission 1991a). There could hardly be a better example of the inter-dependence between a human resource management issue (in this case, certification of skills formation) and the industrial relations framework.

Based on the experiences of the Plastics plant, Ford and the unions reached a Memorandum of Understanding, 'Implementation of Work Reorganisation', in October 1991, spreading the principles developed at the Plastics plant to the rest of Ford Australia. This Memorandum called for participative design of new work structures, namely 'natural work groups', with supervisory staff moving to a new role of 'group facilitator'. The Memorandum was subsequently reinforced by the comprehensive enterprise agreement reached between Ford and the unions in December 1991. Thus the progression to new work structures within Ford continues within the constitutional framework provided by the industrial relations system.

THE FORD Q1 PROGRAMME

The Q1 Programme is a Ford ('Quality First') project that has been implemented world-wide through the 1980s. Ford plants or components suppliers that receive a 'Q1' quality rating are recognised as having achieved a 'level of excellence' and as having in place 'processes and systems for continuous improvement in meeting and exceeding the customer's needs and expectations'. More prosaically, they are judged to be state-of-the-art manufacturers, and they are assumed to be able to feed into the Ford manufacturing process without creating any subsequent defect problems. Several components suppliers in Australia have applied for, and been given, Q1 status under the Ford Supplier Quality Assurance programme. This programme has recently been opened up to include Ford plants themselves, and the Plastics plant was working hard to become the first Ford plant in Australia to be awarded this status. It subsequently achieved this distinction in March 1992, and indeed went on to be presented with an Australian Quality Award in November 1992.

World-wide, Ford has been converted to quality as a manufacturing way of life, just as it has permanently adopted employee involvement as a way of managing. In this, as in many other ways, it has been stimulated to act by the success of the Japanese automotive manufacturers, and the 'lean production system' they have perfected.

Ford global headquarters first issued its *Quality System Standard Q-101* in the late 1960s, outlining procedures for meeting specified quality goals for its own manufacturing operations and outside suppliers of production and service products. This is now backed by a comprehensive Quality System Survey and Scoring Guidelines, to be used in assessing a plant's eligibility for Q1 status, as well as a Supplier Quality Rating System and a Q1 Preferred Quality Supplier Programme. The whole package has been revised several times, and was re-issued in modified and upgraded format from Ford global headquarters at Dearborn, Michigan, in 1990. It is this upgraded Q1 status that the Plastics plant at Broadmeadows achieved.

To receive a Q1 award, a plant has to pass stringent tests covering seven criteria which include:

- the adequacy of the quality system (for example, safety activity review, product review and system survey);
- adequacy of initial sample testing and process potentials (that is, checking for likely defects in a process before they appear repeatedly in full production);
- quality experience with customers (involving formal customer assessments by the plant's 'customers', that is, Ford assembly operations);
- quality experience in the field (for example, warranty performance, marketing research data, and analysis of returned defective parts); and
- plant management quality commitment.

In addition, the Q1 Assessment team (made up of representatives from customers, design and world headquarters) has to give a positive finding regarding adequate use of statistical methods for quality control and regarding the use of manufacturing feasibility studies.

The System Survey covers twenty major questions in great depth. These look at activities such as:

- planning for new models (Advanced Quality Planning);
- use of statistical methods to control significant product and process characteristics;
- implementation of procedures related to quality functions, for example, an audit programme;
- monitoring of the quality of incoming goods and communications with suppliers;
- responses to customer concerns;
- orderliness of handling, storage and packaging practices; and
- attention paid to plant cleanliness, housekeeping and quality of working conditions.

The product review consists of systematic measurement of parts quality against a number of specifications. Typically 2500 measurements are taken; no more than six measurements can be outside specification if maximum points are to be achieved. The product review is summarised in a conformance index which shows the number of defective measurements as a proportion of the total. The aim is to see the index decline to zero. (The Plastic plant's use of this index is discussed below; examples of the rating of different sections of the plant are shown in Figure 7.1 on page 175).

The initial sample review is concerned with establishing whether, for example, the first mouldings made off a new tool are checked for correct shape, size and other characteristics, prior to feeding them into the assembly process, and whether procedures are in place for making modifications in light of the checks. Such an initial sample review is to be succeeded by follow-up checks, for example, after production of 300 parts, and using statistical analysis; this is called the Process Potential Review.

Plastics plant Q1 teams

The use of multi-functional teams to achieve and maintain quality production has been strongly endorsed by Ford. The idea has been taken up in a big way at the Plastics plant, and a series of Q1 teams were established in the latter half of 1990. The Q1 teams are cross-functional groupings of staff, drawn from such functions as engineering, manufacturing supervision, scheduling, and materials; they also include key payroll workers who are prepared to become involved.

At the Plastics plant there are fourteen Q1 teams in operation. There are ten Q1 area teams, as well as four Q1 special task teams, covering advanced engineering and manufacturing feasibility, quality assurance, materials and production, and housekeeping audit. The area teams are mandated to address all the quality issues they can find in a particular process. These cover virtually all plant processes: the mould shop, instrument panel assembly line, heater/console assembly line, polyurethanes production area, fuel tanks assembly, lamp assembly, bumper bars production, extrusion area, bumpers painting area, and small parts painting area.

The Q1 teams have been given a charter by senior plant management. This specifies the process control objectives to be reached, the measures to be taken to achieve continuous improvement, and the methods to be used, namely team-building and participative management.

Q1 Polyurethane area team: steering wheel production

The best way to gain a feel for the activities of the Q1 teams at the Plastics plant is to look at one in detail. A good example is the Q1 Polyurethane area team, which had been operating for around nine months at the time of the study. This team consists of eight members: a leader (an engineer), a facilitator (also an engineer), a training instructor, supervisor, two maintenance staff, and two production staff. This team has met for one hour each week since August 1990. It covers four production areas: steering wheels production, crash pads, foam pads, and reaction injection moulding. The team decided to tackle quality issues in the steering wheel production area as their first project.

The exercise began by looking at what constituted the important characteristics or outcomes for steering wheel production. Hardness was identified as an important outcome; others were the wheels' spline profile (measured by a 'go–no go' gauge), the foam adhesion (checked by twisting), the overall trimming and visual appearance of the wheel (compared with the master sample), and the presence and fit of various components such as the horn ring, switch assemblies, wiring and the Ford badge. Hardness values were established and stabilised within certain tolerance limits. This initiative in itself highlighted a defect in the measuring procedure for hardness, triggering a search for a better method of securing the wheel during measurement. A design for a 'hardness measuring rig' was then commissioned, and submitted to the group. At its fourth meeting, the group sent back the design with some suggested modifications.

With this small step, the group showed that already it was developing a capacity to manage the quality assurance process in an interactive and participative manner. This was remarkable progress, given the culture of the plant and of the automotive industry generally. To enable the operators to better understand the steering wheel process and their job functions, tours through the Assembly Plant at Broadmeadows were arranged and conducted.

In the meantime a cause and effect diagram (or *Ishikawa* chart) was developed for the hardness quality of steering wheels, identifying the materials, equipment, people, environment and method factors involved in the outcome 'hardness'. In addition, regression studies were completed on all machines producing wheels, and batch numbers were noted together with dies used in producing the batch. From the chart, five major factors were identified as contributing to the achievement of hardness, together with their current monitoring procedures: chemical ratio, die temperature,

169

material pressure, material temperature, and raw materials quality. This exercise revealed that some current practices were of marginal significance (for example, date clocking, which duplicated the labelling of each shipment) and led to their discontinuation. Other outcomes previously required as standard, such as putting white highlights on the wheels, were also abandoned after discussions with line supervisors further down the process revealed that they were no longer required. The analyses undertaken by the group were checked against information received from German suppliers of the Integral Skins Systems materials and process.

This steering wheel exercise was a classic case of identifying the activities that 'add value' and eliminating or modifying those that do not; but its significant feature was that the people making these assessments were the staff and operators themselves, not senior management or external consultants. In this way, the Plastics plant was acquiring its own institutional 'memory' built into its shop floor team structures, and thereby building a learning process into its production system.

Inter-team cooperation

The team then went on to consider crash pads, again starting by identifying the important outcomes. This involved the Polyurethane Q1 area team interacting with an Employee Involvement team (calling itself 'Divided Nations' after its multiethnic composition) which was looking at the layout of the Polyurethane area. A *kanban*, Just-In-Time card system for calling up crash pads from storage had been developed by this group, and it was decided to implement this in conjunction with the Q1 team in order to remove the congestion of the area caused by the build-up of empty pallets. With this exercise, a joint solution to a problem was developed by two Employee Involvement groups working together—a small step for the groups involved, but a big step for the Plastics plant as a whole. Inter-group collaboration was now becoming part of the culture of the plant.

A further example of cross-group cooperation arose at a later meeting of this Q1 team, this time involving the Q1 Instrument Panel team. The Instrument Panel area was the downstream 'customer' of the Polyurethane area, and its Q1 team wanted to report to the Polyurethane team on its review of the quality of the components supplied to it. The important characteristics were identified, and issues such as the numbering of lots and cleanliness of pads were highlighted as matters where improvement could be effected. Problems were also found with missing clips. After discussion, the team felt that the problem could be resolved by transferring the fitting operation to the Instrument Panel line itself. Thus this Q1 team was already concerned with its 'customer relations', and was redesigning jobs and recommending transfers of responsibility between departments. But it was also concerning itself with mundane housekeeping matters, such as machines dripping oil on operators, and taking steps to have equipment better maintained to prevent this.

Problems encountered by the group were also very much in evidence. Some matters were raised and solutions identified, only to be postponed apparently indefinitely. One such issue was the problem of the congestion of wooden pallets in the area—this appeared on the minutes of the team meetings for five weeks in a row until some improvement was noted. Thus the regular meetings of the Q1 teams, and the documentation provided by their minutes, acted as a spur to recalcitrant supervisors and operators; this was obviously one of the latent effects which the architects of the Q1 process intended it to have. Consideration of these matters also prompted the Polyurethane Q1 team to consider and review the operations of the areas upstream, for which it was the 'customer', just as the Instrument Panel Assembly Q1 team downstream had reviewed its operations and made recommendations to the Polyurethane team.

Thus the Polyurethane team was being led to clearly identify its *inputs* and *outputs*, and to distinguish between matters over which it had direct control and matters in which it was dependent on others. In this sense, it was acquiring all the characteristics of a semi-autonomous work group, without seeing itself as such or seeking this status (as yet).

At one of its meetings, the group engaged in a debate on the importance of recording data. By now, two performance measures—first-time buy (i.e. getting it right first time), and scrap rate—were being regularly recorded by operators in all Polyurethane areas. Previously operators had been reluctant to record this data, as they felt (perhaps with good reason) that they would be blamed and held responsible for any problems revealed. But the discussions within the Q1 team led to a concentration on these charts as a means of quantifying the effects of changes made or planned. Again, we can see that the questions studied by the team were not only important in themselves, but they had the effect of changing the culture of this workplace.

In general, the Q1 process in the Plastics plant experienced an initial flush of success and enthusiasm, but by the time of our first study (March–May 1991) a degree of jadedness was setting in. The issue of recording 'performance measures' such as machine uptime and scrap parts, was generating resistance and revealing some deep-seated conflicts. Some people on the shop floor referred to Q1 as the 'Quality for Idiots' programme, and there was also a widespread suspicion that once the plant achieved Q1 status, people would be laid off.

On the other hand, the Q1 process was having a demonstrable effect in introducing operators to the notion of the costs involved in running their own section, in terms of labour costs, scrap costs, and materials supplied cost, and where suspicions were overcome, progress had been made in charting these measures. This was seen by the plant manager as an essential prelude to more widespread use of teams, where members of the team would be responsible for managing these cost factors themselves. This is where the Q1 programme merges in with the development of work area teams.

At the end of March 1991, the plant manager stepped up the pressure on Q1. He gave a speech and issued a subsequent memo, putting the plant on 'full alert' to be ready for Q1 assessment by September, that is, within six months. All Q1 area team leaders were asked to concentrate all their resources to define the 'significant characteristics' of their production by 1 June. For each characteristic, they would need to consider how to:

- define an important outcome (e.g. hole diameter);
- establish rational tolerances;
- verify and implement a measurement system;
- investigate the statistical stability and the capability of the operation; and
- develop the documents defining their quality responsibilities.

To assist teams to meet these goals, the plant manager assigned to each team a member of senior plant management as a 'blocker remover'; his or her role was to participate as a team member and assist in removing any obstacles that the team might confront. For example, the Engineering Manager was assigned to the Heater/Console assembly team. The team told him that they had been having difficulty in getting the maintenance department to make up a 'step gauge' for them to be used to measure quality of assembly operations. The manager intervened on the team's behalf, and the gauge was produced without further delay. The plant manager conceived this exercise as benefiting the teams in that they could count on some high-powered assistance, but also benefiting the managers themselves through exposing them to the minutiae of shop floor problems. This has turned out to be a critical factor in bringing plant management to the point where they can play a constructive and supportive role in promoting genuine teamwork.

A SOCIAL CHARTER FOR WORK AREA GROUPS

By the time of our second visit to the Ford Plastics plant in October 1992, the transition to teamwork had advanced to the point where the company was negotiating with the production operatives' union (Vehicle Builders Employees Federation, now the automotive division of the Australian and Metal Engineering Workers Union) a 'social charter' for work area groups. This would complement the previous arrangements, which were designated as the 'technical charter'. A sequence of events for the implementation of work area groups was envisaged by the social charter, oriented around five general principles. These were to make sure that group members:

- have the opportunity to perform a variety of jobs and to learn and practise new skills;
- have a say in the decisions that affect them;
- have a real chance to do different jobs, to learn new skills, and to participate in training and decision making;
- take account of occupational health and safety issues in their decisions; and
- benefit from a new style of supervision.

In this way, the participative design of a new sociotechnical production system is becoming entrenched at the Plastics plant. It is developing according to sound social and technical principles which put the process on a quasi constitutional footing. At the same time, the plant management and unions were grappling with the stresses involved in this transition. A report commissioned from a work reorganisation consultant drew attention to a 'contested boundary of expertise' arising between work area group members and existing professional staff, such as engineers and supervisors. In other words, the traditional skilled groups were wary of and even hostile towards the new team structures.

173

RESULTS ACHIEVED SO FAR

The performance results achieved at the Plastics plant so far are little short of astounding. In areas where teams have had some control over their own operations, such as the bumper bar painting section and the fuel tank assembly section, the achievement of 'first time OK' is approaching 100 per cent. Indifferent results being achieved two and three years ago have been transformed; for example, instrument panel assemblies suffered 40 per cent rejection rates in mid-1990 and now suffer fewer than ten per cent. Examples of the performance improvements, as measured by operatives themselves, are shown in Figure 7.1. Over the entire plant, the conformance with Q1 quality standards *improved by a factor of ten* over a five year period. As shown in Figure 7.2, the conformance index has come down from 3 units rejected out of 10 000 in 1986, to 0.32 in mid-1992.

These are the kind of results that productivity and quality managers used to dream of in the 1980s. They have been achieved at the Ford Plastics plant through its intense focus on devolving responsibility for achieving quality assurance down to the teams themselves. This is 'process intent' in action: motivate staff not with orders but with explanations of the intent or goals of the process they work on, and equip them with the tools and skills needed to do a good job. In the end, it is a matter of reciprocal trust. This is the engine of productivity and quality performance in the new production systems.

CONCLUDING REMARKS: CHANGE STRATEGY

The Ford Plastics plant has had a concentrated experience of workplace reform in the 1990s, bringing the plant to the forefront of organisational change in the automotive industry in Australia. The experimentation with employee involvement is now being taken further, using teamwork in mainstream production. It is part of the transition underway in other areas of manufacturing and services, towards teamworking and devolution of responsibility and authority. Initiatives such as these are tightly constrained by the industrial relations framework governing job classifications, demarcations and procedures. But the plant management have been able to utilise this industrial relations framework to provide support and facilitation to human resources management initiatives that go to the very foundations of work organisation, integrating both industrial relations

Figure 7.1 Ford Plastics plant: Quality index for individual production areas

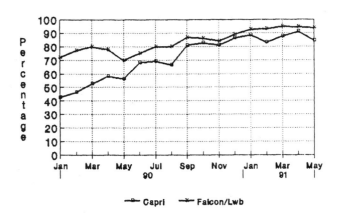

Painted Bumper Bars
Monthly 1st Time Buy

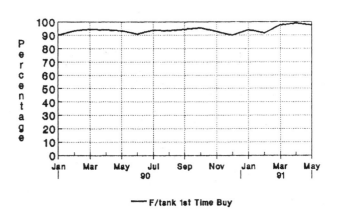

Fuel Tank Assembly
Monthly 1st Time Buy

and human resources management in the wider context of production strategy and enterprise restructuring.

Transitional strategies loom as critical in this epochal process of change. At the Plastics plant, a clear strategic choice appears to have been made: the shift is to be driven by quality enhancement.

Figure 7.2 Ford Plastics plant conformance index

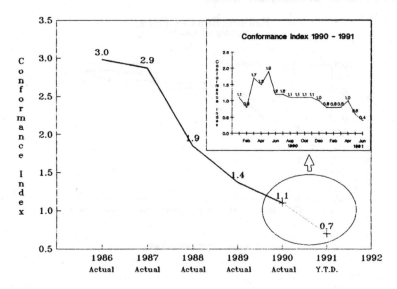

The quality conformance index is a measure used daily by the plant to determine the quality of the parts sent to customers. It signifies the number of defects per 10 000 units, and is based on random audits conducted on parts ready to be shipped.

Source: Ford operational charts

Hence the shift in emphasis from Employee Involvement teams to Q1 teams, and subsequently to work area teams responsible for their own jobs programming and quality assurance procedures. Employee involvement is thus merged with quality assurance in a powerful combination which underpins the commitment to teamwork.

In place of seeing the industrial relations system as a rigid set of rules frustrating initiative, this Ford plant has been able to use it to provide the constitutional foundation for innovation and experimentation, giving such initiatives a legitimacy they could not have hoped to have if they came solely from senior management (or from the union) by fiat. This provides an interesting new context for the inter-dependence of industrial relations, human resources management and organisational change, with wide ramifications and applicability throughout industry.

8

Network organisation
TCG

So far we have been concerned with the internal transformation of enterprises and the roles of industrial relations, human resource management and organisational change strategies. But organisations do not exist as islands. They have multiple connections with other firms so that the boundaries within which organisational innovation takes place become blurred. The International Institute for Labour Studies, Geneva, which has recently been looking intensively at these developments, posed the issue this way: 'Is the single firm vanishing?' (International Institute for Labour Studies 1992). What then are the implications for workplace change strategies and for labour institutions given these inter-organisational networks?

Network organisations, and the small firm clusters that they generate, are coming to be seen as one of the principal organisational innovations that will dominate the twenty-first century. As Snow, Miles and Coleman put it,

> What began quietly, more than a decade ago, has become a revolution. In industry after industry, multilevel hierarchies have given way to clusters of business units coordinated by market mechanisms rather than by layers of middle-management planners and schedulers (Snow et al. 1992, p. 5).

The network organisation is simply an extension of the factory within a factory or manufacturing cells treating each other as customer and vendor.

Network organisations emerge either from the introduction of quasi market forces into large organisations, allowing their component parts to acquire greater levels of autonomy and responsibility, or through small firms clustering and networking with each other to form larger entities that behave like quasi firms but retain the flexibility and responsibility of their small firm constituents. This two-pronged origin accounts for the extraordinary interest shown in this form of organisational innovation over the past decade.

Increasingly it is coming to be realised that such network organisations and small firm clusters play a powerful role in the restructuring and revitalisation of industrial economies. This realisation has been hastened by the recognition of the role of extensive networks of small firms in the successful economies of Japan, Italy, and the East Asian 'Four Tigers'. In Italy whole industrial districts, consisting of thousands of small firms specialising in particular industrial sectors such as ceramic tiles, woollen cloth and agricultural machinery, have been the backbone of much of Italy's post-war export-led industrial success.[1] These districts are superior in terms of innovation and market responsiveness through a combination of competition and cooperation, and group-based service centres offering assistance in technology and market intelligence (Weiss & Mathews 1991). In Japan it is now widely recognised that extensive networks of small firm clusters have driven the success of large international corporations such as Toyota, Honda, Sony and NEC.[2]

These are not seen as passing phenomena or aberrations. On the contrary, organisational theorists now point to cooperative alliances between firms, in clusters or inter-organisational networks, as providing a superior form of economic coordination to that offered by the traditional alternatives of closed-firm hierarchies and atomistic markets.[3] In specialised areas of economic activity such as research and development and new product development, collaboration between small and large firms in various forms of network structures is coming to be seen as 'world best practice' (Teece 1989). In Japan, such alliances are seen as lying behind the phenomenal developments in 'fusion technologies' (i.e. technologies that 'fuse' two separate streams of development, as in mechatronics or optoelectronics), and the adaptation of new materials to new market niches (Kodama 1992).

According to the respected scholar Charles Perrow, the last decade has seen 'dramatic changes in the form of economic organizations in North America, Europe and Japan', characterised generally by a move towards decentralised structures and loose alliances (Perrow 1991, p. 1). Perrow scans the field of these new structures, looking at the rise of non-dependent sub-contracting networks, particularly in Japan where they can involve hundreds of firms, and the emergence of small firm networks which appears to him to be the most radical organisational innovation. Common to all these forms of organisational innovation is a new emphasis on collaboration, either between semi-autonomous units within an integrated firm, or between semi-independent units within a network. What such a model throws up is the issue of the governance of inter-firm networks. While individual firms within the networks maintain their independence and autonomy, their membership of the network imposes certain constraints and obligations. These are borne because membership also confers substantial benefits, as witnessed by the striking success of many of these networks. Governance of networks is rarely formal or 'political' (i.e. through specially constituted boards or committees). Rather it exists in the structuring of transactions between firms that constitute the network. It is the investigation of transactions governance that constitutes the special interest of networks.

This chapter will take the case of TCG, a particularly successful cluster of firms in Australia, as an exemplar of a network organisation. TCG's governance structure will be made explicit with a description of the 'rules' which govern the functioning and growth of the cluster. Seen as axioms, these rules constitute a model of a network within which governance issues can be explored and examined.

In addition, the development of new products and fusion technologies through the extension of the network via a process of triangulation will be examined, and its relevance for wider models of industrial restructuring considered. Such studies lie at the interface between organisational and workplace innovation.[4]

TCG: ORGANISATIONAL BACKGROUND

The TCG group (the name comes from Technical and Computer Graphics) was founded as a small computer services company in 1971 in Sydney. Since then it has grown through new company start-ups to form a highly successful cluster of small firms each specialising in some aspect of information technology applications. The group as a whole numbers around 24 active firms, employing around 200 people, and turning over $43 million per year. It is now one of the largest privately-owned computer supplies groups in Australia.

TCG has built its success on the practice of sharing revenue from external customers. Member firms specialise in different facets of computing, telecommunications and information technology generally, some in software, others in hardware. Each firm seeks business from external customers and fulfils contracts by sub-contracting aspects of the job to sister firms within the network. For example, a firm like TCG Systems Automation Marketing (one of the earliest members of the network) might obtain a contract from a supermarket chain for 10 000 hand-held data loggers. It would be able to fulfil this contract by sub-contracting the development of the design to one TCG firm, the software development to another, the manufacture of the data loggers to a third and the telecommunications aspects to a fourth. It could play the role of broker or coordinator itself, maintain close relations with the customer and ensure that all contractual obligations were met.

To the outside world, TCG appears a coherent entity. But internally, small firms are actively bidding for contracts that would otherwise be beyond them. It is the nimbleness of small firms, and their responsiveness to market opportunities, combined with low overheads, that explain the superior economic performance of networks like TCG as organisational structures.

But a network is not a formless entity. If it were, member firms would drift apart as they started to compete with each other. They might end up sharing some resources, but that would be all. The secret of successful network sustainability is structure and governance. In the case of a network, such a governance structure cannot be imposed by any single party. What then has evolved at TCG to solve this problem?

A MODEL OF TCG's GOVERNANCE STRUCTURE

There is no overall holding company for the TCG group. Rather, it exists as a genuine network, or value-adding partnership, of independent firms. The firms deal with each other on a bilateral basis through commercial contracts.

The independence of the TCG member firms means that the network is under the constant potential threat of dissolution. Indeed it is understood that it will dissolve if member firms believe that they will do better outside the network than within it. The rules that hold it together are therefore the means through which cooperative relations are maximised and dissonance is minimised.

Over the years, relations between TCG's member firms have

come to display certain features that characterise the TCG inter-organisational governance structure.

Mutual independence

The TCG network consists of independent firms whose relations are governed by bilateral commercial contracts. No member firm is under any overriding obligation to the others. The network is open to new entrants who are prepared to abide by the rules. This is a foundation rule that defines the quality of the network. It excludes the formation of an internal hierarchy, where one of the members would play the role of 'lead firm' as in a solar–planetary model.

Mutual preference

The first rule for group cohesiveness is that member firms give preference to each other in the letting of contracts. This rule gives the group its identity. Without it, TCG member firms would simply be atomistic entities sharing some resources. Tendering and contracting are done along strictly commercial lines. Preference does not exclude the possibility that contracts will be let outside the group when circumstances warrant it (such as when a member is overloaded with work, or as a signal to the member firm that it has to lift its game).

Mutual non-competition

The second rule for group cohesiveness is that member firms do not compete head to head with each other. If one member firm is marketing hand-held terminals, another member firm does not acquire rights from another supplier to market similar terminals. This is a form of 'self-denial' that establishes the necessary foundation of trust between members. In the absence of such a rule, member firms would be reluctant to discuss business opportunities with each other, for fear they would take advantage of the information and undercut the originating firm's operations.

Mutual non-exploitation

Member firms do not seek to make profits from transactions among themselves. Instead their goal is to make profits from their dealings with the outside world; dealings with each other are a means towards this end. This is the origin of various forms of 'cost-plus' contracting that TCG member firms have devised for their dealings with each other. The absence of this rule would undermine trust and create a hierarchy of strong and weak members in the group that would lead rapidly to its dissolution.

Flexibility and business autonomy

The flexibility of the group as a whole derives from the capacity of the member firms to respond to opportunities as they see fit. They do not need to seek group approval for entering into any transaction or new line of business, provided their proposed innovation does not breach the accepted rules. This rule allows for maximum flexibility and provides the expansionist dynamic for the network.

Network democracy: no overall 'owner' or controller

There is no holding company formally tying the TCG group together. Nor is there any form of 'central committee' or formal structure giving direction to the network as a whole. It coheres as a result of the commercial ties operating between member firms, and through member firms holding equity in each other as well as in third party joint ventures.

Non-observance of rules leads to expulsion

The network rules provide member firms with positive incentives to cooperate with each other. This is the material basis of the long-term interests that guide transactions, rather than short-term spot transactions which form the model for most economic theorising. These incentives are complemented by the sanction of expulsion if any member wilfully disobeys the rules. Expulsion can be effected simply by severing all commercial ties with a miscreant member. (It has not been necessary at TCG to resort to this sanction in nearly twenty years of network operation.)

Entry

New members are welcome, but they are not to draw resources from the rest of the group. Hence TCG has evolved the practice that start-ups are financed through bank overdrafts (i.e. debt capital) rather than through equity capital from member firms. Start-ups are much easier within the network rather than outside since the network as a whole provides collateral for a loan. This rule allows the network to expand and to continue to renew itself without sacrificing the efforts of more mature members to the improvidence of new entrants.

Exit

Mature members of the group are allowed to leave if they wish. No firm is held within TCG against its will. Since there is no ready market for shares held in TCG member firms, departure arrangements have to be negotiated on a one-by-one basis.[5] All departures have been amicably negotiated. If a firm grows too large, it may depart or adopt some other course such as spinning off a new start-up company.

External relations

All member firms have access to external work. There are no 'sub-contractor only' firms within the TCG group. Each member firm is free (indeed expected) to bring in work from outside. This maximises the market responsiveness of the network and also ensures that no hierarchy emerges between broker firms and sub-contractors, with the incipient exploitation that such a hierarchy would bring with it.

These ten rules form what might be called the TCG constitution. They give it its definitional form, its coherence, and its dynamism. Its constitution provides for both specialisation and flexibility. In terms of the classification of networks introduced by Snow, Miles and Coleman (1992) as internal, stable or dynamic, TCG exhibits all the features of a dynamic entity.

Taken in a more abstract sense, the rules constitute the axioms of an abstract model of a network. They ensure that the network continues to reproduce itself and maintain its coherence over time.

SUSTAINABILITY OF THE TCG GOVERNANCE STRUCTURE

Governance structures are about procedures, due process, and the allocation of rights and responsibilities to the parties that have an interest in a corporate entity. The TCG governance structure is no exception. It has evolved in a manner that allows firms which would otherwise explode into atomistic competitive entities to form well-defined cooperative relations and to cement ties over a sustained period.

Some networks arise in ways that cannot be considered sustainable. For example, a firm might put out the various phases of its operations to sub-contracting firms, linking them to itself in a solar–planetary arrangement. If it imposes norms and obligations on these firms, such as prohibiting them from dealing with third parties, and if it maintains arms-length relations that allow it to withdraw contracts as soon as business falls off, forcing the sub-contracting firms to absorb the business downturns, this cannot be described as a sustainable network. Such arrangements are frequently exploitative in the sense that sub-contractors are allowed simply to cover their costs, while the solar firm takes the profits from contracts negotiated with outside customers.

It is clear that the TCG model avoids these features which is why it may be seen to provide a model of sustainable economic organisation. TCG is successful because of the non-exploitative rules that govern relations between its component parts. Member firms feel safer inside the network than outside it. But to survive, the network has to have the capacity to enforce its own rules. This is where its governance structure is so important. TCG has acquired this structure over time in the form of the legal contracts that member firms enter into with each other and with the outside world. Appeal mechanisms are brought into play if one firm appears to breach a rule (such as by producing a product that threatens to compete head-on with something already marketed by another member firm). Significant and repeated breaches would lead to expulsion.

A representation of the TCG 'transactions map' is given in Figure 8.1. This shows the intensity of transactions between members of the group.

NEW PRODUCT DEVELOPMENT THROUGH NETWORKING

New product development through the use of joint ventures, strategic alliances and other forms of collaborative networking between organisations, has been much discussed over the past decade. The same pressures that drive firms to collaborate in development activities are also forcing them to seek much closer relations with customers and the market, turning innovation towards a demand-driven process. A third ingredient identified with new product development in Japan is that of technology 'fusion', where new products are developed from the coming together of two separate technologies. Thus a picture is emerging of best practice product innovation as *market-articulated, fusion-oriented inter-organisational networking.*[6]

Figure 8.1 TCG Transactions map

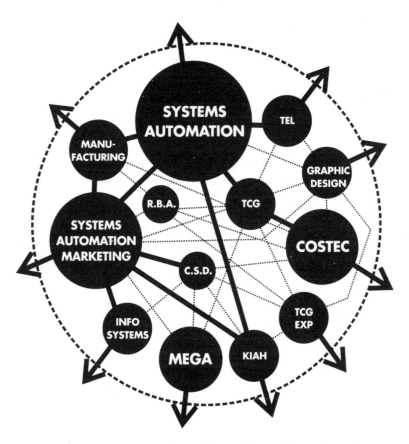

This model is very different from the traditional serial intra-organisational conception of innovation. Teece (1989) for example has pointed to the inadequacies in this traditional model of technological innovation, where new product development is thought of as a sequence of independent steps starting with research concepts and leading through development, design, manufacturing, marketing, sales and service to the final customer. He notes that successful innovators are more likely to engage in parallel product development steps which engage more than one firm or party in the innovation process, bringing the focus of attention to the governance of the inter-organisational linkages involved.

Kodama (1991; 1992) has emphasised the important role that

technology fusion plays in accelerating the process of innovation. New technological areas such as opto-electronics and mechatronics have emerged as a result of firms bringing their expertise in certain technologies together in order to create something greater than the sum of the individual parts.

The TCG group has perfected a method of joint development of new products that exemplifies in a striking way these new tendencies. TCG identifies new market opportunities for adaptations of its existing products, and allies itself with a collaborator and a major customer, in a triangular or three-way joint development strategy that has proven to be a potent commercial success. This strategy builds on the internal networking that links the member companies within the TCG group.

We shall illustrate the TCG approach to triangular collaboration in new product development through several case studies. The key ingredients in the approach will then be identified and compared with other extant models of innovation. The argument is presented that the TCG strategy incorporates all the elements of what is currently considered best practice in new product development. Furthermore, it underscores the significance of networking as a mode of economic coordination or governance of contractual relations. The TCG strategy brings to the fore features which can make networking superior as a mode of organisation to that of open markets and closed hierarchies, the two dominant forms of economic organisation discussed in the influential works of Williamson (1975; 1985).

In this sense, the TCG triangular approach has significance not just as a general strategy for collaborative industrial development that is widely applicable, but also as an exemplar of an emerging third way of economic organisation and governance structure that has fundamental economic and organisational implications.

THE TRIANGULATION STRATEGY OF TCG

Companies in the TCG cluster extend their network outwards in a quite distinctive fashion. The term 'triangulation' has been coined to describe this process, meaning that it involves typically a three-cornered collaboration. The essence of the arrangement is that TCG seeks to extend the capacities of one of its existing products into a new or related market by entering into a partnership with a firm that is already established in this market. The two firms combine their strengths to create a new entity and new product ('fusion') which is greater than the sum of their individual parts. This is where many firms leave the arrangement; they then seek to market their idea as best they can. The TCG approach is to identify a major potential customer for the innovation, and seek to bring this firm into the arrangement as a third partner. This customer firm does more than place an order and put up cash which is used to fund the development; it is offered genuine partnership through licensing and sell-on arrangements.

It is best to look at some examples of how TCG has perfected this triangulation strategy before discussing in more general terms how it combines fusion, networking and market articulation.

Case 1: Fuel monitoring terminal

A TCG company, TCG Systems Automation Marketing (TCG SAM) has developed hand-held data terminals for use in the retail grocery trade. TCG identified a possible extension of this product concept in the idea of providing aviation refuellers with a hand-held fuel metering terminal to keep track of airport refuelling activities. This can lead to better record keeping of aviation fuel supplied to airlines and faster supply of invoices from the fuel company to the airlines. The idea is that in order to record all the necessary data about a plane being refuelled, operators on the tarmac simply punch the plane's flight number into their Remote Data Terminal which they carry in their tarmac vehicle. At the end of the shift, the operators download data from their terminal into a terminal in the airport office; the flight details are sufficient to call up full airline customer details, and invoices billing for the fuel supplied can be on their way within 24 hours.

In order to develop this concept, TCG enlisted the partnership of an established aviation fuel metering supplier, ACME. The basis of the partnership was that TCG acquired access to a new market, while ACME acquired access to a new technology. The joint venturers then brought in a third partner as customer, in this case Mobil Oil, which was persuaded of the project's benefits.

Working to Mobil's specifications, the first version of this product was developed as the Rapid Aviation Refuelling Information System (RARIS). Mobil agreed to purchase the first terminals, putting up the cash that drove the development; it stood to steal a technological march on its aviation fuel competitors. Mobil's Operations group invested a great deal of time and energy in ensuring that the product met its needs.

Mobil turned out to be more than a customer by acquiring rights to license the RARIS product to other airports and to other aviation fuel suppliers. TCG for its part acquired the rights to sell the software driving the product worldwide, while ACME secured manufacturing contracts and acquired the rights to extend the product concept into new areas of fuel metering and data logging. The RARIS system is now available commercially in airports around the world.

Case 2: Field service terminal

Another extension of the data logging concept developed by TCG involves the use of a data terminal by field maintenance engineers working for telephone and other utility companies. Crews go out in their maintenance vans with a certain stock of parts. These are used up as they complete jobs, presenting a logistics problem of resupplying them in timely fashion. The idea for a portable terminal to keep track of the jobs done and parts used arises from this market need.

TCG SAM identified this market niche, and sought to adapt its existing Portable Data Entry Terminal to the needs of utility firms. At the same time, it found that the computer giant Toshiba was seeking to interest an Australian utility in an adaptation of its laptop computer for the same purpose. Each product had its strengths and weaknesses from the point of view of a utility. Telecom Australia became interested, and under its guidance, and instead of competing head to head, TCG and Toshiba formed a technological partnership to develop a hybrid or fusion product that took the best elements of the two existing products. Thus a partnership was formed to produce a field service terminal—a rugged, hand-held data logger using a common communications platform that is compatible with the laptop or any other computing device.

The triangle in this case represents a genuine long-term collaboration or set of relational contracts. TCG gets the rights to manufacture and sell a new product domestically and overseas. Toshiba acquires technology in a new product area, with the option of blending it with a range of its existing products; it also satisfies Australian government offset obligations imposed on it. The Australian utility gets preferential access to a new product that is tailored to its field service requirements, plus preferential access to future enhancements and other commercial advantages.

Case 3: Passive Transponder System

In this case, TCG identified a market niche for electronic identification systems. The idea hinges on a passive transponder being inserted into an object, giving that object a unique electronic identification tag which can be carried by the object for the whole of its existence. The tag is read by a hand-held device which emits a low-frequency magnetic field; this activates the transponder, inducing it to emit a signal carrying a unique code which is received by the device, where it is decoded and displayed on a read-out, and stored in a memory for subsequent processing. The idea, which is a terrestrial application of transponder technology developed originally for satellites, is termed the Passive Transponder System.

This system is capable of virtually endless applications. Everything that is tagged or marked in some way—engine numbers in cars, baggage going through an airline terminal, product serial numbers, animals that are branded, wool bags, plastic personal identification cards—provides a potential application. The transponders themselves take any form, such as tiny glass capsules or plastic devices. The passive transponder needs no power source of its own (since it is activated by the reader device) and so it can last virtually forever. It can be read in the most demanding physical conditions (when visibility for example is zero), from any angle. Each transponder is manufactured with its own unique code; once programmed, this code cannot be altered, giving great security.

TCG has secured the Australian rights to this technology from the developer, Trovan, and AEG/Telefunken, which manufactures Trovan identification systems in Germany. TCG is tackling each potential market through its familiar triangular strategy, bringing in a major customer in each case. For example, tags in the animal livestock market are being developed in conjunction with Leader Products, the world's leading supplier of non-electronic animal ear tags. Thus TCG prises open a market by entering into an alliance with a firm already established in that market, offering the firm enhanced technology in return for market access.

THE STRATEGY GENERALISED: NETWORK INNOVATION THROUGH TRIANGULATION

We may model the TCG triangulation process as a sequence of four steps.

Step 1: Identify the market niche
TCG plays the role of innovator and broker, identifying a market

niche to which one of its existing products can be adapted. TCG researches the application and develops the innovation strategy.

Step 2: Find a development partner

TCG seeks out a firm which has complementary skills, markets or technologies, to be a partner for the development. In the case of the fuel metering terminal, it was an existing (non-electronic) meter supplier, which would otherwise have been a head to head competitor. In the case of the passive transponder ear tag for livestock, it was a firm with markets in plastic ear tags which was anxious to acquire new technology, providing market access in return.

Step 3: Find a major customer

TCG then scours the world looking for likely customers for the envisaged product and tries to convince them of its potential benefits. It seeks to persuade one such firm to enter the partnership arrangement as the principal customer, with relational contractual rights that carry it well beyond the status of simple customer. Step 3 closes the triangle, establishing a three-way network of firms with very different backgrounds but with a common interest in the new product under development.

Step 4: Extend the triangle in new directions

As the product development proceeds, the joint venturers begin to realise their rights to further development. This takes each of them in new directions, and towards an extension of the network already created. TCG in particular seeks to link the development to others it has in the pipeline, generating further ideas and joint ventures which can be 'triangulated' with further customers.

Thus the whole process is evolutionary and dynamic (Nelson 1987), driven by a mechanism that might be described as 'technological leverage' (by analogy with financial leverage). The triangular networks that result are shown in Figure 8.2.

This four-step approach complies with the model of technology fusion as described, for example, by Kodama (1992), blending incremental technical improvements from previously separate fields of technology to create revolutionary new products. It is market-driven by the initial identification of a market niche, and by the involvement of a major customer in the development process. It is an incremental process involving fusion between an existing product (such as an animal ear tag) and a new concept (passive transponder) creating a totally new product with new market potential.

Figure 8.2 TCG customer-driven innovation triangles

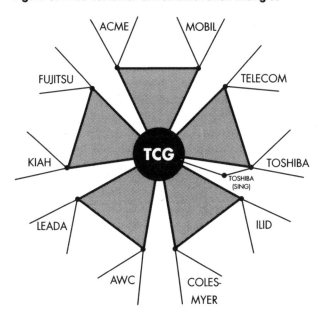

It is driven by networking, where TCG seeks partners in each of the new markets it elects to enter; for TCG, this is merely an extension of the networking it already practises internally. The special feature of the process which makes it distinctive is the role of the customer in shaping the product development, and in providing a source of finance. That is an attractive alternative to other development financing options such as the use of government grants, or funds put up in exchange for equity by a venture capital firm.

ORGANISATIONAL ADVANTAGES OF NETWORKING

What then are the organisational advantages of networking? What are the factors driving the formation of these alternatives to closed firms and atomistic markets as forms of economic coordination? Why are they such an important form of workplace innovation?

The literature on networking and collaborative inter-firm arrangements, while extensive, has been concerned largely with establishing the legitimacy of networking as a third mode of economic coordination, midway between open markets (spot contracting) and closed firms (hierarchical control).[7] The conventional explanations derived from mainstream economics focus on issues such as improved resource use, enhanced flexibility, and access to information. But these factors do not get at the root issues to do with the creation and maintenance of networks.

Clearly TCG enters into joint arrangements with firms like Fujitsu to tap markets that would otherwise be closed to it. The triangular strategy offers a means of accessing markets through mutual value-adding. Within the TCG group itself, membership offers benefits and mutual support in seeking access to finance, for example, and in entering contracts with external customers.

But this is to look at the surface phenomena. What factors can be identified as underlying the perceived superiority of networking in general, and TCG's *modus operandi* in particular?

One line of argument, associated with the work of Oliver Williamson (1975; 1985), is that transaction costs provide the benchmark for discriminating between different forms of economic organisation. Transactions between firms conducted within the market carry associated costs such as the costs of obtaining information about suppliers or customers, prices and reliability, costs of enforcement of contractual obligation, and costs of operational breakdown when transactions fall through. It is the avoidance of such costs that provides the conventional arguments for the original emergence of firms as corporate entities which internalise these transactions and turn the open market into a closed hierarchy.[8]

Application of transactions costs reasoning in the case of networks leads to a surprising result. The members of the TCG network have found ways to economise on transaction costs, through the various forms of long-term commercial contracts they enter into with each other, as well as through enjoying the benefits of financial security and the immediate client base that network membership offers them. Thus reasoning according to transaction costs would favour the network outcome, rather than the internalised hierarchy within a vertically integrated firm as concluded by Williamson (1985).

Similarly, Williamson's argument that internal hierarchies emerge as a protection of sunk investments can be turned on its head in the case of networks. Williamson argues that the specificity of investments incurred through long-term contracts makes firms vulnerable to cancellation of contracts. The desire to protect themselves induces them to internalise transactions within a hierarchy. But not so in the case of TCG. Certainly TCG feels vulnerable to the whims of its major customers, but it protects itself from this by moving *away from* a hierarchical structure; by allowing its constituent member firms to sign contracts with external customers, TCG insulates the rest of the group from any disaster that may befall a constituent if a major contract falls through.

In its triangulation mode, TCG is exploiting its small size and nimbleness in offering to enter consortia or joint ventures with much larger partners; the option of internalising a relationship with, say, Mobil Oil, is obviously no option at all for TCG. From Mobil's perspective, the relationship with TCG offers a convenient way to develop a new product without major internal investment and disruption. Such firms might be tempted to internalise the arrangement by taking over TCG but they probably understand that this would be self-defeating, as they would destroy the very mechanism that makes TCG function so effectively.

Another line of explanation has been developed by Powell (1990). He argues that network modes of coordination offer advantages over their hierarchical equivalents in the quality of the information processing and transfer that takes place within them. He argues that in contrast to information flow within markets or hierarchies where processing alone takes place, within networks new meanings and perspectives are developed that provide the foundation for active 'learning by doing'. It is this, he argues, that constitutes the advantage of networks.

The TCG example provides support for this explanation. In the TCG network, each member firm draws from the collective experience of the others; by becoming part of the network, a new member firm gains access to an enormous repository of knowledge about markets, about suppliers and their products, about contracts: information and experience that it takes small businesses working on their own years to acquire. This is one form of corroboration of Powell's argument. Another lies in the quality of the information transmission within the network. A member company bringing in a contract for outside work involves the participation of another member company (such as when TCG SAM acquired marketing rights to a hand-held terminal and offered customised software through the participation of TCG Software Engineering). This offers the partner company a chance to learn a new skill, and in the process generates a new perspective on the product.

From being a 'transaction', the contract can become an opportunity to develop a new product concept, with the customer perhaps coming to play the role of collaborator in a new development. In this sense TCG sheds light on a network's capacity to opportunistically turn 'transactions' into occasions for collective and interactive learning.

Leanness of a value-adding chain

Study of the TCG network brings out further advantages which have yet to receive adequate recognition in the literature. The most striking feature of the TCG network is its leanness, in the sense that it contains no superfluous elements or superfluous operations. All the constituents of the group provide value-adding operations (i.e. none are purely internal services). And they are all required to take quasi autonomous decisions, bringing in orders from the outside world (with the exception of some elements largely devoted to internal transactions). Thus administrative, coordinating overheads are minimised and local responsiveness at the small firm level is maximised.

Johnston and Lawrence (1988) are at pains to point to these advantages in their notion of the value-adding partnership. Since each operating company in the chain specialises in one task, all the overheads associated with other tasks performed by a general integrated firm are eliminated. They claim that this sense of focus translates into low overheads, lean staff numbers and few middle managers. Certainly TCG's experience would corroborate this claim.

This source of superiority of a network over its conventional rivals is so important that we are tempted to use it as the basis of a definition. As a first approximation, we may define a network as a chain of value-adding activities whose elements all add value as measured by commercial tendering and contracting.

What is the optimal size for such a network? Is TCG at the optimal size? Obviously there can be no definitive answer to this question, but some light can be shed on the issue by looking at the question of returns to scale.

Networks and returns to scale, scope and variety

In traditional accounts of industrial organisation, large firms grow larger in order to capture *economies of scale*. While difficult to define, the general idea is clear enough: unit costs decline as the scale of production increases. This is the core principle and secret of success of the mass production system. Economies of scale are necessarily associated with rigidities. Hence as markets and technologies become fast-moving, competitive advantages are seized by firms that can respond more quickly and with greater variety than traditional mass production giants. This notion is conveyed by saying that such firms capture *economies of scope*, or what Di Bernardo (1991) calls *economies of variety*.

Clearly a network of small firms has an advantage over its integrated rival in terms of economies of scope and of variety. This is another way of saying it is nimble on its feet; it creates diversity, and it devolves maximum responsibility to operating centres.

But a successful network also seeks to capture available economies of scale. This is what distinguishes it from an amorphous *cluster*. Yet economists have made little effort to investigate such economies since the pioneering investigations of Alfred Marshall into industrial districts.[9]

An exception is the investigation made by Italian political economists of industrial districts in Italy where returns to scale have been identified in the form of collective marketing ventures (consortia), information gathering and dissemination services, technology updating services, and training services. All of these features of business can be pooled and provided across the entire network, giving small firms access to services that they would not be able to afford individually. The provision of such services through public infrastructure, on a user-pays basis, is simply one aspect of the sophisticated public policy environment in which small firm networks thrive in countries such as Italy.

Johnston and Lawrence (1988, p. 99) also point to economies of scale as being one of the competitive features of value-adding partnerships which can share such things as purchasing services, warehouses, research and development centres, and of course, information.

TCG clearly captures these economies of scale while being fully alive to the economies of scope and variety that give it its nimbleness. At TCG, economies of scale are reaped through such measures as central invoicing and collective purchasing, sharing development costs as new products are generated through the triangular process, and through repeated cycles of software development in closely related products.

Networks and workplace innovation

Finally, to come back to network organisations and workplace innovation, we may consider how far some firms take the principles of shop floor autonomous teams, and how well they do with these organisational forms. One interesting example is that of Kyocera in Japan.

Kyocera is a very successful supplier of electronics components and office products such as laser printers. Kyocera has developed a remarkable internal network of small self-managing quasi firms that they refer to as 'amoebae'. (Like real amoebae, they change their size and shape depending on the state of the environment.)

Kyocera maintains the same lean internal structure as TCG, with the coordination between self-managing teams effected through quasi market relations of commercial contracts rather than through hierarchical administrative control. The system is described by Kazuki Hamada and Yasuhiro Monden (1989) as follows. Kyocera has around 400 'amoebas', each one having between three and forty workers. They are independent profit centres, but they have the flexibility to divide if work is plentiful and to join with others if it is scarce. When orders from the outside are received, management does not pre-plan all the necessary production steps and hand a production schedule to a manufacturing division. At Kyocera, a final assembly amoeba is given the order, and it calls up the needed sub-assemblies from the appropriate amoebae, which in turn order the components from other amoebae, and so on. Thus the work needed to fulfil the outside order is completed by the propagation of contracts through the Kyocera internal network. This is very much in the manner of TCG group member companies contracting with each other to fulfil the requirements of an order received from an external customer.

At Kyocera, all the details of internal contracts, including price, delivery and quality, are determined by the team members themselves, working under the supervision of a Kyocera sales division. Transfer prices between amoebae are set by considering current market prices, and use formulae such as full cost plus profit, partial costs plus profit, and shadow prices. Again the similarity with the situation at TCG is striking. However, the key difference is that Kyocera is a unitary firm; its amoebae constitute a work organisation innovation, not the creation of separate business entities.

196

Concluding Remarks

The significance of networks as an alternative form of economic decision-making structure to the traditional alternatives of atomistic markets and closed-form hierarchies, is now receiving increasing attention. Such networks of independent and semi-autonomous firms represent a further evolution of what Tricker (1990) calls the 'corporate concept'. To date, the literature on networks has concentrated either on their identification and description (such as the 'discovery' of hundreds of such small firm networks in Italy and Japan), on the patterns of their success, or on the policy frameworks within which they flourish.

This chapter has sought to extend this literature by focusing on the implicit or explicit rules that govern such inter-organisational networks, bringing to the fore the rules that underpin sustainability.

The value of the TCG model is that it has generated a set of rules that have proven over time to be sustainable, in the sense that they provide flexibility and innovative capacity without being exploitative. It is economically sustainable structures such as this that will become increasingly the focus of public policy as the world moves closer to the twenty-first century.

9

Negotiated technological change
Australia Post

The management and negotiation of technological change is one of the most significant aspects of the introduction of the new organisational order. Whether the change be in machines and their layout or operation, in process, or in programming, the associated and complementary changes in organisation, logistics, skills and job design make the highest demands on the parties to workplace negotiations.

Over the past decade, broader participation in change involving new technology has been occurring in firms that have recognised shortcomings in the traditional approaches to change. Participation does not mean that everyone has a say concerning technical decisions. This would be anarchy, not democracy. Rather, it means that the users of the new technological systems are recognised as a constituency and are consulted about the changes at the development stage, prior to implementation. This provides essential *user feedback* to designers and engineers. Rather than diminishing their technical expertise, it actually enhances it, since they now have a well-defined basis on which to introduce their technical changes. It is user-involvement in the design and implementation of new technological systems that has made such a difference in this important facet of workplace innovation.

Australia Post provides an excellent case study in technological change because it embodies both the best and worst extremes. This organisation has suffered the worst of top-down, technocentric, labour-shedding automation in the 1970s and 1980s, leading to bitter disputes and stand-offs with unions and grievous results for the organisation as a whole. More recently it has demonstrated a form of 'best practice' in technological change, in its introduction of optical character recognition (OCR) systems into mail-sorting operations.

The introduction of OCR mail sorting into Australia Post is one of the most encouraging stories of workplace reform and organisational innovation in Australia today. It has placed the postal corporation on a much stronger foundation of efficiency due to the flexible use of the programmable sorting technology and the new levels of motivation and commitment evident among staff. It has been a classic case of technological change accelerating a process of organisational change, in which Australia Post has emerged with a stronger culture of industrial participation, and a stronger sense of itself as an efficient public carrier of mails.

A flavour of the change would have been evident to any observer who attended the open day hosted by the Melbourne Mail Centre for staff and their families on Saturday, 23 March 1991. The obligatory barbecue was provided, together with drinks and presents for the children, in the two year old, single-storey building. Pride of place at this celebration was given to a machine, acquired only four months before, and now fully operational and ready to show its paces. The machine was an optical character recognition mail sorter, or OCR unit as it is called in Australia Post.

The reception given to this machine was remarkable by any standards. It was transforming the way in which mail would be sorted, taking the place of the manual sorting frames which had only recently been redesigned, and complementing the keyboard index machines through which staff entered postcodes in preparation for mechanical sorting. The new machine enables addresses to be read and encoded by computer, and the letters to be sorted in any sequence according to programmes installed in its control unit. No-one at the Melbourne Mail Centre was retrenched as a result of the machine's arrival.

Training on the new high-speed machine started from the day of its arrival on 3 December, and already involved a majority of the centre's 350 staff. Its arrival had been preceded by intensive planning, involving management and staff deciding for themselves the layout and manner of operation of the new equipment in a joint 'action committee' that had been meeting and deliberating for six months. This committee had invited all the staff to contribute to its deliberations, issuing regular 'OCR Bulletins', and posting its proposals and recommendations on a large noticeboard before taking decisions.

This hectic round of activity at the Melbourne centre was complemented by preparations at the state management level, and this in turn was fashioned by years of joint activity and planning by Australia Post at corporate level through its OCR Project team. The Melbourne OCR machine was simply one of 36 units being installed between 1990 and 1993, in the 21 largest mail centres around the country. A further sixteen keyboard-operated Flats Sorting Machines to handle larger mail items were included in the same modernisation programme, costing Australia Post a total of $40 million. Melbourne was expected to bring its OCR unit up to operational level only after a pilot run had been carried out and evaluated at the Brisbane Mail Centre, the first to be equipped with an OCR machine. The units had been carefully selected and modified to Australian specifications in a process involving Australia Post management and unions in intensive consultations. The kind of technology chosen was only settled on after a range of options had been inspected in mail centres around the world, by a joint union–management team (including a consultant ergonomist) that travelled to six countries in June and July 1988.

The whole process of change had started in 1984 and was cemented with an agreement reached in 1985 between Australia Post and its principal union. The Australian Postal and Telecommunications Union (now the Communications Workers Union), sanctioned the new technology for letter sorting, but on the condition that existing jobs were safeguarded. Australia Post gave a ten year commitment that no-one would be retrenched on account of mail sorting modernisation, external conditions permitting. This collaborative approach was publicly confirmed in December 1989, when Australia Post and the union issued their Joint Statement of Understanding on Participative Management.

The contrast with previous episodes of mechanisation of mail sorting at Australia Post could not have been more stark. For a quarter of a century since the mid-1960s, the battle over mechanisation was fought through bans, strikes and sabotage on the unions' side, matched by arrogant and authoritarian decisions being imposed unilaterally on management's side. Australia Post, which had moved to world leadership of postal authorities in the 1960s with its plans for modern, centralised and mechanised mail exchanges, had reached a level of confrontation and dispute that threatened its very survival as a public sector enterprise. The pos-

Manual mail sorting on horizontal frames in the 1970s

An operator loads letters into an OCR machine for letter sorting

sibility of leaping forward technologically with OCR, and the opportunities this would present for burying the old confrontationism and enhancing the flexibility and efficiency of operations, could not be missed.

OCR technology represents a potentially more efficient and flexible system of mail sorting, through its automatic reading of postcodes coupled with sorting capacities. But evidence from around the world indicates that OCR technology can be implemented in very different ways, depending on the organisational culture and the extent to which such a transition is accomplished through participation or coercion. At Australia Post, a clear commitment emerged in the mid-1980s to go with the new computerised technology and make it the vehicle for a fresh start on the industrial relations front.

This case study is concerned with the organisational innovation through which Australia Post has effected this major change in its operating procedures without losing a single day in industrial disputation. The change is placed within its organisational context, leading to the distillation of a nine-step 'model' of participative organisational and technological change.[1]

The story of this seizing of an organisational opportunity, and the saga of negotiation, planning and cooperative endeavour that it entailed, is one of the great episodes in the round of restructuring and workplace reform that is taking place in Australia in the 1990s.[2]

ORGANISATIONAL OVERVIEW OF AUSTRALIA POST

Australia Post is the operating name of the Australian Postal Corporation, a business enterprise wholly owned by the Commonwealth Government under the *Australian Postal Corporation Act 1989*. The Corporation is run as a commercial enterprise and is entirely self-funding; indeed it is one of the few public mail operations in the world to return a profit. It was set up as a separate entity in 1975, when the old Post Master General's Department was split into two statutory corporations, Australia Post and Telecom Australia. Its policies are set by a board of directors accountable for the Corporation's performance to the Government, and particularly to the Minister for Transport and Communications.

Australia Post operates letter and parcel delivery services within Australia and internationally, and a range of related services including acting as an agency for other organisations such as the Commonwealth Bank, the Passports Office of the Department of

202

Immigration, and for gas, electricity and water utilities. As a business enterprise, Australia Post operates its courier, parcel and retail services in a highly competitive market. Under the Act, Australia Post has a community service obligation to provide all Australians with access to a letter service charging uniform rates. The total assets of Australia Post amount to more than $2 billion. Annual revenue is just on $2 billion, with a profit of $57 million in 1990 exceeding expectations by more than $20 million. The corporation employs 35 000 full-time staff and 8000 part-time staff and contractors. It retails its services through 1400 post offices and 3100 post office agencies.

Australia Post is actually a number of businesses, but the one we are concerned with is the mail sorting operation. Within mail sorting, there have been significant organisational and technological changes. Organisationally, the attempts of the 1960s to centralise operations in single state mail exchanges were reversed in the 1970s into a forward-thinking strategy of sorting mail in smaller centres linked together in state and national networks. This has resulted in the establishment of a network of 47 mail centres; of these, there are 22 metropolitan centres carrying daily loads of up to 1 million letters, and 19 country mail centres handling up to 300 000 letters each. In addition, there are delivery centres in the heart of six capital cities. This organisational initiative has been followed up in the later 1980s with reforms to staff selection and promotion procedures, devolving powers from state level to the level of mail centres and facilities management. Thus a substantial level of organisational decentralisation has been achieved.

In technological terms, Australia Post has pursued a fluctuating strategy of electro-mechanisation of mail handling operations. Moves to introduce new electro-mechanical sorting systems in the late 1960s and 1970s met with great resistance. A later generation of letter indexing machines introduced at the beginning of the 1980s were also introduced in a way that fomented great unrest. Now Australia Post is moving into the era of electronic and computerised information technology on a number of fronts. In the mail sorting network, the most significant development is the introduction of computerised mail sorting systems involving OCR technology. This is set to further enhance the efficiency of Australia Post operations, enabling it to cope with increasing volumes of mail at costs which are acceptable to the community.

Australia Post appears to have learnt an important organisational lesson from the experience with mechanised letter sorting initiatives that came to grief in the past. The introduction of OCR equipment, unlike its electro-mechanical predecessors, is being managed on the basis of extensive consultation and agreement, at national, state divisional and mail centre level. The OCR Project is now into its seventh year, and has reached the stage of implementation, following intensive staff and union involvement processes in planning and designing the transition to the new system.

By 1993, some 85 per cent of standard letters are being sorted using the OCR equipment. The introduction of the new systems is being accompanied by an intensive public promotion urging the use of postcode squares on hand-addressed envelopes (35 per cent of all letters) to facilitate their sorting by OCR technology. Computer-based management information systems are also being developed to improve the flow of mail and allow for the more productive use of mail processing resources.

The mail processing network is labour intensive and has a history of industrial volatility. The 47 centres together employ around 9000 sorting staff and approximately 1000 technical and administrative staff. Each centre typically employs between 200 and 600 staff. Like other Australian government business enterprises, Australia Post is heavily unionised. In the mail centres, the Communications Workers Union (which at the time of our study was still called the Australian Postal and Telecommunications Union) represents about 90 per cent of the staff. Other unions with members in mail centres were the Australian Telecommunication Employees Association, the Postal Supervisory Officers Association (all now part of the Communications Workers Union) and the Public Sector Union. Relations between Australia Post and the postal unions have been pivotal in determining success or failure in the technological change process. Significant productivity-related industrial relations agreements were reached in 1987 (*Restructuring and Efficiency: Postal Levels Structure*), and 1989 (*Structural Efficiency: Introduction of OCR*).

The OCR Project has been at the forefront of Australia Post's adoption of industrial participation and consultation. It has done this in a conscious effort to involve employees and their unions in decision-making processes, to enhance their knowledge of the system and their commitment to the outcomes. This approach was a feature of the OCR 'Log of Claims' served on Australia Post by the Australian Postal and Telecommunications Union. It is enshrined in a *Joint Statement of Understanding on Industrial Participation*, reached in December 1989, agreed to by the corporation and the postal unions and endorsed by the Australian Industrial Relations Commission. It recognises the need for Australia Post to provide reliable and efficient services, and the need for consultation and participation in the workplace to achieve this goal. Industrial participation programmes have been developed by joint union–management steering committees, facilitated by external consultants.[3]

This form of direct consultation and negotiation has complemented, and in some respects surpassed, the frameworks for consultation established at peak council level. The major forum is the Postal Industry Development Council, which evolved out of the Postal Consultative Council established in 1975 when Australia Post was set up as a statutory Commission. However, the Council has never had the OCR Project on its agenda—not because there has been no consultation on OCR, but because the level of consultation has been too intense to be confined to the periodic meetings of a peak-level council.

MAIL SORTING BY OCR

From being at the forefront of modernisation in the 1960s when Redfern and its electro-mechanical sorting systems were widely applauded by engineers, by the late 1980s Australia Post had slipped badly behind. It paid a heavy price for the human relations bungling involved in the Redfern centralisation episode and in the letter indexing debacle. In 1990, prior to the introduction of the first OCR machines, and even with the use of letter indexing machines and letter sorting machines, the majority of mail sorting in Australia Post was conducted manually, albeit on ergonomically well-designed sorting frames.

Precisely because of this relative backwardness, Australia Post was presented with a unique opportunity to once again assume a leading position, by learning from the extensive experience with computerised sorting equipment clocked up by postal authorities around the world. Mail sorting equipment involving OCR is now widely used, so Australia Post has much experience to learn from in making its own transition to the new technology. Issues have been debated regularly at the International Postal Mechanisation Conferences, held approximately every two years.

Optical Character Recognition technology differs fundamentally from previous forms of mechanisation. Letters can be coded directly within a machine, rather than through an operator reading the address and coding via a keyboard. If OCR is combined with programmable sorting routines through computerisation, a powerful and flexible system is possible. By analogy with Flexible Manufacturing Systems that employ programmable computer numerically controlled machine tools, we could call these programmable mail sorting set-ups Flexible Mail Sorting Systems.[4]

How OCR works

In an OCR machine, a video image of the envelope's address is formed and the characters in it are identified by comparing them with standard characters in the computer memory. This is the means through which the OCR device 'recognises' both the locality name and postcode in typed addresses (and the postcode only in hand-written addresses). The machine then prints the postcode on the envelope in the form of a machine-readable barcode, similar to the price code on supermarket goods. (This barcode is now visible on sorted mail in Australia, printed on the face of the envelope.) The letter is then directed by a barcode-reading sorter to the output stacker which corresponds to the postcode.

If the brain of the OCR is its computer, then its heart is the scanning, delay, printing and verifying module which carries out the sorting preliminaries. This unit takes a digitised (or video) picture of the address side of the envelope (scanning); it then diverts letters along an extended circular letter path to give the computer time to recognise and act on the address (delay); it then sprays a barcode index on the envelope (printing); and subsequently re-reads the printed index to verify that this index is in fact correct (verifier). The splitting of the optical scanning and barcode printing process from the barcode reading process means that letters can be sorted electronically more than once, without being rescanned each time. Letters might be sorted two or more times, as the streams are 'broken' into finer and finer postcode divisions. Australia Post has made maximum use of this facility which has had a profound impact on its network planning, and offered it great efficiency potential that has not been so fully captured by overseas postal authorities.

A picture of an OCR machine is shown on page 201. The typical machine with 40 stacking points is about fifteen metres long and two metres wide, rising to waist height. At its head there is an input stacker module, into which an operator places bundles of culled, faced and cancelled letters. A pick-off point sweeps the letters away individually, at a rate of between 25 000 and 35 000 per hour, into the scanning and printer module. Controls and sorting programmes are set at an operator's panel located just above the feeder module;

this panel also gives digital readouts of current sorting rates, recognition rates and cumulative totals. Letters pass from the scanning and printing module to the stacker control module, and are sorted to output stackers; these are cleared regularly by operating staff. Letters which are non-readable, such as handwritten addresses without postcodes or typewritten addresses which are faulty in some way, are diverted to a 'reject' stacker and taken away for manual sorting (or letter indexing and electronic barcode sorting).

Because computerised mail sorting is by now a relatively mature technology, there are established designers and manufacturers of the equipment. Leading manufacturers who were shortlisted by Australia Post include AEG, Toshiba, NEC and Alcatel. AEG was eventually selected as the preferred supplier by Australia Post, subject to Australian manufacture of the technology.[5]

Technological alternatives: video coding

Video coding is a related technology that can be used to process mail that is rejected as unreadable by OCR machines. It is a hybrid technology in that it uses video scanning (as in OCR) combined with operator coding (as in letter indexing). Machines developed by AEG and NEC are in use in many postal systems around the world. They generally consist of a transport section similar to an OCR machine (or part of an OCR unit), combined with a series of terminals displaying video images of the scanned envelopes; operators sit at these terminals, and key in the postcode of the address they see *on the screen*. This is the important point; operators are indexing letters from a *video image of a letter*, presented on a television-type screen, rather than from the letter itself, as at the presently used letter indexing desks. Indexing from a video image presents major ergonomic and staff morale issues.

There is a further twist to video coding. In most mail sorting applications, the video terminals are located close to the scanning and printing module of the machine. But in principle there is no reason why this should be so, and indeed the viewing terminals could be located hundreds of miles from the actual letter handling systems. This is the 'attractive' feature of video coding; it has strong centralising tendencies built into it, encouraging postal authorities to centralise all coding in a few key locations. This is precisely what the US postal system is doing, with its notion of 'remote barcoding'. There are also ergonomic problems in coding from a video image which have led Australian postal unions to oppose the introduction of this technology.

International experience

While OCR equipment is looked on most favourably by managements and unions throughout the world, there are very different ways of introducing it and managing it.

In the United Kingdom, OCR machines were used during the 1980s in conjunction with letter sorting machines. OCR machines were first ordered in 1980, and were trialled in 1982 at the Mt Pleasant sorting office in central London, provoking disputes with the union. OCR equipment was only introduced there in 1984 after a confrontation with the union in which management resorted to the use of legal sanctions made available by the Conservative government. When agreement was eventually reached with the unions in 1985, the equipment was introduced in an atmosphere of 'management victory', with extensive use of part-time workers to provide the labour flexibility that was sought.[6]

As further OCR machines were introduced in the late 1980s, again consultation with staff associations was minimal; potential privatisation by the Thatcher government was the whip that drove this process. The general direction of change in mail sorting in Britain has been towards task specialisation and the intensification of work associated with computerisation. Operators are being trained to specialise and work with OCR equipment only—a strategy which is strikingly at variance with the pursuit of flexible multi-skilling at Australia Post. Intensification of work is such that the independent ergonomist who travelled on the 1988 joint Australia Post overseas mission reported: 'One mail centre in particular placed emphasis on throughput in such a strong way that video cameras were trained on the operators as they worked'. This is certainly a novel twist to the notion of 'video coding'!

In Sweden, a quite different approach has been taken. Flagship of the Swedish mail sorting centre is the Tomteboda centre, located in the northern suburbs of Stockholm. This is a futuristic centre, opened in 1983 and imbued with the technological logic of centralisation. OCR equipment has been used from the outset at Tomteboda, but in a manner which broadens skills and with some job rotation as a means of providing task variety. Efforts have been made to introduce teamwork at Tomteboda, but so far these have not yielded the results anticipated (Lofgren 1986, pp. 86–7). Early enthusiasm for the new technology has been observed to give way to a tendency towards simplification and routinisation of work. Lansbury gives a 'more qualified view of the mail centre's success', where teamwork and job rotation have been abandoned and 'employees have preferred to stay in the one work area doing the same type of job' (Lansbury 1987, p. 154). OCR equipment was introduced into the Swedish postal service with guarantees of continued employment; the productivity gains have been accompanied by increasing volumes of mail.

At Tomteboda, video coding is again being utilised after a prolonged period of non-use, but only in a limited way. It was not in use when the Australia Post delegation visited Tomteboda in 1988 but they heard reports that its use was unpopular with staff; viewing letters on a screen demanded great concentration, with resulting problems of eyestrain and back and shoulder pain. One of the informants at Tomteboda remarked that the video coding equipment had at least one positive function—it was providing spare parts for the rest of the equipment at the mail centre!

In Switzerland, OCR equipment is used extensively, frequently in conjunction with video coding machines. Some mail sorting centres in Switzerland seemed to be moving towards multi-skilling with OCR, while others seemed to be following the British path towards task specialisation. In either case, the OCR equipment had been introduced without job losses and with productivity increases. The Swiss postal service employs large numbers of female part-time staff. Work on the OCRs is rotated; operators work for three and a half hours then have a fifteen minute break. The use of OCRs has facilitated improvements in postal delivery service.

In the United States, the US Postal Service is engaged in a major programme to upgrade its mail sorting equipment, using index-printing OCRs and index-reading letter sorting machines. These are referred to in the USA as barcode sorters. By the end of the 1980s, the US Postal Service deployed 400 OCR units capable of reading five digit ZIP codes; an additional 350 are in the process of being installed, with capacity to read and code by the enhanced nine digit 'ZIP + 4' postcode (United States Postal Service 1991).

The US Postal Service is taking barcoding of addresses to new limits (and other countries are likely to follow suit). It uses barcoding not just to define postal districts, but with extended ZIP codes it can define streets and even street numbers. The explicit aim is to reduce and ultimately eliminate manual sorting in delivery offices, which is seen as the last bastion of manual procedures in the postal service. OCR units are adapted for this purpose in what is called *multi-line OCR*. In the mid-1980s a first attempt was made to extend the ZIP code with a further four digits, embodying the street and street number information. This was vigorously opposed by the postal union, on grounds of massive threatened job losses, but it was introduced for the key market segment of business mail.

In the 1990s, the US Postal Service is relentlessly pursuing this automated delivery sorting option, through what it calls the Advanced Bar Code concept which adds a further two digits to the ZIP + 4 barcode, these representing the last two numerals of the street address; the length of the barcode itself increases from 52 to 62 bars. By 1995 it envisages that all letters will be sorted to delivery points, using Advanced Bar Code techniques (USPS 1991). Indeed the postal service anticipates that by 1995, 40 per cent of letters will be barcoded to this degree by customers, thus eliminating the need for OCR operations within the postal service; such letters can be put directly into barcoded sorting machines. There will be a financial incentive in the form of reduced rates applying to customer-barcoded mail.

The US Postal Service is also pursuing centralised video coding, through what it calls its *Remote Bar Coding System*. Images of letters scanned by OCR units are stored in computers, then transmitted to operator workstations anywhere in the USA for coding through a keyboard. The code is then in turn transmitted back to the sorter for printing on the letter and sorting. The two steps, remote video encoding and remote computer reading, are combined in what is now called remote barcoding. This kind of system became operational in two US postal facilities in late 1990, and it was planned to install a further 40 such systems in 1991, with 300 systems being the eventual goal (United States Postal Service 1991).

These developments in the USA take the automation of mail sorting in a direction which I would characterise as intensifying technological control, extending computer surveillance, and displacing traditional quality control over deliveries by mail deliverers (postmen) through the automation of final sorting. These are what I would call anti-labour technological options that other postal administrations, such as Australia Post, have managed to avoid and, in the process, have achieved better organisational performance. It is to these issues that we now turn.

Efficiency and quality of service

Already there is a clear indication of the benefits Australia Post is reaping from the operational flexibility offered by programmed OCR and the new level of staff commitment and morale engendered by the participative approach to its introduction. In April 1991, Australia Post launched a public efficiency campaign, centred on a new and unprecedented commitment to provide next day delivery for postal items lodged within metropolitan areas by 6.00 p.m. This is a standard of efficiency that few postal services can hope to reach. It represents a fundamental shift in attitude on the part of Australia Post, from a 'supply-driven' organisation telling its users what services were available, to a 'demand-driven' organisation asking its customers what they want. It has required, in the case of Australia with its vast distances, new organisational arrangements involving use of air freight transport through the night, for example, but it also depends critically on the enhanced mail processing capacity offered by the OCR equipment.

It remains to be seen whether Australia Post will, in practice, be able to achieve these new standards of service and productivity. As part of the new package, it intends to subject itself to independent monthly audits, as long demanded by customers and bodies such as the Prices Surveillance Authority; these audits will involve a separate organisation sending articles in planned sequence through the mail and monitoring their delivery. Again it is the new levels of staff motivation and commitment, achieved through the OCR Project, that give Australia Post the confidence to subject itself to such external scrutiny.

New technology and participation

The Australia Post OCR Project was self-consciously one of participative change involving the introduction of new technology. It provides an interesting test of some theories of organisational change—just as it was itself partly guided by such theories. This is the inescapably 'self-reflexive' feature of change in any self-managed social process (Baumgartner 1986).

The introduction of new technology has sparked a tremendous international debate. There is now widespread agreement that many of the negative features which have been associated with a transition to work with new technology have had more to do with the authoritarian nature of its introduction than any intrinsic properties of computerisation. Employee participation in change has been found to be a positive factor in numerous studies.[7]

The Australia Post OCR Project has provided a further definitive confirmation of this organisational perspective. The enthusiasm with which the OCR equipment was received in mail sorting centres had very little to do with its novelty (after all, previous indexing technology which had been roundly rejected had been novel) and very much to do with the conscious structures established to allow staff some measure of control over the way it was introduced (layout, work design, rosters) and then subsequently over the way it was used (formation of work teams).

Within the OCR Project, there was a clear understanding of the difference between what Herzberg (1968) called 'hygiene' and 'motivator' factors. Herzberg argued that humans experience two kinds of needs: there are basic security issues (safety, job security, money) and aspirational issues (such as achievement, recognition for achievement, responsibility and growth). The point of making this distinction was to argue that satisfaction of hygiene needs did not of itself lead to employee motivation; what was needed was enriched *job content* over and above the satisfaction of basic needs. Herzberg claimed to have demonstrated this distinction empirically through attitude surveys; whether he did or not is a moot point, but his argument has certainly been influential, and its plausibility has been further underlined in the Australia Post experience. The extraordinary levels of staff commitment evident in the OCR Action Groups set up in mail centres, could only have been unleashed in a situation where basic security issues had been taken care of, and moreover, like justice, had been seen to be taken care of. This was the significance of the 'no retrenchment' guarantees and the constant references to independent assessments of Occupational Health and Safety issues to do with OCR.

This in itself is a powerful lesson from the Australia Post experience. Organisations which go about the process of change without first securing satisfaction of the hygiene factors are doomed to fail. This discussion leads us to ask what have been the substantive effects of the new technology, in terms of working conditions, productivity and efficiency.

Worker experience of OCR technology

The literature on the subjective impact of new technologies is polarised. On the one hand, there are triumphal accounts which celebrate the efficiency and novelty of handling vast quantities of data and controlling armies of plant and equipment, such as in power plants or chemical refineries, through keyboards and display screens. On the other hand, there is a pessimistic stream of scholarship which laments the passing of direct, physical interaction between workers and the material on which they are working, exemplified in David Noble's or Harley Shaiken's accounts of the use of Computer Numeric Controlled metalworking equipment

(Noble 1984; Shaiken 1984). Shoshana Zuboff's studies of clerical workers and paper mill workers utilising new information technology were generally pessimistic as well, claiming that it distanced them from sentient experience of their work, but she also looked forward to an 'informating' strategy that would bring the full intellectual dimension of skills to the fore (Zuboff 1988).

The case of mail sorting with OCR falls somewhere between these two extremes, and to date has been relatively under-investigated, apart from some surveys carried out by Australia Post and the consultant ergonomist as part of the OCR Project. The experience obtained to date does not support Zuboff's notion of a 'mediated unreality' involved in the distancing of worker from task with automating systems. On the contrary, OCR keeps workers closely in touch with the letters they are handling (they physically stack them and move them in and out of the processing machine) but they are saved the essentially monotonous and deadening task of sorting each letter individually, or keying in a code for each letter individually.

Instead, the OCR machine allows workers to *manage* the process of sorting; their work becomes one of ensuring that sorting is done efficiently, promptly and in a programmed sequence by a machine which takes the drudgery out of the process. The rotation of work provides variety, while social interaction while performing tasks has been built in as a deliberate design strategy. Thus the introduction of OCR technology into Australia Post conforms more to Zuboff's 'optimistic' scenario of information technology being used to stretch and complement the intellectual skills of workers without deadening their physical experience of control.

Seen from this perspective, further increases in flexibility and efficiency are likely to come from refinements to the programming of the OCR machines, rather than from 'automating' mail handling functions by building conveyor belts, automatic feeds and the other paraphernalia familiar from the worst kinds of factory mechanisation. This is the essence of computerised OCR mail sorting: it is programmable, and as staff gain more familiarity with the equipment, they are likely to come up with programming innovations (for example, different routines for sorting mail into various postal districts, termed 'breaking' the mail) that further increase efficiency. Such refinements are likely to be developed through worker input, as skilled operators think about how and why they are sorting in particular sequences. An example is provided by a suggestion from a worker at the Melbourne Mail Centre for coloured lights to indicate the current sorting programme being utilised by the machine. This is a suggestion of great import in that such initiatives promise a process of incremental innovation to improve the efficiency of programmed mail sorting within Australia Post.

Contrast this perspective with that which informs the development of video coding, particularly in its remote, centralised version, with a suite of keyboard coders in one part of the country being presented with video images of letters being sorted mechanically in centres all around the rest of the country. This is certainly a case of 'mediated unreality', reaching new depths of alienation and surveillance as workers are paced by the machine as it presents letters to them, and even explicitly 'watched' by video cameras, as in the example of the British postal service and no doubt others as well. Here is a case of technology potentially increasing the intensity and demeaning aspects of work in quite stark contrast to the benign effects of programmed OCR sorting.

Cooperation and business strategy: the political dimension of change

In the OCR Project, it may be argued that management and unions in Australia Post have resorted to a cooperative strategy in the face of overwhelming common threats, such as rising competition from private mail carriers and the possibility of loss of the public monopoly over general services. In effect, the two sides have formed a coalition in defence of the continuance of Australia Post as a public sector carrier.

Within a wider political perspective, it can be argued that the union has been able to stamp the industrial relations agenda with its demands for co-determination because of a favourable political environment. This has included the existence of a federal Labor government with Ministers promoting the notion of cooperation with staff organisations. The Accord between the ACTU and the Labor government favoured co-determination of issues rather than confrontation. The 'Joint Statement on Participative Practices' developed by the ACTU with the Confederation of Australian Industry, was freely referred to by the union in its correspondence with Australia Post on OCR matters.

These have all contributed to an environment in which a kind of 'political exchange' takes place, with the union giving up its disruptive (negative) powers in return for positive influence over the management of the enterprise. This notion of 'political exchange' was introduced by the Italian theorist Pizzorno (1978) to describe union–state relations under social democracy, and extended by Regini (1984) to describe its implications for the relations between union leaderships and their rank and file members.

It took several years for the Australian Postal and Telecommunications Union to embrace the notion of co-determination, and the same may be said of Australia Post, particularly its middle management levels. The OCR Project provided the catalyst which accelerated this process that was already underway. The lineaments of a 'political exchange' between the union and Australia Post are now quite manifest and they extend into regions undreamed of by Pizzorno. An example is the insistence by Australia Post that the OCR equipment being utilised in this technological transformation be manufactured in Australia (under sub-contract from the successful tenderer, AEG); this is a clear extension of the issue to encompass questions of industry policy. The specifications of the equipment were also altered to conform with the independently developed ergonomic criteria. This is an extension of the political exchange bargain that encapsulates the interests of the manufacturing unions and of Australian industry. It has ensured that there is a genuine transfer of OCR technological know-how to Australian industry. This is critical in providing for the capacity to extend and modify the technology, particularly its programming features, as ideas for improvement continue to be generated within the ranks of Australia Post employees as they become familiar with the operation of the OCR equipment.

The scope for influence of Australia Post unions, catalysed by the OCR Project, compares markedly with the diminishing prospects facing the British Union of Communication Workers as it confronts an increasingly militant Post Office buttressed by the privatisation plans of the British government (Ferner & Terry 1985; Terry & Ferner 1986).

Rosabeth Moss Kanter, in her book *When Giants Learn to Dance*, discusses a strategic alliance between a union and employer in the communications services field in the USA. The case, involving Pacific Bell and the Communications Workers of America, bears a striking resemblance to the 'political exchange' negotiated in Australia (Kanter 1990, pp. 131–2). She calls this a 'complementary partnership', equating it in strategic terms to joint ventures and other inter-company cooperative ventures. Whether the Australian parties would want to characterise their experience with Industrial Participation and OCR technology in these terms is a moot point, but there can be little doubt that she is correct in pointing to such alliances as being the key to business success in the future. As she describes the situation, Pácific Bell entered into cooperation with the union as a business proposition, seeing it as a 'business partnership', in order to be able to develop its strategy of introducing new technologies and operating methods and keeping a lid on costs. For its part, the union was able to increase its influence within the company and with its own members, through the establishment of local common interest forums involving managements and union officials at operating level. In her later work on organisational change (1992) she laments the passing of this partnership; it lasted only as long as the individuals involved in its creation. In contrast, the strength of the Australia Post innovation lies in its being embedded in the organisational structures and routines of the corporation, beyond the powers of any particular individual.

The changing role of supervisors

Supervisors at Australia Post, as at virtually all enterprises undergoing restructuring, have found it hard to accommodate the new regime of participation. Most supervisors were appointed in the past for their capacity to keep the 'troops' in line; they were the sergeants in the industrial army. They were appointed on the basis of seniority, and most of them (with honourable exceptions) regarded their elevation as a farewell to working 'on the tools'. There is no role for the sergeant in the participative workplace, and the new team leaders are expected to be working members of the team, not arm's-length superiors.

Again, the OCR Project has accelerated a process of change that was already underway. Its successful resolution has demanded that the problem be addressed by offering inducements to cooperative supervisors and finding ways to marginalise those supervisors who remain unaccommodating. The issue has been tackled in different ways at the various mail centres but in all cases it has not been allowed to go unresolved. Further developments using teams in mail centres will settle the issue once and for all.

The changing role of the union

The experience of participative change with the OCR Project, and the adoption and extension of Industrial Participation which it has triggered, has already had profound effects on the postal unions. The Australian Postal and Telecommunications Union effected a quite remarkable turnaround from a confrontationist approach to cooperative accommodation. There have been enormous demands on union leadership, requiring it to follow and monitor the technical and organisational issues generated by the OCR Project, and to find a way to convey these to the membership in comprehensible terms that would encourage member involvement and minimise the chances of backlash. This was an extremely complex political exercise for the union leadership.

Like their counterparts elsewhere, union officials all around Australia are struggling with the problem: what is the role of the union when centralised negotiations of wages and conditions give way to enterprise-focused negotiations which link wages and skill formation and job design to the strategic goals of the organisation? The OCR Project has demonstrated that in the course of this change the status of workplace delegates increases while that of central officials is diminished.

The role of external agencies

As a statutory authority, Australia Post operates under constant surveillance from public and private institutions, starting with Parliament itself. The recent move towards greater public commitment to mail collection services, and independent audit of mail clearing efficiency, is clearly the product of external pressure brought by agencies such as the Prices Surveillance Authority (Prices Surveillance Authority 1991).

The lesson of the OCR story is that the institutions of the industrial relations system in Australia still have a significant role to play. While in the past, the rigidities of awards and tribunal procedures have hampered enterprise flexibility and efficiency, the changes registered in the later 1980s have been remarkable, and Australia Post has provided a good testing ground to assess their significance. The Postal Levels Structure review could not be implemented in 1984 due to the unwieldiness of the national wage guidelines at the time, but with the easing of this restraint and the move towards productivity bargaining in 1987, Australia Post was able to institute a massive process of job reclassification which was the prelude to the success of OCR. Subsequently, the national wage guidelines, through the Structural Efficiency Principle, were able to offer an appropriate framework for the resolution of the union's Log of Claims on OCR and Flats Sorting Machines equipment, thereby providing the structural framework within which participative initiatives at mail centre level could be pursued. The Australian Industrial Relations Commission was also instrumental in assisting

Australia Post to adopt its culture of industrial participation in the first place.

In these ways, the OCR story underlines the dependence of any organisation, even one as large and seemingly autonomous as Australia Post, on its regulatory and commercial environment.

In the wake of the OCR Project, Australia Post has negotiated an enterprise agreement with its staff which delivers pay increases as further productivity standards are reached. A one-off payment is made as each workplace (such as a mail sorting centre) reaches higher quality and service standards under the Q1 (Quality First) programme. Talks are proceeding on the introduction of gainsharing arrangements which will further distribute the fruits of higher levels of productivity. All of these initiatives would have been impossible without the change in culture brought about by the OCR Project and industrial participation.

Team-based performance pay and gainsharing

CIG Gas Cylinders

So far, our case studies have been concerned with process and structure. Where does money fit in? Money remains a prime motivator in the workplace. Wage systems are important, not because they provide the sole cause of satisfaction from work as in the mass production system, but because in the best practice firms workers who are more productive and committed expect to be allocated a share of the improvements. Otherwise, they will suspect, and usually with good reason, that someone else is benefiting at their expense. Money can also be an important factor in the sense that Taylorist wages schemes, such as individual incentive payments systems, act as negative influences on the introduction of workplace innovations like teamwork. In fact, individual incentive payments are incompatible with group-based performance measurement. The structuring of financial rewards through the wages system is an essential component of best practice management.

In Australia, there have been many examples of restructured wage systems linking wages with skills and group performance. One of the most notable is the gainsharing system which has operated for over ten years at the firm CIG Gas Cylinders. This system has proven to be an extremely flexible arrangement within which the company has continuously sought productivity improvements, sharing the benefits at each stage with a workforce that is cooperative, but which protects its interests through union membership and collective bargaining over the structure of the scheme.

Pay remains the principal motivator, and sends strong messages as to how the firm really regards its own employees. If senior management are talking in terms of cooperation and continuous improvement while keeping all employees on individual incentive payments, they are unlikely to find their message being taken seriously. Nevertheless, changes to pay systems are notoriously difficult to effect. Most organisations find they can cope with skills-based pay or performance-based pay but rarely with the two together, at least at first. But the innovative organisation aims to move in the direction of establishing a link between people's collective accomplishments and what they find in their pay packets. The scope for improvement in wage systems is certainly great.

Payment systems in the traditional firm are based on the 'rate for the job', enshrined in award structures in Australia as in most other industrial countries. Innovative organisations are now seeking to link payment systems to employees' skills and performance rather than tying wage rates to the jobs that people perform.

Gainsharing systems are designed explicitly to link employee remuneration with measured organisational performance, at the team level and at the plant level. It is a way of distributing the gains, or value-added, which is attributable to superior performance. It differs from profit-sharing in that it is much more immediately tied to people's efforts, and is unaffected by extraneous factors such as interest and exchange rates, overseas customers, sales efforts and so on, all of which can have a marked influence on profits.

Issues to be resolved in installing a gainsharing system include the following.

- How is the value-added to be calculated? The easiest formula is to assign a value to output and deduct the cost of all inputs. A charge might be made for overheads such as accommodation, power consumption and management services.
- How is the share to be settled on? Some schemes adopt a 50:50 approach, while others allocate a smaller proportion to employees on the grounds that the firm wishes to retain a good proportion of the value-added for investment.
- How are employees to allocate their share among themselves? This can usually be left to the employees themselves to determine. One simple way is for all employees to share equally in the increment. Alternatively, shares might be weighted by employees' current classification.

In Australia, gainsharing schemes were pioneered using Common Interest Programmes, schemes installed in many companies in the 1970s and 1980s by the consultancy firm, Effective

Management Systems. This programme combined employee participation in productivity improvement (before 'quality circles' became fashionable) with sharing in the rewards made available through productivity enhancement. 'Productivity' was defined in terms of controllable costs per unit of production, for example, cents per kilogram of product. Controllable costs covered those which were under the control of participants, such as labour costs, material wastage, maintenance and so on; it excluded factors such as energy costs which were beyond their control. Improvement in controllable costs per unit of production over a previously agreed baseline, formed a money pool each month which was shared equally between the organisation and the participants. The participants' share was allocated equally to all members of the Common Interest group. (This was not strictly adhered to; an alternative explored was the setting up of a foundation or trust which would then administer the pool and make payments for agreed projects, such as workers' housing.)

CIG Gas Cylinders was one of the most important firms to install a Common Interest programme. After ten years it still works very well, albeit with some modifications and most recently a simplification to bring it into line with other best practice changes introduced by CIG Gas Cylinders. It is worth exploring just how this has been done, since this is a case where industrial relations and organisational innovation are totally intertwined.[1]

CIG GAS CYLINDERS: ORGANISATIONAL BACKGROUND

CIG Gas Cylinders has sustained ten years of collaborative workplace reform, bringing it to a point of productive efficiency matched by few comparable organisations. The firm is now an international success story, exporting two-thirds of its output into the highly competitive markets of Asia, and in particular into Japan, where it holds a commanding 60 per cent of the market for aluminium gas cylinders.

CIG Gas Cylinders has achieved this manufacturing success, so rare in Australia, on the strength of a long-term cooperative approach to its workforce, exemplified in a gainsharing system that has delivered productivity-linked bonuses to the workforce since 1985. It has acquired long-term customers in Asia on the strength of its capacity to deliver quickly, on time, and to a level of quality that keeps the company constantly striving for improvement. Its cooperative industrial relations, and long-term commitment to continuous improvement through workforce participation, backed by the gainsharing system that has increased employees' wages by ten to fifteen per cent each year, has paid handsome dividends.

The company's workplace reforms have been recognised in the Federal government's Best Practice Programme, with CIG Gas Cylinders being designated a Best Practice organisation in the second round in early 1992. The grant received is helping CIG Gas Cylinders accomplish its present stage of reform of moving towards self-managing shop floor teams. Once these are in place, the company confidently expects to double its output and further expand its export activity.

CIG Gas Cylinders is an autonomous division within the Commonwealth Industrial Gases (CIG) group which was founded in Australia by the British Oxygen Corporation. CIG Gas Cylinders was given a degree of autonomy with the parent taking 100 per cent control only in the late 1980s. CIG Gas Cylinders is part of CIG's Manufacturing Businesses Division, which is allowed to operate independently of the company's major industrial gases business.

It manufactures seamless aluminium cylinders for a range of industrial gases, as well as producing cylinders for acetylene. Current production levels are around 200 000 cylinders per year, with sales of around $35 million in 1991, dropping back to around $30 million in 1992 due to recession in Australia and Japan. The workforce at the Kings Park site has fluctuated from a peak of around 130 in 1982 to 110 now.

The company services a variety of markets for gas containers: cylinders for scuba diving, for medical and industrial use, and carbon dioxide bottles for use in pubs and clubs. In all, it produces a range of nearly 150 different types of cylinders. Although the plant appears to be a 'single product' operation, in reality there is great variety within this product range. This is a deliberate marketing strategy on the part of CIG Gas Cylinders, and one of the reasons why it continues to dominate the Australian market for aluminium gas cylinders.

Production of seamless aluminium cylinders started at the Kings Park, Sydney, site in 1975 with CIG as the sole customer. This in itself was an interesting exercise in vertical integration on the part of CIG, which wished to secure its own supply of gas cylinders, but had the foresight to establish the plant as a separate business entity that would be able to expand and take outside orders as the opportunities presented themselves.

The technology used at the plant, cold extrusion, was also

secured in an interesting way, under a long-term licensing agreement from the UK developer, Luxfer (the leading aluminium cylinder producer in the world and now a wholly-owned subsidiary of British Alcan). CIG Gas Cylinders has paid royalties under this agreement to Luxfer for the past sixteen years. It has worked to the advantage of both parties in that CIG Gas Cylinders has access to improvements developed by Luxfer and Luxfer has access to improvements developed by CIG Gas Cylinders. The two companies maintain a close relationship; indeed in 1992 a group of CIG Gas Cylinders employees, including shop floor staff, went on a 'benchmarking' tour to the UK with Luxfer as their primary port of call.

The licensing agreement with Luxfer also allocated potential markets to the parties with CIG Gas Cylinders being given the Asia-Pacific region, Japan and South-East Asia. Within six years of starting production, CIG Gas Cylinders was involved in finding export customers in these markets with spectacular success, to the point that it now exports two-thirds of its output.

In 1980, CIG Gas Cylinders embarked on the production of cylinders to hold acetylene. These have to be made of steel with a 'massing' material wound around them to provide extra strength. Again CIG Gas Cylinders bought state-of-the-art technology under a licensing agreement with the world leader, Norris Industries in the USA. This agreement, like that with Luxfer, was flexible and long term, offering upgrades as they were developed. Indeed Norris discarded the original asbestos base and substituted a fibreglass winding material which CIG Gas Cylinders was able to appropriate five years ago. Acetylene cylinders are now an important part of the production at the Kings Park site.

These technology licensing agreements have provided CIG Gas Cylinders with the state-of-the-art production platform it needed to launch its export drive. They are classic examples of what Williamson (1985) calls 'relational contracting', where competitors find common ground and join forces over a limited range of activities, on a flexible contractual basis that can accommodate changes. Whether CIG Gas Cylinders would have been allowed to enter into these innovative agreements when it was 100 per cent owned by the British Oxygen Corporation, must remain a matter of speculation.

PRODUCTIVITY IMPROVEMENT AND THE EXPORT MARKET

The first decade at Kings Park was spent bringing the production system up to world standards. The foundations were laid by the technology licensing agreements but a lot of work had to go into implementing the technology to best effect. Much time and energy was spent investigating comparable plants around the world; CIG Gas Cylinders was 'benchmarking' before the term had been invented.

It was soon realised that CIG Gas Cylinders was not getting the levels of productivity from its technology that comparable plants overseas were obtaining. Some attempts were made to redress the situation in traditional mode. For example, work and production standards were introduced in 1978 based on time and motion studies but the measurements had been 'fudged' and the targets were too easily achieved. In a frank discussion with a manager who was a technical superintendent at that time, it was acknowledged that productivity improvements achieved had plateaued after only one year and then began to decline.

At this point, management decided to break with Australian tradition and seek a direct accommodation with its workforce. After shopping around, an approach was made to the Effective Management Systems group to introduce participative management and gainsharing.[2] This Australian consultancy firm had already installed such systems in a number of companies; they were called Common Interest Programmes.

These schemes are among the great unsung success stories of workplace reform in Australia. They are just as innovative as the US Scanlon Plans which they resemble, but they go further in their identification of the 'common interests' that drive workplace participation and productivity improvement. They have arguably achieved their most successful implementation at CIG Gas Cylinders.

As described by Dennis Pratt in the book which first expounded this novelty:

> In essence, the Common Interest Programme . . . is based on a participative decision-making process, with people being invited to share information and ideas for improving productivity. Managers and workers meet regularly (usually monthly) using a system of representatives' meetings to review productivity over the past month and to put forward proposals for improving productivity in coming months . . . The second part of the Common Interest Programme involves rewards. These are both psychological, in terms of gaining job satisfaction, and financial, in terms of sharing the money generated by increased productivity (Pratt 1977, p. 1).

The development of a bonus scheme tailored to CIG Gas Cylinders's circumstances took the best part of a year. The new system was introduced in 1982 but really only began to run smoothly in 1985. It has proved to be a flexible instrument and motivator ever since.

WORKPLACE INNOVATION AT CIG GAS CYLINDERS

With the gainsharing system providing the incentive, CIG Gas Cylinders embarked on a programme of productivity enhancements. In striving to improve its efficiency, the company went through the alphabet soup of workplace reform in the 1980s. In 1984/85, a full-scale Total Quality Control programme was implemented, based on shop floor participation and using the guidance and leadership of the Common Interest Committee which had been established to implement the Common Interest Programme. This had some success, such as in improving some machine efficiencies, but it was seen to be limited in its appeal and approach and something better was needed as CIG Gas Cylinders started to make headway in the Japanese market.

Early contacts were made with potential Japanese customers, such as breweries, in 1984/85 during the Total Quality Control improvement programme. Eventually a large order for approximately 10 000 carbon dioxide cylinders was placed by Asahi brewery, followed by further orders from Kirin brewery, the largest in Japan. CIG Gas Cylinders was now established as a competitor with Japanese cylinder suppliers but it was hampered by its long delivery times.

At this stage, CIG Gas Cylinders was able to respond to customer orders for cylinders within 24 days. When added to the 28 days needed for shipping to Japan, this lag made it difficult to secure orders even though CIG Gas Cylinders was meeting quality standards. Hence the company embarked on an all-out effort to improve its turnaround. It committed itself to becoming a Just-In-Time producer.

The year 1987 was therefore devoted to improving the time management of the production system, in a programme called Value-Adding Management. Again external consultants were called in to assist, this time from the Technology Transfer Council. All the elements of the production system were subjected to analysis by project teams drawn from management and the shop floor. It was found that discontinuities in production meant that cylinders spent days waiting in stacks between production steps. Changes were implemented, such as ensuring that certain procedures were carried

CIG cylinders are inspected before export to Japan

out only when the next stage was ready to receive the output (e.g. machining heads on billets only when they had been trimmed).

Through paying attention to such details, the production system was geared to customer orders rather than to production for stock. Turnaround time was reduced eventually to seven days—a 400 per cent improvement. Stock levels of finished cylinders were also drastically reduced. When the programme started, CIG Gas Cylinders had 33 000 cylinders in stock; in March 1992 this figure had dropped to 11 000—a 300 per cent improvement.

The pay-off in terms of business was almost immediate. In 1987, CIG Gas Cylinders learnt that Coca-Cola Japan was in the market for gas cylinders. The company was asked to supply samples 'live' from its production system, and was able to get them to Japan before its competitors. It got the contract, and hasn't looked back since. Japan is now the company's major overseas market, and CIG Gas Cylinders is able to beat the Japanese cylinder producers on quality and delivery; it has no price advantage over its Japanese competitors. It estimates it has a third of the Japanese market for beverage cylinders and fully half of the market for scuba diving cylinders.

Forty-two per cent of its sales go to Asia. This exceeds sales in Australia and is considerably more than sales to traditional Anglo-Saxon markets such as the UK and New Zealand. CIG Gas Cylinders already looks like the manufacturing organisation called for by repeated government statements and reports.

The pay-off from these Asian export sales can be counted as more than dollars. The Japanese customers continue to place the highest demands for quality, stimulating staff to seek continuous improvement. Some leading customers have been sponsored by CIG Gas Cylinders to visit the plant in Australia to talk to management and shop floor representatives. This direct contact with customers has had a marked effect on staff morale. Representatives of one of the Japanese breweries which buys carbon dioxide cylinders from CIG Gas Cylinders were brought to the plant and they explained directly to staff why they place so much importance on stencilled Japanese characters on their cylinders. Quality problems were solved through this direct face-to-face contact.

The firm has also promoted direct contact with its suppliers through exchange visits between Kings Park and the Alcan aluminium smelter at Kurri Kurri. From the acetylene cylinders plant there has also been close contact with the cylinder supplier Rheem. These improvements have resulted in CIG Gas Cylinders winning a Total Quality Management award in 1991/92 and a federal government Best Practice award in 1992.

The company has recognised that its traditional workplace organisational structure stood in the way of further improvements and had to be tackled if the momentum of change was to be sustained. This has been, if anything, the hardest challenge tackled by CIG Gas Cylinders in a decade of sustained workplace reform. It has meant dismantling the previous hierarchical supervisory structure, and moving instead to self-managing shop floor teams. This has been accomplished under the Sociotechnical Systems programme implemented in 1991.

SOCIOTECHNICAL REFORM

Major changes in the work organisation at CIG Gas Cylinders were launched in July 1991. The positions of supervisor, foreman and leading hand were eliminated, and in their place, semi-autonomous teams covering the production of aluminium cylinders and acetylene cylinders were installed. A degree of self-management was introduced, with coordination being provided by designated team coordinators.

At the same time, annualised salaries were introduced, incorporating estimates of overtime paid under the previous system, and hours were made much more flexible. Attendance was no longer regulated, with the hated bundy clock being scrapped. Overtime rates have plunged. A new skills-based job classification system has been introduced, with workers now being paid for the skills they have acquired rather than for the job they were required to perform.

Again under the guidance of the Technology Transfer Council, a project team was formed, with full union support, to subject the plant to a total sociotechnical review, looking for all possible ways of improving collaboration and teamwork. It was the recommendations of this group that were implemented in July 1991.

Flexible hours, multi-skilling, teamwork, annualised salaries: these are the ingredients of the new sociotechnical workplace reforms which have now evolved over a period of eighteen months. Performance measures have been introduced for the individual teams. The acetylene plant team in particular has shown marked improvements, producing ten per cent more each week in five days than previously was produced in six.

CONCLUDING REMARKS

Thus the change process evolves at CIG Gas Cylinders. New market opportunities are anticipated in Japan while relations with both suppliers and customers continue to grow closer. The teamwork arrangements are still in their infancy, and cannot yet be said to have made the improvements anticipated. But this will come. The awarding of a Best Practice demonstration grant of $0.5 million in 1992, matched by company investments in sociotechnical reform of $1.5 million, augur well for the future.

CIG Gas Cylinders has shown that concentrated attention to the fundamentals of workplace design, quality assurance and productivity enhancement, all conducted within a framework of sociotechnical innovation, is feasible in a typical, relatively small, established manufacturing operation that is totally unionised and part of a larger corporate group. Positive elements have made the CIG Gas Cylinders story a success: a degree of business autonomy within the larger corporate group, a sound business strategy oriented towards exports and niche markets, a sound use of technological advantages combined with a focus on skills enhancement in human resources management to utilise these technological advantages to the full, and above all, a trust and openness with the workforce and a preparedness to distribute the benefits of improved productivity with them in a negotiated, transparent and fair scheme for sharing the financial gains. There could hardly be a better illustration of the inter-connectedness of industrial relations and organisational innovation in achieving world best practice in manufacturing.

11

People, technology and organisational change
The Australian Taxation Office

The public sector in Australia is providing some of the most interesting and far-reaching examples of sociotechnical organisational
change. Our final case study is one of total organisational change.
The Modernisation Programme of the Australian Taxation Office
(ATO) is an ambitious ten year programme that will utterly change
the way in which the organisation operates, and in which
sociotechnical principles of participative design and implementation
of the new systems have been followed almost to the letter.

The Electronic Lodgment Service (ELS) was the flagship of
modernisation at the ATO, and provides a fascinating insight into the
approach taken to redesigning the organisation's systems. ELS was
also the first public demonstration of modernisation in action. It was
the first 'deliverable' to the public and returns processing staff and
showed that the ATO was on the move. ELS has been an outstanding
organisational success, meeting and even bettering its very ambitious
performance targets, and receiving acclaim—it won the Gold Award
in the 1991 Government Technology Productivity Awards.

ELS has enabled the ATO to deliver on its promises to the public
to improve efficiency and service: in its first year it reduced the
turnaround time for mailing refunds from an average of ten weeks
to two weeks in 80 per cent of cases. ELS has also been an
organisational success in that it was developed through highly
participative methods. It saw through changes to job and work
design (building on prior experience with Office Structures
Implementation) that have contributed to further changes that point
the way to the 'ATO of the Future'.[1] But the Electronic Lodgment

Service must not be oversold; in effect, it represented an automation of the existing paper-based returns processing system, rather than a leap forward in integration of tasks with computer systems.

It is the external dimensions of ELS which have been such a success—the relations with tax agents and the improved turnaround time. How exactly was this achieved? ELS is a nationally integrated computer network that allows tax agents to prepare and lodge their clients' tax returns electronically instead of through paper-based traditional returns. The system allows tax agents to transmit individual tax returns directly from their computers via an electronic network to the ATO's systems.

The system was trialled in South Australia in successively larger steps from 1987 to 1989. ELS went national late in 1989, commencing formally on 1 July 1990. In its first year, it involved more than 3000 registered tax agents who were expected to lodge around 1.7 million tax returns electronically. In the event, almost 3 million returns were lodged electronically in 1990/91, which is over 30 per cent of the total returns lodged that year and just on 50 per cent of the returns lodged by tax agents. A total of 3800 tax agents have become involved. For many of them, ELS has been their first introduction to computerisation. This is an unheard of degree of penetration for a new system.

The mode of introduction of ELS was a classic piece of sociotechnical trial and evaluation. A small trial commenced in South Australia in 1987 involving one tax agent lodging 150 returns. The volume increased in 1988 with more tax agents participating and lodging 27 000 returns. These trials were critical in ironing out bugs in the system and in testing its feasibility.

During the first year of trials in Adelaide, for example, it was noted that there was a high incidence of errors in the electronic data transmitted from tax agents, and that the ATO staff were engaged in a great deal of verification work that would be sufficient to 'gum up' the whole system nationally if not corrected in advance. The solution adopted was to 'tighten up' the software specifications produced by the ATO. Initially these had been fashioned purely to structure data from the tax returns; they were now expanded to embody cross-referencing and internal consistency checks. This meant that simple transcription errors could be picked up in the tax agent's office prior to transmission, and the ATO was thus presented with 'cleaner' data through transmission. Further refinements led to some of the ATO's own edit procedures being embodied in the software packages sold to tax agents.

This approach carried the ATO into a closer relationship with the software suppliers, working with them to achieve standards for software packages that were both fair and which met the ATO's requirements. This was a novel experience for both the ATO and the software industry in Australia. It also involved the ATO in closer liaison with tax agents themselves which also had spin-off effects in terms of greater mutual understanding. This generation of techniques and procedures with commercial ramifications has become characteristic of the Modernisation Programme, bringing the ATO to the fore of commercial innovation in information technology. ELS also demonstrates the impact the ATO has had in diffusing computer innovation through the Australian services sector. In this way it has demonstrated flexibility in adopting the new information technology as predicted by the paradigm shift mentioned in Chapter 3. The ATO is now becoming a fifth paradigm organisation.

ELS represents a major transformation of the returns processing function of the ATO, which constituted the core, or 'factory', of the previous organisational system. Before ELS, all returns had to be lodged on paper forms; it took ten to twelve weeks to issue assessment notices, and often far longer. The jobs associated with returns processing had been fragmented, repetitive and boring, with high rates of staff turnover. With ELS, the turnaround time was reduced to two weeks for more than 80 per cent of tax returns lodged electronically. An added benefit is that the turnaround time was also reduced to an average of six weeks for 50 per cent of the remaining paper returns. Returns processing staff throughout Australia have been reduced from around 3500 to around 2800 (a twenty per cent reduction) and a large proportion of staff are being used more creatively, such as to solve problems that ELS cannot handle and to provide a more responsive service to taxpayers and tax agents. Displaced staff have been redeployed within the ATO.

The achievement of ELS, and the wider changes associated with modernisation, are all the more remarkable when set against the moribund state of the ATO a decade ago when it languished through government neglect and sought efficiencies through computerised automation using mainframe systems and the familiar functional division of labour.[2]

THE AUSTRALIAN TAXATION OFFICE: ORGANISATIONAL BACKGROUND

The ATO is required by various acts of the Australian Parliament to collect taxes. This makes it the core agency that drives the rest of government.[3] Its vicissitudes in the post-war years have reflected the vicissitudes of Australian democracy itself.

In the post-war 'golden years', the taxes in Australia seemed more or less to collect themselves; no special competence on the part of the ATO was called for. However, as people became more affluent, paying taxes fully and fairly came to seem old-fashioned, and tax evasion schemes multiplied. The dark years of tax evasion reached their nadir in the late 1970s and early 1980s, when the ATO itself suffered a crisis of demoralisation, inefficiency and loss of direction. So too in the wider polity, as Australia was racked by serious disputes and bitter confrontations.

Over the past decade, all that has changed. New laws and regulations have clamped down on tax avoidance and tightened up collection systems, while the national mood has turned against the get-rich-quick mentality that induced frauds like the 'bottom of the harbour' schemes publicised by the 1983 Costigan Royal Commission. This new sense of social solidarity has been reflected in a renaissance within the ATO itself, which is now actively overhauling its collection systems, its management procedures, and its staffing arrangements in a complex sequence of organisational projects called the Modernisation Programme.

Central to the changes is a new confidence in building an organisation on foundations of efficient and effective use of information technology. Over the ten years 1989 to 1999, the ATO is committed to expenditure of $1.2 billion to realise this ambitious programme. In another society such expenditure might be channelled towards surveillance systems to spy on citizens or staff (or both), whereas in the confident, thriving Australian democracy it is creating a world-class, sociotechnically-aware organisation of skilled staff utilising computer systems as tools to better serve a public that is given every facility to pay the taxes that are due. These tools provide new avenues for payment, such as through electronic lodgment and electronic transfer of funds, new avenues for taxpayer service, such as through rapid turnaround in producing assessments and rapid response to queries regarding the status of lodged returns, and new avenues for efficient audit to identify and crack down on cheats while giving every support to those citizens who pay their due.

MODERNISATION AT THE AUSTRALIAN TAXATION OFFICE

What then is notable about the ATO modernisation story? What makes it worthy of extended attention? One factor is certainly the

233

scale of the changes. By any standards, the ATO Modernisation Programme is large. It involves an organisation with just under 20 000 staff, processing of over 12 million tax returns each year, involvement in over 80 million transactions each year, and entering an era of full utilisation of information technology. This is a big ship to turn around. A nationwide network of 10 500 computer terminals has already been created—the largest in the world—and the network is due to get larger as the ATO develops its vision of a single, integrated electronic taxation system accessible by fully-trained and multi-skilled staff from anywhere in the country. It is big in terms of its time-frame—a programme planned to last ten years, from 1989 to 1999. It is big in terms of its budget, with expenditure of $1.2 billion allocated to it over the ten year period of modernisation (comparable to the current operating budget of the ATO, which stands at $1.16 billion per year, of which $0.6 billion is spent on salaries—all expended to collect tax revenues of $77.5 billion per year).

A second factor is the *contrast* between the organisation today and what it was only a few years ago, and the even sharper contrast with what it will be in 1999. In the early 1980s, the ATO would certainly not have been seen as a candidate for revolutionary organisational innovation. The public record tells the story, warts and all. Years of tax evasion in Australia had left the organisation in a state of demoralisation. In 1983/84, the level of outstanding, uncollected taxes stood at 26 per cent of the collectable revenue (compared with only fourteen per cent today); the backlog of disputes choking the courts stood at over 100 000 cases (compared with fewer than 2000 today); the turnaround time for assessments stood at around five to six weeks on average (and much longer in some cases), compared with the fourteen day target met in over 96 per cent of cases lodged electronically today.[4]

Internally, the ATO was close to breaking point. It was adding new computer systems to an increasingly rickety structure. In the fashion of the 1960s and 1970s, these systems were hierarchical, centralised and insulated from the rest of the organisation, accessible only through computing specialists and armies of data processing operators who made up an increasing proportion of the swelling ATO staff numbers.

I visited the ATO's Melbourne office in 1982 and saw for myself the conditions that led to widespread worker alienation and stress, and ultimately to the breaching of physiological limits with the appearance of repetitive strain injuries. Data processing operators were goaded to work at unnaturally fast speeds (over 12 000 keystrokes per hour) through work systems that provided the excuse for introducing electronic monitoring through which every pause and departure from set routine was recorded and subsequently analysed.[5] The ATO was not alone in installing these systems in the early 1980s but it took them further than most, and the battle with the unions over repetitive strain injury and its prevention, as well as the compensation of sufferers, was fought harder in the ATO than almost anywhere else. A watershed case in 1985 was fought almost to a standstill, with the Commonwealth going to extraordinary lengths to prevent a precedent case being established, and the Tax Officers Branch of the Federated Clerks Union almost bankrupting itself to pursue the case and the cause. After this, both sides realised that there must be a better way of utilising the new information technology. These were the bitter origins of the current approach to modernisation.

Externally, new demands on the ATO forced a re-evaluation of operating systems by senior management. The clamp down on tax avoidance led to the introduction of new taxes such as Fringe Benefits Tax and the Recoupment Tax (aimed at tax avoidance schemes that were eventually found by the courts to be illegal). Concern over the tax-avoiding 'cash economy' in the building industry led to the innovation of the Prescribed Payments Scheme. These innovations all required an ATO with efficient procedures, which was not being achieved with the internal tensions generated by the then current approaches. On top of this, the government elected to make life easier for taxpayers, encouraging them to pay lawfully due taxes through innovations such as quarterly rather than annual payment of provisional tax. This lightened the burden on taxpayers—but it made life that much more difficult for the already overstretched ATO which had to conduct four times as many transactions in order to collect the same volume of revenue from provisional taxation. These were the external pressures that led to the change of direction that is now called modernisation.

As predicted by organisational theory, a new champion of change was needed at the top to act as the vehicle for the profound adjustments needed. This champion emerged in the person of the new Commissioner of Taxation, Trevor Boucher, appointed in June 1984 for a seven year term. It was Commissioner Boucher who seized on the internal and external pressures, arguing that they could only be accommodated through fundamental changes to operating procedures and, more profoundly, operating philosophies. Artfully, he worked by persuasion, bringing in new people, setting up internal enquiries and investigations, and only moving to effect changes when a consensus, or at least the beginnings of a consensus, had been established—and then moving swiftly and decisively to install the new.[6]

Commissioner Boucher began his assault by confronting the core of the culture of the ATO: its assessment procedures. Here the bulk of the technical work was performed, with banks of assessors looking over tax returns but having the time to give them only the most cursory of glances. The Joint Committee of Public Accounts that looked at ATO procedures in 1985 reported on the assessment operations of the Sydney branch. The Auditor-General had found that of 1.8 million individuals' returns assessed in 1983/84, no more than six had been referred to the Compliance Branch for investigation or tax auditing. The Parliamentary Committee expressed its amazement that assessment was so cursory, and yielded so little return, and that it involved so little computerised assistance—even though, as noted, so much effort was expended in entering all tax return data into vast, centralised computer systems.[7]

It was this sorry state of affairs that the Commissioner and his senior executives tackled, not through requesting more assessors (the traditional approach) but through taking a radically different tack. Since it was impossible for the ATO to manually assess each and every return, and since there were no computer systems which could undertake this skilled task, the solution was to trust taxpayers to do the right thing, and in place of expending resources in futile assessment, it was argued that these resources were better directed towards taxpayer service (assisting taxpayers to do the right thing) and taxpayer audit (checking on a systematic basis that they were doing so). Thus self-assessment was born as a new operational concept in the ATO, backed by taxpayer service, treating taxpayers as clients rather than enemies, and taxpayer audit, targeted at the biggest companies and at strategic areas of known non-compliance such as failure to declare income from interest payments on bank deposits.

These changes were not wrought overnight. They involved confrontation with established procedures and culture. There were counter-revolutions staged to the Boucher initiatives but they were fought to preserve an inadequate past rather than through any conception of a better future. The counter-revolutions were extinguished. By a combination of direct argument and strategic appointments, by the formation of alliances among stakeholders, by bolstering his position with the use of consultants, and by using the damning evidence of public investigations (such as those of parliamentary committees) as ammunition in the campaign for change, Commissioner Boucher led from the front to execute a change in the culture of the ATO, thus laying the foundations for a change in structures and strategies.

The changes in procedures were accompanied by assaults on the narrow specialisations and fragmentation of tasks that had been engendered by the computer systems. The Office Structures Review launched by the second tier decision of the national wages system in 1987 led to a review, covering the entire public service, of narrow jobs in clerical work, and was seized on within the ATO to initiate wide-ranging participative job redesign exercises. The unions were embraced as partners in these exercises, thus overcoming another bitter legacy from the past. Structural barriers to promotion, such as the Section 33A impediment to ATO clerical staff advancing to technical positions, were tackled head-on as part of this exercise and, again in the face of considerable resistance, the barriers were removed. Thus keyboard staff were offered new opportunities to broaden their skills, and career paths were opened up, supported by a series of skills formation initiatives such as the Taxation Officer Development programmes and the Australian Taxation Studies project at the University of New South Wales.

These procedural, job design and skills formation initiatives provided the context for a novel approach to the redevelopment of the ATO's antiquated computer systems. What started as a purely technical review of hardware systems in the early 1980s, went through successive transformations to become a fundamental reconceptualisation of the purposes and functions of the ATO. Again leading from the front, Commissioner Boucher dismissed computer reviews that merely offered tinkering solutions, and instead brought in new staff and ideas from outside to provide the heavy artillery in a programme of total redevelopment. Cabinet approval was sought and obtained in 1987 for a major upgrading of equipment and systems (as urged by parliamentary enquiries) and thus the ATO was launched on a new technological trajectory. Its novelty was demonstrated at the outset in the fashioning of a most unusual Request for Tender document issued in August 1987.

This Request for Tender broke with tradition in several ways. Rather than the usual specification of certain items of hardware and software, it called for functions and objectives for a new system and invited tenderers to explain how they would meet these objectives.

237

This brought tenderers into the ATO for extensive discussions, making them privy to internal problems and procedures in order to facilitate their offering more competent service. Above all, the document broke with tradition in calling for a total system concept, with new products such as mainframes, terminals, network elements and software all contributing to an over-riding set of core functions and capacities. These requirements were spelt out in the Request for Tender in ambitious terms:

- the development of a single taxation system integrating existing revenue lines and to which new revenue lines could be added as needed;
- the provision for staff access to this system through terminals located all around the country;
- provision for staff to obtain access to all aspects of the system from their own terminal, to enable them to concentrate on client (taxpayer) service;
- provision of the ability to obtain a consolidated picture of the taxation affairs of a taxpayer across different revenue lines;
- the move away from batch processing towards on-line processing by staff themselves; and
- provision for management information systems such as accounting functions and personnel systems as part of the system redevelopment.

After extensive evaluation, the redevelopment and re-equipment tenders were let to the Computer Power Group, which in October 1989 entered into a joint endeavour with the ATO to provide a massive injection of new information technology along the lines of the philosophy specified in the Request for Tender. These were the formal beginnings of a series of projects now called modernisation.

THE ELEMENTS OF MODERNISATION

The Modernisation Programme has evolved along a number of dimensions. It has included features such as providing for a constitutional foundation through enabling agreements, basing redevelopment on participative project management, and developing an innovative systems design framework. Let us explore these three features in greater depth.

Enabling agreements

From the outset, the entire project has been covered by agreements with the major stakeholders, in particular the government and the ATO employees. The government, through the Department of Finance, negotiated a ten year enabling agreement on financing with the ATO, through an exchange of letters in August 1989, allowing both sides to plan their commitments well in advance but building in flexibility through the capacity to advance or retard particular financing elements. This 'Resource Agreement' is itself seen as highly innovatory by informed public service circles.[8]

Prolonged discussions with unions over the lineaments of modernisation, taking the Office Structures Implementation programme as a starting point, led eventually to the negotiation of an enabling Modernisation Agreement with the Public Sector Union in March 1990. Again this was a pioneering step, being the first Section 115 enterprise agreement to be certified by the Australian Industrial Relations Commission applying to the Commonwealth public service. This agreement defined the aims of modernisation, gave guarantees of no redundancies arising from the modernisation process, and spelt out the consultative and participative structures that would be established to ensure maximum staff input to the redevelopment process. It embodied the spirit of award restructuring in spelling out key objectives of job redesign and the reorganisation of work.

These agreements subsequently provided the constitutional foundations for the Modernisation Programme and were the instruments through which the principal stakeholders protected their interests and ensured their contribution to the process. The agreements established that modernisation was to be an inclusionary organisational process rather than one based on coercion and exclusion of affected parties.

Participative project management

The Modernisation Programme is an umbrella plan containing details of the scope, objectives, milestones and inter-relationships of over 130 projects identified as falling within the ambit of the programme. These projects extend beyond the business systems redevelopment to encompass building and accommodation issues, as well as a wide range of standards and guidelines (e.g. covering security, internal audit), management procedures (management information systems) and people issues (training and skills development, participative work and job redesign, employment impact assessments, personnel reporting).

From the outset, the ATO has approached the Modernisation Programme as an organisational learning experience, with carriage of the major projects being entrusted to multi-functional teams operating out of branch offices and the national office. Thus project teams have been established to investigate and report on such issues as systems design (for example, client registration spanning revenue lines), systems integration (for example, experimenting with client-focused teams handling all aspects of business taxes in a particular geographical area) and systems development (for example, experimentally evaluating alternative approaches to the delivery of a particular service, as in the Integrated Processing and Services project).

The teams are accountable at branch office level to their local branch office steering committees, established under the Modernisation Agreement, and nationally to their project steering committees. All projects are overseen ultimately by the ATO's board, chaired by the Commissioner.

This is a distinctive approach to organisational change, showing a high level of trust in the ability of staff to manage complex projects and deliver outcomes on time and within budget. While there have inevitably been a few hiccups, the process has worked so far with astonishing efficiency. Its strength, and the source of its superiority to a coercive, top-down approach to change, is the consensus it builds in favour of the adopted policy, and the rapidity of implementation once the consensus policy is ratified.

Systems development framework

The technical goal for the redevelopment of the ATO's computer systems was identified in the Request for Tender document as a single system integrating the key features of the present revenue processing systems and accommodating any future tax systems that governments may develop. This goal has come to be articulated in the ATO's technical documentation as the 'target system'; it is to be approached by an ingenious 'tacking strategy' that started in July 1993 and gets closer and closer to the full system each year until completion in 1999. Along one axis, work proceeds to develop the core functions of the target system, such as comprehensive registration of taxpayers to enable them to be tracked across different revenue lines, and full accounting systems computing revenues across different revenue lines in uniform formats designed for ease of reporting. Along another axis, work proceeds to adapt the different revenue lines, or collection systems, to these core functionalities.

The 'tacking' strategy works like this. In July 1993, a subset of core functions (including client registration) was to be introduced for a subset of taxes, namely PAYE and Sales Tax. The next year, this would be extended along the collection systems axis to include Income Tax. The year after, it would be extended along the functional axis to incorporate more functional features. In this way, the operating system tacks in zig-zag fashion, like a yacht coaxing impetus from a breeze, between the two axes, getting closer at each step to the full target system. As this process unfolds, the existing systems have to be interfaced with the emerging target system, without contaminating it. With a system the size of that being operated by the ATO, this is a technological challenge of the first order. The 'tacking strategy' is illustrated in Figure 11.1.

All the elements of the Modernisation Programme come together in this mature version of the redevelopment strategy. Each module of the system is designed through participative processes, with full user involvement providing the means to anticipate future problems and to design in 'user-friendliness' at the outset. This makes for high staff morale as well as for organisational efficiency.

Confidence in the achievement of the projected timetable for redevelopment is founded on the success of early modernisation projects. There was the Electronic Lodgment System which opened up the existing income tax system to electronic data input beyond all expectations. There have been other projects such as the Office Automation System (OASYS) which provided software tools to staff using the thousands of new terminals located throughout the ATO, and which has accelerated computer literacy to the point where staff are impatient for the fruits of full redevelopment. At the conclusion of modernisation, they will have full on-line access to the integrated taxation system through their own terminals.

There have been dozens of singular initiatives and achievements as part of modernisation but perhaps none reflects the spirit of the process as well as ELS. It was also one of the first of the redeveloped systems, achieved before there were any working computer tools which have since made life easier for project teams.

THE ELECTRONIC LODGMENT SYSTEM

As we have seen above, ELS involves the preparation of individual

Figure 11.1 Australian Taxation Office: 'tacking strategy'

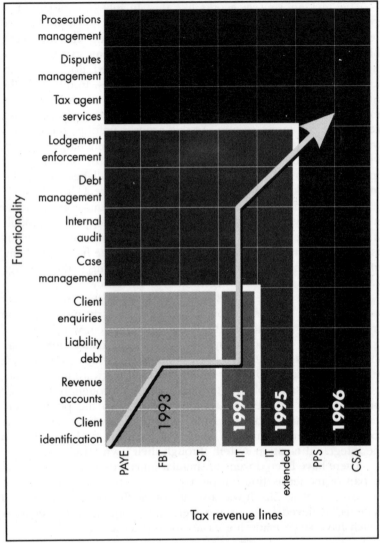

Through the Modernisation Programme, the ATO is set to achieve the 'target system' covering all tax lines and all tax functions, by 1996.

income tax returns on a tax agent's own computer and the transfer of data to the ATO via electronic means.

The ELS processing system controls the movement of data from the lodged tax return through the ATO's processing systems, creating an 'electronic highway' along which data sets move into and out of the National Taxpayer computer system, taking the place of the paper chain which originally constituted the Returns Processing system. Staff gain access to the tax returns data within the ELS processing system through their own terminals, in exactly the same way that staff gain access to returns which have been keyed in to the computer system by ATO operators, for purposes of controlling discrepancies, gathering statistical data and other functions. Eventually the 'highway' leads to the ATO's Automated Document Despatch facility, which prints and despatches the taxpayer's assessment notice. In the meantime, the details of the assessment have been stored in an electronic data bank from where they can be retrieved in the event of any query such as from the tax agent, the taxpayer, or from audit.

The technical scope of ELS

The technical problems involved in moving towards electronic lodgment were formidable. Early experience was obtained from a visit to the USA in 1985 where electronic lodgment was being planned by the Internal Revenue Service, stimulating thought as to how it could be done in Australia. Tax agents were also increasingly using 'computer generated' tax returns for their clients and lodging them in this form instead of on standard ATO stationery; a small market for software used in preparing tax returns had been created and was serviced by around 60 software suppliers in Australia.

As in the Modernisation Programme overall, technical debates at the outset of the ELS project carried strong organisational overtones. The Information Technology Systems Group argued strongly for the connection of ELS direct to the ATO's mainframe systems. The Modernisation Director argued instead that ELS should be seen as a 'one-off' venture that could be serviced in a 'stop-gap' way by Prime mini-computers set up in key branch offices. This was a more piecemeal option, but one which would allow ELS to be developed quickly as a high profile project and act virtually as the flagship of modernisation proper. After all, it was argued, the general public didn't really care whether their tax return was being received by a mainframe in Canberra or a mini-computer in a local branch; what was important was that a return lodged electronically should be processed quickly and accurately. In this case the 'stop-gap' option was the one that emerged as successful, in keeping with the general preference of modernisation strategists for a phased and careful evolution towards the new systems.

Organisational issues

The ELS project has proven to be a trial run for the rest of modernisation in many ways, not the least significant of which is its organisational dimension. It was managed from inception to implementation by a cross-disciplinary project team formed for the specific purpose of getting ELS up and running. The team leader reported direct to the Commissioner, and was guided by a steering committee chaired by Second Commissioner Carmody.[9]

Organisationally, ELS stood alone. While it was formally part of the Revenue Collection Group, in effect it functioned as an independent project team or task force assembled for a specific purpose. Other functional groups had an interest in the way that ELS developed, and had their own people involved in the development team, directly or indirectly. In this sense, ELS resembled the project organisation and method used for developing new products in the most advanced areas of industry, such as in the automotive sector (a point we expand on below).

People issues

The jobs of thousands of ATO Returns Processing staff were affected by the ELS project; it was also their first taste of modernisation in action. On top of the job redesign experience of the Office Structures Implementation project which had followed a relatively 'open' agenda in 1988 and 1989, the ELS project called for further upheavals in late 1989 and 1990, following a strict timetable in order to be ready to go 'live' nationally in July 1990. There was an acceleration in the supply of computer terminals to staff sections designated as dealing with ELS and training to go with the shift to computer-based working. This in itself was a massive undertaking.

Nationally, ELS was expected to reduce staff requirements by around 725 in its first three years of operation, from 1990 to 1993. After that, staff savings were expected to be more modest. As mentioned above, all displaced staff were being redeployed within the ATO.

The biggest impact has been on the work of Returns Processing staff. In the beginning in some branch offices, ELS was separated out as a specific job, but it is generally now fully integrated with returns processing, which covers electronic and paper-based lodgment. Many staff have volunteered for ELS training and the jobs to go with them, leading to an upgrading of their skills and, in most cases, their classification levels.[10]

Fewer numbers are being employed within ELS than for paper-based processing, with the reductions being absorbed through internal redeployment. To date there has not been a major need for redeployment and the new skills acquisition that would go with it, although this is now coming to be more of an issue as ELS becomes widely accepted and takes over a majority of returns being lodged.

Although staff appear to have been coping with the rapid changes unleashed by ELS, nevertheless the pace of change appears to have been dictated more by a sense of political urgency than strict organisational requirements. The Public Service Union has protested at the rapid pace, arguing that it has created problems which would have been avoided if a more measured transition had been effected. Job design has also arguably been sacrificed in the rush to implement ELS, with the result that its operation can still be dull and unsatisfying. Nevertheless, all parties seem to be agreed that ELS has been a success as an indication of the power of modernisation, and that it represents simply a first step in a long journey of technical and organisational co-evolution.

STRATEGIC CHOICE OR TECHNOLOGICAL DETERMINISM?

There is a school of thought that holds that organisations merely reflect the technologies they adopt. Thus the choice to 'go with new technology' is held to carry certain necessary organisational implications. This was certainly a popular management point of view in the 1970s and 1980s. It informed the approach of Telecom, for example, in the installation of its computerised telephone exchanges in the 1970s, when its engineers insisted that maintenance functions had to be centralised under such an arrangement; they were forced in the end to recognise the validity of an alternative way of organising maintenance operations with the same technology that actually turned out to be more efficient.[11]

In the case of modernisation within the ATO, it is clear that organisational choices presented themselves at every stage of the process. Indeed, these choices were inescapable. For example, in place of opting for 'self-assessment', which after all is a gamble in favour of the public's basic honesty, the ATO could have pursued a policy of greater reliance on electronic surveillance of both tax-payers and of its own staff, in a bid to 'crack down' on tax evasion. This would have resulted in a very different approach to modernisation, utilising information technology as a routine, automated substitute for skilled work rather than as the interactive tool being developed in the current approach. Such an approach would be technologically 'brittle', and require a hard-nosed approach to personnel management as its complement. This would be little different from the position the ATO found itself in in the early 1980s.

The 'surveillance' approach would have led to further choices. In place of the network model adopted, with staff exercising competence at all levels in accessing the single, consolidated national tax system, the ATO could have gone down a very different path. It could have chosen the model of the 'dual' organisation, consisting of a small, professional core, serviced by a network of processing 'bunkers'. These bunkers, established in suburban or regional locations, away from the professional offices in central city locations, would perform all the document processing operations by semi-skilled staff exercising keyboard skills and little else. In this scenario there would be no continuity of career development between staff in the bunkers and those in the professional offices, with the implication that the bunker staff are seen as, and treated as, cogs in a larger processing machine.

This is the route being chosen by other Commonwealth public agencies, such as the Australian Securities Commission.[12] That it is *not* the route being chosen by the ATO can be attributed partly to the pressure from the staff themselves for job enlargement and variety, partly to the willingness of the unions to engage in discussions concerning productivity and efficiency, partly to the strong preference expressed by the unions that decentralised branch offices should perform a variety of functions, and of course partly to the leadership exercised by the Commissioner himself. In the end, the route chosen by the ATO reflects a macro vision of organisational efficiency combined with a micro approach to job design, all within the framework of a more advanced concept of management leadership.

Another option that the ATO could have chosen is the purchase of a 'black box' computer system off the shelf. Such a scenario would have had the superficial attraction of avoiding all the in-house development work that constitutes the Modernisation Programmes that some would call 're-inventing the wheel'. But it carries the implication that the adopting organisation learns nothing from the experience of change, and furthermore is tied to the procedures embodied in the software that runs the purchased system. Thus one set of rigidities is traded for another, and the purchasing organisation places itself in a position of permanent dependence on the vendor organisation.

Such an option was actually presented to the ATO at a critical juncture in the Modernisation Programme. In November 1990, the international consulting firm, Andersen Consulting, offered the ATO its 'Tax Administration Software' package. This package, developed by Andersen's in conjunction with the New York Department of Finance, embodied the procedures (and 'values' associated with them) of a different way of administering a taxation system. If adopted, it would inevitably have given the ATO's modernisation process a very different flavour.

In the event, the ATO's Management Advisory Committee rejected this option. In an all-day session on 27 August 1991, the Management Advisory Committee considered the report submitted by an evaluation team, the recommendations of a steering committee, and additional information previously requested. Eventually it was decided to reject the Andersen offer. The Management Advisory Committee concluded that it was 'preferable for the ATO to stay on its existing path of in-house redevelopment of its processing systems'.

This choice has been critical in maintaining the spirit of modernisation as an organisational learning experience, expanding the net of people affected by the process and thus able to contribute expertise and experience to the task of making procedures as efficient as possible.

These are just some of the most obvious organisational choices involved in the modernisation process. The idea that technology could actually determine organisational form is a fantasy concocted by theorists who have presumably never been close to a real process of change. In the case of the ATO, the technical and social choices have at each stage of the process been seen as 'separate but linked': the technical choices set the limits on what is available socially, but the social choices likewise set limits to what is feasible technically.

As a result of the choices made, the ATO's Modernisation Programme is leading in the direction of what it calls a 'learning organisation'. The ATO has a new face, characterised by:

- a new approach to offering efficient service to taxpayers through initiatives such as the Electronic Lodgment Service, over-the-counter payment of business taxes in Post Offices, and the decentralisation of branch offices with a commitment to maintain a spread of expertise in each;

- a new sense of staff involvement and empowerment, through the use of project teams for the development of modernisation initiatives, through the micro-approach to job design that blends technological and organisational considerations, and through the over-riding commitment to participative change embodied in the Modernisation Agreement and its implementation;
- a new capacity to audit taxpayer affairs, through intelligent use of computer tools such as income matching software packages;
- a new capacity to monitor and measure organisational performance through such achievements as the success of the fourteen day turnaround commitment with ELS, and the lower level of outstanding taxes in relation to total revenue collected; and
- a new approach to management development, offering organisational support and encouragement to managers prepared to rethink their role and meet the challenge of passing from being administrators to leaders of organisational change.

It is important to emphasise that all this has been achieved *before any of the core redeveloped systems have come on stream.* To date, the development work has been conducted through teams working with antiquated systems in largely batch mode; processing is slow, and usually involves waiting for responses overnight. Job redesign initiatives have been hampered by the failure of the existing systems to support initiatives such as teamwork. It is arguable that the potential power of modernisation could be felt only after July 1993, when staff had direct, on-line access to redeveloped systems for the first time. It would only be then, for example, that client-focused teams would enjoy full access to taxpayer information and be able to respond quickly and accurately to queries in the spirit of customer service that is pervading the ATO.

THE ATO MODEL OF ORGANISATIONAL INNOVATION

When the University of New South Wales study of modernisation at the ATO began, my interest was aroused by the prospect of studying an organisation in the throes of total organisational change. In the event, the ATO has exceeded even these grand expectations. The Modernisation Programme is unquestionably the most far-reaching, most visionary and most exciting project of organisational change ever undertaken in Australia. It is innovation in the best sense of the word: renewal of an organisation through its own participative learning processes. Our exposition has focused on the unique blend of technological, organisational and 'people-oriented' innovation that constitutes modernisation. Here in this final section we shall look briefly at the highlights of the process, in an effort to unravel the 'model' or set of procedures that can be said to characterise this remarkable programme of change.

I claim then that through modernisation, the Australian Taxation Office exhibits elements of world best practice in the way it has approached organisational innovation. It does this in a number of ways. Let me illustrate how by choosing six of them.

Client focus and segmentation

Within an astonishingly short span of time, the ATO has shifted its external orientation from one where 'the ATO knows best' and 'everyone is a tax cheat' to a situation where it goes to extraordinary lengths to enquire into the needs and aspirations of its 'client base', namely the citizens of Australia as taxpayers, and to develop a long-term relationship with them.[13]

The ATO has pioneered a totally new conception of its role, starting with self-assessment and moving on to audit and taxpayer assistance, using modernisation to deliver real improvements in service through such measures as electronic lodgment with its fourteen day turnaround time for assessment. This new approach to the taxpayer, as potentially cooperative and law-abiding given fair treatment and fair tax laws, has proven to be the essential prelude to the development of a new approach to the ATO's own staff.[14]

Continuous process innovation and 're-engineering' of work systems

Through modernisation, the ATO is perfecting an approach to innovation that draws in the first instance on the organisation's own staff, equipped with the skills and technical resources they need to make their contribution to change. There can be no better foundation than this for a 'learning organisation', that is, an organisation which embodies within the skills and experience of its staff an aptitude and capacity for responding to new and unexpected situations. It is this responsiveness that stems from a skilled and committed staff that provides organisations like Toyota with their competitive edge.

The ATO has made a choice, through modernisation, to utilise information technology as a means of extending the capacities of its staff, rather than bypassing them or eliminating them as is so frequently the option taken. In this, it is not merely 'automating' the previous processing procedures but 're-engineering' them through full utilisation of the integrating potential of information technology.[15]

In its service delivery organisation, the ATO is abreast of world best practice in its formation of *client-centred, complete-cycle cells.* Through the Collection Systems Modernisation Programme, for example, the ATO is moving to establish such teams or cells throughout its revenue lines, offering 'one-stop' service to clearly identified client segment groups. In this, the ATO parallels the experience of other best practice financial services organisations such as Colonial Mutual.

Continuous product innovation

The ATO is engaged in a constant process of 'new product development'. It is required to have up and running each year a new version of the income tax collection system, together with other tax systems that are modified or are introduced as new developments, such as the Training Guarantee. From this perspective, it is interesting to compare ATO organisational initiatives with those in firms already recognised as leading the way in new product development, such as Japanese manufacturers.

A particularly illuminating study of the practices of Japanese companies that have revolutionised their product development processes and turned them into a potent competitive weapon, has been published by Imai, Nonaka and Takeuchi (1988). They looked at the approach taken by Honda, NEC, Fuji–Xerox, Canon and Epson. They noted, for example, that:

> Product development breaks down the hierarchy or rigidity normally associated with Japanese organizations such as the seniority system or lifetime employment. Management gives the development team very broad but challenging goals as well as full autonomy to come up with something new. It uproots a competent middle manager from the hierarchical organizational structure and assigns innovative young talents to the team. Management gives unconditional support and legitimizes these unconventional moves by declaring a state of emergency or crisis . . . These changes are institutionalized within the entire organization until another crisis situation forces it to unlearn the lessons of the past (Imai et al. 1988, pp. 559–60).

It is surely striking that this could be read, word for word, as a description of the process followed within the ATO for the introduction of the Electronic Lodgment Service, and for each modernisation initiative thereafter. In the case of the ELS, the restraints applying within the conventional functional lines were overthrown in the formation of the original project team. The leader of this team was plucked out from his conventional position and given very broad latitude in recruiting bright staff and in working under pressure-cooker conditions to come up with a workable system for electronic lodgment. The whole of the ATO was placed on a virtual 'war footing' by the Commissioner to ensure the success of ELS. And so the parallels go on.

Hence I would claim that the ATO is engaged not in a process of 'modernisation' so much as in a transition to a permanent state of new product development, where the 'products' are new tax collection systems embodying features imposed on the ATO as a public body by Parliament and the courts. It is interesting in this context to observe what Imai, Nonaka and Takeuchi highlight as the organisational underpinnings of new product development in successful Japanese firms. They claim that the process is one of rapid organisational learning *and unlearning.* This is the essence of the creation *and destruction* of task-oriented project teams which are formed for the purpose of creating a new product and are then disbanded, with a totally new team being assembled for the next new product. It would appear that this is the path down which the ATO is headed. It represents a revolutionary new organisational form in Australia.

Continuous performance measurement

While some modernisation projects have developed means to monitor their own outcomes, the ATO as a whole has been moving steadily towards a new outward focus, measuring not just inputs (in classic Public Service fashion) but now measuring its outputs, such as cycle completion times (in ELS), tax collected as a proportion of collectable total, and responsiveness to client demands. Such continuous performance measurement combined with benchmarking against world best practice, is the hallmark of 'lean production' of goods or services.

The ATO is taking the concept further. Through modernisation, it is building performance measurement into its operating systems—not in the alienating spirit of surveillance of individuals utilised in the early 1980s, but in the spirit of providing performance feedback

251

to teams and to the organisation as a whole. Thus the new Accounting Systems being developed as part of modernisation will capture financial data at the point where it is entered, through ELS or through electronic funds transfer more generally, and feed this into accounting systems that will be structured to provide transparent reporting mechanisms for staff as well as public oversight agencies. At the micro level, new computer-based tools being introduced as part of modernisation, such as the Computer-Assisted Taxation Audit, generate data that are fed back immediately to the user, acting as an 'expert' extension of the professional skills of the auditor. This is world best practice design of computer systems.

Building equity into efficiency

Through its 'people policies', the ATO is using modernisation to lay the foundations for an organisation that will permanently seek its efficiency gains through the contributions of a skilled and committed staff. It is these 'people policies', with their emphases on continuous skills formation, the development of career paths, the opening up of positions to minorities, the development of jobs that challenge and fulfil, and the building of structures that allow for participation and involvement that have been critical. It is these policies that act as the best defence against a future shift in political direction that might seek to return the ATO to the dark days of a dual organisation, split down the middle into professional and processing staff, and divided further by computer-based systems that reflect and reinforce the separation. The further the ATO goes down its present road, the more solid becomes its foundation of people on which a flexible and efficient public agency can be built.

These are the features of the ATO operations, as transformed by modernisation, that constitute the relevant points of comparison with other organisations. Important as it is for the ATO to benchmark itself against the performance of similar tax collection agencies around the world (a comparison in which the ATO comes out looking very good), it is even more important for it to subject its individual operations, such as 'new product development', to comparison with the best practices in these operations around the world, no matter what kind of organisation utilises them. This in itself is 'best practice' benchmarking.

Sociotechnical design and experimental validation

Finally, we may note that through modernisation, the ATO has

252

developed a totally original approach to sociotechnical participative design of new work systems, and a means for their evaluation and validation that draws on the best practices of social science. In place of the incoherent and fortuitous pilot project experience that passes for 'experimentation' in most situations of organisational change, the ATO has instead developed a means for testing and evaluating the contribution of different factors to the success or otherwise of its change projects. We have already seen how this worked in the case of ELS. It has since been followed in numerous other modernisation projects as well.

In the Client Interface Project, for example, the project team developed a number of different approaches to the formation of client-focused teams for the administration of business tax revenue collection and then tested these different approaches under what amounts to experimental conditions through conducting parallel pilots in different branch offices, namely Adelaide, Hobart and Penrith. Common performance criteria were developed to measure the effects of structuring the teams according to different 'market segmentations' and according to the inclusion of different tasks within the teams. The results of these pilots were evaluated, thus feeding into the development of an 'optimal' configuration for such teams when the redeveloped computer systems came on-line in 1993. Rarely does one find an agency that goes about its organisational innovation in such a systematic and sophisticated fashion.

This approach to sociotechnical design is a demonstration of the power of *participation* as a means of getting things done efficiently and, even more importantly, as a means of tapping into people's creativity and providing a structure within which their contributions can be realised. It also provides an effective response to critics of the sociotechnical approach who see it as jaded, outmoded and unable to cope with the redesign of professional work.[16]

The experience of the Australian Taxation Office shows that the full power of the sociotechnical approach to organisational change is still being explored and indeed continues to be invented; it will itself be subject to a process of continuous improvement over the course of the 1990s, as the benefits flowing from its approach become more widely known.

Part 3

Sociotechnical organisational innovation

12

Industrial relations and organisational innovation
The costs and benefits of negotiated change

The stories of workplace reform and organisational change discussed so far are notable for the successes achieved. These are world class companies achieving world class performance. Yet it also has to be pointed out that these stories are exceptions.

The brute fact of the matter is that most programmes of organisational change are abject failures. They fail usually because the protagonists of change do not take into account the complexities of the process they are embarked upon. They fail to formulate clear goals, or to communicate the goals when they have them. They seek to impose new techno-organisational systems that have been bought off the shelf, and then rail against people's 'resistance to change' when the new systems do not perform to expectations. They fail to offer people basic reassurances to do with their employment, their skills, or their relevance.

In one major Australian organisation I saw a programme of change launched by a video from the chief executive, shown to all staff, in which he demonstrated why it was essential for the organisation to change, and how exciting the whole process was going to be. It was an energising, well produced message. In the final seconds of the video, he mentioned that, of course, there would have to be staff cuts. This change programme turned out to be a monumental failure, and its collapse cost the organisation dearly, resulting in lost market share and the loss of highly-skilled staff. A moment's reflection should have alerted the chief executive to the stupid mistake he was making in beginning a programme of change with threats of redundancy.

I claim that the programmes of change in our selected case studies have succeeded because of the clarity of the vision informing the reasons for the change, the openness of the approach taken to legitimising the change among the stakeholders, and the painstaking attention paid to the details of the change process.

At Colonial Mutual, the shift in the Client Services Division was informed by a clear vision of the new customer service teams and how their operations would differ from the existing 'production line' organisation of tasks. The whole process was driven by the design object of bringing staff into teams that would have a clear customer focus and sufficient control over a sequence of tasks to improve the level of service to that focused group of customers. The details of the change were clearly envisaged in advance and project teams assigned to tackle each facet of the programme.

The Ford Plastics plant clearly made a substantial commitment to grounding its workplace changes in structures of employee participation. At the plant, a clear strategic choice was made: the change programme was to be driven by quality enhancement. Hence the shift in emphasis from Employee Involvement teams to the Q1 (Quality First) teams with a work area focus. These teams have successfully retained the spirit of involvement inherited from the Employee Involvement teams, but transferred it, or refocused it, to the enhancement of quality in specific work area processes. At the same time, workers in these areas are being given greater scope to regulate, monitor and control the quality of their own work. This is a powerful strategy in which twin components converge on the work area and the need for team cooperation to maintain and improve quality; it thereby lays the foundation for a successful shift to genuine 'on-line' self-managing teamwork.

The reason for the collapse of many change programmes is that they fail to make a connection between process re-engineering or restructuring and industrial relations. They fail, in other words, because they are not conceived of in terms of negotiated outcomes. Rather than seeing industrial relations systems as 'the enemy', in the successful cases the negotiating process is seen as one which fashions consensus and commitment.

Industrial relations systems provide the institutional framework within which production strategies and organisational change strategies can be negotiated and legitimated. If there is a single lesson to be wrung from the Australian case studies, it is surely that industrial relations can make or break programmes of organisational change.

It is easy to nominate examples of the ways in which traditional industrial relations can frustrate the best-laid processes of organisational renewal. Wage systems, for example, that reward individuals for their productive performance (such as the piece-rate payments which still dominate in the textile, clothing and footwear industries) operate on principles completely at variance with those which support the shift to new work organisation structures such as teamwork. It is impossible to get a group of people working as a team if they are all paid according to their individual efforts. Incentive payments systems were invented within the context of Taylorist, highly fragmented work organisation systems, in an effort to motivate people to work hard in conditions where job satisfaction is zero. They simply have no place in the new workplace culture; indeed, their continuation actively frustrates the achievement of a new, collaborative productive culture.

Union demarcations offer another well-known obstacle to the introduction of cross-functional teams. While firms created the job divisions in the first place, along with the standardisation of labour, unions were able to 'colonise' the divisions and now defend them vigorously. Again firms need to find innovative ways around this legacy from the mass production paradigm if they are to navigate their way to the new workplace culture.

The chief impediment to organisational renewal bequeathed by mass production industrial relations, is the low trust it engendered between employers and their workforce. In extreme cases, unions stood in the way of employers even communicating directly with employees (such as on the waterfront and in the construction industry, but also in several parts of manufacturing industry). The mass production paradigm promotes the kind of bargaining situation where the only issues are pay levels and immediate working conditions (leaving aside questions of skill, work organisation, technology, and work culture); the protagonists are unions and employer peak councils whose officials engage in ritualised confrontations, leaving employees to play the role of shock troops to be called out whenever the unions feel a little pressure needs to be applied. In such a situation, trust could not be allowed to grow and complicate otherwise clearcut hostilities.

The Australian case studies provide plenty of rich examples of these kinds of industrial relations at work in the past. In Australia Post and the ATO, efforts were made to mechanise and automate operations in the early 1980s by driving ahead along technologically supremacist lines, marginalising union representations and provoking ugly disputes that sometimes dragged on for years, totally frustrating the change programmes.

Against these negative examples, the case studies provide examples of how industrial relations can facilitate the process of organisational renewal. It does this by providing a negotiated and agreed framework within which the details of work organisation, skills formation and technology may be changed.

Teamwork arrangements were explicitly the subject of innovative industrial relations agreements at both the Ford Plastics plant and at Colonial Mutual. In both manufacturing and services, the same issues needed to be resolved: the scope and timing of teamwork arrangements, the composition and cross-functionality of teams, team members' control over such matters as work allocation, performance monitoring, and personnel issues (their degree of self-management) the training to be offered, and other such issues.

Work organisation arrangements more generally were the subject of numerous industrial agreements. At Ford, Colonial Mutual, Australia Post and the Australian Taxation Office, previous fragmented job classification systems were reformed as the prelude to major organisational change. This was effected through the arrangements handed down nationally by the Australian Industrial Relations Commission, through its various wage-fixing principles such as the Restructuring and Efficiency Principle (the 'second tier') in 1987, followed by the Structural Efficiency Principle ('award restructuring') in August 1989, and the Enterprise Bargaining Principle of October 1992. It was the Structural Efficiency Principle, in particular, which provided the framework within which new skills-based job classification systems were negotiated and implemented in these organisations.

Skill formation arrangements were explicitly the subject of industrial agreement in a number of cases. At the ATO, as an extension of the Modernisation Agreement, new skills and training modules were developed via negotiation, with agreements reached on Tax Officer Development training modules Level One, and then Level Two, and so on. At Colonial Mutual, a link between competencies and job classifications was explicitly developed, and displayed in a job classifications/competencies matrix (as discussed in Chapter 3). In the automotive industry, Ford Plastics' extensive negotiations resulted in an agreed production workers' qualification which was to be recognised throughout the industry, in the form of the Vehicle Industry Certificate (see Chapter 3).

Technological change was the subject of negotiation and industrial agreement in a number of cases, notably at Australia Post and the ATO, where the whole project of change was encompassed in the Modernisation Agreement. This comprehensive agreement (the first 'enterprise agreement' negotiated under Section 115 of the federal Industrial Relations Act) provided the structures and processes to be followed in the change programme; in addition it offered basic guarantees of employment security (within the parameters laid down by the ten year Resource Agreement negotiated with the Department of Finance) and skills upgrading.

Unions showed that they can play an important role in all these change programmes. After coming in from the cold where previous 'mass production' attitudes had cast them, they were able to play a positive role in terms of diffusing an understanding of the change process, providing a means through which options could be tested and explored, and in some cases, an avenue through which support for change could be mobilised. At the same time, unions were able to exercise their strength and influence outcomes, such as at Australia Post where they ensured that video coding was discarded as an option.

Industrial Relations and the New Workplace Culture

It is clear, then, that industrial relations, and unions themselves, can play an important role in facilitating organisational change. This has been achieved through an extension of the traditional negotiating arena to encompass such issues as skills formation, work design, and the introduction of new technology—matters previously covered by managerial prerogative, or by the emerging profession of human resources management (where they are treated as non-negotiable issues). Indeed I claim that organisational renewal, and the rise of new production systems, has led to the extension of the very idea of industrial relations, so that we can now talk meaningfully of a shift to the industrial relations of skills formation, or the industrial relations of technological change, or the industrial relations of job design.

The industrial relations of skills formation, for example, is concerned with the negotiated procedures for the acquisition of skills and their component competencies, their standardisation, and the processes to be observed as workers acquire skills and claim recognition for their competencies.[1]

The industrial relations of technological change, in contrast, covers such matters as the negotiation of agreements concerned with change programmes, the consultation procedures to be employed, the reskilling to be involved; generally they deal with the issues raised whenever established procedures are to be dispensed with and new procedures introduced.

The industrial relations of job design covers such matters as the criteria to be respected whenever jobs are being restructured, either because of technological change or organisational change (or both). This is where sociotechnical systems have made significant contributions going back several decades (Emery 1974).

The extension of the industrial relations agenda in the case of best practice firms and industries, and by contrast its limitation within traditional collective bargaining arrangements (hemmed in as they were by the claims of 'managerial prerogative') invites us to set these industrial relations arrangements within a production system setting.

In line with the discussion given above concerning the influence of production system paradigms on production strategy decisions, I claim that we can refer to the *industrial relations of the mass production system*; to the *industrial relations of the lean production system*; and in the case of best practice, to the *industrial relations of the sociotechnical production system*. Let us establish the comparisons, to make these abstractions more precise.

Industrial relations and the Mass Production System

The canonical principles governing industrial relations in the MPS start with the standardisation of labour, that is, with Taylorist work organisation systems that break jobs down into meaningless fragments calling for task coordination to be provided through professional groups and supervisory hierarchies. Thus the classic ingredients of an MPS industrial relations collective bargaining agreement are:

- narrow and numerous job classifications, based on machines rather than skills;
- wages geared to individual performance and job classifications;
- standardisation and specification of conditions of employment, with anomalies to be processed through complex grievance procedures;
- concentration of skills formation in one-off 'front-end' training programmes such as apprenticeship, and defence of such skills through strong union demarcations; and

- limitation of the sphere of collective bargaining, with union interventions limited to disputes resolution and grievance procedures.

This 'ideal type' of the MPS industrial relations is given its clearest expression in collective bargaining contracts in the USA, but it is also expressed in Australian 'awards' handed down to cover entire industries by the industrial relations tribunals. We can see how such a system was functional within the MPS (given the recognition of unions, which was of course only very reluctantly conceded, particularly in the heartlands of American mass production): it established stable and rigid demarcations and procedures, and institutionalised the exclusion of labour from production decision-making. But the question that immediately arises is how efficient it might be in the context of changing production systems, when rigidity, standardisation and worker exclusion might not be so advantageous. The answer is clear: it is not efficient; indeed, it is a stumbling block to superior performance. Cases abound of companies in Australia which have failed in their attempts to install change because of their reluctance to tackle their existing MPS industrial relations system.

Industrial relations and the Lean Production System

The emergence of the LPS as a more flexible and innovative rival of the MPS, brought with it a characteristic set of industrial relations arrangements. Perfected first in Japan and still dominant in that country, they have become institutionalised as part of the national economy. The essential features of industrial relations under the LPS are:

- broad, skill-based job classifications (providing maximum flexibility in the allocation of workers to tasks and teams);
- enterprise unions (thus eliminating demarcations within the enterprise);
- seniority wages system;
- career paths for workers ('internal labour markets');
- worker involvement via Employee Involvement groups, or quality control circles; and
- employment security guarantees.

As Koike (1988) has subtly observed, this industrial relations system is essentially an extension to blue-collar factory workers of the conditions applying traditionally to white-collar workers; it represents the 'professionalisation' of workers. Along with the superior recognition and promotion of skills, the employment security guarantees and the seniority wages system, there was created an important element of commitment to the enterprise that underwrites all the improvements in quality, productivity and product and process innovation that are the characteristic strengths of the LPS.[2]

Industrial relations and the Sociotechnical Production System

Against the background of a widespread shift in production strategies undertaken by firms in the USA, Europe and Australia, major efforts have also been expended to broaden the narrow agenda of industrial relations, to encompass skills, work organisation, technology and culture, and to build trust and commitment into the system through institutionalising positive sum outcomes (in place of the zero sum features of the MPS system, where a win for one side was at the expense of a loss for the other).

The ideal form that the emerging industrial relations system has taken in innovative firms and sectors organised along STPS lines, features the following:

- broad job classifications linked to levels of skill rather than to machines or technology;
- skills formation made a central feature of negotiated arrangements, e.g. creation of career paths, skills acquisition, time off for training, etc.;
- work organisation arrangements made a feature of negotiated outcomes, such as explicit processes for forming and operating teams;
- wages based on skills acquired, as well as on group performance;
- participative structures used to complement and enhance the levels of responsibility built into new job structures;
- single bargaining units at enterprise level and enterprise-specific agreements; and
- national and sectoral standards providing a framework within which enterprises reach their own agreements on the above elements.

All these elements can be found in the Australian best practice case studies (with the exception of TCG, where the emphasis is on inter-organisational links). For workers, these arrangements offer obvious benefits such as an end to alienating and degrading labour, and a sense of involvement, commitment and responsibility. It spells the end to the 'psychosis of labour' that threatened workers in the meaningless jobs of the mass production system. For employers, the benefits are also substantial—in terms of functional flexibility, enhanced rates of product and process innovation, higher levels of quality assurance, and the improvements in measured performance criteria demonstrated in the case studies.

This is an industrial relations structure orientated towards innovation, responsiveness and flexibility through eliminating previous impediments (such as fragmented jobs and demarcations), and providing enterprise-level flexibility within a framework laid down at the national or sectoral level. It also encourages the trust and commitment needed to secure high performance production, by making both parties to the agreement dependent on its successful operation for their rewards. This is the cybernetic, 'feedback' feature of STPS enterprise agreements that is one of their most dynamic features. The agreement is predicated on its being implemented successfully, so both sides have an interest in ensuring that it *is* implemented in the way envisaged.[3]

It is worth commenting on the strong enterprise focus of the STPS industrial relations framework. The above characterisation, together with the model of skills formation in the new workplace culture exhibited in Chapter 3, brings to the fore the enterprise character of many of the categories involved in skills formation, job design and technological change.

While sector level and national negotiations can set overall standards and qualifications, the details still need to be worked out at enterprise level. This focus on the industrial relations of the STPS thus provides us with an unexpected but plausible explanation for the current trend in industrial relations towards enterprise bargaining. Most discussions of this matter take the 'rigidities' of the industrial relations system as their starting point and pose enterprise bargaining as a flexible solution to these rigidities.[4] This is what might be called the 'endogenous' explanation, locating the impetus towards enterprise negotiation *within* the present industrial relations system.

In contrast, the argument I am developing is 'exogenous', in that it locates the impetus towards an enterprise focus in the changes that are occurring in the production system, with shifts in industrial relations reflecting and registering these changes. This is a 'base' and 'superstructure' matter, dressed in new clothes, with the production system constituting the base, and the industrial relations system the superstructure; trends within the superstructure can be aligned with developments in the base. However it is not a determinist argument. Rather than the developments in the productive base 'causing' certain phenomena in the industrial relations superstructure, it is a question of developments in the base setting certain limits on what can be achieved through industrial relations, with strategy and the balance of forces accounting for the eventual negotiated outcome.

Let us return to the question of the frameworks, models or 'patterns' of industrial relations and associated theories of bargaining. Within standardised, low value-added production systems, where industrial relations is largely concerned with the resolution of matters to do with 'labour costs', there is little incentive for the parties to identify common interests, and indeed the process of negotiation is fruitfully modelled as a zero-sum game. In contrast, the industrial relations of skills formation creates a bias towards what Walton and McKersie (1965) have called 'integrative bargaining', or what Walton (1985) has more recently called 'mutual commitment', and I have called 'cooperative accommodation' (Mathews 1989c) since employer and employees have a common interest in the enhancement of productivity and efficiency.

The 'style' of negotiation within the industrial relations of the STPS is also distinctive. In the 1960s and 1970s, it could be argued that collective bargaining arrangements were predominantly concerned with revising labour contracts every few years, and were handled by industrial relations professionals on both sides of the negotiating table. STPS industrial relations, such as the negotiation of skills formation, in contrast, is a much more continuous, enterprise-based process, in which industrial relations professionals play a less significant role, and where traditional disputes such as over 'interests' and 'rights' become less relevant.[5]

Ultimately, it can be argued that in the new sociotechnical production systems, industrial relations is concerned with measures to enhance and reward productive efficiency. If this is the case, then theoretical frameworks devised for the description and analysis of industrial relations processes need to reflect this. For example, as much attention needs to be given in the new systems to the constitutional foundations of consensus, as was given in the previous industrial relations system under MPS to grievance and dispute handling procedures. This is not to abandon the notion of separate interests (for there will always be divergences between the interests of employees and managements, even in employee-owned firms); rather it invites us to focus on the collective aspects of skills formation and the other attributes of the new production systems, and on their susceptibility to collective resolution through bargaining (as opposed to individual resolution, according to managerial prerogative). This in the end is what industrial relations is all about.

A MODEL OF THE CHANGE PROCESS

Drawing together the threads of this discussion, I wish to present a model of the change process that is grounded in negotiation and agreement, providing it with legitimation. This model is based originally on the experience of Australia Post, and each step can be illustrated with respect to the OCR Project at Australia Post, but also with respect to the other successful programmes discussed.

The OCR Project is successful, and therefore provides more appealing guidance than that gleaned from unsuccessful programmes subjected to post-failure audit. It is also a special kind of process of change; it is a change stemming from a technological shift, demarcated in time and space, and involving one section only of the total organisation. It is therefore easier to pin down the essential features of the process of change than in more open-ended cases of private organisational transformation which dominate the literature on change.

A NINE STEP PROCESS OF CHANGE

We shall attempt to distil the essence of the Australia Post 'model' into a generalised nine step process, and then subject it to critical discussion in the light of the extensive literature on organisational change. The process is displayed in Table 12.1.

Step 1: Secure broad goals in a negotiated agreement

The overall goals of the process of change need to be spelt out, and the limits of the change demarcated at the outset, to define the process that people are being asked to become involved in. Guarantees need to be spelt out, such as job security, commitment to consultation, and a graduated approach to change (insofar as management has the power to give such guarantees). Without such matters being dealt with at the outset, the scope for mobilising the support and commitment of people who will be involved in the change programme is virtually nil.

In Australia Post this was achieved explicitly through the 'Modernisation Agreement' reached with the Australian Postal and Tele-

---

Table 12.1 Nine steps to negotiated organisational renewal

1 Secure broad goals in a negotiated agreement
2 Establish clear executive lines of responsibility and accountability
3 Underpin the process of change with promotion of a culture
   of Industrial Participation
4 Establish a mechanism for joint identification of options
5 Establish an overall negotiating framework
6 Establish regional and local implementation structures
7 Pilot all changes and subject them to evaluation and audit
8 Implement changes as agreed
9 Subject the whole process to review: this is how organisations
   learn

---

communications Workers' Union (APTU: now the Communication Workers Union) in 1985, and in its subsequent re-endorsements. An agreement negotiated with recognised staff unions carries more credibility with staff than a unilateral management assurance, no matter how well intentioned. Implicitly, Australia Post signalled that it was prepared to make the change to OCR a *negotiable issue*, not in the sense that it could be refused (for all parties agreed on its necessity) but in the sense that its implementation would respect the existing industrial relations frameworks within Australia Post, and use them to advantage rather than seeking to avoid them or get around them. In this way, the ground was prepared for wide-spread support.

Such an agreement need be no more than a few lines, spelling out the goals and establishing the broad procedures to be respected. But the value of such an agreement in granting legitimacy to the process of change cannot be overstated. In effect, such an agreement provides the constitutional foundations of the change process.

Step 2: Establish clear executive lines of responsibility and accountability

Organisational commitment to the change must be shown at the outset through the clear identification of executive accountability and responsibility. A top-level manager needs to be given respon-sibility and authority to go with it, to bring together the various elements within the organisation likely to be affected or able to make a contribution to the change. This is best done in the form of an ad hoc grouping, or task force, rather than through a line division which will end up 'owning' the change and seek to exclude the involvement of others.

In Australia Post this was achieved with the setting up of the OCR project team early in the process, and the designation of a senior manager, Mr Ross Lennon, as being responsible for its successful conclusion. The OCR project team was a textbook example of a task force, bringing together different kinds of expertise and acting as a rallying point for the rest of the organisation, without ever trying or being seen to try to take over line responsibility for the operation of electronic sorting equipment; that always remained the firm prerogative of the state administrations of Australia Post. Continuity of management on this task force was rightly seen as critical; in the event the senior people have all been involved continuously since 1986 or 1987. Thus the OCR Project provided all parties in the organisation, and particularly the unions involved in negotiating the details of change, with a constant reference point that was authoritative without being authoritarian.

If the initial agreement provides the constitutional instrument that guides the change process, then the second step establishes the executive powers and lines of responsibility needed to ensure that change actually occurs.

Step 3: Underpin the process of change with promotion of a culture of Industrial Participation through workshops and joint problem solving

Rather than simply establishing consultative committees, which is the common approach to change, it is far more effective to establish a cultural change at the outset by holding joint workshops with open agendas on the model of a 'search conference'.[6]

These workshops and focused problem-solving sessions break down the barriers that bedevil traditional industrial relations processes, and establish a degree of trust and reveal areas of common interest, prior to the initiation of formal negotiation. They can take place at appropriate levels, from the national, through regional, to local levels.

At Australia Post this strategy has been followed through in textbook fashion, starting with an Industrial Participation workshop held in May 1989, followed by 'OCR conferences' staged at state level (in NSW) and at mail centres subsequently. No-one started the OCR process with the thought that it could be made the vehicle for Industrial Participation, but as the process evolved it became clear that circuit breakers were needed to liberate the potential support locked away in the organisational hierarchy and the industrial relations 'divide'. Australia Post now has a vigorous programme of Industrial Participation underway, with coordinators in each state. It is significant that the participation process in Australia Post could rely for its fundamentals on the initial joint statement, and for technical input from the OCR project team. Thus Industrial Participation never became bogged down in rambling indecisive discussions, which is frequently its fate, and was always kept sharply focused on the technological process of change.

This step recognises that an organisational culture of participation must precede the pursuit of formal negotiations and procedures. There are many ways through which a culture of intolerance, suspicion and resistance can be created and sustained; unfortunately this is all too easy. But to create a culture of trust and participation requires vision and leadership from an intelligent and far-sighted management. This is a much more difficult task, but one which gives much greater satisfaction in its achievement.

Step 4: Establish a mechanism for joint identification of the major technical issues and options

The culture of participative change only gets into its stride as it engages with the real issues of identification and selection of technological options and associated organisational and job design structures. At the outset, the basic issues need to be identified and the values informing choices need to be explored, again prior to formal negotiations taking place. This joint exploration needs to precede the formal negotiation of the specific parameters of change. It is also the most difficult step for most organisations to accomplish, because it involves a sacrifice of the 'technical prerogative' that was formerly claimed by engineering departments.

At Australia Post this was achieved through widespread discussion, sparked by joint overseas missions looking at various technical options for electronic mail sorting, and various job design structures to go with them. This was no 'junket', but a hard-headed appraisal of the experience that the best postal authorities around the world had to offer. This produced a consensus view at the outset that was vital to the subsequent smooth transition to new ways of working. It established some options as essential, and killed off others such as video coding. The engineers were won to this formula in Australia Post by placing them in the role of consultants to the process, as part of the project but not driving it; this offered them full recognition of their technical expertise, and drew on it continuously, without ever forcing them to make the social choices which were previously taken implicitly under the banner of technical prerogative.

Step four recognises that meaningful participation is experienced in the details of change, not in the broad abstractions like 'empowerment' or 'devolution'. It also builds in the essential feedback quality of participation at the beginning, when technical and organisational choices are being made. While it slows down the process, it builds in correctives that could prevent enormous problems from occurring later.

Step 5: Establish an overall negotiating framework and use it to establish the 'milestones' of change

A formal negotiating framework needs to be set in place, in which the parties can present their agendas and negotiate the agreements or contracts which will provide the constitutional foundation of the change. This could be through established industrial relations procedures, or through a separately constituted negotiating committee. Such a process provides a means of tying together all the loose threads generated by the consultative mechanisms, gives direction to the process, and lends legitimacy to the efforts of the participants. What these 'development agreements', or 'change agreements' or 'joint statements' on the process of change achieve, is a spelling out of the agreed goals and scope of the process, the agreed processes and procedures, as well as the agreed substance of the change, in terms of jobs, skills, responsibilities, interfaces and such issues. It is this attention to industrial relations formalities that is missing from so much of the organisational change literature, giving it an air of unreality in the Australian context.

At Australia Post this formal process of negotiation was central to the success of the OCR Project. At every step, the legitimacy of the consultations and the planning was underpinned by formal agreement, which in turn legitimised the constructive involvement of the unions in the process of change. Negotiations were conducted initially under the auspices of the Restructuring and Efficiency Principle (the 'second tier') and subsequently as part of the Structural Efficiency Principle laid down by the national wage guidelines in 1989. The formal negotiation process was kept clear of the Industrial Participation process, thus allowing maximum cooperation and exploration of options, free of the responsibility to stick to rigid positions. However the negotiating framework provided a 'court of appeal' in which disputes generated through the process could be resolved.

Of course, this step can only be achieved if unions are prepared to take a constructive approach to the change process. If the ground-work has been done through the preceding four steps, then it is unlikely that such a constructive approach would be withheld. If it is, then a different strategy is called for.

Step 6: Establish regional and local implementation structures

It is essential to have channels for implementation that reflect local operating conditions, and which involve people at the level of their local working conditions. This builds flexibility into what would otherwise be a rigid top-down process of change. Local working parties operating within guidelines laid down through the agree-ments and structures established through steps one to five above, provide for flexibility in implementation and maximum involvement, consistent with national or overall goals and procedures. It thus achieves a blend of centralised direction and decentralised implementation.

This step was achieved at Australia Post through the setting up of OCR committees at state level and OCR implementation teams within each mail centre. Significant discretion was left to these bodies to organise things according to their own needs and proce-dures, provided they maintained consistency with the overall guide-lines that were developed nationally through the project and the formal negotiations. This discretion acted as a positive force for the process of change in two ways: it provided the flexibility that the national project could not hope to build into centralised plans; and it mobilised the interests and creativity of people at all levels of the organisation. Particularly at mail centres, this was expressed in some surprising and spectacular ways, as we saw in Chapter 9.

Step 7: Pilot all changes first and subject them to evaluation and audit before generalising the process

Steps one to six might be followed to the letter, and then the whole process ruined by attempting to implement change across the board without first 'testing' the model under real but controlled conditions. All change in an established large organisation is threatening, no matter how much consultation is involved, and it needs to be 'tasted' in small portions before the whole meal is consumed. Pilot programmes are therefore essential, as is their evaluation by independent assessment procedures.

At Australia Post this step was the subject of formal agreement; it figured highly in the Log of Claims presented by the APTU. It was achieved in various ways, such as through the setting up of mock OCR and flexible mail sorting systems workstations, to familiarise operators with the new technology, and through the running of pilot programmes in certain mail centres and subjecting them to independent ergonomic audit. The results of these were fed back to the various state and local working parties, and conditioned their finalisation of implementation plans. Again, Australia Post was able to accomplish a smooth piloting of the OCR process because of the established negotiating frameworks that allowed agreement to be reached on phased implementation. Thus feedback mechanisms were built into the process, allowing for corrective action to be taken without its threatening to bring down the whole process of change.

Exactly the same process of 'learning by doing' was evident in the introduction of teamwork at Colonial Mutual, and in the formulation of the Electronic Lodgment Service at the ATO. There are general principles of organisational learning in play here, which we shall explore in the final chapter.

Step 8: Implement changes as agreed and through the structures established

There is no point in establishing elaborate frameworks for the negotiation of change if the actual changes are then driven through in the time-honoured authoritarian fashion, under pressure of unrealistic deadlines, chief executive enthusiasm or some other intervening factor. The strength of participative change, that gives it an edge over its coercive rival, is that it secures acceptance of change in advance; it appears to be slow while issues are sorted through, but implementation can then be rapid and relatively problem-free. Coercive change, on the contrary, offers the illusion of rapid adjustment by crashing through the opposition that it generates, but it is followed by endless skirmishes and disputes that can prove to be crippling; they are avoided by the participative route.

At Australia Post the established procedures were followed to the letter, and the results speak for themselves. The transition to totally new ways of working has been accomplished in exemplary fashion. Considerable care was taken to ensure that commitments were honoured, particularly in regard to the modifications of the equipment demanded by ergonomic consideration, the training of operators and in the expenditure of funds in preparing mail centres for the changes. This is not to say that implementation at Australia Post has been trouble-free. But the bans and restrictive practices that bedevilled previous exercises in technological change at Australia Post were markedly absent this time. More to the point, the experience of cooperative accommodation established through the OCR process is now spreading its influence to other facets of work in Australia Post, laying the foundations for further efficiency gains.

Step 9: Subject the whole process to review: this is how organisations learn

An organisation learns from a successful process of change, but this learning can only be consolidated and disseminated if the process of change is subjected to adequate review by all the parties and forums established to facilitate the change. The change itself is a reflexive process, exerting its own effect on the existing processes and structures, giving them new content as the change is digested.

At Australia Post this has been achieved, not by staging some self-congratulatory conference, but by quietly maintaining the national, state and mail centre structures right through the process of change, rather than dismantling them after the first OCR was installed, and monitoring the acceptance of the new equipment and ways of working through systematic investigation and feedback to the various levels of the consultative structures. Thus the different parts of the organisation are learning from each other's experience. This has had some surprising effects. The success of the OCR Project has done much to enhance the reputation of Industrial Participation as part of the organisational culture at Australia Post, and to diminish the credibility of the 'crash through or crash' proponents of change. This is its real legacy to the organisation.[7]

SUPERIORITY OF THE NEGOTIATED CHANGE MODEL

Let us explore this model of change in terms of its costs and benefits. There are costs and gains associated with the issue of legitimacy and the participative approach to change. Just as some texts offer a detailed analysis of the 'costs of quality', meaning by this the costs associated with not achieving and maintaining adequate quality standards, so we might attempt to list the costs entailed in embarking on a programme of organisational change without seeking some form of mandate or legitimising the process in some way. In contrast, we might list the gains, in terms of organisational efficiency, flexibility, adaptivity and creativity, of placing the process of organisational change on a secure constitutional foundation.

The nub of my argument is that while there are costs to be borne by following the steps of this change model, there are organisational benefits flowing from it that ultimately far outweigh the costs. This participative model of change actually works; it delivers the goods. It is superior to models of change grounded in alternative concepts and values, such as top-down autocratic change delivered by a charismatic leader overcoming resistance and obstacles in a display of will and determination.

The top-down approach has its attractions. Apart from the gut feeling of satisfaction that company chiefs derive from barking out orders (the 'sex appeal' of top-down change, not to be underestimated), it does offer rapid development of plans and change that 'cuts through' tradition and resistance. But the costs are all too real, and are frequently borne by the organisation after the corporate hit man who implemented it all has moved on to other pastures.

The costs are felt in terms of inflexibility of the process (driven entirely from the top) and its non-adaptability; this can turn out to be a grievous cost if the plans are formulated to deal with a certain situation which actually no longer applies when the changes are implemented—an all too common occurrence. Organisational change programmes are big ships that need a lot of time and energy to change course.

Costs are also felt in terms of people's sullen lack of cooperation; their failure to offer ideas for a programme that is foisted on them, even when it has glaring faults that everyone can see; their rigidity in implementing orders to the letter ('working to rule') when it is clear that better ways are available. Frequently the status quo is maintained anyway behind the facade of the new forms, or it is actively undermined by middle level managers who offer apparent support to their 'leaders'.

These costs are well known; they are the stuff of nightmare case studies in the organisational behaviour literature. They are taken as revealing the 'difficulties' of change, and the 'resistance' mounted by otherwise rational people.

My approach, in contrast, is to characterise these costly programmes as the fruits of failed leadership. Crash-through programmes are implemented by managers who are afraid of dealing with people as equals; they are afraid of allowing people an involvement in the process for fear that their errors might be exposed; they are jealous of other people's accomplishments and wish to reserve all credit for themselves. The list of such failures could go on. This is what I was getting at in my cryptic character-isation of leadership as being the capacity to allow people to become involved.

From this perspective, what then are the benefits of a high-involvement process of change that is negotiated, agreed, and thus legitimated? The case studies illustrate both costs and benefits of the participative approach.

The most significant cost of participation is evidently the time it takes to reach agreement. At Australia Post, with its bitter prior experiences of technological change, the time taken to reach agree-ment was a constant issue in internal discussions. There was always a management party in favour of dropping 'participation' and going in with the heavy boot, and the longer it took to reach agreement on the fundamentals of the OCR process, the more this party gained a hearing. In the end, it was touch and go at Australia Post whether the participative approach would prevail; clearly the time taken to reach agreement was the maximum that the organisation could afford. At the ATO, there was more adroit leadership by the Com-missioner, and the agreements reached were correspondingly more comprehensive. But again it took time. Initial discussions over a Modernisation Agreement were stalled by the industrial relations 'old guard', attempting to secure agreement to a range of measures they had been pushing for years (such as freedom to move staff around the country, freedom to change rosters, and other elements of 'flexibility'). Even when this agenda was dispensed with, it still took several months of intensive negotiations to reach agreement, with the prospect of an election concentrating the participants' minds towards the end.

Another cost of participation is the danger of drift. This was avoided in most of our case studies by placing the participative arrangements firmly within an industrial relations framework, pre-cisely to anticipate and cut off drifting tendencies. But leadership is exercised in such anticipation and in making arrangements that keep drift under control, without sacrificing the underlying participation.

So participative change can take time in reaching agreement, and it runs the risk of drifting off the rails in the absence of active leadership to keep it on track. These are its costs. What of the benefits?

The case studies are in a sense testimony to the benefits of legitimated change. We may identify at least three such benefits in the measured performance superiority, reflecting:

- self-correction and adaptability;
- cooperation in the planning and execution of change; and
- rapid implementation.

Self-correction and adaptability

A participative programme of change is one which takes self-correcting action in mid-course. Unlike a top-down programme which is formulated by a group of managers and then 'rolled out', that is, implemented to the letter, which in cybernetic terms can be seen as a form of 'open loop' control, the participative approach offers the advantages of 'closed loop control', where feedback offers mid-course corrections.

This feature of change could be seen in the case of the ATO, where numerous corrections have been made to original plans as the experience of change unfolds, induced through the wider involvement of those who will be called on to implement changes. The introduction of the Electronic Lodgment Service was a classic example, where a number of different approaches were tried (for example, in lodgment procedures) within the participative framework.

Cooperation in the planning and execution of change

The change programmes are hard enough to manage in the best circumstances; when they provoke the active hostility and non-cooperation of the organisation's members, then change can only be effected through resort to coercive, dictatorial tactics, including the 'organisational terrorism' of threatened job loss.

If presented in a better way, the very same goals for change might command widespread support and people's full cooperation in the implementation process. The Australia Post example provides an outstanding example of this in the way that regional mail centres were not allowed to feel that they were simply implementing a programme that had been developed elsewhere, by having real control over their local environment built into the implementation process.

Rapid implementation

The feature of all the change programmes described is the rapid implementation once agreement was secured. At Colonial Mutual, for example, the process of planning and consultation was lengthy, but the implementation of the plans and the establishment of client-focused teams was in fact very rapid, given the scale of the changes envisaged. The reason for rapid implementation is not hard to divine. People who have participated in reaching a plan of action are committed to its success, and will work to make it a success— rather than as is so often the case, work to slow it down or sabotage it altogether.

What preconditions are called for if these benefits are to be realised in all cases? We may highlight some of the most obvious as:

- paying attention to hygiene factors;
- sharing of sacrifices; and
- offering representation to those involved.

Hygiene factors

Frederick Herzberg's insights regarding the necessity to attend to people's basic security issues (employment, remuneration, acquisition and practice of skill)—termed hygiene factors—prior to calling for enhanced levels of organisational commitment or self-actualisation, remain as valid today as when they were written in the 1960s.

The high-involvement model of change provides a means of ensuring that the hygiene factors will not be ignored. They can indeed be made a source or trigger for involvement, in a way which breaks down the mistrust engendered by traditional industrial relations. For example, a firm's senior management might establish their bona fides with the workforce at the outset of a process of major change by establishing a consultative committee (in itself a ho-hum initiative) and giving this committee the task of determining priorities for expenditure of funds to make the workplace safer and more congenial. Announcing a budget for such an initiative at the outset of the process, on a topic not normally seen as contributing to 'productivity' (although of course the link is very real), and involving the consultative committee in determining priorities, is a way of utilising the hygiene factors and building them into the foundations of the participative process.

Sharing of sacrifice

In any change programme, there will be winners and losers. Usually the losers are supervisors and middle level managers whose jobs

278

disappear as teamworking arrangements are introduced. The way that these potential losers are handled can make the critical difference to a programme's success or failure.

Colonial Mutual showed understanding of this issue in the way that existing supervisors were offered positions in the new structure, either as team leaders (after appropriate training), or as professional support, or as members of newly-formed teams. Those who didn't take to the new regime were allowed to 'exit with dignity'. It turned out in this case that many of the previous supervisors were only too happy to throw off their 'command and control' approach and move into a new role as team leader. In other cases, supervisors may not be so amenable. There are also other professionals such as maintenance staff, or laboratory staff, or software engineers, who do not see themselves as gaining by being required to join shop floor multi-functional teams. Again it is a question of leadership, and appropriate industrial agreement, to show such people the potential gains from the anticipated moves, and to minimise the personal losses involved.

Representation

The rallying cry of republican government and democracy was issued by the American Revolution: no taxation without representation. The insight was as simple as it was profound: those who were called on to support the state apparatus demanded a say in how that apparatus was to be run. Why has it taken so long for the same insight to work its way through the organisational change literature? The key issue is one of legitimation. Senior managers can issue no end of calls to action, challenges, even threats, regarding the necessity of change; however, it cuts little ice if the demands are unilateral. In any organisational change where people are going to be called on to make sacrifices (at the least, in terms of upheaval and dislocation; at worst, loss of jobs, skills or roles) it is a matter of the highest strategic importance to seek an agreed platform for the change, through the industrial relations process. Hence the nine step change model places this agreed position at the outset of the process; its significance lies in the legitimacy it grants to the subsequent process of change as a whole.

THE FUTURE ROLE FOR TRADE UNIONS

So far we have been stressing the positive role that unions can play in the negotiated process of organisational change, once they are seen as legitimate partners in the process. But unions are organisations in their own right, with their own goals and their own agenda for survival. What does legitimated organisational change offer to unions? There are two cases to consider.

In advocating collaboration at the workplace, I am not blind to the possibility that some employers will be unwilling or unable to cooperate with their workforce or their union. For such employers, there is only one 'best way'—their own way. In these cases, unions would be expected to deploy all the resources at their command to curb such employers' excesses. This is what I see as the proper role for union militancy in the era when sophisticated competitive strategies require sophisticated approaches to workplace cooperation. This role calls for the continued existence of strong, independent and well-resourced unions to act as a bulwark against employer malpractices, and to act as a vehicle for the democratic participation of their members in organisational restructuring.

The latter point raises the issue as to whether unions can expect to thrive in the new workplace culture, or will they 'wither away' in the era of collaboration. Because my perspective is grounded in organisational democracy, I see a proper and everlasting role for unions in providing the vehicle for the participation of workers in organisational institutions. But this means that unions themselves have to change quite drastically.[8]

Hierarchical union organisations were adapted to putting pressure on employers in wage negotiations (the essential industrial relations ritual of mass production) and offering no role to the membership other than that of being troops in an industrial army. These organisations have to change into participative structures themselves. Their workplace delegates will come to play more and more of a direct role as negotiations shift increasingly towards the enterprise level, while the union corporate office, and union officials, will come increasingly to play support roles. They will, in effect, come to act as consultants to the true change agents, who are the workplace delegates. But in the process—and this is the nub of my argument—the union itself grows stronger. It is no longer a brittle, top-down organisation, but an organic structure with a strong base and an infrastructure that can be called into play whenever needed. And by focusing its resources, it can play a strong policy-oriented role through the process of 'political exchange' at the macro level.[9]

This is already the pattern discernible in the case studies. At the

ATO, the PSU was initially a most reluctant partner in the process of modernisation, preferring to play its more familiar role of opposition. But this option was exhausted with the compensation battle over repetitive strain injury in the mid-1980s, and the union henceforth sought to play a role in influencing modernisation developments. It has done this so successfully that it is now seen by the ATO staff, and its own members, as an integral part of the process. The ATO has even gone to the lengths of funding the union's own research centre, URCOT (the Union Research Centre on Office Technologies) to help it provide an active agenda for the process of change and thereby help to prevent it running out of steam.

Similarly at Australia Post, the OCR Project came in the end to rely on union input for its successful diffusion to mail centre level, while at the national level, the union was able to focus its influence on the policy question of Australian manufacture of the new equipment—a position which was eventually acceded to. This was a perfect example of 'political exchange'.

In the private sector cases, unions have come out of the process of change stronger than when they entered it. In the case of Colonial Mutual, the union has achieved a measure of participation unprecedented in an industry notorious for its anti-unionism, while at the Ford Plastics plant and at Bendix Mintex, the union delegates were able to play a constructive role and bring their union with them, in an industry that had until recently a bloody industrial relations record. In both cases, unions have achieved industrial agreements covering the introduction of teamwork that are among the first of their kind in Australia. These place the unions in a position of strategic influence over subsequent developments in the evolution of the STPS.

I claim that unions have everything to gain by entering wholeheartedly into the new workplace culture and negotiating its transition. They lose their old militant posturing (while retaining their fire power for when it is needed, in cases of blatant employer recalcitrance) but gain instead an organic strength that grows from well-informed and committed workplace delegates who can make sophisticated judgments in balancing the interests of their enterprise with those of sectoral and national considerations. My argument certainly has no truck with 'company unions', which have no basis for making such judgments, and which can offer their members no resources other than those provided by the company itself.

This discussion brings us to another point, namely the role that unions play, and industrial relations frameworks more generally, in the economic performance of enterprises and nations. In the era of mass production, their economic role (real but rarely acknowledged) was to maintain purchasing power which in turn provided the mass markets that mass producers relied on. We have seen how this was a burden that unions could not bear on their own, and the mass production system spread rapidly in the post-war era only with the assistance of state-sponsored social security and income maintenance measures together with fiscal policies to iron out economic recessions.

In the era of the sociotechnical production system, what is the economic role of unions and of industrial relations systems?

MACRO FACTORS AND INDUSTRIAL RELATIONS

Industrial relations provides the setting or framework, I have argued, for the formulation and elaboration of change programmes at the enterprise level. But it goes beyond this. I now wish to claim that countries which have national and sectoral industrial relations systems enjoy a competitive advantage over those which do not, in the sense that such frameworks enforce the recognition of minimum standards. The economic advantages of this have long been overlooked, but they are now starting to be recognised. This brings us to debates over the shape of industrial relations systems, and the issue of 'deregulation of the labour market', which has dominated the turn to enterprise bargaining.

Industrial relations and polarisation: counter tendencies

One problem that is generated by the enterprise-focus of STPS industrial relations negotiations is the threat of polarisation. In the context of the new production systems, the emphasis on skills creates the potential to offer a privileged group of highly-skilled workers satisfying conditions, employment security and high salary levels, while excluding large numbers of under-skilled and underemployed people from such conditions. This is the threat of incipient polarisation, and it is already evident in countries where governments have not taken steps to combat it, such as in the UK.

The enterprise-specific mechanisms that promote incipient polarisation are enterprise-specific skills, internal labour markets, and stringent personnel policies covering recruitment and training. The counter-mechanisms that can be negotiated within a broadened industrial relations agenda include aligning enterprise competencies with public education and training curricula, accrediting enterprise training programmes to grant public recognition to their qualifications or credentials, and setting negotiated sectoral and national standards with which enterprise skills formation can comply.

Beyond these matters, it is open to governments and public authorities to intervene and ensure that the offerings of public education and training institutions meet the needs of the new production systems by ensuring, for example, that courses are offered in modular format, that they are aligned with enterprise offerings, and that they form generic skills which can then be adapted to specific requirements at enterprise level. This is the interface between the industrial relations and the politics of skills formation, as part of a politics of the transformation of production systems.

All these matters are central to the question of the diffusion of the new organisational models, and they highlight once again the central role played in this process by the industrial relations system. The same arguments apply at a more general level, in terms of economic outcomes for industrial sectors and for the country as a whole.

Influence of the industrial relations system on enterprise decisions

In the field of consumer behaviour, for example, it is now coming to be understood that active, alert and demanding consumers keep firms on their toes. As Michael Porter has argued in his *Competitive Advantage of Nations*, customers demanding quality and responsiveness from firms in the home market create the conditions for national competitive advantage. Thus a concern with consumer rights need not necessarily stem exclusively from a sympathy with the under-dog, or with creating countervailing power, but can carry important economic and industrial implications. So it is with industrial relations, which provides the framework within which firms make decisions.

The regulated system that is emerging in countries such as Australia plays an important economic role. By loosening the previous rigidities, and introducing workplace and enterprise flexibility, it taps productivity potential that was previously dammed up. But by placing a relatively high floor to wages and conditions, it prevents employers from resorting to sweating and cost-cutting as their sole competitive strategy.

The key to industrial success, I have argued, is the competitive strategy pursued by firms. Either they seek to compete along a spectrum of issues, including quality and its assurance, customer service, responsiveness and innovation, as well as cost (the STPS approach), or they seek to compete in terms of quantity and cost alone (the MPS model). Increasingly firms choosing the latter option are simply holding their heads above the tide of Third World imports. It is from this quarter that the clamour for protective tariffs is loudest.

The industrial relations system provides the framework or structure within which these choices of competitive strategy are made. A system that keeps employers on their toes is to the advantage of the country as a whole.

The issue is best understood if we move from a national perspective to one of small industrial districts. Consider the example of the highly successful industrial districts in Italy, where thousands of small firms have been the powerhouse of Italy's striking industrial success of the past two decades. Breaking with the model of mass production and its reliance on low-cost competitive strength through long runs of standardised products, the small firms in these districts (such as in Emilia-Romagna) have succeeded through nimbly attacking market niches as they open up within mature mass markets.

In Emilia-Romagna, for example, any single firm is offered the temptation of stealing a march on competitors by cutting its costs; if one firm did so all the other firms would have to follow suit and the competitive advantage of the entire district would be lost. Many districts in Italy, such as the footwear towns of The Marches region, have perished through precisely this mechanism. The Emilian industrial districts guard against such an eventuality partly by common culture and moral pressure, but also by reaching hard-headed agreements with trade unions to maintain high levels of wages and working conditions. These force employers to look for competitive advantages through innovation rather than through cost cutting.[10]

Thus industrial relations and negotiated agreements with unions play a uniquely significant economic role in Italy, helping to shape the trade and industry strategy of thousands of export-oriented small firms away from cost minimisation towards productivity enhancement and quality assurance.

The same process is underway in Australia. The revolution in award structures accomplished through award restructuring and enterprise negotiation, with the linkage established between payment and workers' productivity, skill and performance, provides a real incentive to firms to seek to maximise their productivity through building on the skills of their workers.

This is where we come back to the political options in industrial relations policy. There is an approach that calls for 'more flexibility' at the level of the firm. By removing the 'brakes' of award conditions on employers, they certainly enable good firms to reward productivity as they see fit. But the system has been evolving to allow this anyway. The problem is that the open slather approach also takes the constraints off the bad employers who lack the wit or imagination to compete on anything other than low cost grounds.

The concern is not so much that such employers will offer poor conditions to their employees (something which no-one would welcome) but rather that such employers will undermine the competitive strategy of their more far-sighted and sophisticated colleagues. A spiral of cost-cutting simply drags the whole country down, making it harder than ever for a country like Australia to compete in sophisticated markets where cost is not the whole or even a significant consideration.[11]

Hence the productivity paradox at the heart of industrial relations policy. By maximising the freedom of choice of individual employers, a loose regime in effect minimises the freedom of choice of the country as a whole to shift itself onto a high-wage, high-skill, high-productivity trajectory. Conversely, a tight regime of negotiated arrangements that forces employers to pay good wages, to offer training, to engage in consultation, and with unions ensuring that these agreements are respected, offers a country as a whole maximum freedom to choose its own economic strategy.

This is ultimately the economic significance of a regime of industrial relations. It sets the limits to the decisions taken by the major economic actors. It shapes the processes of organisational change, at both macro and micro level. It provides the constitutional foundations for the programmes of change that firms need to embark on as they adapt to external forces. It sets the rules, but does not determine the outcomes. These are the product of the strategies, insights and intelligence deployed by the economic actors themselves. It is in this context that 'learning by doing' acquires such economic and competitive significance. It is to this matter that we turn in the final chapter.

13

Organisational learning and innovation

The workplace and organisation of the future

In this book, I have placed the project of organisational innovation at the centre of my analysis. I have claimed that firms need to embrace innovative strategies if they are to prosper in conditions which differ radically from those which obtained in the days of mass markets and mass production. Furthermore I have gone on to argue that there is an emerging range of 'best practices' in organisational change that embody notions of experimentation, probing, and controlled testing. In the real world (as opposed to the fantasy world of neoclassical economics) firms grope their way forward in a sea of uncertainties, tacking between strategies as they discern short- and long-term advantages. I have argued that employee involvement, together with negotiated, legitimated change, offers real advantages in a world of intrinsic uncertainty, through its self-adjusting, feedback capacity to take corrective action as circumstances change.

Let us now draw the threads of our story together. We started the book with some propositions concerning the way in which organisations could be expected to achieve outstanding improvements in productivity and efficiency, if they were prepared to countenance radical restructuring of their operations. We used the image of a giant bound hand and foot by dwarves, as Gulliver found himself to be in Lilliput. In our case, the giant is the potential productivity that skilled workers can achieve, while the dwarves are the myriad restrictions imposed on workers by the structures and rules which are a legacy of the mass production system. It is not rules themselves that are the problem—for every production system must operate according to rules which derive from the wider purposes of the organisation in which the production system is embedded. The problem lies in the petty rules that derive from fundamental lack of trust, rules embodied in hierarchical chains of command, in the ranks of the non-commissioned officers (supervisors and foremen) and in the technologies themselves such as computer surveillance of work and its regulation through moving conveyor assembly lines that divide tasks into endlessly repeated, meaningless cycles.

My purpose has been to show how productivity can be unleashed by the relaxing of these iron rules, and putting in their place a more open and flexible structuring of production. The gist of this reorganisation is the structuring of work around the goals to be achieved, through organising the production system into teams of operators who are empowered to achieve the goals by being equipped with the physical and intellectual tools needed. I have sought to demonstrate the validity of this approach through consideration of real case studies, probing them to understand what is really happening behind the bland recital of improved performance and production statistics.

These successful change programmes in Australia—at Ford, at Colonial Mutual, at Bendix Mintex, at the ATO and elsewhere—are distinguished by the scope of their change programmes, by the vision that has driven them, and by the institutionalised trust that has been engendered through the harnessing of organisational members themselves to the change programme. Unlike many other programmes that do not pay attention to such factors, these change programmes actually worked, and they have helped to create vibrant organisations that continue to evolve in the direction of becoming ever more flexible, adaptive and responsive.[1]

This notion of continuous adaptation to a changing environment—rather than reliance on any single static 'optimal' structure—lies at the heart of what I have been calling the 'best practice' sociotechnical production system. Continuous adaptation is akin to the process of learning, hence the phrase 'learning organisation' which is now coming into vogue.[2] The term is useful because of the paradox that lies behind it: we associate learning with people, not with inanimate objects like organisations. But if we think of learning as a process of intelligent continuous adaptation, in the more general setting employed by artificial intelligence (AI) theory, then the phrase 'learning organisation' makes sense, and indeed captures a central feature of the viable systems I have been describing in this book.

The ultimate achievement of the process of organisational innovation is a spectrum of 'learning organisations' which are able endlessly to invent new forms in response to new circumstances, utilising their full complement of people's skills, experience and imagination in doing so. Their repertoire of such responses, and the skills and creativity on which they rest, is their real 'competitive advantage'.

Of course the concept of the 'learning organisation' is quite distinct from the process of learning undertaken by its individual members. People embody their learning in their own minds. But organisations have no 'mind' except in a metaphorical sense. Organisations have to develop the institutional structures through which experience can be gathered and accumulated, and embodied in what Nelson and Winter (1984) aptly termed 'organisational routines'. This is what is meant by 'organisational memory'.

We can see this process at work in our best practice case studies. At the Australian Taxation Office, for example, the process of new product development (which in this case means the adjustment of tax systems each year in accordance with legislative and judicial fiat) has been internalised and institutionalised in cross-functional teams that are formed and disbanded as the need arises. Teams work in the structures established by the experience of earlier teams, developing new 'products' such as in the Electronic Lodgment System. The ELS project is now part of the ATO's institutional memory. In the same way, the goal of sociotechnical change programmes, which involve as many participants as possible, can be seen to be directed towards creating such an institutional memory that can be called upon in developing organisational responses to new situations that may arise in the future.

I have found the notion of the 'learning organisation' to be an attractive one, and I use it as a means of testing the claims of real organisations to have become continuously adaptive entities. The notion of the 'learning' organisation emphasises how organisations in practice improve their performance through a probing of their environment, testing first one approach then another, gathering data in this way, processing these data, and trying to make sense of the resulting picture. It also emphasises the cumulative character of organisational routines and procedures, thus bringing us closer to a realistic conception of the firm as an entity that 'knows how to get certain things done'—as opposed to the ludicrous model of the firm as a 'black box', processing inputs into outputs to maximise a profit function, bequeathed to us by neoclassical economics.

But the discipline of economics has itself started to come to grips with these notions, starting with the pioneering analyses by Kenneth Arrow of 'learning by doing', through the so-called 'new growth theory' of the 1980s, and in the 1990s with the fundamental theoretical investigations of Luigi Pasinetti in structural economic dynamics.[3]

The description of the learning organisation bears many striking parallels with Piaget's analysis of the processes through which a child learns by interacting with its world.

Indeed, the Italian organisational theorists Barbara Di Bernardo and Enzo Rullani (1990) have drawn out explicit parallels between the process of organisational learning and human infant development, basing their exposition on the genetic psychology of Piaget. They describe the process in these terms:

> After many attempts in which the desired effect is either not attained or is attained by accident (in a non-reproducible way) the infant begins to learn when, not only is it able to obtain from a certain action the desired result, but—having conceptualised its behaviour in abstract terms—it is able also *to reproduce it* at will. Once the infant has achieved the capacity to reproduce an abstract pattern of behaviour, without variation, it then poses to itself the problem of extending the field of application of its knowledge. Through successive attempts, it will learn to vary its action with ad hoc solutions, which it will adapt to the particular environmental conditions in which it finds itself or to the particular results which are sought. The set of abstract rules remains, but it becomes more *complex* through many ad hoc adaptations, each of which calls for some experimentation. The third stage will be one where the infant seeks to move beyond ad hoc solutions, from case by case variation, to a state of *reversibility*, where the infant has grasped the conditions which enable it to rapidly produce flexible responses which are appropriate to the circumstances. In other words, the experimental solutions are inserted in a practical sense in a field of variations which in turn are comprehended within a space of *formal, quasi abstract knowledge*, valid for all the potential variations that may occur within that field (Di Bernardo & Rullani 1990).[4]

The relevance of this description to that of a firm seeking to adapt intelligently to its changing environment, is indeed striking. Di Bernardo and Rullani go on to posit three steps through which firms must pass as they 'learn' to cope with the complexity of their environment. These entail the capacity to:

- develop abstract solutions to particular problems and be able to reproduce them;
- add complexity to these abstract solutions, transforming them into ad hoc solutions, in such a way as to extend their field of application; and
- make these ad hoc solutions reversible within a given field of variation.

Thus for Di Bèrnardo and Rullani, the three processes of reproduction, complication and reversibility, lie at the heart of a notion of 'organisational learning'.

Such an approach makes the assumption that organisations are free to construct quite different solutions to the problems they are presented with, subject to the constraints of efficiency and effectiveness—in clear opposition to the barren doctrines of social and technological determinism, on the one hand, and to the doctrines of organisational contingency on the other.

I conceive this notion of organisational learning as an 'engagement' between a strategy and reality, drawing an analogy between this managerial process and that of elaborating scientific theories and testing them against reality, or drafting technological designs that likewise are subject to the constraints of performance criteria in the real world. It is in this context that I introduce the broad notion of *organisational innovation*, as the social process of variation and selection of organisational novelties in the face of constantly changing commercial and technological environments. I insist that this process of variation and selection, far from being 'blind', is in fact a conscious and intelligent process of learning through trial and error, through controlled experimentation, where the norms of experiment are contained in particular organisational routines and capacities that we identify as a firm's 'competitive advantage'.

The notion of organisational innovation therefore provides a framework for analysis that I have found helpful in making sense of the cumulative, evolutionary, adaptive and learning character of organisational change, as firms deploy successive and competing models of productive efficiency. It provides us with an abstract description of organisational behaviour which may be elaborated concisely in the following terms.

Organisational innovations arise through imaginative responses to new commercial conditions. These responses are not programmed in advance, as if they were brought forth like so many 'contingencies'. Rather, they represent genuine novelties of adaptation, achieved by managerial, entrepreneurial, or workplace 'learning by doing'. It is the process through which firms become more efficient in doing the same thing over and over, and through which they capture 'economies of scope' as they vary these routines and extend them to new applications, thus creating the possibilities for capturing new markets.

This accounts for the generation of organisational variations. Whether they 'survive' or not depends basically on whether they add a competitive edge to the originating firm, or group of firms in a cluster. If so, the innovation is likely to be emulated by other firms, seeking to assimilate the innovation to their own organisational milieux and practices. Thus a process of organisational diffusion is set up, mediated through market competition, or (more commonly) through interactive learning across inter-firm networks.

This accounts, then, for the selection of organisational variants, via a process of diffusion and competitive filtering of novel processes or procedures. Firms will be driven by competition to adopt innovations that are giving their competitors an advantage. These innovations might be technical, such as CNC machine tools, or organisational, such as manufacturing cells.

The two processes, viz the generation of organisational variants, and their selection through institutional, market, and indeed political mechanisms, constitute the evolutionary framework through which organisational innovation proceeds.

Unlike biological evolution, from which this model is generalised, there is no 'random generation' of organisational variants, nor does selection take place through a blind process of Darwinian 'natural selection'. On the contrary, in the organisational domain, the generation of innovations is purposive and adaptive, and is best described as a process of organisational learning.[5]

Organisational learning, then, is a purposive, adaptive, and cumulative series of responses to changes in the environment of an organisation or network of organisations. The learning takes place both within the individual organisations, and as a collective activity across inter-organisational networks. These networks link suppliers, users and customers in complex, value-adding chains that span the economy. They provide the setting in which interactive learning takes place across and between firms. In a striking phrase, Lundvall et al. (1992) refer to this as the 'learning economy', and thus pinpoint one of the critical factors in the generation of wealth by nations.[6]

One feature of this description is its capacity to provide a focus on the flexibility and responsiveness that firms need to develop if they are to adapt to and survive in changing circumstances. This in turn provides a focus on the organisational and human dimensions of the processes engaged in by the firm to develop and secure its core competencies that define the business or markets in which it is located.[7] The innovative firm is one then that incorporates such structures of adaptation. Hence the significance of organisational devices like product and service cells that form semi-autonomous business units, each with a clear product or service focus, a clear system of performance measurement, and a clear framework of accountability to the organisation as a whole. This process of continuous adaptation, with cells being formed as the need arises, and dismantled as the need changes, is the essence of the 'learning organisation'.[8]

A second important feature of the description given is its insistence on the complexity and social character of processes of adaptation. They involve not just the bland 'formulation' of organisational goals, but their negotiation through complex processes of organisational politics in which coalitions will form and parties compete for support. What makes this process so distinctive, and places a constraint on the formation of self-serving coalitions, is the necessity to maintain adequate levels of production or service demanded by the market and enforced by competitors. As Kochan and Useem (1992) put it, the 'learning organisation' is the metaphor that captures 'the vision of individuals, groups and organisational networks committed to and capable of continuous learning through information exchange, experimentation, dialogue, negotiation and consensus building' (1992, p. 391). Thus notions of industrial relations and organisational development all find their home in the concept of organisational learning.

The opposite condition is one of organisational stasis.[9] This is what afflicts organisations which are incapable of generating the changes needed for adaptation and survival. To return to our initial discussion of production systems, firms that cling to a model of productive efficiency grounded in obsolete mass production notions, suffer from 'organisational stasis'; they will pay for such conservatism by losing business to their more innovative competitors.

The third feature of this kind of description that I wish to bring out is its emphasis on the 'match' that a firm can attain between its organisational architecture and the conditions in which it finds itself. This is the macro dimension of innovation that I keep coming back to as the necessary ingredient in understanding why some 'national systems of innovation' (Lundvall et al. 1992) are better than others. If there is no escaping the necessity for organisational choice at the level of the firm, neither is there any possibility for avoiding political and social choices at the national and sectoral levels; these infrastructural and policy frameworks matter.[10]

THE LEARNING ORGANISATION OF THE TWENTY-FIRST CENTURY

So what then can we say of substance concerning the likely evolution of the learning organisation? What will such organisations look like by the year 2001?

Intelligent production systems

The first point to establish is that work and management will have converged, so that what are currently called 'flat organisations' (such a clumsy term!) will come to resemble 'intelligent organisations'. Indeed, the workplace of the future will be one characterised by the application of intelligence to manufacturing and service operations. Thus we will speak of the 'intelligent manufacturing system' and the 'intelligent service organisation'; these are already phrases that are coming into general use, such as in the Japanese-inspired international collaborative research programme on the Intelligent Manufacturing System.[11]

In manufacturing, the trend will be away from the vision of 'unmanned factories' or workerless factories where automation and robots take over all activities, and 'manual tasks' are reduced to meaningless operations pending their elimination via automation. Experience to date with such concepts has shown them to be brittle, rigid and very expensive; they are in fact exaggerated versions of the engineering approach that seeks to take the skill out of work and place it in machines or in software programmes. This trend towards automation will no doubt continue, due to being deeply embedded in management ideologies and engineering design approaches; but it will increasingly be challenged by an alternative trend towards 'intelligent' manufacturing systems which bring together tools, logistics and people in a flexible, integrated whole. This latter will be responsive and adaptive precisely because it puts people and their skills at the centre of the system.

This manufacturing system will be 'intelligent' in the sense that its responses (e.g. activities to deliver a customer order) will be informed by reasoning and not just by rote or technical, deterministic routines. Such a vision calls on advanced forms of information technology architecture and artificial intelligence, and on more pragmatic elements such as standardised interfaces that allow different elements to 'speak' with each other.

Let us take the architecture first. The most advanced thinking on the future of intelligent manufacturing refers to 'distributed autonomous manufacturing systems', 'fractal factories' or 'holonic manufacturing'.[12] It is holonic in the sense that it is formed of 'holons' or semi-autonomous modules that have a degree of independence but which also derive certain parameters from a central coordinator. (Holon comes from the Greek 'holos', meaning whole, and '-on', denoting a part or particle, as in proton or neutron; hence an entity that shares the attributes of a part and of a whole.[13])

Such holonic architectures have been developed for computer systems where the traditional command–control hierarchical relationships have given way to whole–part relationships. Computer programs were originally developed along strikingly hierarchical lines, with 'master programmes' calling up 'slave' routines and sub-routines as circumstances warranted. These systems suffered from the rigidity that now bedevils manufacturing systems organised along the same lines. The new holonic architectures for computer systems embody what is called 'Object-Oriented Programming', where the 'objects' are independent, semi-autonomous routines or data sets that come into play depending on the use to which the programme, or machine, is put. 'Objects' communicate by sending each other messages to perform operations. 'Objects' may learn from experience, in strong contrast with traditional computer functions which have no memory.[14]

While such non-hierarchical models have been deployed for many years in data processing, their use in manufacturing has been limited by the very much greater complexity encountered in processing materials as opposed to pure data. However the advent of 'intelligent manufacturing' brings the concept of enterprise modelling and process representation that much nearer reality, on the understanding that people and their skills are at the centre of the system.

Again the most advanced thinking on these topics insists that each part of the system be modelled in the same way as the overall system. This implies that each processing unit within the greater whole uses a similar model of the system and captures data structured in the same way, so that aggregation and disaggregation do not present insuperable problems as at present. This 'self-similarity' or recursivity, has always been the hallmark of holonic systems. The same idea is captured physically by holograms in optics; in mathematics it is captured by fractal geometry and by recursive functions. Thus the idea has an attractive universality that makes it worth pursuing in the context of advanced manufacturing.[15]

The other aspect of the Intelligent Manufacturing Systems deserving of comment concerns standards. Everyone knows that computer systems vendors tried in the 1970s to lock customers into their proprietary architectures and networks, but that this attempt broke down with the advent of open systems architectures in the 1980s. In the field of manufacturing, an area of greater complexity than that of data processing, the standardisation issue is still without resolution. Brave attempts by manufacturers such as General Motors to produce interface standards such as Manufacturing Automation Protocol (MAP) were in effect nothing but bandaids that continually fell behind new manufacturing automation developments.[16]

The Japanese initiative to create an international Intelligent Manufacturing System programme, launched in 1989, was partly an attempt to remedy this problem and ensure that integrated factories of the future would have universal and transparent interface standards. These standards would allow small and medium-sized firms to purchase advanced manufacturing systems and adapt them to their own purposes, without having to make the huge investments that confined the field to large firms until relatively recently. At the time of writing this question of standardisation is still without resolution; it remains a crucial element in the development of universal manufacturing systems that can be used by small firms and by developing countries to leapfrog their larger competitors.

So learning organisations of the twenty-first century can be expected to possess 'holonic' organisational architectures, giving them a powerful modular structure and the capacity to form and disband cellular units as needs arise or disappear. The heart of these cellular structures will be the collaborative efforts of skilled people, working together to accomplish well-defined tasks and cross-skilling each other in the process. Thus the manufacturing or service cells will provide units of organisational learning, as we have seen them do so in our case studies of Bendix Mintex in manufacturing, and Colonial Mutual in the services sector. This is the foundation of interactive learning which will lie at the heart of intelligent production systems in future.

Network organisations

A second point to note about learning organisations, and their interaction through networks into a learning economy, is that collaboration and cooperation will be seen as just as important for economic success as competition. The case of TCG is instructive, in that it is not only a lean and efficient cluster, or network structure in itself, but its mode of developing new products and gaining entry to new markets (the 'triangular strategy'), also involves networking with larger players. A generalisation of the TCG model of networks as outlined here leads one to posit the concept of an economy as a 'network of networks'. This has far-reaching ramifications both for theory and practice.

It brings our attention back to the important issues that have been neglected by the dominant atomistic paradigm. The balance between competition and cooperation becomes a prime subject of inquiry (just as it is in studies of natural ecology) in relation to important topics such as product and process innovation.[17] Networks can be examined from the point of view of equity, efficiency and public policy. For example, what kind of legal regimes are needed to prevent non-sustainable and exploitative networks from becoming a dominant form? The 'life cycle' of networks also becomes the topic of sustained interest, focusing on the conditions that favour the birth, maturing and decline of firms themselves, and of networks of such firms.

Above all, the study of the governance structure of networks brings the issue of trust back to the centre of attention. Trust is not natural, but a social construct. It is produced from the norms that govern people's behaviour and their commercial interactions. Trust in this context may be defined as that state between parties where they can afford to delete the clauses forming the preamble to a neoclassical contract, thereby saving considerably on transaction costs.[18] Conventional economics has marginalised the study of trust, seeing it as antithetical to atomistic competition. Conventional approaches to corporate governance likewise marginalise trust, seeing it as antithetical to the adversarialism that is seen as central to western institutions. But real and successful economies have shown the importance and significance of trust in cementing economic ties.[19] The network model of corporate governance developed at TCG can be interpreted in this light as an explicit means of structuring trust between contracting parties, allowing them to act according to the dictates of long-term sustainable interests rather than short-term spot calculations.

Organisational ownership

A third point to make about learning organisations of the twenty-first century, is that they will take a much more sophisticated approach to the sharing of productivity gains, and thereby tackle the vexed issues of motivation and control. Already firms around the world are experimenting with various models of employee ownership such as Employee Stock Ownership Plans (ESOPs). Experimentation with these forms, and their legislative mandating, backed by favourable taxation incentives, is likely to wax rather than wane in advanced industrial countries.[20]

This issue of the broadening of ownership in industry is clearly linked to the parallel development of the notion of stewardship of resources, as pressures on firms to take a more responsible attitude to the natural environment, and to recycling, are mounting. Indeed it may be foreseen that the best way to guarantee environmental and resource responsibility on the part of firms is to ensure that their ownership and control is shared by many stakeholders, including employees themselves.

Organisational experimentation

A final point to make about learning organisations in the twenty-first century, is that they will operate much more systematically as experimental entities. In place of the myopic probing of the environment that characterises the first steps of even the most progressive firms engaging in workplace reform and organisational innovation, there will be a much more sophisticated and 'managed' process of experimentation to determine new strategic directions and tactical responses, as much at the level of the firm itself as at the level of individual work cells.

In the 1980s, the Italian firm, Benneton, showed how systematic 'probing' of the market could lead to dramatic results. Benneton would offer a range of goods in its retail outlets around the world, linking the sales data to its production systems electronically so that production could be 'tuned' almost instantaneously to slight shifts in demand. This is the prototype of market-led production in which virtually all learning organisations of the twenty-first century will engage. But on a broader level, all change will be piloted in a conscious 'experimental' fashion, with the reasons for the change being discussed with all relevant parties, the change strategy settled on through discussion and negotiation, the change piloted in one or two experimental 'probes' and then carefully evaluated, before the full change is then swiftly and comprehensively implemented. This is ultimately what we mean by 'sociotechnical organisational change'.

A COMMON MODEL FOR INNOVATION IN SCIENCE, TECHNOLOGY AND ORGANISATION?

In my approach to 'innovation', I am drawing no hard and fast distinction between innovation in 'science', 'technology' and 'organisation'. Instead I am appealing to a rational process of innovation that is common to all three enterprises.[21] In all three, what is involved is a process of controlled experimentation and rigorous testing of one or more rational structures—a theory, a design, a strategy—and a rational process for selection of the desirable option.

There is the imaginative and creative component of this rational process, in the development of new concepts, theories, designs or organisational strategies, conceived as responses to identified problems. These problems might be so serious as to demand revolutionary breaks, involving genuine paradigm shifts, or they might be instances of continuous improvement or adaptation. As the Asian societies have shown, improvement and adaptation are central to the process of innovation. The 'big bangs' occur only rarely and only in response to great stress in the rational framework.

There is the set of received or accepted methods for testing the validity of these rational constructs against the counter claims of other constructs, according to the results registered by controlled encounters with the 'real world'. In the case of science, this 'canonical' set of methods has itself evolved over several centuries, and it now contains its own criteria such as public demonstration, repeatability of results, and peer review. In the case of technological artifacts, the process of innovation has likewise developed characteristic institutional features such as the patenting system, and a set of professional engineering rules of 'common sense' that separate successful from unsuccessful designs. In the case of organisational designs and strategies, the testing process is a management responsibility, and one of the most difficult that any group of managers will ever have to face. But as to whether controlled experimentation and rigorous evaluation are becoming part of the management discourse, there can be no doubt.

Take the case of Benneton, the Italian-based and now multinational clothing and knitwear company. As noted above, when

Benneton develops a new product line in knitwear, it tests consumer response in a most rigorous manner through the collection and evaluation of data. Variations on the new theme are introduced to retail outlets in a controlled sequence (very much in the way that drugs are administered in a controlled trial of efficacy); the data on sales (and other responses) are fed back promptly through computerised information networks. The timeliness of these responses is ensured by keeping the trial quantities small, and by establishing the information channels and feedback routes prior to the process of market experimentation. The market responses are then evaluated and product options chosen, in the knowledge that there is an expressed (hence, real) consumer demand for that product line. Since this whole process is conducted over a period not exceeding a few weeks, the response can be developed in time for a season's clothing lines, giving Benneton a marked commercial advantage over competitors who base their product lines on last year's tastes and 'hunches' about the direction of tastes in the current year.

The emphasis in most accounts of Benneton's strategy is on the real-time computer linkage between the retail distribution and the production activities. While this is certainly significant, it is merely the vehicle for the process which I wish to emphasise, namely controlled experimentation and evaluation as a rational, disciplined business strategy. My point is that this is a process which can be discerned as much in good business and organisational practice as in laboratories and in engineering design establishments. It is a rational process of innovation that yields the same high results in business as it has yielded impressive gains in knowledge and technique in the cognate fields of science and technology.

The generalised rational approach I am describing is now fairly well established as the new 'received view' of what happens in science and technology (that is, in certain history and philosophy of science and sociotechnical systems circles). But it is still far from being the received view of the process of organisational innovation.

Rather, in the business or management literature, organisational innovation is still conceived of generally in terms of the characters, personalities and qualities of the people involved. Adjustments are viewed in terms of personal success or failure, with those who manage a successful programme reaping praise and promotion and those who manage a failure finding themselves looking for another· job. Yet this is equivalent to the 'great man' perspective of scientific and technological progress (yes, most of them are men); while undoubtedly there are 'great men' involved in the process of innovation, we have learnt that we develop a most distorted understanding of the process if this is all we focus on. Alternatively there is a tendency to attribute success or failure to the spirit of cooperation, or lack of it, in the people involved. This again is to ignore the process in favour of concentrating exclusively on the natural endowments of the participants; it is equivalent to the naturalist fallacy in the human sciences (which emphasises nature always over nurture and culture) or to the metaphysical tendency in the physical sciences to seek explanations of change in terms of the 'essences' of interacting bodies rather than in the structured relations between them.

The significance of my argument now becomes clear. I am claiming that organisations are successful, in terms of adapting to their changing environment and operating successfully within a given environment, when they probe and evaluate their options in a controlled and rational fashion. Such a process gives equal weight to the creative and imaginative development of the options themselves (the right half brain activity) and the logical, rational and methodical evaluation of these options according to specified and explicit criteria (the left half brain activity). I claim that this is a strategy that was first developed in the modern era in the case of science, and perfected in the case of technology.

The same powerful method, then, is available to organisations as they seek to keep ahead in the competitive race. The secret is not the adoption of a single 'model' of organisational success, no matter how clever or tested it might be, but the adoption of a method of innovation that combines imaginative generation of options together with their rigorous testing and evaluation.

A knowledge system consists of sets of statements concerning an 'environment' that lies outside the domain of the statements. Inferences or predictions generated from the statements (hypotheses) are then compared, under usually artificially induced conditions, with events in the 'environment'. (A realist philosophy of science insists on the separate reality of these events; the statements have an epistemological rather than an ontological character.) The goal is to produce statements of regularity that are called 'laws', specifying what can be expected to happen under certain conditions. These statements can then be applied to real world situations with predictive value, provided the assumptions on which the theory is built do not depart too radically from the real world conditions.[22]

A technology, in contrast, consists of a set of rationally assembled or integrated components or statements (as in a computer programme) whose behaviour is, via design, brought to approximate a stated and preconceived goal. Thus design is a central category that is present in technologies but not in knowledge systems.

An organisation consists of a set of rationally integrated relations or structures, linking people via information and control; in this case the behaviour sought will again approximate to a goal, but this goal cannot be imposed by 'design' unilaterally onto the organisation. Instead what we have are 'strategies' that are pursued by the stakeholders within the organisation, with outcomes that are far from or close to the goals, depending on the arrangements reached or negotiated between the parties.

In all three cases, evolution or adaptation occurs through the strategic processes of developing new internal relations, such as conjectures or hypotheses in the case of science, or design structures in the case of technology, or communication and control strategies in the case of organisations. These are the rational processes of innovation and selection common to all three systems.

CATCHING THE WAVE

So we have come full circle. The sleeping giant of worker productivity that lies imprisoned in inappropriate production systems in so many organisations today is being liberated. Productivity is being unleashed as firms come to recognise the superiority of organisational architectures based on cellular, modular, or 'holonic' structures, staffed by skilled people working towards well-specified goals and equipped with the appropriate tools and information. These are the firms that are catching the wave of 'world best practice' and are riding it to commercial and organisational success.

The propositions advanced at the start of our journey, which seemed so radical in conception in the context of existing production systems, seem obvious in the context of the learning organisations that are emerging around the world. In the learning organisation, there is a conscious dependence on people and their skills. It is unthinkable to impose on such people 'black box' technological innovations, or 'top down' organisational innovations, without involving them in the development of such innovations. In the learning organisation, 'learning by doing' is translated into continuous improvement and continuous testing of new organisational forms, designs and strategies. At the same time, the rights of organisational members to be consulted in these changes will be underwritten by their growing influence over the management of the firm through ownership, as forms of control embodying

301

various stakeholder interests come to prominence. Thus our conception of the learning organisation will move from the mechanical ideas that have been so prevalent in economics and management science, to more organic notions and, latterly, more cybernetic ideals of balanced regulation and systemic viability.

There is no escaping our personal responsibility for the emerging learning organisation and for the learning economy that is being created as its commercial environment. Ultimately, it has to be recognised that these are conscious structures, created as an act of will to achieve specified objectives. There is no escaping our responsibility for these organisational choices, nor for the social choices that must frame them.

Endnotes

Chapter 1

1 There is by now an extensive literature on cellular manufacturing principles and experiences. On the human aspects of cellular manufacturing or group technology, see, for example, J. Burbridge (1992) and V. Huber and K. Brown (1991).

2 Such a system was first developed in Japan by the Toyota subsidiary Aisin Seiki and is now marketed world-wide as the Toyota Sewing System, contributing to 'best practice' in clothing factories throughout the world.

3 See the description of just such a system in G. Fyfe and B. Curran (1993).

4 The descriptions of the new production systems are by now numerous. See, for example, the MIT Commission on Industrial Productivity and their text *Made in America* (Dertouzos et al. 1989); the International Motor Vehicle Programme, also based at MIT, and their text *The Machine that Changed the World* (Womack et al. 1990) which introduced the notion of the 'lean production system' as a generalisation of the Toyota organisational innovations; the German industrial sociologists Kern and Schumann (1984), with their notion of the 'new production concepts'; and the US scholars Piore and Sabel (1984), who introduced the notion of 'flexible specialisation' in their influential text *The Second Industrial Divide*. Many of the issues are canvassed in the context of a global framework of 'new competition' by Best (1990).

5 See Chandler (1977; 1990) for the most authoritative account of the rise of the mass production organisations and the systems that sustained them.

6 See Skinner (1986). His earlier works were collected in Skinner (1985).

7 The terminology of 'paradigm shift' is common to authors such as

303

Piore and Sabel (1984) who characterise the emergence of a new form of 'flexible specialisation' as a shift in production system paradigm analogous to the shift (or divide, a parting of the ways) that occurred at the time of the rise of mass production and the suppression of the craft system of production. Similarly Perez and Freeman (1988) characterise the present turbulence as the emergence of a new 'technoeconomic paradigm' that effects a break with the paradigm based on mass production; for them, this is the fifth rupture since the original Industrial Revolution saw the rise of mechanisation and factories. Other authors utilise this terminology in discussing the rise of a new 'technological paradigm', such as Roobeek (1987) and Mahon (1987). I prefer the term 'techno-organisational paradigm' since it is in the complementary character of technology and organisation that the shift in design and operation is occurring. The framework used by Perez and Freeman is further explored in Chapter 4.

8 Hammer introduced the phrase 're-engineering' of organisational processes in his influential 1990 *Harvard Business Review* article. It has since been popularised as 'business process re-engineering' or as 'core process re-engineering'; a number of examples are given by Hammer and Champy in their 1993 book.

9 The phrase 'new production concepts', meaning a break with the concepts of Taylorism, was introduced by the German industrial sociologists, Kern and Schumann (1984; 1987; 1989). Their work is discussed in Chapter 2.

10 There is by now an enormous literature on the kinds of industrial and production systems that are possible once the shackles of mass production rigidities are dispensed with. See, for example, the discussions given in Dertouzos et al. (1989); Lane (1988); Hirst & Zeitlin (1990); and in Australia, Department of Industrial Relations/Australian Manufacturing Council (1992).

11 See Badham and Mathews (1989) for an elaboration of these arguments.

12 The staggering feature of Emery's 1974 article, prescient as it was in almost every respect, is that it never once mentioned the rise of small firm networks, nor hinted at the 'wind from the east' that was already blowing stronger than the westerly and was about to blow so hard that it would humble the giants that Emery saw as already being too strong.

13 See Plowman (1992).

14 The 1980s have seen much debate in Australia over the nature of the unique Australian Council of Trade Unions–Australian Labor Party Accord, which has provided a framework for the relations between the two wings of the labour movement for over a decade. There is a strong school of thought which sees the Accord as a 'neo-corporatist' arrangement, after similar incomes policy agreements established in Europe in the 1970s. See Regini (1984) for a useful discussion.

15 For the Structural Efficiency Principle, see the decision of the National Wage Case (Australian Conciliation and Arbitration Commission 1987) and for the Enterprise Bargaining Principle, the October 1991 decision (Australian Industrial Relations Commission 1991b). An earlier form of the enterprise bargaining principle was enunciated by the New South Wales State Industrial Commission under Justice Fisher (Industrial Commission of New South Wales 1991). For a discussion of these developments, see Davis and Lansbury (1993). For a discussion that links the industrial relations issues with workplace reform, see Curtain (1992).

16 The debate on enterprise bargaining in particular has been long and bitter. One position has been strongly put by the Business Council of Australia (1989); for a discussion, see Frenkel and Peetz (1990). Many of the features of the enterprise-based system that is emerging in Australia were foreshadowed by Niland in his Green Paper for the State of NSW (Niland 1990).

17 See, for example, the studies conducted under the auspices of the Business Council of Australia (Rimmer & Verevis 1990), those conducted for the Australian Productivity Council by the National Institute of Labour Studies (Kriegler & Dawkins 1988), and those conducted under the auspices of the Centre for Corporate Change at the University of NSW by Dunphy and Stace. Evidence of a more quantitative kind has been provided by the publication of the Australian Workplace Industrial Relations Survey (Callus et al. 1991).

18 There have been joint study missions conducted by several sectoral working parties. A recent cross-sectoral mission produced the 1992 report *International Best Practice: Report of the Overseas Study Mission* (Australian Department of Industrial Relations/Australian Manufacturing Council).

19 The Australian pioneers of workplace reform and enterprise restructuring include Fred Emery, Dexter Dunphy, Bill Ford and Hollis Peter. See Emery (1974), Dunphy (1986), Ford (1975), and Dick and Peter (1978) for representative texts.

20 In terms of methodology, the case study is an essential means of obtaining insight into real processes of change. It offers results that complement those found through survey methods. For an interesting discussion of the significance of case histories for organisations themselves, see Barrett and Srivastva (1991).

21 The monographs on which the following chapters are based are as follows:

• Bendix Mintex: Mathews, Griffiths and Watson (1993)
• Colonial Mutual: Mathews (1991)
• Ford Plastics plant: Mathews (1991)
• TCG: Mathews (1992)
• Australia Post OCR Project: Mathews (1992)

- CIG Gas Cylinders: Mathews and Griffiths (1993)
- Australian Taxation Office: Mathews (1992).

In each case, the story has been checked with the organisation concerned, sometimes through numerous revisions. All the monographs are obtainable from the Industrial Relations Research Centre at the University of New South Wales, Sydney.

22 For an exposition of this view, see a recent paper on the industrial relations of skills formation (Mathews 1993a).

Chapter 2

1 Ford of course was not the first to practise this principle. It had been followed in the 1840s by Rowland Hill with the introduction of the penny post, designed explicitly to expand the market for postal services.

2 The literature on the mass production system as it emerged in the USA includes Chandler (1977), Abernathy et al. (1981), Hounshell (1984), Piore and Sabel (1984), Sabel and Zeitlin (1985), Chandler and Tedlow (1985), Hughes (1989), Glyn et al. (1989), and most recently the contributions of Chandler (1990) and Lazonick (1991).

3 In our study of the textile industry in Italy and Australia, Linda Weiss and I characterised these choices in terms of the strategy being pursued by firms, the structure of the industry in which they compete, and the ramifications of public policy on the choices they are forced to make (Weiss & Mathews 1991).

4 On the Toyota production system, see the seminal work by Monden (1984; 1993) and the series of texts by such Toyota pioneers as Shingo (1985). On the reception in Europe of this system as 'Toyotism', see, for example, Dohse, Juergens and Malsch (1985), Kaplinsky (1988) and MacDuffie and Krafcik (1992).

5 Starting in 1993, the European Automotive Initiative Group from Richmond, Surrey, UK, began publishing a regular 'management digest for lean enterprise practices', called *Lean Enterprise* (ISSN 0968 4263).

6 Lucas Engineering Systems, for example, have produced a Manufacturing Systems Handbook based on lean production concepts and techniques, designed for use in shop floor environments in any industry; these principles are explicitly contrasted with those derived from mass production. (We look at these Lucas principles in some detail in the next chapter.)

7 For a perceptive discussion of these issues, see the report from a symposium staged by the International Institute for Labour Studies, Geneva, in Sengenberger and Campbell (1993).

8 This case has not been helped, of course, by the announcement by Volvo in Sweden that it intends to close both Kalmar and Uddevalla, in 1993 and 1994. For a discussion of this decision, and its ramifications, see Berggren (1993).

9   See K. Sheridan, paper delivered to UNSW Symposium on the future of the public sector, University of New South Wales, 19 March 1993.

10 M. Nomura (1992).

11 In the case of the United States, see the numerous examples discussed by Appelbaum and Batt (1994) collected under their rubric of the 'new American workplace'. In the case of Europe, see the studies prepared for the European Commission by Dietrich Brandt (1991). For a fascinating discussion of enterprise-level change in the German automotive industry, that brings together organisational and industrial relations issues, see Turner (1991).

12 The term 'mutual commitment' was introduced by Walton (1985), as part of his extensive contribution to the industrial relations foundations of new, collaborative forms of production. It has since been picked up by Kochan and Dyer (1992) and as 'high involvement' by such authors as Lawler (1992). The term 'mutual commitment' is developed further in the UK literature as the 'open-ended employment contract' (see, for example, Brown & Nolan 1988) and in the US literature as 'intensity of collaboration'. For a most useful discussion of these issues, see the survey on workplace productivity by Alexander and Green (1992).

13 On the difficulties involved in assimilating LPS systems to workplaces which have cultivated a 'new workplace culture', see, for example, the work of Harvard Business School researcher Janice Klein (1989).

14 On the human relations school and Lewin's contributions in particular, see the recent magisterial survey by Weisbord (1990). The human relations school reached its highest expression in the work of Douglas McGregor, with his ground breaking text, *The Human Side of Enterprise* (1960). He was succeeded by such scholars as Rensis Likert and his text *The Human Organization* (1967).

15 For a useful introduction to the debates that took place between various schools within the QWL movement in the 1970s, see Emery (1991).

16 Two important books which document the origins and subsequent development of the sociotechnical school, were published in 1993. See van Eijnatten (1993) for a comprehensive treatment of the school, and an analysis of its divergent trends as they are practised today (to be discussed below); and Trist and Murray (1993) for an invaluable compilation of early and more recent sociotechnical writings.

17 In 1949 some government funds were made available to the Tavistock Institute to investigate productivity issues in industry. The Institute had on hand some postgraduate research fellows who were encouraged to revisit their old worksites to review them in the light of their new concepts. A former miner, Ken Bamforth, revisited his old colliery and was astonished to find that along with mechanisation, the colliery manager and workers had quite autonomously re-introduced a group method of mining that predated mechanisation. This was quite differ-

ent from the standardisation that went with mechanised 'longwall' methods as normally seen. When Bamforth reported back to his Tavistock colleagues, they seized its significance at once, and initiated a study of the emergence of this efficient alternative to Taylorisation of work accompanying mechanisation. The resulting study has become a classic in the work organisation literature (Trist & Bamforth 1951).

18   Emery formulated the principal theoretical contributions of sociotechnical systems in the form of two principles: the principle of joint optimisation of the social and technical systems of an organisation (Emery 1959) and the principle that the redundancy of parts in traditional organisations should be superseded by the redundancy of functions (Emery 1967). The application to the redesign of jobs was spelt out as 'democracy at work' (Emery & Thorsrud 1977).

19   Outstanding contributors to the sociotechnical tradition include Eric Trist, Fred Emery, A.T.M. Wilson, A.K. Rice, David Herbst and many others in centres established elsewhere. On the sociotechnical approach, see E. Trist et al. (1963), Herbst (1974), Emery (1978, pp. 448–57). On the Norwegian Industrial Democracy Programme, see Emery and Thorsrud (1977). For a more recent example of how the sociotechnical tradition has been taken up and extended in Scandinavia as 'participative design', see Ehn (1988).

      For a retrospective on the contributions of the Tavistock Institute over 40 years, see the three-volume collection *The Social Engagement of Social Science*, edited by Eric Trist and Hugh Murray.

20   For an account of this programme, see Emery and Thorsrud (1977) as well as the more recent survey by van Eijnatten (1993).

21   See my earlier book, *Tools of Change* (Mathews 1989a) for a description of these developments.

22   For Gustavsen's account of his notion of 'democratic dialogue' as the key to workplace reform, see Gustavsen (1992).

23   Principal contributors to the stream of thought, investigation and workplace intervention that make up 'Action Regulation Theory', are Volpert and Hacker. See Volpert (1982) and Volpert et al. (1989).

24   See Lane (1988). Other work was done, for example, by Juergens and colleagues from the WZB, Berlin: Juergens (1989).

25   On the concept of the 'anthropocentric production system' and its elaboration by the FAST Programme of the European Commission, see the reports by Wobbe (1992), Kidd (1992) and Lehner (1992). This work, coordinated on behalf of the FAST Programme by the Institut Arbeit und Technik [Work and Technology Institute], Gelsenkirchen, has drawn on a European network of researchers and a broad collection of case studies of organisational and technological innovations. The content of the case studies makes it clear that FAST uses the term anthropocentric production system to refer to the same set of characteristics that I call STPS. In my view the term anthropocentric is too clumsy to enter popular usage, and should be abandoned by Brussels.

26 Rosenbrock was a professor of control engineering at Manchester's UMIST, and had early expressed his dissatisfaction at the direction in which control systems were going (Rosenbrock 1977). Cooley was a design engineer who had led the union-inspired Lucas Aerospace 'Alternative Plan' for socially useful production; although the plan was never accepted by Lucas, the ideas became well known as a counterpoint to dominant trends in technological development.

27 See Badham and Schallock (1990), Martin (1988) and Broedner (1985a; 1985b; 1987) for a discussion of these developments, with specific reference to Germany; see Majchrzak (1988) for a more general discussion.

28 The Esprit project 1217 (1199) 'Human-Centred Computer-Integrated Manufacturing' continued the work begun in Manchester, and brought together design and manufacturing partners from Germany, Denmark and Britain (Hamlin 1989).

29 Similar studies are being conducted under Esprit project 2415 on software development for 'Distributed Manufacturing Planning and Control', and the SERC/ACME project 'Operation and Management of Flexible Human-Centred Machining Cells' at Imperial College, London; see Hancke (1989), 'Human-centred design for the Imperial College demonstrator cell', Research report, Imperial College, London. This was linked to a demonstration site near Frankfurt, Germany, producing precision gear drives (Slatter et al. 1989).

30 See, for example, Kidd (1988), Corbett (1988) as well as Kidd and Corbett (1988). For an approach to advanced manufacturing systems conceived as 'integrated factories' from an explicitly sociotechnical perspective, see Susman and Chase (1986).

31 For an exposition of the approach, see the extensive review provided by de Sitter and den Hartog (1990). The whole sociotechnical tradition, including the contributions of the Dutch school, has been expounded in a new book (Eijnatten 1993) which contains the author's reconstruction of the intellectual history of what he calls the Socio-Technical Systems Design paradigm, documenting the period from 1951 to 1993.

32 Different terms have been used for these dualities or triads of strategies. For example, Piore and Sabel (1984) characterised what I am calling STPS as 'flexible specialisation', emphasising the capacity of small firms to link their activities together. More recently, Appelbaum and Batt (1994) have framed their discussion of the emergent 'new American workplace' in terms of a contrast between an American version of lean production, and an American development of team production, which corresponds reasonably closely to my distinction between the LPS and the STPS. I myself have characterised the STPS as 'post-Fordist', and a variant of the LPS, emphasising its control features and short-cycle operations as 'neo-Fordist' (Mathews 1989), as have other authors. I no longer find these terms to be very helpful, and have abandoned their usage in this text. For a description of the

controversies involved, which need not detain us here, see Badham and Mathews (1989) and Mathews (1992e).

33 This study looked at such cases as the design of the viewfinder assembly machine at Polaroid, the spindle/cuff machining cell at Sikorsky Aircraft, the FMS established by Westinghouse Electrical Systems to produce aircraft power generators, and the series of assembly lines designed and operated by Whirlpool Corporation for the production of washing machines (Lund et al. 1993).

34 See, for example, the interesting discussion of the role that sociotechnical design criteria can play in the design of Computer-Integrated Manufacturing systems, in Eichener (1992), in Broedner and Karwowski (1992). On the application of sociotechnical ideas in the design of software systems, see Salzman and Rosenthal (1993).

35 See the fascinating paper by Hancke and Braune (1993).

36 On the challenge of the LPS, see the FAST report by Rauner and Ruth (1991). The same theme has been tackled by the ILO's International Institute for Labour Studies in Geneva, in its Forum on 'Lean production and beyond: Labour aspects of a new production concept', 5–6 November 1992; see Sengenberger (1992).

37 Here I draw on the model developed in Badham and Mathews (1989).

38 For a searching discussion of the state–space representation of dynamic systems that is becoming standard throughout the engineering and technological sciences, see Bunge (1979).

39 Critics have seized on this model and used it to parade all their antagonism to the idea that firms, including managements and unions, might have some control over their own destiny. For a response to these critics, and a re-evaluation of the theoretical origins of these arguments, see Mathews (1992e).

Chapter 3

1 A variety of terms are used to describe 'best practice': 'high commitment' (Walton 1980); 'excellent' (Peters & Waterman 1982); 'best practice' (Dertouzos et al. 1988); 'transformed' (Kochan, Katz, McKersie 1986); 'high involvement' (Lawler 1986); 'mutual commitment' (Walton 1985; Kochan & Dyer 1992). I shall use the terms 'world best practice' and 'sociotechnical production systems', but will freely refer also to cases of 'mutual commitment' or 'cooperative accommodation'.

2 I have in mind such texts as Harmon and Peterson (1990) and the challenging sequel by Harmon (1992), as well as the numerous texts produced by Japanese masters such as Ohno and Shingo in the Productivity Press series. In the services sector, I have in mind such texts as Heskett, Sasser and Hart (1990) and Schlesinger and Heskett (1991).

3 See the outstanding report on this theme from the Royal Swedish

Academy of Engineering Sciences by Erik Hornell (1992). This report makes systematic comparisons between Scandinavian and such world-class firms as Motorola and Ericsson, Nippondenso and Luxor, Singapore Airlines and SAS.

4   See Boyer (1990). On Boyer's more general formulations, and the approach of the Regulation School of which he is a member, see Boyer 1988; 1989. See also the review by Juniper in Green and Genoff (1993).

5   For the USA, see the propositions advanced by the MIT Commission on Industrial Productivity in their influential text *Made in America* (Dertouzos et al. 1989); for the OECD countries, see the positions taken in such influential texts as *New Technologies in the 1990s* (OECD 1988); *New Directions in Work Organisation* (OECD 1992); and the report on the OECD Technology/Economy Programme, *Technology in a Changing World* (OECD 1991); for the European community, see reports on the Anthropocentric Production System, such as in Lehner (1992); for Australia see the Australian Manufacturing Council (1990) and most recently its report on International Best Practice (Australia, Department of Industrial Relations/Australian Manufacturing Council 1992).

6   There is by now an enormous literature on teams and teamwork. For representative examples, see Pearce and Ravlin (1987); Versteg (1990); and Wellins et al. (1991).

7   On the distinction, and on the general foundations of the approach to the segmentation of the flow of product through a production system, see the contributions of the Dutch sociotechnical school, such as in de Sitter and den Hartog (1990).

8   On the effects of teamwork, and the phases they move through, see Wellins et al. (1991). On the approach to 'distributed leadership' in teamwork, see Barry (1991).

9   See the *Lucas Manufacturing Systems Engineering Handbook*, produced by Lucas Engineering & Systems Ltd, Solihull, UK. The ten points are taken from Szczygiel (1993).

10 A fascinating contrast can be drawn between the system embodied in the *Lucas Manufacturing Systems Handbook*, and that espoused by the German firm Bosch in their comprehensive *Flexible Automation System* handbooks. In the Bosch system, it would appear that skills-displacing automation is still the dominant aim, while lean production principles are conspicuous by their absence. The study of production systems design principles, embodied in such handbooks, remains a fascinating but little-researched topic.

11 Quality certification is provided under the International Standards Organisation's ISO 9000 series, which appear as Australian Standards in the AS 3900 series. The standards comprise the following elements:

- AS 3900 Quality Systems: Guide to Selection and Use;
- AS 3901 Quality Systems: Model for Quality Assurance in Design/Development, Production, Installation and Servicing;

- AS 3902 Quality Systems: Model for Quality Assurance in Production and Installation;
- AS 3903 Quality Systems: Model for Quality Assurance in Final Inspection and Test;
- AS 3904 Quality Management and Quality System Elements: Guidelines.

These are being amplified with such sector-specific documents as:

- AS 3904.2 Quality Management and Quality System Elements. Part 2: Guidelines for Services.

The ISO 9000 standards series have been adopted, without change, in at least 53 countries, including Japan, all the EU and EFTA countries, and the USA.

12 On performance monitoring, see Eccles (1991) for an overview of the issues. For an exposition of the Objectives Matrix and how it can be used as a flexible performance monitoring tool by team members, see Riggs and Felix (1983). On benchmarking, see Walleck et al. (1991).

13 On banking experiences, see Bertrand and Noyelle (1988); on CNC machine tools, see Sorge et al. (1983, p. 155).

14 On the models of efficiency that inform different approaches to award restructuring, see Curtain and Mathews (1990).

15 On the role of skills in the new production systems, see Streeck (1989); for a comparison between Germany and the UK in this regard, see the interesting work by Steedman and Wagner (1989).

16 For an exposition of skills formation, see Ford 1988.

17 For an outline of the model, see Mathews (1993a). The approach taken offers advantages over indirect modelling exercises such as the extensions of neoclassical economics into 'human capital' theory or 'multi-factor productivity', all of which introduce needless confusion with their reliance on an undefined and (virtually) unmeasurable notion of 'capital'.

18 The Vehicle Industry Certificate was formally ratified by the Industrial Relations Commission; see Australian Industrial Relations Commission (1991a). It is discussed in Chapter 7, on the Ford Plastics plant.

19 For an illustration of the confusion that can occur when the different roles of supervisors in traditional, participative and 'lean' production systems are scrambled, see Klein (1989). On the marginalisation of supervisors in the Australian context, see Lansbury and Gilmour (1986).

20 On 'cluster' organisations, which are made up of cells (or clusters) linked in supportive arrangements, see Mills (1991). On the similarly inspired notion of a spider's web bringing together business units or service cells in a 'web' rather than a hierarchy, see Quinn (1992). I have come across these two books only after formulating the DISC model of organisational structure. They capture (up to a point) many

of the ideas I find Australian best practice firms successfully developing. I add 'up to a point', because Mills has little to say on the legitimation of cluster innovations through negotiations, while Quinn has a fascination with 'core competencies' and 'outsourcing' that could end up turning the 'intelligent enterprise' into the 'hollow enterprise'.

21 This figure was first displayed in the case study on Colonial Mutual, Mathews (1991).

22 See R. Likert (1967). Chapter 10 in particular discusses the achievement of 'effective coordination in a highly functionalized company'; Likert's Fig. 10-2a displays vertical, overlapping group linkages of customary line and staff departments.

23 On this topic, see the works of Stafford Beer and his recursive Viable Systems Model: in particular, Beer (1985).

24 See the summary exposition of McGregor's and Likert's views in Pugh et al. (1983) which states: 'The essential concept which both Likert and McGregor are propounding is that modern organizations, to be effective, must regard themselves as interacting groups of people with supportive relationships to each other' (1983, p. 168).

Chapter 4

1 For their original elaboration of this framework, see Freeman and Perez (1988); for earlier forms of the thesis, see Perez (1985) as well as Freeman's work on long waves, Freeman (1983). For a recent exposition that is concerned more with the economic impact of paradigm shifts, see Tylecote (1992).

2 In the biological sciences, a process of co-evolution describes a system where one species evolves in relation to another species. Common examples include flowers and insects which co-evolve so that the flower depends on the insect for pollination, while the insect depends on the flower for food. This biological concept has been adapted for organisational use, in the notion of 'sociotechnical' or 'techno-organisational' co-evolution.

3 On this point, see Marglin (1974). I take the modern view to favour the social origins of the factory as an organisational innovation which paved the way, or created the opportunity, for a series of technical innovations.

4 See, for example, the work of Lazonick (1979) on the reassertion of skilled workers' organisation in the British textile industry after the introduction of the technological innovation of the self-acting mule in the 1830s.

5 For Freeman's original formulation of the revised 'long wave' thesis, see Freeman (1983). For a discussion, see Grubler and Nowotny (1990). On the 'national system of innovation', see Lundvall et al. (1992).

6 Kuhn's original concept has been much elaborated and discussed by

313

philosophers of science (for example, in Lakatos and Musgrave (1970); and in Toulmin (1972)) but its core feature of a shift in the 'rules of the game' introduced through a subtle reformulation of existing categories, remains intact. This is what has been transposed across to the discussion of changes in technological systems; a shift in technological paradigm involves a change in the common assumptions informing design processes, as for example occurred with the introduction of a small steam engine by Watt (making only small modifications, centred on the introduction of a separate condenser, to existing atmospheric steam engines). This aspect of technoeconomic paradigm theory, involving the transposition of a conceptual framework developed to explain changes in scientific theories across to changes in technological systems which differ from science in their being open to rational design, has also been discussed at length (Clark 1987).

7   There is evidence, for example, provided by Jaikumar (1986) on the diffusion of computer numeric controlled (CNC) flexible manufacturing systems in Japan and the USA, highlighting the impediments to their take-up by firms in the USA who only understand one way of utilising automated systems.

8   There has been much criticism of the framework of 'paradigm shift' in industrial firms, focusing more particularly on Piore and Sabel than on Freeman and Perez. A typical example is that of Williams et al. (1987). I do not intend to engage with these criticisms here; they have been discussed in Badham and Mathews (1989) and Mathews (1992e).

9   On the topic of organisational 'ecology,' viewing organisations as members of populations, see the seminal contribution by Hannan and Freeman (1989).

10   The problem of promoting diffusion of new organisational forms and new industrial relations practices was the subject of an interesting symposium staged in Washington D.C. in March 1994. Richard Locke, from MIT's Sloan School of Management, introduced the discussion by contrasting the 'passive' (market-led) with the 'active' (institutionally-based) models of diffusion. He concluded that best practice would be expected to spread through mainstream firms in America—and, by the same reasoning, in Australia—only with the aid of specific institutional mechanisms, such as mandatory enterprise-level consultative structures. The symposium was organised by the Work and Technology Institute (Washington D.C.) under the auspices of the Dunlop Commission's inquiry into reform of industrial relations in the USA.

11   Building on their work in *Under New Management* (1990), Dunphy and Stace have developed further categories regarding 'scale of change'. Type one is 'fine tuning'; type two is 'incremental adjustment'; type three is 'modular transformation'; and type four is total organisational change, or 'corporate transformation'. These categories are exemplified in a further series of case studies prepared within the Centre for Corporate Change at the Australian Graduate School of

Management, University of NSW. These studies, on organisations such as Alcan Australia Ltd, the NSW State Library, Comalco, AGL and FAI, have been issued as CCC working papers between 1991 and 1993. They will form the basis of a forthcoming book by Stace and Dunphy.

12   On the learning organisation, see the influential book by Senge (1990), and the earlier text by Hayes, Wheelwright and Clark (1988). These ideas are explored in greater detail in the final chapter.

Chapter 5

1   The term 'focused factory' derives from the Harvard theorist and observer, Wickham Skinner, who has done so much to revitalise manufacturing concepts in the west. His 1985 book is now a classic. In this text, he denounces the 'anachronistic factory' and traces the outlines of a 'focused factory' which simplifies the complexity of traditional hierarchies through driving responsibility and authority into self-managing teams. He also introduced the idea of 'reinventing the factory' as a catch-all for manufacturing organisational innovation. These terms have been picked up and extended by Roy Harmon based on the case files of the consulting firm Arthur Andersen & Co. I take up the concept of the 'focused factory' in my final chapter, and embed it in the deeper concept of the 'holonic organisation' or 'fractal factory' (Warnecke 1993).

2   The literature on team-based cellular manufacturing is growing quickly. I discuss some of the more important contributions in Chapter 3. See Burbridge (1985) in particular for an extensive discussion.

3   The study on which this chapter is based was published as no. 10 in the UNSW Studies in Organisational Analysis and Innovation series: see Mathews, Griffiths and Watson (1993). The study takes the Bendix Mintex story up to the end of 1992.

4   The Australian Best Practice Demonstration programme is a federal government initiative, offering support for selected companies that are prepared to invest in various forms of organisational innovation. A brief description of workplace reform at thirteen Australian companies, including Bendix Mintex, was published by the Australian Trade Commission in 1992.

5   In 1984 the Minister for Industry in the new Hawke Labor government, Senator John Button, launched an 'industry plan' for the automotive industry, envisaging a wind-down of tariff protection, an increase in restructuring assistance, and a rationalisation of producers. This has provided the framework for automotive industry operations in Australia for the past decade.

6   The components of the package were anticipated as being: capital works, $3.24 million; consultancy and contract engineering, $0.67 million; non-capital expenses, $0.89 million; and labour, $0.44 million.

7   The consulting engineers' contract had been terminated by the time

of our second visit in October 1992. It seems that cells were launched without adequate attention being paid to the logistics side of their operations which accounts for the difficulties they found themselves in.

8   The terminology 'Process Intent' is the same at Ford (see Chapter 7 on the Ford Plastics plant).

9   Technical issues tackled by the project team in conjunction with the consulting engineers concerned: friction material automatic weighing; new pad grinding machines; automatic moulding presses for latest friction materials technologies; direct gauging and computerised on-line statistical quality control facilities; the automated material handling system; and automated grinding, grooving and clipping equipment.

Chapter 6

1   This chapter is based on the study published as no. 5 in the UNSW Studies in Organisational Analysis and Innovation: J. Mathews (1991c), *Colonial Mutual Life Australia: Service quality through self-managing teamwork*, Industrial Relations Research Centre, UNSW. This chapter takes the Colonial Mutual story up to the end of 1992. In 1993 there were changes in management in the Client Services Division following the arrival of a new chief executive and the operation of the team-based innovations was subject to review.

2   For the initial exposition of business process re-engineering, see Hammer (1990) and Hammer and Champy (1993). The underlying ideas conform exactly with the notion of the sociotechnical production system interpreted as an organisational construct, and not just as an instrument of work design.

3   Whether this timetable will be met depends on the actions of the new management team installed by Colonial Mutual in 1993.

4   See the report by Levine (1986).

5   See Schlesinger and Heskett (1991) who call these systems examples of the 'industrial model' of service organisation, meaning that they conform to what we have called the mass production system. See also the MIT studies reported in Scott Morton (1991).

Chapter 7

1   This chapter is based on study no. 3 in the UNSW Studies in Organisational Analysis and Innovation: J. Mathews (1991b), *Ford Australia Plastics Plant: Transition to Teamwork through Quality Enhancement*. The chapter takes the story up to the end of 1992. The plant manager at the time of the study was Tom Pettigrew; he has since gone into private consultancy.

2   See the reports concerned such as that of Automotive Industry Authority (1991).

3   For a discussion of the Vehicle Industry Certificate and its significance,

see the example given in Chapter 3. The formal statement of the certificate is given in Australian Industrial Relations Commission (1991a).

Chapter 8

1   On the Italian experience, see the collection of studies commissioned by the International Institute for Labour Studies: Pyke, Becattini and Sengenberger (1990) as well as original contributions by Brusco (1982), Inzerilli (1990), Becattini (1991), and more recently, in a review of several such examples, Pyke and Sengenberger (1992) and Pyke (1994).

2   On the experience of Japan's small firm networks, see, for example, Kenney and Florida (1993).

3   See, for example, Thorelli (1986) and Powell (1990).

4   This chapter is based on study no. 7 in the UNSW Studies in Organisational Analysis and Innovation: J. Mathews (1992b), *TCG: Sustainable Economic Organisation through Networking*. Research assistance was provided by Andrew Griffiths. For an account of the TCG story by its founder, Peter Fritz, see Fritz and Ellercamp (1989). Aspects of the study have been published in Mathews (1993b; 1994).

5   This was the situation in 1992. Since then, three TCG member firms have been floated.

6   On networking as a mode of stimulating new product development, see Teece (1989). On innovation as a 'demand driven' process, see Kline and Rosenberg (1986). On 'fusion' technologies, see Kodama (1992), and Subramanian and Subramanian (1991).

7   The Australian Bureau of Industry Economics has recently considered the role of networks as a 'third form of organisation' (Australia. Bureau of Industry Economics 1991). The Bureau, basing itself on the work of Powell (1990), identifies three areas where networks offer significant advantages.

   • To improve resource use and spread risk
   Here the advantage of networks lies in avoiding costly duplication in areas such as research, product development and promotion. It is recognised that partnerships form around ventures with limited objects; partners may well be competitors in other areas.
   • To enhance flexibility and adaptability
   Relative to integration through merger or takeover, networks can be seen as offering advantages where product life-cycles are short-term; they are less costly and irreversible than mergers, and they retain a flexibility based on the continued self-interest of all the partners.
   • To access information and know-how
   Because much information about emerging technologies is tacit in character, the scope to exploit it through licensing arrangements is limited. Technological transfer through collaborative arrangements

provides a more flexible instrument for sharing the costs of development.

These reasons I take to be the conventional explanations for the success of networks.

8 This line of argument has been developed since the work of Coase (1937) and in Williamson (1985) it has been extended to include explicit recognition of intermediate forms between markets and hierarchies such as joint ventures.

9 See Marshall (1919). For a discussion of his significance in the context of Italian industrial districts, see Bianchi (1993).

Chapter 9

1 This model is developed in Chapter 12. For an account of an earlier experience with sociotechnical reform in Australia Post at the Brisbane Mail Centre, see Dick and Peter (1978).

2 This chapter is based on study no. 2 in the UNSW Studies in Organisational Analysis and Innovation: Mathews (1991a), *Australia Post: Introduction of Optical Character Recognition Mail Sorting Technology.* The study takes the story of the OCR Project to mid-1991.

3 The consultancy organisation chosen was the Industrial Participation Unit at the Royal Melbourne Institute of Technology.

4 This is my own terminology, introduced by analogy with programmable Flexible Manufacturing Systems. For a description of the OCR Project by Australia Post itself see Australia Post (1991).

5 The bulk of the Australia Post equipment is actually being manufactured in South Australia, sub-contracted by AEG to British Aerospace (Aust) Pty Ltd. The equipment has been modified to meet Australian operating standards, including health and safety standards. The first machine was handed over in January 1991.

6 For a description, see Ferner and Terry (1985, p. 7).

7 See, for example, Hedberg (1980), and Buchanan and Boddy (1984). Wall et al. (1984) found that it is organisational structuring and managerial strategies which determine the control of work, rather than the technological characteristics of the new equipment being operated. In a study of computerised typesetting at Adelaide Newspapers, Patrickson (1986) found that the control issue was central to employees accepting the new technology. On the broader issues of technological change and its negotiation through a broadened industrial relations system, see Sorge and Streeck (1988).

Chapter 10

1 This chapter is based on study no. 11 in the UNSW Studies in Organisational Analysis and Innovation: Mathews and Griffiths (1993), *CIG Gas Cylinders: A decade of gainsharing through the Common Interest Model.* It takes the story up to mid-1993.

2 The Common Interest Programme was originally developed by three associates, Colin Harrison, Dennis Pratt, and Paul Carey. They founded the consultancy group Effective Management Systems, which installed the gainsharing system at CIG Gas Cylinders. For the definitive exposition of the Common Interest Programme, as developed in the 1970s, see Dennis Pratt (1977). For a more recent exposition of the Programme as part of a wider organisational renewal, see Pratt (1993).

Chapter 11

1 Office Structures Implementation was a reform of job structures implemented across the entire public sector, resulting in a new eight tier job classification structure and career path for the Australian Public Service. It was negotiated with the various public sector unions under the terms of the 'Second Tier' wage principles, and ratified by the Australian Conciliation and Arbitration Commission in 1987.

2 This chapter is based on study no. 6 in the UNSW Studies in Organisational Analysis and Innovation: Mathews (1992a), *The Australian Taxation Office: Modernisation through People, Structures and Technology*. Research assistance was provided by Andrew Griffiths. Only a fraction of this 194 page monograph can be given here. The chapter takes the story of the Modernisation Programme up to the end of 1992.

3 Taxes mandated by Parliament for collection by the ATO are currently specified as:

- Income Tax—the *Income Tax Assessment Act 1936* and various amendments and regulations issued under it;
- Medicare Levy—the *Medicare Levy Amendment Act 1989*;
- Fringe Benefits Tax—the *FBT Assessment Act 1986*;
- Sales Tax—the *Sales Tax Assessment Act 1930* and amendments and regulations;
- Company Recoupment Tax—*Taxation (Unpaid Company Tax) Assessment Act 1982* (passed for the purpose of imposing a once-only tax on former promoters of tax evasion schemes);
- Debits Tax—*Debits Tax Act 1982* (formerly known as the bank account debits tax);
- Wool Tax—*Wool Tax Act 1964* (levied to finance R&D in the wool industry, and to support the Australian Wool Corporation; this arrangement was modified with the break-up of the Corporation in 1991);
- Tobacco Charge—*Tobacco Charges Assessment Act 1955*;
- Petroleum Resource Rent Tax—*Petroleum Resource Rent Tax Act 1987* (levied on profits from certain offshore petroleum projects);
- Child Support—*Child Support Act 1988*, amended by the *Child Support Assessment Act 1989* which established the Child Support

Agency (set up to collect child maintenance payments awarded by the Family Court);

- Higher Education Contributions Scheme—*Higher Education Funding Act 1989* (requiring students to contribute towards the cost of their higher education when they are in a position financially to do so);

- Training Guarantee Scheme—*Training Guarantee Act 1990* (imposing a levy on firms which fail to spend 1.5 per cent of their payroll on training-related activities). In a test case, the Act was challenged as unconstitutional in the High Court in August 1991.

4 See Australian Taxation Office, *Annual Report 1990/91*.

5 See the reference to ATO electronic monitoring and pacing of Returns Processing operators in 1982, in my 1985 occupational health and safety handbook (p. 315 of the second edition: J. Mathews (1993) *Health and Safety at Work: Australian Trade Union Safety Representatives Handbook*, Pluto Press Australia, Sydney).

6 Commissioner Boucher himself insists that he was simply the catalyst who brought together a very talented management team. While it is undoubtedly the case that he could not do everything himself, and was able to call on very able senior managers, he nevertheless provided the leadership that was an essential ingredient. Commissioner Boucher retired in 1993, and took up a posting as Australian Ambassador to the OECD, in Paris.

7 See Australia. Parliament. House of Representatives. Standing Committee on Public Accounts, *A Taxing Problem: Review of Five Auditor-General's Efficiency Audit Reports into the Australian Taxation Office*, AGPS, Canberra, 1986.

8 See, for example, the discussion of the Agreement in the public sector innovation review: Australia. Management Advisory Board, *Resource Agreements*, Joint Report of the Management Advisory Board and its Management Improvement Advisory Committee, no. 4, AGPS, Canberra, 1991.

9 On the retirement of Commissioner Boucher, Michael Carmody took over at the end of 1992, fresh from his experience directing the Modernisation Project. For his own account of the project up to 1989, see Carmody (1989).

10 For example, at the Penrith branch office on the western extremities of Sydney, the ELS returns processing team consists of twelve staff, ten of whom are at level 2 in the Administrative Services Officer (ASO) ladder, one at level 3 and one team leader at level 4; whereas the three paper-based returns processing units each have a staff complement of fifteen, seven of whom are at level 1, six at level 2, one at level 3 and again a team leader at level 4.

11 See the discussion of this Telecom dispute which led to a national telephone strike in Australia in 1978, in Mathews 1989a, pp. 71–2.

12 For a description of the establishment of a centralised Document

Processing Centre by the Australian Securities Commission in the Latrobe Valley in Victoria, see the study by Belinda Probert (1991). She characterises the choice as one of organisational segmentation, splitting the Commission into professional and processing operations.

13 On the influence of long-term relationships between organisations and their clients, a topic which is called 'relational marketing' or more generally 'relational contracting', see the interesting paper by Dwyer, Schurr & Oh (1987). This thinking, along with that on 'market segmentation', has had a great influence in the ATO, particularly through Deputy Commissioner Bill Godfrey.

14 Note the striking similarity between this approach to tax collection, and McGregor's arguments concerning a Theory X or Theory Y approach to management, discussed in Chapter 3. Using McGregor's framework, one could argue that the ATO under Commissioner Boucher is moving from a Theory X view of the taxpayer as someone who wishes to cheat and subvert the system, to a Theory Y approach which sees people as willing to pay their fair share of taxes if given the opportunity and incentive to do so. This is a theoretical approach that one can see underpinning the current programmes of the ATO.

15 For an exposition of the 're-engineering' approach to the utilisation of information technology, see Hammer (1990, pp. 104–12). As Hammer says on page 110:

> Nearly all of our processes originated before the advent of modern computer and communications technology. They are replete with mechanisms designed to compensate for 'information poverty'. Although we are now information affluent, we still use those mechanisms, which are now deeply embedded in automated systems.

16 For such critiques, see Pava (1986). For a more recent discussion, see the book by van Eijnatten (1993).

Chapter 12

1 For a more extended treatment of the industrial relations of skills formation, see Mathews (1993a); for an introduction to the issues of skill formation generally, see Mathews (1994).

2 On the Japanese industrial relations and labour systems, see the seminal text by Koike (1988); this establishes the lineaments of the Japanese system as one which extends to blue-collar workers conditions which have traditionally been accorded white-collar workers in the West. For recent expositions of the state of the Japanese system, see Koshiro (1992) and Kuwahara (1993).

3 Similar points have been made in relation to the development of union–management common ground, at the enterprise level, in the USA, by such authors as Applebaum and Batt (1994); Cohen-Rosenthal

and Burton (1993); Bluestone and Bluestone (1992); and Herrick (1990).

4   In Australia, such a position has been forcefully put by the Business Council of Australia (1989). It calls for the dismantling of the centralised system of awards in favour of largely unregulated enterprise negotiation. A similar position has been spelt out by Niland (1989), in his Green paper on industrial relations reform prepared for the NSW government, again locating the impetus for enterprise agreements in the 'rigidities' of the present industrial relations system, without much, if any, discussion of underlying production systems. For a discussion of the Business Council of Australia position, see Frenkel and Peetz (1990).

5   On the distinction, which has been central to industrial relations theory, see Niland (1989).

6   The open agenda 'search conference' was pioneered in Australia by Fred and Merrelyn Emery, as a tool of transformative organisational change. On the technique of such conferences, see Emery and Emery (1978).

7   The nine step model elaborated can be fruitfully compared with the sociotechnical approach to organisational change developed in The Netherlands, where it has come to be called the 'Integrated Organisational Renewal' model of change. This model likewise emphasises participation as a learning tool and as a means of engaging in 'structural exploration'. See the review by de Sitter and den Hartog (1990), and the exposition by Eijnatten (1993).

8   I have expounded these views at length in my *Tools of Change* and in the chapter 'The Future for Trade Unions' in my *Age of Democracy*. For the definitive exposition of the role that unions can play in the new competitive conditions, with special reference to the United States, see Marshall (1988).

9   The notion of political exchange was introduced by the Italian theorist Pizzorno (1978) to describe union–state relations under conditions of social pacts, and extended by Regini (1984) to describe its implications for the relations between union leaderships and their rank and file members. See Crouch (1990; 1993) for an extended discussion of its applicability in other European contexts. The term has been adopted in Australia in the 1980s to describe the relations cemented between the Australian Labor Party and the Australian Council of Trade Unions under the ALP–ACTU Accord, first reached in 1983 and still in operation at the time of writing.

10   On these Italian industrial relations arrangements, see, for example, Perulli (1990).

11   The position expounded here has been contested by the Business Council of Australia, especially in the third report of the BCA Employee Relations Study Commission (Hilmer 1993). In this report, the argument that industrial relations frameworks provide an important floor below

which employers will not be allowed to sink, thereby forcing them to compete on other than least cost grounds, is never met head on; it is simply dismissed! On page 127, for example, it is claimed *tout court* that such a view 'is firmly based on the application of classical economics to the market for employment'; four pages on, the argument is again dismissed on grounds that it 'rests on assumptions about the nature of product markets and consumers' preferences that are not found in the real world'. This is an extraordinary statement, given the experience of most of the twentieth century with the repeated success of low-cost market strategies, first in manufacturing and then in services. The BCA's Employee Relations Study Commission has yet to make any serious response to the arguments (such as in Chapter 2 of this book) where product markets and consumer preferences are treated in a decidedly real world fashion. To date, the BCA's Employee Relations Study Commission has sought refuge from these arguments in abstract economic theorising, treating the firm as a 'nexus of contracts' and thereby seeking to undermine the case for any form of negotiated collective agreements at the enterprise level. A very different approach is taken by the BCA's Innovation Study Commission (Carnegie & Butlin 1993).

Chapter 13

1   I do not wish to give a hostage to fortune with this remark. These 'best practice' companies are subject to the buffeting of their commercial environments, and are likely to enjoy periods of downturn as well as prosperity. But the point is that they seem to have recovered from the pits of alienation and despair that many of them reached at the worst points of their existence prior to restructuring and workplace reform.

2   The term 'learning organisation' has taken off, and now has considerable literature behind it. See the popular exposition by Peter Senge (1990), as well as the works by Lundvall (1992). This literature tends to be rather Anglo-centric. For a description of the powerful organisational learning systems developed by the successful East Asian economies, see, for example, Amsden (1989) and her description of the Korean learning organisation, Hyundai.

3   See, for example, Pasinetti (1993). This book presents a theoretical investigation of the dynamics of production which are placed at the centre of analysis instead of exchange, in the context of a 'pure labour' economy, but one which grasps the essential features of modern industrial systems. On the 'new growth theory', see the OECD study (1992).

4   Di Bernardo and Rullani (1990). This is my own translation from Note 49, page 425.

5 The process is thus much closer in spirit to Lamarckian evolution with its notion of learned adaptations than to neo-Darwinian accounts.

6 See the ground breaking work edited by Bengt-Ake Lundvall (1992). The 'learning economy' in particular is discussed in the final chapter, 'Public policy in the learning society', by Bent Dalum, Bjorn Johnson and Bengt-Ake Lundvall. See also the paper 'The learning economy' delivered by Bengt-Ake Lundvall and Bjorn Johnson to the EAEPE 1992 conference 'Structural change and the regulation of economic systems', Paris, 4–6 November.

7 See the discussion of 'core competencies' in Prahalad and Hamel (1990). This paper won a 1990 McKinsey Award for excellence.

8 These are the issues that Mills (1991) brings out in his notion of the 'cluster organisation'. In an apt characterisation of the 'learning organisation' based on clusters (or cells), Mills and Friesen (1992) identify four key features of the successful learning organisation. First, it should possess mechanisms which transfer learning from the individual to the group, meaning that there is a net gain in knowledge when someone joins a cluster. Second, there must be a commitment to knowledge, and to knowledge-based systems. Third, it needs a mechanism for renewal, such as in dismantling clusters that are no longer needed, or which have become demoralised, and starting new ones. And fourth, it needs to possess an openness to the outside world, such as through direct contact between clusters and customers.

9 I do not use the term 'organisational inertia' for this condition, as I wish to reserve this term for the phenomenon of 'institutional lag' that holds back the diffusion of organisational innovations from one firm to another. Such a concept of inertia, when embedded in the broader notion of diffusion, is much more satisfying as a scientific term than the slightly petulant notion of 'resistance to change'.

10 This is emphasised by Freeman and Perez (1988) in their account of technoeconomic paradigm shifts, as discussed earlier, and by many other OECD publications, such as the recent influential text, *Technology and the Economy: The Key Relationships* (Paris 1992a). For a discussion of this issue in the context of the textile industry, probing the reasons for the successful adjustment strategies in Italy and the unsuccessful strategies in Australia, see Weiss and Mathews (1991).

11 The Intelligent Manufacturing System (IMS) programme was proposed by Japan as a trilateral collaborative research venture involving Japan, the United States and Europe, in 1989. Following initial hostility from the Americans and Europeans, who harboured suspicions that this programme would be a Trojan Horse planted by Japan in their economies to spirit away their supposed technological lead, it has now evolved to encompass a wider agenda and a wider group of participants, including Australia. On the IMS see the Proceedings of the three International Symposia staged to date (the third being staged in Vienna in November 1993), as well as the Proceedings of the Workshop held

by the IMS International Technical Committee in Sydney, 22 February 1993.

12 On these concepts, see, for example, Ranta (1993); Moriwaki (1993); and Warnecke (1993). The essential point of the 'fractal factory' is that it consists of recursive 'cells' whose composition reflects the overall composition of the production system.

13 The term 'holon' was coined originally by Arthur Koestler in his book *The Ghost in the Machine* (1967). It was intended as a term for biological notions such as 'cell', which are at the same time both 'parts' and 'wholes', with the aim of combatting reductionist thinking in the human sciences. Its application in the organisational arena is surely long overdue.

14 There is now an extensive literature on Object-Oriented Programming (OOP). See, for example, Shriver and Wegner (1987). Niklaus Wirth, the developer of the computer language PASCAL, has now developed a first generation Object-Oriented language called Oberon. This is a set of 'objects' that work as a team, providing the services of both an operating system and applications programmes. 'Objects' are essentially self-contained programmes that perform a single function, such as word processing, drawing charts, or running the operating system. The conceptual links between OOP and cell-based manufacturing are clear, although they have yet to be drawn out in any depth.

15 It is worth noting that the cybernetics pioneer Stafford Beer insisted on the same property in his organisational model based on living systems, called the Viable Systems Model. See Beer's trilogy 'The managerial cybernetics of organization': Beer (1979; 1981; 1985).

16 For a fascinating account of the MAP initiative and the wider attempts to develop an open CIM standard, see Dankbar and van Tulder (1989). On the early formulation of the Intelligent Manufacturing System concept that emphasises the issue of global, transparent standards, see Yoshikawa (1990).

17 On innovation networks, see the seminal contributions of Mariti and Smiley (1983), of Imai (1985) in the context of Japan, of Mariotti and Cainarca (1986) in the context of Italy, and of Pisano and Teece (1989) in the context of the USA.

18 On neoclassical contracts, and an alternative termed 'relational contracting' that reflects long-term relationships, see Macneil (1978). This idea is elaborated into a theory of inter-firm relationships based on transactions costs by Williamson (1985).

19 On the economic significance of trust, see Sabel (1992).

20 On ESOPs, there is by now a voluminous literature documenting their many forms, and the superior performance of firms which have installed them. See, for example, Hyde (1992). It is noteworthy that in Australia, the union peak council, the ACTU, issued a comprehensive guide for its affiliated unions in 1993 (*Handle With Care: Employee Share Ownership Plans*), urging them to enter into negotia-

tions with firms to establish preferred model ESOPs that would give Australian workers a substantial ownership stake in the nation's industry by the year 2001.

21 Toulmin (1972) appealed to an entity he called 'rational enterprise' that is common to science, technology and law. However Toulmin paid no attention to organisation, and did not attempt to include it in his common model. Nevertheless I wish to acknowledge him as the source for this idea.

22 This is a highly compressed account of scientific reasoning that draws on a vast literature. A classic statement is that given by Lakatos and Musgrave (1970), while more recent discussions that canvass a variety of approaches are those by Chalmers (1990) and Turnbull (1991). My point is not to take a position in the elaboration of science, but to underline the similarities in rational procedure between scientific theory formation, technological design, and the formulation of organisational strategies.

Bibliography

Abernathy, W. 1978, *The Productivity Dilemma*, The Johns Hopkins University Press, Baltimore, Mass.

Abernathy, W., Clark, K. and Kantrow, A. 1981, 'The New Industrial Competition', *Harvard Business Review*, Sept.–Oct. 1981, pp. 68–81

ACTU/TDC Mission to Western Europe 1987, *Australia Reconstructed: ACTU/TDC Mission to Western Europe. A Report by the Mission Members to the ACTU and TDC*, AGPS, Canberra

Ainger, A. 1988, 'CIM—The Human-Centred Approach', *Technology in Action*, Jan. 1988, pp. 28–31, BICC plc, London

Alexander, M. and Green, R. 1992, 'Workplace Productivity: Issues and Evidence', in M. Alexander et al., *Industrial Relations and Workplace Productivity* (Industrial Relations Research Series, no. 2), Department of Industrial Relations, Canberra

Amsden, A.H. 1989, *Asia's Next Giant: South Korea and Late Industrialization*, Oxford University Press, New York

Appelbaum, R. and Batt, R. 1994, *The New American Workplace: Transforming Work Systems in the United States*, ILR Press, Cornell University, Ithaca

Atkinson, J. 1987, 'Flexibility or fragmentation? The UK labour market in the 1980s', *Labour and Society*, vol. 12, no. 1, pp. 87–105

Australia, Bureau of Industry Economics 1991, *Networks: A Third Form of Organisation* (Discussion Paper no. 14), AGPS, Canberra

Australia, Department of Industrial Relations/Australian Manufacturing Council 1992, *International Best Practice: Report of the Overseas Study Mission*, AGPS, Canberra

Australia, Management Advisory Board 1991, *Resource Agreements* (Report of Management Improvement Advisory Committee (MAB–MIAC), no. 4), AGPS, Canberra

Australia, Parliament, House of Representatives, Standing Committee on

Public Accounts 1986, *A Taxing Problem: Review of Five Auditor General's efficiency audit reports into the Australian Taxation Office*, AGPS, Canberra

Australia, Parliament, Senate, Standing Committee on Industry Science and Technology 1990, *People and Technology: New Management Techniques in Manufacturing Industry*, AGPS, Canberra

Australia Post 1991, 'Application of OCRs in Australia as Combined Address and Barcode Reader Sorters', paper presented to 10th International Conference on Postal Mechanization, Tokyo

Australian Conciliation and Arbitration Commission 1987, *National Wage Case: Decision* ('Second Tier decision'), Print G6800, Melbourne

——1988, *National Wage Case: Decision* ('Structural Efficiency Principle decision'), Print H4000, Melbourne

Australian Council of Trade Unions 1993, *Handle With Care: Employee Share Ownership Plans*, Melbourne

Australian Industrial Relations Commission 1989a, *National Wage Case: Decision*, Print H9100, Melbourne

——1989b, *Structural Efficiency Principle, Vehicle Builders' Employees Federation–Ford Australia: Decision*, Print H9654, 19 September, Melbourne

——1991a, *Endorsed Vehicle Industry Certificate, VBEF–Ford Australia: Decision*, Print J8021, 5 June 1991, Melbourne

——1991b, *National Wage Case: Decision*, Print K0300, 11 December 1991, Melbourne

Australian Manufacturing Council 1990, *The Global Challenge: Australian Manufacturing in the 1990s: Final report of the Pappas Carter Evans & Koop/Telesis study*, Melbourne

Australian Taxation Office 1991, *Annual Report 1990/91*, AGPS, Canberra

Australian Trade Commission 1992, *Best Practice for World Competitiveness: Thirteen Australian Success Stories*, AGPS, Canberra

Automotive Industry Authority 1991, *Report on the State of the Automotive Industry 1990*, AGPS, Canberra

Axelrod, S. 1984, *The Evolution of Cooperation*, Penguin Books, London

Babbage, C. 1832, *On the Economy of Machinery and Manufactures*, London, reprinted 1963, Kelley, New York

Badham, R. and Mathews, J. 1989, 'The "New Production Systems" debate', *Labour & Industry*, vol. 2, no. 2, pp. 194–246

Badham, R. and Schallock, B. 1990, *Human Factors in CIM development: A Human-Centred Perspective from Europe*, Fraunhofer IPK, Berlin

Bamber, G. and Lansbury, R. (eds) 1993, *International and Comparative Industrial Relations: A Study of Industrialised Market Economies*, Allen & Unwin, Sydney

Barrett, F. and Srivastva, S. 1991, 'History as a mode of inquiry in organizational life: A role for human cosmogony', *Human Relations*, vol. 44, no. 3, Mar. 1991, pp. 211–308

Barry, D. 1991, 'Managing the bossless team: Lessons in distributed leadership', *Organizational Dynamics*, Summer, pp. 31–47

Baumgartner, T. 1986, 'Actors, models and limits to societal self-steering', in F. Geyer and J. van der Zouwen (eds), *Sociocybernetic Paradoxes: Observation, Control and Evolution of Self-Steering Systems*, Sage, London

Becattini, G. 1991, 'Italian industrial districts: Problems and perspectives', *International Studies of Management & Organization*, vol. 21, no. 1, pp. 83–90

Beer, M., Eisenstat, R. and Spector, B. 1990, 'Why change programs don't produce change', *Harvard Business Review*, Nov.–Dec., pp. 158–66

Beer, S. 1979, *The Heart of Enterprise*, John Wiley, New York

——1981, *Brain of the Firm*, 2nd edn, John Wiley, New York

——1985, *Diagnosing the System for Organizations*, John Wiley, New York

Berggren, C. 1992, *Alternatives to Lean Production: Work Organization in the Swedish Auto Industry*, ILR Press, Cornell University, Ithaca

——1993, 'The Volvo Uddevalla plant: why the decision to close it is mistaken', *Journal of Industry Studies*, vol. 1, no. 1, pp. 75–87

Bertrand, O. and Noyelle, T. 1988, *Human Resources and Corporate Strategy: Technological Change in Banks and Insurance Companies*, OECD, Paris

Best, M. 1990, *The New Competition: Institutions of Industrial Restructuring*, Harvard University Press, Cambridge, Mass.

Bianchi, P. 1993, 'The promotion of small-firm clusters and industrial districts: European policy perspectives', *Journal of Industry Studies*, vol. 1, no. 1, pp. 16–29

Bijker, W., Hughes, T. and Pinch, T. (eds) 1988, *Social Construction of Technological Systems: New Directions in the Sociology and History of Technology*, MIT Press, Cambridge, Mass.

Bluestone, B. and Bluestone, I. 1992, *Negotiating the Future: A Labor Perspective on American Business*, Basic Books, New York

Boyer, R. (ed.) 1988, *The Search for Labour Market Flexibility: The European Economies in Transition*, Clarendon Press, Oxford

——1989, *The Transformations of Modern Capitalism by the Light of the Regulation Approach and Other Political Economy Theories*, CEPREMAP, Paris

——1990, *New Management Practices and Work Organisation*, Report to OECD Conference on Industry Structure and Strategy, Helsinki, CEPREMAP, Paris

Brandt, D. 1991, *Advanced Experiences with APS Concepts, Design Strategies, Experiences: Thirty European Case Studies* (APS Research Papers, vol. 2), FAST Programme, European Commission, Brussels

Broedner, P. 1985a, 'Options for CIM: "unmanned factory" versus skill-based manufacturing', *Computer-Integrated Manufacturing Systems*, vol. 1, pp. 67–74

———1985b, *Fabrik 2000: Alternative Entwicklungspfade in die Zukunft der Fabrik*, Ed. Sigma Bohn Verlag, Berlin

———(ed.) 1987, *Strategic Options for 'New Production Systems': Computer and Human Integrated Manufacturing (CHIM)* (FAST Paper 150), European Commission, Brussels

Broedner, P. and Karwowski, W. (eds) 1992, *Ergonomics of Hybrid Automated Systems III*, Elsevier Science Publishers, Amsterdam

Brown, W. and Nolan, P. 1988, 'Wages and labour productivity: The contribution of industrial relations research to the understanding of pay determination', *British Journal of Industrial Relations*, vol. 26, no. 3, pp. 339–61

Brusco, S. 1982, 'The Emilian Model: Productive decentralisation and social integration', *Cambridge Journal of Economics*, vol. 6, pp. 167–84

Buchanan D. and Boddy, D. 1984, 'Skills, motivation and interdependencies: The effective use of new computing technology', *Journal of Organisational Behaviour Management*, vol. 6, pp. 99–107

Bunge, M. 1979, *A World of Systems (Treatise on Basic Philosophy*, vol. 4*)*, D. Reidel, Dordrecht

Burbridge, J. 1985, *The Introduction of Group Technology*, Wiley, New York

———1992, 'Change to group technology: Process organization is obsolete', *International Journal of Production Research*, vol. 30, no. 5, pp. 1209–19

Business Council of Australia 1989, *Enterprise-Based Bargaining Units: A Better Way of Working*, Melbourne

Callus, R., Morehead, A., Cully, M. and Buchanan, J. 1991, *Industrial Relations at Work: The Australian Workplace Industrial Relations Survey*, Department of Industrial Relations, AGPS, Canberra

Carmody, M. 1989, 'Modernisation: The Australian Taxation Office, Approach to Introducing New Technology', in R. Clarke and J. Cameron (eds), *Proc. SOST 1989*, Australian Computer Society, Sydney

Carnegie, R. and Butlin, M. 1993, *Managing the Innovative Enterprise: Australian Companies Competing with the World's Best*, Business Council of Australia, Report of the Innovation Study Commission, The Business Library, Sydney

Centro d'Informazione Tessile Emilia-Romagna (CITER) 1989, *Information Paper*, Centre for Textiles Information Emilia-Romagna, Carpi

Chalmers, A. 1990, *Science and its Fabrication*, Open University Press, Milton Keynes

Chandler, A. 1977, *The Visible Hand*, Harvard University Press, Cambridge, Mass.

———1990, *Scale and Scope: The Dynamics of Industrial Capitalism*, The Belknap Press of Harvard University Press, Cambridge, Mass.

Chandler, A. and Tedlow, R. 1985, *The Coming of Managerial Capitalism: A Casebook on the History of American Economic Institutions*, Irwin, Homewood, Ill.

Clark, N. 1987, 'Similarities and differences between scientific and technological paradigms', *Futures*, Feb., pp. 26–42

Clark, N. and Juma, C. 1987, *Long-Run Economics: An Evolutionary Approach to Economic Growth*, Pinter Publishers, London

Coase, R. 1937, 'The Nature of the Firm', *Economica* N.S., vol. 4, pp. 386–405; reprinted in G. Stigler and K. Boulding (eds) 1952, *Readings in Price Theory*, Irwin, Homewood, Ill.

Cohen-Rosenthal, E. and Burton, C. 1993, *Mutual Gains: A Guide to Union–Management Cooperation*, 2nd edn, ILR Press, Cornell University, Ithaca, NY

Cooley, M. 1981, *Architect or Bee? The Human Price of Technology* (reissued 1987), Hogarth Press, London

Cooley, M. and Crampton, S. 1984, 'Criteria for human-centred systems', in B. Hirsch and M. Actis-Data (eds), *Esprit CIM, Design, Engineering, Management and Control of Production Systems*, Elsevier, Amsterdam

Corbett, J. 1988, 'Ergonomics in the Development of Human Centred Advanced Manufacturing Technology', *Applied Ergonomics*, vol. 19, no. 1, pp. 35–9

Cressey, P. and Williams, R. 1990, *Participation in Change: New Technology and the Role of Employee Involvement: Research Results on Participation in Technological Change*, European Foundation for the Improvement of Living and Working Conditions, Dublin

Crouch, C. 1990, 'Generalized political exchange in industrial relations in Europe during the twentieth century', in B. Marin (ed.), *Governance and Generalised Exchange*, Campus, Frankfurt-am-Main

——1993, *Industrial Relations and European State Traditions*, Clarendon Press, Oxford

Cummings, T. 1978, 'Self-regulating work groups: A socio-technical synthesis', *Academy of Management Review*, vol. 3, July, pp. 625–34

Curtain, R. 1992, 'Emergence of workplace bargaining within a centralised wage system: The new industrial relations in Australia', in *New Directions in Work Organisation: The Industrial Relations Response*, OECD, Paris

Curtain, R. and Mathews, J. 1990, 'Two Models of Award Restructuring in Australia', *Labour & Industry*, vol. 3, no. 1, pp. 58–75

Dankbar, B. 1993, *Economic Crisis and Institutional Change: The Crisis of Fordism from the Perspective of the Automobile Industry*, University Press Maastricht, Maastricht, The Netherlands

Dankbar, B. and Tulder, R. van 1989, *The Construction of an Open Standard: Process and Implications of Specifying the Manufacturing Automation Protocol (MAP)*, Netherlands Organisation for Technology Assessment (NOTA), The Hague

Davis, E. and Lansbury, R. 1993, 'Industrial relations in Australia', in Bamber and Lansbury (eds), *International and Comparative Industrial Relations: A study of Industrialised Market Economies*, Allen & Unwin, Sydney

331

de Sitter, L.U. and den Hartog, J.F. 1990, 'Simple Organizations, Complex Jobs: The Dutch Sociotechnical Approach', paper presented at Annual Conference of the American Academy of Management, August 1990, San Francisco

Dertouzos, M. et al. 1989, *Made in America: Regaining the Productive Edge*, MIT Press, Cambridge, Mass.

Di Bernardo, B. 1991, *Le Dimensioni d'Impresa: Scala, Scopo, Varieta* (The Size of Firms: Economies of Scale, Scope and Variety), Franco Angeli, Milan

Di Bernardo, B. and Rullani, E. 1990, *Il Management e le Macchine: Teoria evolutiva dell'impresa* (Management and Machinery: An evolutionary theory of the firm), Il Mulino, Bologna

Dick, R. and Peter, H. 1978, *Changing Attitudes to Work: Participative Survey Feedback in the Brisbane Mail Exchange*, Organisation Studies Unit, University of Queensland, St Lucia

Dohse, K., Juergens, U. and Malsch, T. 1985, 'From "Fordism" to "Toyotism"? The social organization of the labour process in the Japanese automobile industry', *Politics and Society*, vol. 14, no. 2, pp. 115–46

Dore, R. 1990, 'Two kinds of rigidity: corporatist communities and collectivism', in Brunetta and Dell'Aringa (eds), *Labour Relations and Economic Performance*, Macmillan, London

Drucker, P. 1990, 'The emerging theory of manufacturing', *Harvard Business Review*, May–June, pp. 94–102

Dunphy, D. 1986, *Organisational Change by Choice*, McGraw-Hill, Sydney

Dunphy, D. and Stace, D. 1990, *Under New Management: Australian Organisations in Transition*, McGraw-Hill, Sydney

Dwyer, R., Schurr, P. and Oh, S. 1987, 'Developing buyer–seller relationships', *Journal of Marketing*, vol. 51, April, pp. 11–27

Eccles, R. 1991, 'The performance measurement manifesto', *Harvard Business Review*, Jan.–Feb., pp. 131–7

Ehn, P. 1988, *Work-Oriented Design of Computer Artifacts*, Centre for Working Life, Stockholm

Eichener, V. 1992, 'The impact of technical standards on the diffusion of anthropocentric CIM systems', in P. Broedner and W. Karwowski (eds), *Ergonomics of Hybrid Automated Systems III*, Elsevier Science Publishers, Amsterdam

Eijnatten, Frans van 1993, *The Paradigm that Changed the Workplace* (Social Science for Social Action: Toward Organisational Renewal, vol. 4), Van Gorcum Publishers, Assen/Maastricht

Emery, F. 1959, *Characteristics of Socio-Technical Systems* (Document 527), Tavistock Institute, London

——1967, 'The Next Thirty Years: Concepts, Methods and Anticipations', *Human Relations*, vol. 20, pp. 199–237

——1974, 'Bureaucracy and beyond', *Organizational Dynamics*, vol. 2, no. 3, pp. 2–13

——1978, *The Emergence of a New Paradigm of Work*, Centre for Continuing Education, Canberra

——1991, 'The search for more democratic/productive workplaces', in P. Thompson and K. Nash (eds), *Designing the Future: Workplace Reform in Australia*, Workplace Australia, Melbourne

Emery, F. and Emery, M. 1978, 'Searching', in J. Sutherland (ed.), *Management Handbook for Public Administrators*, Van Nostrand, New York

Emery, F. and Thorsrud, E. 1977, *Democracy at Work*, Martinus Nijhoff, Leiden

Federal Chamber of Automotive Industries/Federation of Vehicle Industry Unions 1989, *Meeting the Challenge: What Award Restructuring Really Means*, Report of Overseas Mission of the Australian Vehicle Manufacturing Industry, Melbourne

Ferner, A. and Terry, M. 1985, *'The crunch had come': A case study of changing industrial relations in the Post Office* (Warwick Papers in Industrial Relations, no. 1), Industrial Relations Research Unit, University of Warwick, Coventry

Ford, W.G. 1976, 'A study of human resources and industrial relations at the plant level in seven selected industries in Australia', Committee to Advise on Policies for Manufacturing Industry (Chair: R.G.R. Gordon Jackson), *Policies for Development of Manufacturing Industry: A Green Paper*, Volume 4: Commissioned Studies, AGPS, Canberra

——1988, 'Reconstruction and skill formation', *Unicorn*, vol. 14, no. 4, pp. 208–18

Freeman, C. (ed.) 1983, *Long Waves in the World Economy*, Butterworths, London

Freeman, C. and Perez, C. 1988, 'Structural crises of adjustment: Business cycles and investment behaviour', in G. Dosi et al. (eds), *Technical Change and Economic Theory*, Pinter Publishers, London

Frenkel, S. and Peetz, D. 1990, 'Enterprise bargaining: The BCA's report on industrial relations reform', *The Journal of Industrial Relations*, vol. 32, no. 1, pp. 69–99

Fritz, P. with Ellercamp, P. 1988, *The Possible Dream. TCG: An Australian Business Success Story*, Penguin Books, Melbourne

Fyfe, G. and Curran, B. 1993, 'Computer-aided telemarketing in an insurance company', in J. Mathews (ed.), *Technology, Work and Organisation: Case Studies* (UNSW Studies in Organisational Analysis and Innovation, no. 9), Industrial Relations Research Centre, The University of New South Wales, Sydney

Gjerding, A., Johnson, B., Kallehauge, L., Lundvall, B. and Madsen, P. 1992, *The Productivity Mystery: Industrial Development in Denmark in the Eighties*, Oekonomforbundets Forlag/DJOF Publishing, Copenhagen

Green, R. and Genoff, R. (eds) 1993, *Making the Future Work*, Allen & Unwin, Sydney

Grubler, A. and Nowotny, H. 1990, 'Towards the fifth Kondratiev upswing: elements of an emerging new growth phase and possible development trajectories', *International Journal of Technology Management*, vol. 5, no. 4, pp. 431–71

Gustavsen, B. 1992, *Dialogue and Development: Theory of Communication, Action Research and the Restructuring of Working Life*, Van Gorcum, Assen, in conjunction with the Swedish Centre for Working Life, Stockholm

Hamada, K. and Monden, Y. 1989, 'Profit management at Kyocera Corporation: The amoeba system', in Y. Monden and M. Sakurai (eds), *Japanese Management Accounting: A World Class Approach to Profit Management*, Productivity Press, Cambridge, Mass.

Hamlin, M. 1989, *Human-Centred CIM Systems: BICC Final Report*, Esprit Project 1217 (1199), BICC Technologies, London

Hammer, M. 1990, 'Re-engineering work: Don't automate, obliterate', *Harvard Business Review*, July–Aug., pp. 104–12

Hammer, M. and Champy, J. 1993, *Reengineering the Corporation: A Manifesto for Business Revolution*, Nicholas Brearley, London

Hancke, T. 1989, *Human Centred Design for the Imperial College Demonstrator Cell*, Department of Computing and Control, Imperial College, London

Hancke, T. and Braune, R. 1993, 'Human Centred Design of Human–Machine Systems and Examples from Air Transport', *Proc. International Federation Automatic Control (IFAC) 12th World Congress*, July, Sydney

Handy, C. 1990, *The Age of Unreason*, Harvard Business School Press, Boston

Hannan, M. and Freeman, J. 1989, *Organizational Ecology*, Harvard University Press, Cambridge, Mass.

Harmon, R. and Peterson, L. 1990, *Reinventing the Factory: Productivity Breakthroughs in Manufacturing Today*, Free Press Collier Macmillan, New York

Harvey, D. 1989, *The Condition of Post-Modernity: An Enquiry into the Origins of Cultural Change*, Basil Blackwell, Oxford

Hayes, R. and Jaikumar, R. 1988, 'Manufacturing's crisis: New technologies, obsolete organizations', *Harvard Business Review*, Sept.–Oct., pp. 77–85

Hayes, R., Wheelwright, S. and Clark, K. 1988, *Dynamic Manufacturing: Creating the Learning Organization*, The Free Press, New York

Hedberg, B. 1980, 'Using computerised information systems to design better organisations and jobs', in N. Bjorn-Andersen (ed.), *The Human Side of Information Processing*, North Holland, Amsterdam

Herbst, P. 1974, *Socio-technical Design*, Tavistock Publications, London

Herrick, N. 1990, *Joint Management and Employee Participation: Labor and Management at the Crossroads*, Jossey-Bass Publishers, San Francisco

Herzberg, F. 1966, *Work and the Nature of Man*, World Publishing Company, New York

——1968 'One more time: How do you motivate employees?', *Harvard Business Review*, Jan.–Feb. 1968, pp. 53–62

Heskett, J., Sasser, W. and Hart, C. 1990, *Service Breakthroughs: Changing the Rules of the Game*, Free Press, New York

Hilmer, F. (chair) 1993, *Working Relations: A Fresh Start for Australian Enterprises*, Report of the Employee Relations Study Commission of the Business Council of Australia, The Business Library, Sydney

Hirst, P. and Zeitlin, J. (eds) 1990, *Reversing Industrial Decline? Industrial Structure and Policy in Britain and her Competitors*, Berg, Oxford

Hornell, E. 1992, *Improving Productivity for Competitive Advantage: Lessons from the Best in the World*, Longman/Pitman Publishing, London

Hounshell, D. 1984, *From the American System to Mass Production 1800–1932: The Development of Manufacturing Technology in the United States*, The Johns Hopkins University Press, Baltimore

Huber, V. and Brown, K. 1991, 'Human resource issues in cellular manufacturing: A sociotechnical analysis', *Journal of Operations Management*, vol. 10, no. 1, pp. 138–59

Hughes, T. 1989, *American Genesis: A Century of Invention and Technological Enthusiasm 1870–1970*, Viking, New York

Hyde, A. 1992, 'In defense of employee ownership', *Chicago–Kent Law Review*, vol. 67, no. 1, pp. 159–211

Imai, Ken-Ichi 1985, *Network Organization and Incremental Innovation in Japan* (Discussion Paper no. 122), Institute of Business Research, Hitotsubashi University, Tokyo

Imai, Ken-Ichi, Nonaka, I. and Takeuchi, H. 1988, 'Managing the new product development process: How Japanese companies learn and unlearn', in M. Tushman and W. Moore (eds), *Readings in the Management of Innovation,* 2nd edn, Ballinger Publishing, Cambridge, Mass.

Industrial Commission of New South Wales 1991, *State Wage Case: Decision*, Justice W. Fisher, President, Sydney

Industry Commission 1991, *The Automotive Industry* (Report no. 5), AGPS, Canberra

International Institute for Labour Studies 1992, *Is the Single Firm Vanishing? Inter-enterprise Networks, Labour and Labour Institutions* (Forum Series on Labour in a Changing World Economy, Number 1), Geneva

Inzerilli, G. 1990, 'The Italian alternative: flexible organization and social management', *International Studies of Management & Organization*, vol. 20, no. 4, pp. 6–21

Jaques, E. 1951, *The Changing Culture of a Factory*, Tavistock Publications, London

Jaikumar, J. 1986, 'Post-industrial manufacturing', *Harvard Business Review*, Nov.–Dec., pp. 69–76

Johnson, H. and Kaplan, R. 1987, *Relevance Lost: The Rise and Fall of Management Accounting*, Harvard Business School Press, Boston

Johnston, R. and Lawrence, P. 1988, 'Beyond vertical integration—The rise of·the Value-Adding Partnership', *Harvard Business Review*, Jul.–Aug., pp. 94–101

Juergens, U., Dohse, K. and Malsch, T. 1986, 'New production concepts in West German car plants', in S. Tolliday and J. Zeitlin (eds), *The Automobile Industry and its Workers*, Polity Press, Cambridge

Juniper, J. 1993, 'Production systems debate', in R. Green and R. Genoff (eds), *Making The Future Work*, Allen & Unwin, Sydney

Kanter, R.M. 1990, *When Giants Learn to Dance: Mastering the Challenges of Strategy, Management and Careers in the 1990s*, Unwin Hyman, London

Kaplinsky, R. 1988, 'Restructuring the capitalist labour process: some lessons from the car industry', *Cambridge Journal of Economics*, vol. 12, pp. 451–70

Kenney, M. and Florida, R. 1993, *Beyond Mass Production: The Japanese System and its Transfer to the US*, Oxford University Press, New York

Kern, H. and Schumann, M. 1984, *Das Ende der Arbeitsteilung?* (End of the Division of Labour?), Verlag Beck, Munich

——1987, 'Limits of the division of labour: new production and employment concepts in West German industry', *Economic and Industrial Democracy*, vol. 8, pp. 151–70

——1989, 'New concepts of production in West German plants', in P. Katzenstein (ed.), *The Third West German Republic*, Cornell University Press, Ithaca, NY

Kidd, P. 1988, 'Human and Computer-aided Manufacturing: The End of Taylorism?', in W. Karwowski et al. (eds), *Ergonomics of Hybrid Systems*, Elsevier, Amsterdam

——1992, *Organization, People and Technology in European Manufacturing*, Report EUR 13967, FAST/MONITOR Programme, Commission of the European Communities, Brussels

Kidd, P. and Corbett, M. 1988, 'Towards the joint social and technical design of Advanced Manufacturing Systems', *International Journal of Industrial Ergonomics*, vol. 2, pp. 305–13

Klein, J. 1989, 'The human costs of manufacturing reform', *Harvard Business Review*, Mar.–Apr., pp. 60–6

Kline, S.J. and Rosenberg, N. 1986, 'An overview of innovation', in N. Rosenberg and R. Landau (eds), *The Positive Sum Strategy*, National Academy Press, Washington, DC

Kochan, T. and Dyer, L. 1992, 'Managing transformational change: The role of human resource professionals', in *Proceedings*, 9th International Industrial Relations Association World Congress, Sydney

Kochan, T., Katz, H. and McKersie, R. 1986, *The Transformation of American Industrial Relations*, Basic Books, New York

Kochan, T. and Useem, M. (eds) 1992, *Transforming Organizations*, Oxford University Press, New York

Kodama, F. 1991, *Analyzing Japanese High Technologies: The Techno-Paradigm Shift*, Pinter Publishers, London

——1992, 'Technology fusion and the new R&D', *Harvard Business Review*, July–Aug., pp. 70–8

Koestler, A. 1967, *The Ghost in the Machine*, Hutchinson, London

Koike, K. 1988, *Understanding Industrial Relations in Modern Japan*, St Martins Press, New York

Koshiro, K. 1992, 'The organisation of work and internal labour market flexibility in Japanese industrial relations', in OECD, *New Directions in Work Organisation: The Industrial Relations Response*, Paris

Kotter, J. 1990, 'What leaders really do', *Harvard Business Review*, May–June, pp. 103–11

Krafcik, J. 1988, 'The triumph of the lean production system', *Sloan Management Review*, vol. 30, pp. 41–52

Kriegler, R. and Dawkins, P. (eds) 1988, *Achieving Organizational Effectiveness: Case Studies in the Australian Services Sector*, Oxford University Press, Melbourne

Kuhn, T. 1962, *The Structure of Scientific Revolutions*, University of Chicago Press, Chicago

Kuwahara, Y. 1993, 'Industrial relations in Japan', in G. Bamber and R. Lansbury (eds), *International and Comparative Industrial Relations: A study of Industrialised Market Economies*, Allen & Unwin, Sydney

Lakatos, I. and Musgrave, A. (eds) 1970, *Criticism and the Growth of Knowledge*, Cambridge University Press, Cambridge

Lane, C. 1988, 'Industrial Change in Europe: The Pursuit of Flexible Specialisation in Britain and West Germany', *Work, Employment and Society*, vol. 2, no. 2, pp. 141–68

Lansbury, R. 1987, 'The Tomteboda mail centre revisited', *New Technology, Work and Employment*, vol. 2, no. 2, pp. 154–6

Lansbury, R. and Gilmour, P. 1986, *Marginal Manager: The changing role of supervisors in Australia*, University of Queensland Press, St Lucia

Lawler, E. 1991, *High-Involvement Management: Participative Strategies for Improving Organizational Performance*, Jossey-Bass Publishers, San Francisco

Lawrence, P. and Lorsch, J. 1969, *Organization and Environment*, Irwin Publishers, Homewood, Ill.

Lazonick, W. 1979, 'Industrial relations and technological change: The case of the self-acting mule', *Cambridge Journal of Economics*, vol. 3, pp. 231–62

——1991, *Business Organization and the Myth of the Market Economy*, Cambridge University Press, Cambridge

Lean Enterprise, European Automotive Initiative Group, Richmond, Surrey, UK, vol. 1, 1993+

Lehner, F. 1992, *Anthropocentric Production Systems: The European response to advanced manufacturing and globalisation*, FAST/MONITOR Programme, Report EUR 13969, Commission of the European Communities, Brussels

Lever-Tracy, C. 1990, 'Fordism transformed? Employee involvement and workplace industrial relations at Ford', *Journal of Industrial Relations,* vol. 32, no. 2, pp. 179–96

Levine, H. 1986, 'Highlights of AMA's 57th Annual Human Resources Conference', *Personnel,* vol. 63, no. 10, pp. 41–5

Lewin, K. 1947, 'Group decision and social change', *Readings in Social Psychology,* Henry Holt, New York

Likert, R. 1967, *The Human Organization: Its Management and Value,* McGraw-Hill, New York

Lofgren, M. 1986, 'A Swedish workplace of the future?: The Tomteboda mail centre', *New Technology, Work and Employment,* vol. 1, no. 1, pp. 84–7

Lund, R. et al. 1993, *Designed to Work: Production Systems and People,* PTR Prentice Hall, Englewood Cliffs, NJ

Lundvall, B.-A. (ed.) 1992, *National Systems of Innovation: Towards a Theory of Innovation and Interactive Learning,* Pinter Publishers, London

MacDuffie, J.P. and Krafcik, J.F. 1992, 'Integrating technology and human resources for high-performance manufacturing: Evidence from the international auto industry', in T. Kochan and M. Useem (eds), *Transforming Organizations,* Oxford University Press, New York

Macneil, I. 1978, 'Contracts: adjustment of long-term economic relations under classical, neo-classical and relational contract law', *Northwestern University Law Review,* vol. 72, no. 6, pp. 854–905

Mahon, R. 1987, 'From Fordism to ?: New technology, labour markets and unions', *Economic and Industrial Democracy,* vol. 8, no. 1, pp. 5–60

Majchrzak, A. 1988, *The Human Side of Factory Automation,* Jossey-Bass, San Francisco

Manz, C. and Sims, H. 1986, 'Leading self-managed groups: A conceptual analysis of a paradox', *Economic and Industrial Democracy,* vol. 7, pp. 141–65

Marglin, S. 1974, 'What do bosses do? The origins and functions of hierarchy in capitalist production', in T. Nichols (ed.) 1980, *Capital and Labour: Studies in the capitalist labour process,* Fontana, London

Marglin, S. and Schor, J. (eds) 1990, *The Golden Age of Capitalism: Reinterpreting the Post-War Experience,* Clarendon Press/ Oxford University Press, Oxford/New York

Marin, B. (ed.) 1990, *Governance and Generalised Exchange,* Campus, Frankfurt-am-Main

Mariotti, S. and Cainarca, G.C. 1986, 'The evolution of transaction governance in the textile-clothing industry', *Journal of Economic Behaviour and Organization,* vol. 7, pp. 351–74

Mariti, P. and Smiley, R.H. 1983, 'Cooperative agreements and the organization of industry', *The Journal of Industrial Economics,* vol. 31, no. 4, pp. 437–51

Marrow, A.J. 1964, 'Risks and uncertainties in action research: Kurt Lewin Memorial Address 1964', *Journal of Social Issues*, vol. 20, pp. 5–20

Marshall, A. 1919, *Industry and Trade: A Study of Industrial Technique and Business Organization; and of their Influences on the Conditions of various Classes and Nations*, Macmillan, London

Marshall, R. 1988, *Unheard Voices: Labor and Economic Policy in a Competitive World*, Basic Books, New York

Mathews, J. 1989a, *Tools of Change: New Technology and the Democratisation of Work*, Pluto Press, Sydney

——1989b, *Age of Democracy: The Politics of Post-Fordism*, Oxford University Press, Melbourne

——1989c, *Towards an 'Australian Model' of Wages-Linked Regulated Structural Adjustment*, Swedish Centre for Working Life, Stockholm

——1989d, 'New production concepts', *Prometheus*, vol. 7, no. 1, pp. 129–48

——1990, 'Theoretical perspectives on enterprise and award restructuring in Australia', *Asia Pacific Human Resource Management*, vol. 28, no. 4, pp. 30–9

——1991a, *Australia Post: Introduction of Optical Character Recognition Mail Sorting Technology* (UNSW Studies in Organisational Analysis and Innovation, no. 2), Industrial Relations Research Centre, The University of New South Wales, Sydney

——1991b, *Ford Australia Plastics Plant: Transition to Teamwork through Quality Enhancement* (UNSW Studies in Organisational Analysis and Innovation, no. 3), Industrial Relations Research Centre, The University of New South Wales, Sydney

——1991c, *Colonial Mutual Life Australia: Service Quality through Self-Managing Teamwork* (UNSW Studies in Organisational Analysis and Innovation, no. 5), Industrial Relations Research Centre, The University of New South Wales, Sydney

——1992a, *The Australian Taxation Office: Modernisation through People, Structures and Technology* (UNSW Studies in Organisational Analysis and Innovation, no. 6), Industrial Relations Research Centre, The University of New South Wales, Sydney

——1992b, *TCG: Sustainable Economic Organisation Through Networking* (UNSW Studies in Organisational Analysis and Innovation, no. 7), Industrial Relations Research Centre, The University of New South Wales, Sydney

——1992c, 'An Australian Model of Industrial Restructuring', in J. Marceau (ed.), *Reworking the World: Organizations, Technologies and Cultures*, De Gruyter, The Hague

——1992d, 'New production systems: a response to critics and a re-evaluation', *Journal of Australian Political Economy*, no. 30, pp. 91–128

——1992e, 'Social construction of technology', Review of Bijke, Hughes and Pinch (eds), *Social Construction of Technological Systems* (MIT Press, 1988), *Metascience*, Issue One, pp. 121–4

——1993a, 'The industrial relations of skills formation', *The International Journal of Human Resource Management*, vol. 4, no. 3, pp. 591–609

——1993b, 'TCG R&D networks: the triangulation strategy', *Journal of Industry Studies*, vol. 1, no. 1, pp. 65–74

——1994, 'The governance of inter-organisational networks', *Corporate Governance*, vol. 2, no. 1, pp. 14–19

Mathews, J. and Griffiths, A. 1993, *A Decade of Gainsharing: The Case of CIG Gas Cylinders* (UNSW Studies in Organisational Analysis and Innovation, no. 11), Industrial Relations Research Centre, The University of New South Wales, Sydney

Mathews, J., Griffiths, A. and Watson, N. 1993, *Socio-Technical Redesign: The Case of Cellular Manufacturing at Bendix Mintex* (UNSW Studies in Organisational Analysis and Innovation, no. 10), Industrial Relations Research Centre, The University of New South Wales, Sydney

McGregor, D. 1960, *The Human Side of Enterprise* (re-issued 1985), McGraw-Hill, New York

McKersie, R. and Walton, R. 1991, 'Organizational Change', in M. Morton (ed.), *The Corporation of the 1990s: Information Technology and Organizational Transformation*, Oxford University Press, New York

Miles, R. and Snow, C. 1986, 'Organisations: New concepts for new forms', *California Management Review*, vol. 28, no. 3, pp. 62–73

——1992, 'Causes of failure in network organizations', *California Management Review*, vol. 34, no. 4, pp. 53–72

Mills, D.Q. 1991, *Rebirth of the Corporation*, John Wiley, New York

Mills, D.Q. and Friesen, B. 1992, 'The learning organization', *European Management Journal*, vol. 10, no. 2, June, pp. 146–56

Monden, Y. 1993, *Toyota Production System: An Integrated Approach to Just-In-Time*, 2nd edn, Industrial Engineering and Management Press, Norcross, Georgia

Morgan, G. 1986, *Images of Organization*, Sage, London

Moriwaki, T. 1993, 'Autonomous distributed manufacturing systems', paper delivered to International Workshop on Intelligent Manufacturing Systems, 22 February, Sydney

Nadler, D., Gerstein. M., Shaw, R. and Associates 1992, *Organizational Architecture: Designs for Changing Organizations*, Jossey-Bass, San Francisco

Nelson, R. 1987, *Understanding Technological Change as an Evolutionary Process*, North Holland, Amsterdam

Niland, J. 1989, *Transforming Industrial Relations in New South Wales. A Green Paper*, NSW· Government, Sydney

Noble, D. 1984, *Forces of Production: A Social History of Industrial Automation*, Alfred Knopf, New York

Nomura, M. 1992, 'Assembly automation and division of labour in Japan: Can Japanese production concept be an alternative?', in P. Broedner and W. Karwowski (eds), *Ergonomics of Hybrid Automated Systems III*, Elsevier Science Publishers, Amsterdam

OECD 1988, *New Technologies in the 1990s: A Socioeconomic Strategy* (Sundqvist Report), Organisation for Economic Cooperation and Development, Paris

——1991, *Technology in a Changing World*, Report from the Technology/Economy Programme, Paris

——1992a, *Technology and the Economy: The Key Relationships*, Synthesis Report from the Technology/Economy Programme, Paris

——1992b, *New Directions in Work Organisation: The Industrial Relations Response*, Paris.

Ohno, T. 1988, *Toyota Production System: Beyond Large Scale Production*, Productivity Press, Cambridge, Mass.

Pasinetti, L. 1993, *Structural Economic Dynamics: A Theory of the Economic Consequences of Human Learning*, Cambridge University Press, Cambridge

Patrickson, M. 1986, 'Adaptation by employees to new technology', *Journal of Occupational Psychology*, vol. 59, pp. 1–11

Pava, C. 1986, 'Redesigning socio-technical systems design: concepts and methods for the 1990s', *The Journal of Applied Behavioral Science*, vol. 22, no. 3, pp. 201–21

Pearce, J. and Ravlin, E. 1987, 'The design and activation of self-regulating work groups', *Human Relations*, vol. 40, no. 11, pp. 751–82

Perez, C. 1985, 'Microelectronics, long waves and world structural change: new perspectives for developing countries', *World Development*, vol. 13, no. 3, pp. 441–63

Perrow, C. 1991, 'Small firm networks', keynote speech, IAREP/SASE Conference 'Interdisciplinary approaches to the study of economic problems', June, Stockholm School of Economics

Perulli, P. 1990, 'Industrial flexibility and small firm districts: the Italian case', *Economic and Industrial Democracy*, vol. 11, no. 3, pp. 337–54

Peters, T. and Waterman, R. 1982, *In Search of Excellence*, Harper & Row, New York

Pettigrew, T. 1983, 'Process Quality Control: The new approach to the management of quality in Ford', *The SAE–Australasia (Journal of the Society of Automotive Engineers—-Australasia)*, vol. 43, July–Aug., pp. 172–80

——1988, 'Process intent, statistics and participative management in a new model programme: The EA26 experience', paper delivered to International Workshop on Engineering Design and Manufacturing Management, November, University of Melbourne

Piore, M. and Sabel, C. 1984, *The Second Industrial Divide: Prospects for Prosperity*, Basic Books, New York

Pisano, G. and Teece, D. 1989, 'Collaborative arrangements and global technology strategy: Some evidence from the telecommunications equipment industry', in R. Rosenbloom and R. Burgelman (eds),

Research on Technological Innovation, Management and Policy, vol. 4, pp. 227–56

Pizzorno, A. 1978, 'Political exchange and collective identity in industrial conflict', in C. Crouch and A. Pizzorno (eds), *The Resurgence of Class Conflict in Western Europe Since 1968*, Volume 2: Comparative Analyses, Macmillan, London

Plowman, D. 1992, 'Industrial relations and the legacy of New Protection', *The Journal of Industrial Relations*, vol. 34, no. 1, pp. 48–65

Porter, M. 1990, *The Competitive Advantage of Nations*, Macmillan, New York

Powell, W. 1990, 'Neither market nor hierarchy: Network forms of organization', in B. Staw and L. Cummings (eds), *Research in Organizational Behaviour*, vol. 12, pp. 295–336

Prahalad, C. and Hamel, G. 1990 'The core competence of the corporation', *Harvard Business Review*, May–June, pp. 79–91

Pratt, D. 1977, *The Common Interest Programme: Motivation, Participation and Rewards*, Effective Management Systems, Terrigal, NSW 2260

——1993, *Aspiring to Greatness: Above and Beyond Total Quality Management*, Dennis Pratt & Associates, Peakhurst, NSW 2210

Probert, B. 1991, *Remote Office Work and Regional Development: The Australian Securities Commission in the LaTrobe Valley* (CIRCIT Policy Research Paper no. 13), Centre for International Research on Communication and Information Technologies, Melbourne

Pugh, D., Hickson, D. and Hinings, C. 1983, *Writers on Organizations*, 3rd edn, Penguin Books, Harmondsworth

Pyke, F. 1994, *Small Firms, Technical Services and Inter-firm Cooperation*, International Institute for Labour Studies, Geneva

Pyke, F., Becattini, G. and Sengenberger, W. (eds) 1990, *Industrial Districts and Inter-Firm Cooperation in Italy*, International Institute for Labour Studies, Geneva

Pyke, F. and Sengenberger, W. (eds) 1992, *Industrial Districts and Local Economic Regeneration*, International Institute for Labour Studies, Geneva

Quinn, J.B. 1992, *Intelligent Enterprise: A Knowledge and Service Based Paradigm for Industry*, The Free Press, New York

Ranta, J. 1993, 'Evolution and diffusion of advanced manufacturing', in W. Karwowski and G. Salvendy (eds), *Human Factors of Advanced Manufacturing*, John Wiley, New York

Rauner, F., Rasmussen, L. and Corbett, J.M. 1988, 'The social shaping of technology and work: Human centred CIM systems', *AI & Society*, vol. 2, pp. 47–61

Rauner, F. and Ruth, K. 1991, *The Prospects of Anthropocentric Production Systems: A World Comparison of Production Models* (APS Research Papers, vol. 5), FAST Programme, European Commission, Brussels

Regini, M. 1984, 'The conditions for political exchange: How concertation emerged and collapsed in Italy and Great Britain', in J. Goldthorpe (ed.), *Order and Conflict in Contemporary Capitalism*, Clarendon Press, Oxford

Riggs, J. and Felix, G. 1983, *Productivity by Objectives*, Prentice-Hall, New York

Rimmer, M. and Verevis, C. (eds) 1990, *Progress of Award Restructuring: Case Studies*, Industrial Relations Research Centre, The University of New South Wales, Sydney

Rockart, J. and Short, J. 1991, 'The networked organization and the management of interdependence', in M. Morton (ed.), *The Corporation of the 1990s: Information technology and organizational transformation*, Oxford University Press, New York

Roobeek, A. 1987, 'The crisis in Fordism and the rise of a new technological paradigm', *Futures*, April 1987, pp. 129–54

Rosenbrock, H. 1977, 'The future of control', *Automatica*, vol. 13, pp. 775–83

——1979, 'The redirection of technology', paper given to IFAC Symposium, Bari, Italy

——1982, 'Technology policies and options', in N. Bjorn-Anderson et al. (eds), *Information Society: For Richer, For Poorer*, North Holland, Amsterdam

Sabel, C. 1989, 'Flexible specialisation and the re-emergence of regional economies', in P. Hirst and J. Zeitlin (eds), *Reversing Industrial Decline? Industrial structure and policy in Britain and her competitors*, Berg, Oxford

——1992, 'Studied trust: Building new forms of co-operation in a volatile economy', in F. Pyke and W. Sengenberger (eds), *Industrial Districts and Local Economic Regeneration*, International Institute for Labour Studies, Geneva

Sabel, C. and Zeitlin, J. 1985, 'Historical alternatives to mass production: Politics, markets and technology in nineteenth century industrialisation', *Past and Present*, no. 108, pp. 133–76

Salzman, H. and Rosenthal, S. 1993, *Software by Design: Shaping Technology and the Workplace*, Oxford University Press, New York

Schlesinger, L. and Heskett, J. 1991, 'The service-driven service company', *Harvard Business Review*, Sept.–Oct., pp. 71–81

Schonberger, R. 1990, *Building a Chain of Customers: Linking Business Functions to Create the World Class Company*, The Free Press, New York

Scott Morton, M. (ed.) 1991, *The Corporation of the 1990s: Information Technology and Organizational Transformation*, Oxford University Press, New York

Semler, R. 1989, 'Managing without managers', *Harvard Business Review*, Sept.–Oct., pp. 76–84

——1993, *Maverick: The Success Story behind the World's Most Unusual Workplace*, Century, London

Senge, P. 1990, *The Fifth Discipline: The Art & Practice of The Learning Organization*, Doubleday/Currency, New York

Sengenberger, W. and Campbell, D. (eds) 1993, *Lean Production and Beyond: Labour Aspects of a New Production Concept* (Forum Series on Labour in a Changing World Economy, no. 2), International Institute for Labour Studies, Geneva

Shaiken, H., Herzenberg, S. and Kuhn, S. 1986, 'The work process under more flexible production', *Industrial Relations*, vol. 25, no. 2, pp. 167–83

Shapin, S. and Schaffer, S. 1985, *Leviathan and the Air Pump: Hobbes, Boyle and the Experimental Life*, Princeton University Press, Princeton, NJ

Shimada, H. and MacDuffie, J. 1986, 'Industrial Relations and "Humanware": Japanese investments in automobile manufacturing in the United States' (Working paper, International Motor Vehicle Program), Sloan School of Management, MIT, Cambridge, Mass.

Shingo, S. 1985, *A Revolution in Manufacturing: The SMED System*, Productivity Press, Cambridge, Mass.

Shriver, B. and Wegner, P. (eds) 1987, *Research Directions in Object-Oriented Programming*, MIT Press, Cambridge, Mass.

Skinner, W. 1985, *Manufacturing: The Formidable Competitive Weapon*, John Wiley, New York

——1986, 'The productivity paradox', *Harvard Business Review*, July–Aug., pp. 55–9

Slatter, R-R., Husband, T., Besant, C. and Ristic, M. 1989, 'A human-centred approach to the design of advanced manufacturing systems', *Annals of the CIRP*, vol. 38, no. 1, pp. 461–4

Snow, C., Miles, R. and Coleman, H. 1992, 'Managing 21st century network organizations', *Organizational Dynamics*, Winter 1992, pp. 5–20

Sorge, A. et al. 1983, *Microelectronics and Manpower in Manufacturing: Applications of CNC in Great Britain and West Germany*, Gower Publishing, Aldershot

Sorge, A. and Streeck, W. 1988, 'Industrial relations and technical change: The case for an extended perspective', in R. Hyman and W. Streeck (eds), *New Technology and Industrial Relations*, Basil Blackwell, Oxford

Steedman, H. and Wagner, K. 1989, 'Productivity, machinery and skills: Clothing manufacture in Britain and Germany', *National Institute Economic Review*, May, pp. 40–57

Streeck, W. 1989, 'Skills and the limits of neo-liberalism: the enterprise of the future as a place of learning', *Work, Employment and Society*, vol. 3, no. 1, pp. 89–104

Subramanian, S.K. and Subramanian, Y. 1991, 'Managing technology fusion through synergy circles in Japan', *Journal of Engineering and Technology Management*, vol. 8, pp. 313–37

Susman, G. and Chase, R. 1986, 'A sociotechnical analysis of the integrated factory', *The Journal of Applied Behavioral Science*, vol. 22, no. 3, pp. 257–70

Szczygiel, M. 1993, 'Information technology in lean production', *Lean Enterprise*, vol. 1, no. 1, pp. 9–11

Teece, D. 1989, 'Inter-organizational requirements of the innovation process', *Managerial and Decision Economics*, Special Issue, pp. 35–42

Terry, M. and Ferner, A. 1986, *Political Change and Union Democracy: The Negotiation of Internal Order in the Union of Communication Workers* (Warwick Papers in Industrial Relations, no. 10), Industrial Relations Research Unit, University of Warwick, Coventry

Thorelli, H. 1986, 'Networks: Between markets and hierarchies', *Strategic Management Journal*, vol. 7, pp. 37–51

Toulmin, S. 1972, *Human Understanding, Volume 1: General Introduction and Part 1: The Collective Use and Evolution of Concepts*, Clarendon Press, Oxford

Tricker, R. 1990, 'The corporate concept: Redesigning a successful system', *Human Systems Management*, vol. 9, pp. 65–76

Trist, E. 1981, *The Evolution of Socio-technical Systems: A Conceptual Framework and an Action Research Program* (Occasional paper no. 2), Ontario Quality of Working Life Centre, Ottawa

——1983, 'Referent organizations and the development of inter-organizational domains', *Human Relations*, vol. 36, no. 3, pp. 269–84

Trist, E. and Bamforth, K. 1951, 'Some social and psychological consequences of the longwall method of coal getting', *Human Relations*, vol. 4, pp. 3–38

Trist, E. et al. 1963, *Organisational Choice: The Loss, Rediscovery and Transformation of a Work Tradition*, Tavistock Publications, London

Trist, E. and Murray, H. (eds) 1990, *The Social Engagement of Social Science, Volume I: The Socio-Psychological Perspective*, Free Association Books, London

——1993, *The Social Engagement of Social Science, Volume II: The Socio-Technical Perspective*, University of Pennsylvania Press, Philadelphia

Turnbull, D. 1991, *Technoscience Worlds*, Deakin University Press, Geelong

Turner, L. 1991, *Democracy at Work: Changing World Markets and the Future of Labor Unions*, Studies in Political Economy, Cornell University Press, Ithaca

Tylecote, A. 1992, *The Long Wave in the World Economy: The Present Crisis in Historical Perspective*, Routledge, London

United States Postal Service 1991, 'OCR applications: remote bar coding system', paper presented to 10th International Conference on Postal Mechanization, Tokyo

Venkatraman, N. 1991, 'IT-induced business reconfiguration', in M. Morton (ed.), *The Corporation of the 1990s: Information Technology and Organizational Transformation*, Oxford University Press, New York

Versteeg, A. 1990, 'Self-directed work teams yield long-term benefits', *The Journal of Business Strategy*, Nov.–Dec., pp. 9–12

Volpert, W. 1982, 'The model of the hierarchical–sequential organisation of action', in W. Hacker et al. (eds), *Cognitive and Motivational Aspects of Action*, North Holland, Amsterdam

Volpert, W., Koetter, W., Gohde, H. and Weber, W. 1989, 'Psychological evaluation and design of work tasks: Two examples', *Ergonomics*, vol. 32, no. 7, pp. 881–90

Wall, T., Burns, B., Clegg, C. and Kemp, N. 1984, 'New technology, old jobs', *Work and People*, vol. 10, pp. 15–24

Walleck, A., O'Halloran, J. and Leader, C. 1991, 'Benchmarking world-class performance', *McKinsey Quarterly*, no. 1, pp. 3–24

Walton, R. 1980, 'Establishing and maintaining high commitment work systems', in Kimberly and Miles (eds), *The Organisational Life Cycle*, Jossey-Bass, San Francisco

——1985, 'Toward a strategy of eliciting employee commitment based on policies of mutuality', in R. Walton and P. Lawrence (eds), *HRM Trends and Challenges*, Harvard Business School Press, Boston

Walton, R. and McKersie, R. 1965, *A Behavioral Theory of Labor Negotiations*, McGraw-Hill, New York

Warnecke, H.J. in collaboration with Manfred Hueser 1993, *The Fractal Company: A Revolution in Corporate Culture* (translation of 1992 German text *Die Fraktale Fabrik*), Springer Verlag, Berlin

Weisbord, M. 1990, *Productive Workplaces: Organizing and Managing for Dignity, Meaning and Community*, Jossey-Bass, San Francisco

Weiss, L. 1988, *Creating Capitalism: The State and Small Business Since 1945*, Basil Blackwell, Oxford

Weiss, L. and Mathews, J. 1991, *Structure, Strategy and Public Policy: Lessons from the Italian Textile Industry for Australia* (UNSW Studies in Organisational Analysis and Innovation, no. 4), Industrial Relations Research Centre, The University of New South Wales, Sydney

Wellins, R., Byham, W. and Wilson, J. 1991, *Empowered Teams: Creating Self-Directed Work Groups that Improve Quality, Productivity and Participation*, Jossey-Bass, San Francisco

Wemmerlor, U. and Hyer, N. 1987, 'Research issues in Cellular Manufacturing', *International Journal of Production Research*, vol. 25, no. 3, pp. 413–31

Williams, K. et al. 1987, 'The end of mass production?', *Economy and Class*, vol. 16, no. 3, pp. 405–39

Williamson, O. 1975, *Markets and Hierarchies: Analysis and Anti-Trust Implications*, The Free Press, New York

——1985, *The Economic Institutions of Capitalism: Firms, Markets, Relational Contracting*, Macmillan, London

Williamson, O. and Winter, S. (eds) 1991, *The Nature of the Firm: Origins, Evolution, and Development*, Oxford University Press, New York

Winner, L. 1977, *Autonomous Technology: Technics-out-of-Control as a Theme in Political Thought*, MIT Press, Cambridge, Mass.

——1986, *The Whale and the Reactor: A Search for Limits in an Age of High Technology*, University of Chicago Press, Chicago

Winter, S. 1987, 'Knowledge and competence as strategic assets', in D. Teece (ed.), *The Competitive Challenge: Strategies for Industrial Innovation and Renewal*, Harper & Row, New York

Wobbe, W. 1992, *What are Anthropocentric Production Systems? Why are They a Strategic Issue for Europe?* (Report EUR 13968, FAST/MONITOR Programme), Commission of the European Communities, Brussels

Womack, J., Jones, D. and Roos, D. 1990, *The Machine that Changed the World*, Maxwell Macmillan International, New York

Yoshikawa, H. 1990, 'An Intelligent Manufacturing System', Committee on Joint International Research Programs into an Intelligent Manufacturing System, International Robotics and Factory Automation Center, University of Tokyo

Zuboff, S. 1988, *In the Age of the Smart Machine: The Future of Work and Power*, Basic Books, New York

Index

Page numbers in italics indicate figures